# Woman's "True" Profession

## Voices from the History of Teaching

# Woman's "True" Profession

## Voices from the History of Teaching

SECOND EDITION

—◦◦◦—

NANCY HOFFMAN

Dear Carol,

This book is loaded with primary sources that reveal teaching as "women's work." The book inspires me to talk about the history of American education, using the lens of feminist theories. I hope it inspires you as well.

HARVARD EDUCATION PRESS

With deep gratitude,

Kendra Moore
Ph.D. 2010

Library of Congress Control Number 2003106678
ISBN 1-891792-13-X (paperback)
ISBN 1-891792-15-6 (library edition)

Published by Harvard Education Press,
an imprint of the Harvard Education Publishing Group

Harvard Education Press
8 Story Street
Cambridge, MA 02138

Cover Photograph: From the Penn School Collection.
Permission granted by Penn Center, Inc., St. Helena Island, SC

Cover Design: Alyssa Morris

The typefaces used in this book are Belucian, Old Claude, and Perpetua.

# DEDICATION

To the next generation of teachers, that you might know and build on the accomplishments of the redoubtable women who came before you.

# Table of Contents

*Dedication*    v

*Acknowledgments*    xi

## INTRODUCTION
*1*

—⟨❦⟩—

## CHAPTER ONE

—⟨❦⟩—

### Seminary for Social Power:
### The Classroom Becomes Woman's Sphere
*Nancy Hoffman*
*23*

Pioneering the Education of Young Women
*Emma Hart Willard*
*49*

Teaching in the Little Red Schoolhouse
*Lucia B. Downing*
*58*

Remedy for Wrongs to Women
*Catherine Beecher*
*66*

"Civilizing" the West: Letters from the Frontier
*Ellen P. Lee and Mary S. Adams*
*79*

Preparing to Teach: A Journal
*Mary Swift*
*85*

Reminiscences of School Life, and Hints on Teaching
*Fanny Jackson-Coppin*
*93*

The Schooolmarm
*Anna Fuller*
*103*

CHAPTER TWO

A Noble Work Done Earnestly:
Missionary Teachers in the Civil War South
*Nancy Hoffman*
119

Teaching During the Civil War: A Fourteen-Year-Old's Story
*Susie King Taylor*
141

Missionary Maidens
*Mary Clemmer Ames*
146

From Northern Home to Southern Dangers
*Maria S. Waterbury*
149

Sisters in the Service
*Sarah Chase, Lucy Chase, Julia Rutledge*
159

Hard Work Every Day: A New England Woman's Diary in Dixie
*Mary Ames*
165

An African American Teacher in South Carolina
*Charlotte L. Forten*
170

Emancipation's Primer: *The Freedmen's Book*
*Lydia Maria Child*
181

New Rules for African American and White
*Elizabeth Hyde Botume*
185

An African American Oberlin Student Goes South
*Sara Stanley*
192

A Good Life, Staying On
*Laura M. Towne*
209

The March of Progress
*Charles W. Chesnutt*
217


CHAPTER THREE
⁓❦⁓

# Teaching in the Big City: Women, the Education Bureaucracy, and Teacher Organizing

*Nancy Hoffman*
227

The True Character of the New York Public Schools
*Adele Marie Shaw*
251

The Inquisition of the Teacher, or, "Gum Shoe Tim"
on the War-Path
*Myra Kelly*
265

Schoolteacher's Nightmare
*Mary Abigail Dodge*
269

The First Class: A Reminiscence
*Marian Dogherty*
272

An Immigrant Student and Her Teacher
*Mary Antin*
280

My Mother's Principal and Mine:
A Personal Interview with Mary Agnes Dwyer
*Nancy Hoffman*
286

Teaching in an African American Boarding School
*Frances O. Grant*
*292*

Public Schools "Owned" by Politicians
*"Amelia Allison"*
*304*

Why Teachers Should Organize
*Margaret Haley*
*308*

Equal Pay for Equal Work
*Grace C. Strachan*
*316*


Notes     *321*

About the Author     *333*

Index     *335*

Photo Credits     *339*

# ACKNOWLEDGMENTS

My thanks to two sets of people who helped this book come to life: Florence Howe and the staff of the Feminist Press, who had the prescience to create the series "Women's Lives/Women's Work" in the 1970s, and to make *Woman's "True" Profession* one of the volumes; and Doug Clayton and Dody Riggs of the Harvard Education Publishing Group, who gave *WTP* a second life. I would also like to acknowledge those scholars of African American history who enabled me to reframe the new edition of *WTP* to include the stories of the many African American teachers who dedicated themselves to the children of their communities in the nineteenth and early twentieth centuries. If the voices of white women teachers from this period have been little heard, African American women teacher's voices were almost totally silenced until the scholarship of the last several decades restored their place in history. And finally, my gratitude to doctoral student and historian Jen De Forest, who stepped in from her perch at the *Harvard Educational Review* with expert researcher's queries and high spirits just when I needed help with the second edition; and Wanda Hunter, administrative assistant in the Brown University Education department, who generously created an electronic version of *WTP* without compensation, saying she enjoyed learning about these redoubtable women while typing their words.

# Introduction

*We hold the pointer to the words, the numbers, the alphabet.*
*Love for another generation.*
*Shelter of hope for another generation,*
*Life for our children.*
    —Tillie Olsen, "Utterance"[1]

WOMEN HAVE ALWAYS BEEN TEACHERS. Our mothers, sisters, aunts, grandmothers, women friends — rare are the women who have not instructed children. Yet it is only in the last 150 years that teaching has been a paid profession for women, and much more recently that women teachers have become a subject of scholarly study. *Woman's "True" Profession* explores some important episodes in the development of teaching as paid work for women.

Until the mid-nineteenth century, when this book begins, teaching was an activity largely embedded in family life, as it had been for most of human history. Most learning occurred as the occasion warranted. Children were taught skills by an older person who needed help with certain tasks, or, learning from observation, they accomplished new tasks on their own. Particularly in rural areas, schooling was casual. Young children learned reading, writing, and arithmetic in a "dame school," gathering in a neighbor's kitchen or parlor for an introduction to the three Rs. Older students were usually taught by a male teacher who was supplementing his income during a vacation from studying for the ministry or the law.

While informal teaching and learning will always be the primary way children learn, over the course of the nineteenth century there rose to supplement household and self-instruction a system of common schooling where none had existed previously. Concerned with the nation's future, the "schoolmen," as our first professional educators were called, saw that if citizens were to respond to economic forces modernizing American society, they would need increasingly complex knowledge. Aware as well that the pace of change and influx of immigrants no longer ensured continuity with past practices and beliefs, these leaders articulated an educational philosophy that attended not simply to rudimentary skills, but also to the formation of character and conscience — qualities needed for participation in a highly decentralized, democratic society.

At the beginning of the nineteenth century, before schooling gained this serious new kind of attention, one in ten teachers was a woman; in the 1920s, when this book ends, out of the greatly expanded force of 657,000 public school teachers, 86 percent were women, including almost all teachers in elementary schools. How did it come about, then, that casual teaching was the work of men, but when the nation needed a system of schools the work of teaching was entrusted to women?

The story of woman's "true" profession is the story both of the development of the first middle-class profession for women and the building of the massive educational system we know today. Yet it is interesting that, until the last several decades, the history of public schooling ignored the fact that teachers are women. With a few exceptions, male and female historians alike considered "woman" and "teacher" one identity that was so much a part of the landscape, so "natural," that gender remained unremarked. Until the 1980s, the single book-length work on women teachers was a 1938 sociological study called *The Schoolma'am*.[2] The civil rights movement and the women's movement spawned two new fields of study — African American studies and women's studies. The first edition of *Woman's "True" Profession* was one of a very few analyses of women teachers published in the late 1970s and early 1980s, and was influenced by these new fields.

Today there is a small scholarly industry devoted to teaching and accounting for gender, including three historical works, *American Teachers: Histories of a Profession at Work* (Warren), *"Everybody's Paid but the Teacher": The Teaching Profession and the Women's Movement* (Carter), and *City Teachers: Teaching and School Reform in Historical Perspective* (Rousmaniere). Works on contemporary women teachers include *Women Teaching for Change* (Weiler), *School Work: Gender and the Cultural Construction of Teaching* (Biklen), *Bitter Milk: Women and Teaching* (Grumet), *Black Teachers on Teaching* (Foster) and *School for Women* (Miller). Scholarly biographies of women educators include Catherine Beecher, Emma Willard, Fanny Jackson-Coppin, and Prudence Crandall, and academic conferences are held on such issues as gender and teacher education.[3] But even today, *Woman's "True" Profession* fills a special niche in this literature as a documentary history in which women teachers speak for themselves — from Emma Hart Willard, a visionary who, in 1814, dreamed of a school for girls; to the African American Oberlin student and anti-slavery activist Sara Stanley, who went south just after the Civil War to teach "her people"; to Grace Strachan, who counted herself one of the 14,000 female elementary school teachers in New York City, whom, in 1907, she was keen on unionizing.

We might ask what can we learn from and about women teachers that might distinguish them from teachers in general? Why focus on gender in the study of a profession? During the period in which the work of teaching was being transformed from casual work for men into a profession for women, a discourse or a way of thinking, speaking, and writing, developed that bound stereotypic female qualities intricately together with teacher qualities. In the early 1800s, one could count as a common kind of statement, "Teaching is not 'a woman's job, anymore than milkin' a cow [is] a man's job.'"[4] At mid-century, Horace Mann, then secretary of the Massachusetts Board of Education, asked a rhetorical question that had already been answered in the affirmative: "Is not woman destined to conduct the rising generation, of both sexes, at least through all the primary stages of education? Has not the Author of nature preadapted her, by constitution, and faculty, and temperament for this noble work?"[5] The woman teacher had come to be mythologized as naturally suited to work as civilizer, moral exemplar, and caregiver, bringing the virtues of the pious Christian home into the schoolroom. The father of the kindergarten movement, Friedrich Froebel, called teachers "mother[s] made conscious."[6] When the woman teacher failed to meet this idealized view, she became the school marm, the spinster, the shrewish disciplinarian, an asexual failure, and the butt of humor.

A focus on gender, then, in the history of teaching should make the familiar discourse about teachers "strange"; it should raise questions about why "woman" and "teacher" are so natural a pairing as to be an invisible part of the landscape. It should disentangle the qualifications for teaching from the set of attributes considered to define "true" woman, and those attributes from the variousness among real women themselves. And yet it should also reveal the pleasures and satisfying challenges of teaching. In this traditional woman's field, the sisterhood of teachers was freed in their choices and ways of living, as much fulfilled as constrained by gender.

A century or more ago, women had few career options; indeed, working at a profession was teaching. Today, however, the questions women ask when considering a career in teaching are more complex. Am I choosing to be with children or have I just fallen into doing "what women do"? Will I be able to teach a subject that I love under circumstances in which I can truly use my intellect and continue to grow and learn? Will I be able to influence children? And, more practically, Is this the best way to move into the middle class or to sustain myself after a divorce or in widowhood? What is the consequence of being a poorly paid "do-gooder" in a "semi-profession" of ambiguous status — highly regarded by some, but in general more honored in theory than in actuality? Despite the often-inspiring story it tells, this book will probably not provide answers to these questions. It will, however, demonstrate that women who chose to teach have a rich tradition on which to draw for guidance and inspiration.

Chapter One tells the story of plucky women setting out on a new course: to found a profession that provided a living wage, independence, and greater access to the civic arena than was acknowledged at the time. Despite the rhetoric of separate spheres for women and men, teaching allowed women to act in public life. Chapter Two recounts the experiences of the many women, African American and white, who dedicated themselves to teaching newly freed people in the Civil War South. They faced physical danger, racism, and immense intellectual and emotional challenges as they set out to found and run schools under conditions that would challenge even the most intrepid. Chapter Three paints a portrait of the constraints and triumphs of the early days of the bureaucratized education system we know today — the system in which women teachers were excluded from decision-making about their work and fought back by organizing unions. *Woman's "True" Profession* ends with the voices of those women teachers and teacher organizers who seized power for themselves, and in so doing won some significant battles for better working conditions and control over their work.

## Organizing Questions

Each chapter in *Woman's "True" Profession* raises key questions about what was possible for women in the teacher labor force between the 1840s and 1920s, taking into account race, class, and geographical location, as well as gender. These questions fall into three groups: First, what is the motivation to teach: Did women choose teaching, as popular rhetoric suggests, because this relational and mothering work was "natural"? If not, how do they explain the motivation that led them to this work? Second, if one were to set up poles with liberating work at one end and conserving work at the other, what would characterize the work of teaching in the nineteenth and early twentieth centuries? As I explain in greater detail below, debate continues among teachers, scholars, and critics about whether teachers — to caricature — are complicit in the agenda of the bureaucratic state to control and mold children to be compliant citizens and workers, or whether teachers exercising their own independent agency, help children attain the critical consciousness that no state can take away. And there is a related question: Did the experience of teaching radicalize teachers or at least sufficiently disrupt gender conformity so that they exercised a broader repertoire of choices than their peers of similar background? The third set of questions that shapes this book is of a different order: What are the characteristics of teachers' constructions of self? How does contemporary feminist analysis shape the reader's analysis of these selves? This introduction suggests approaches to these questions that may be useful to the reader in making her own analysis of the teacher writings in this book.

## *"To wrest a living from the world": Motivation to Teach*

Historians of American education consistently link the feminization of teaching with the bureaucratization of schools, noting that what was casual work for men through the early nineteenth century became a regulated, mass profession for women.[7] As the country began to industrialize in the mid-nineteenth century, common school leaders began to argue for a greater investment in public schooling — more schools, better trained teachers, and some uniformity across states about the conduct of schools. By the 1850s and 1860s, almost all children between the ages of seven and thirteen were receiving some schooling (at least ten weeks in the summer and in the winter), placing much greater demands on what had been a somewhat haphazard institution. The new position of state superintendent of schools had also become a bully pulpit from which to exhort the population to improve the quality of schooling. Thus, while urbanization and industrialization were opening new employment possibilities for men, there was a growing need for teachers for common schools, which were increasingly seen not just as a village or township responsibility but a commitment of state and local governments. Not surprisingly, this moment coincided with two persistent arguments for hiring women: they were cheaper, and they were naturally suited to teaching young children.[8] Indeed, records of school meetings are quite forthright about the efficiency of hiring two female teachers for the price of one male, thereby permitting funds to be used for other educational purposes like school buildings and equipment. Said Indiana's first state superintendent of schools in 1853, "Blessed be he who invented female teachers."[9] And Horace Mann asked rhetorically: "Is [woman] not fitted to commence the first work in the Temple of Education?"[10]

Women took over one-room schools, and, once it was accepted practice that in towns and cities a male principal could supervise a number of female teacher "assistants," heading off any discipline problems with rowdy older boys, females became the backbone of multi-classroom schools. The availability of teaching positions coupled with the argument of women's special suitability to this work explains why women flocked into teaching in such numbers. Indeed, the question of motivation must be analyzed through both the lens of women's labor force participation and the ideology of the time — that woman's true calling was in caring for and educating young children. If there is one major argument in this book it is that women were entering the labor market for the same reasons as men — to earn a living, to take part in public life, and to take on challenges in order to test themselves. But because women were taking teaching jobs just at the historical moment when the doctrine of separate spheres issued from pulpits and printed tracts, public rhetoric exaggerated women's motivation to lead children to virtue and downplayed the commonalties they had with male professionals in the labor market. In truth, women were public employees, negotiating contracts with school committees, exercising authority over children and adolescents (often young men) close to their age, speaking before school boards, and leading public school exercises before the gathered townspeople.

And unlike the unmarried male who might go off with the ambiguous goal of seeking his fortune, a woman's choice of work was constrained by her primary obligations to contribute to her family's domestic economy, to care for siblings and do household and farm work until she married. Once a family made a decision to encourage or permit a young woman to work for wages, or if a young woman fell on hard times and had to make her way in the world, there were relatively few choices available. In antebellum New England, women could be domestic servants, governesses in private service, laundresses, mill workers in some regions, and teachers almost everywhere.

Teaching, while a shared experience of legions of women, occupied only a short time in the working lives of most antebellum women, whose true destiny was marriage and work in the home. In Massachusetts, for example, women filled a vast majority of the state's teaching posts. According to the historian of education Geraldine Clifford, between 1830 and 1880, one in four of all native-born white women in the state had been a teacher at some time in her life. At no time between 1870 and 1970 did teaching fall below fifth place among the occupations of all women workers. In 1912, 74 percent of Mount Holyoke graduates who had ever been employed were teachers, and a 1912 report of the Association of Collegiate Alumnae (afterward the American Association of University Women) concluded that of all college women at work, 70.5 percent were teachers.[11] Only for single women or those sharing a life-long partnership with a female companion was teaching a long-lasting career.

However short a woman's tenure as a teacher, teaching permitted both freedom and autonomy, which most women were unlikely to have gained at home. Teachers could live independently, with one other woman or several. They could travel. They could engage in intellectual activity in the public world. For some women, teaching provided a platform for doing good and speaking out in the classroom and the community. For others, teaching made the difference between poverty and survival for the teacher and her family, and conferred prestige and status. African American teachers in particular saw themselves and were seen as highly respected agents of progress who were leading their young people to a better life.

When teaching changed from being considered a substitute for marriage and children to being considered as extending the mother's knowledge of childrearing into the classroom — married women with children were permitted to teach toward the mid-twentieth century — the job became even more attractive because it allowed women to balance childrearing and career, an attraction that remains today. But choosing teaching because working with children is more palatable than working in a factory or because the hours and summer vacations can accommodate unpaid work in the family does not mean that teaching is an extension of mothering or that women do it out of love for children. Indeed, given the sheer numbers who taught, one cannot believe that all these women were attracted to a "mothering" profession rather than to having stable work, some autonomy, and a modicum of power.

That women themselves exploited the rhetoric that presented teaching as public motherhood is undeniable. They used it to justify paying work with children, decisions to travel far from home on missions to save children from barbarism, and even to reject marriage itself, as one could inculcate virtue in a greater number of children as a teacher than as a mother. Although one might argue that allowing teaching to be considered "not real work" had consequences that teachers live with today — if teaching is like caring for children in the family, then it is done more for love than money and low pay is justified — in the nineteenth and early twentieth centuries the "cover" such rhetoric provided was quite functional. Ambitious for their sex, both Emma Willard and Catherine Beecher, whose writings appear in the first chapter of this book, exemplified users of such arguments.

Beecher wrote voluminously on women as "true" or "born" teachers. Rather than argue that women should be able to enter the labor market, she made teaching into a profession that was, in her lexicon, mothering and not work. And yet her own work, like that of many women teachers, was carried out with a competitiveness and determination as close to "masculine" as one could get in the nineteenth century. Beecher (1800–1878), who never married, ran a school in Connecticut, raised money for her work, organized and prepared teachers for the western states, published prolifically, and traveled tirelessly as a lecturer. In a fascinating passage from the "Remedy for Wrongs to Women" (included in this volume), she argues first that mothers, by transmitting "what they receive to their children, to pass on again," finally are responsible for "the character and destiny [of] the whole nation." Continuing the theme of female superiority, she argues — using audaciously male metaphors— that mothers are "kings and priests unto God. Kings, to rule the destiny of all their descendants — priests by sacrifices and suffering to work out such sublime results!" (see p. 77). She then chides parents for allowing their intelligent daughters to suffer idly at home rather than taking on the next best occupation to mothering — teaching. Finally, she argues that if there were more teaching jobs for women, "capitalists" would no longer be able to "use their power of wealth to oppress our sex" in factories, as seamstresses, as laundresses, and farm hands.

As a proselytizer for the woman's true profession, Beecher said little of the way school committeemen exercised their power over female teachers. If teachers were "public mothers," then schoolmen were "public fathers." Many school committees forbade such activities as riding in a carriage with a man, frequenting confectionery shops, and being out after 8 P.M. And in most states well into the twentieth century, teachers were legally required to resign when they married, since home was considered the proper place for a married woman. While these regulations are chilling in what they reveal about male preoccupation with regulating the behavior of unmarried females, writing by teachers does not reveal either protest against such rules or much interest in them.

The issue of teachers' marriage, so charged with significance among male educators, only emerges in stories of schoolmarms pressured reluctantly into marriage by families fearful of having an "old maid" on their hands. There are also explicit statements in these accounts of teachers choosing work and independence over a married life that appeared to them to signify domestic servitude or social uselessness. As one teacher herself said, teaching was her "husband and children," a remark ambiguous in the extreme. Interestingly, the single piece in which a woman explicitly makes teaching a second best to "husband and children" is a short story by the African American writer Charles Chesnutt. He imagines a failed romantic relationship of a northern white woman as her reason to seek employment as a teacher in the South.

### "Training citizens . . . to free and intelligent action": Teacher Autonomy, Teacher Power

The period covered by this book falls into two blocks: the period of feminization that goes through the 1880s; and the period of bureaucratization that goes through the 1920s. Viewed through the frame of teacher agency — the ability of the working woman to choose her own path, to resist imposed power as necessary, and to authorize her students to act — the two periods differ dramatically. In the first, teachers could have great autonomy; in the second, autonomy was limited. These differences raise several questions: In the feminization period did teaching attract feisty women? Did they encourage their students to think critically, to act on behalf of their beliefs? In the period of bureaucratization, how did women engage the anonymous power of the system? As a greater number of professions opened to women, did willing conformists choose teaching? This section examines these interesting questions in light of the limited evidence available in the historical record.

For the pre-bureaucratization period, despite the few choices of work, one could plausibly argue that a young woman's decision to leave home to teach was already nonconforming or rebellious. When she declined to remain a worker within the family circle until marriage and chose instead to rule over a classroom, her behavior was an indication of the exercise of unusual agency. While it is difficult to generalize, the documents in this book provide some evidence to support that argument. Lucia Downing (1868–1945), for example, itches to compete with her older sister on the teacher exam, and then vies for a school of her own at age thirteen. The fictional character in Anna Fuller's short story "The Schoolmarm" (1892) argues her way out of the household and into a teaching position against her grandmother's assertion that she did not "approve of young women gettin' dissatisfied with the sphere to which they've been called" (see p. 104).

Drawing on a wide range of letters, diaries, and memoirs, historian Geraldine Clifford, takes the more radical view that "teaching was a seedbed of feminism." Clifford argues that teaching attracted "rather unexceptional young women of modest daring — many of whom were changed . . . by the experience and made supporters of feminism, and a surprising number of whom were radicalized and became the left wing of the organized feminist movements of the later nineteenth and twentieth centuries."[12] She also argues that the opportunity to exercise power in the classroom changed male-female power relations, conferred economic and psychic independence, and developed assertiveness in young women. Clifford cites as evidence the fact that, among the teachers who went South to teach during and after the Civil War, many thought of themselves as the nineteenth century equivalent of "feminist," and some assumed activist roles in the progressive movements of the day both from their homes in the South and upon return to the North. As Clifford and others have pointed out, major leaders in the early "woman movement" such as Lucretia Mott, Susan B. Anthony, Amelia Bloomer, Lucy Stone, Abigail Scott Duniway, Anna Dickinson, and Mary Church Terrell were all teachers for some period. Whether teaching itself radicalized them or simply allowed them to exercise critical powers previously repressed is an open question.

African American teachers in the post–Civil War South, where schools were largely rural and not bureaucratized as quickly as those in the North, were under extreme pressure to exercise not only agency but also leadership in their communities. African American teachers were expected to develop their students' intellectual competence, dispel white notions that African Americans were of inferior intelligence, and lead racial uplift. They were to be moral exemplars with responsibilities that included everything from the physical care of the schoolhouse to teaching the largely unwritten history of the race, to modeling appropriate behavior and setting the tone for spiritual life.[13] While teachers themselves endorsed these goals, they were largely unreachable. African American teachers suffered poor preparation for teaching, deplorable physical conditions within schools, meager pay, and endured the organized efforts of white racists to undermine the development of an African American educated class. W. E. B. DuBois and Augustus Granville Dill underscore this tragic irony:

> Broadly trained Negro teachers are feared by many school authorities because they have "too much egotism" or "individuality" and because they can not be depended upon "to teach the Negro his place." The result is that many superintendents and trustees will, therefore, hire a half-trained graduate of an industrial school who can teach a few industries and then complain that the teacher lacks education and culture.[14]

African American teachers were thus placed in an impossible situation in regard to their own abilities to lead social change. Michael Fultz argues in "African American Teachers in the South, 1890–1940: Powerlessness and the Ironies of Expectations and Protest," that

> African American teachers were caught in a racially and ideologically

*charged middle. Their status and abilities were of interest and concern to their fellow African Americans in the drive for justice and equality. Their performance was also of interest to southern whites determined to maintain the status quo. Without question, southern whites tried to control the contours of African American education and to degrade its condition just as African Americans strove for reform and improvement.*[15]

While some white teachers and many African American teachers in the pre-bureaucratization period might have been activists and outspoken individualists, it is not inevitable that they would pass on their views of social change to their students or inculcate in them the critical thinking skills necessary for autonomous decisionmaking. Finding evidence to make even an informed guess about this question is a challenge. With the exception of both African American and white teachers who taught formerly enslaved students in the South, adhered to an ideology that celebrated freedom and preparation for active citizenship, and had access to materials such as Lydia Maria Child's *The Freedmen's Book,* we have few resources to which to turn. Young women entered schoolhouses intent on teaching penmanship, spelling, and commonplace pieties that they themselves had been taught. There had been little national concern about a philosophy of education, let alone agreement about subject matter beyond the three Rs. What uniformity existed resulted de facto from the widespread use of such texts as *McGuffey's Reader.* Learning by rote recitation was the common pedagogy. Even accounts of end-of-year exhibitions of student learning tell us little about the values and views communicated by teachers to their students in everyday schoolroom practice. Very young teachers were more apt to record their prowess at discipline than to ponder the fine points of what we today call curriculum, and school boards seem to have been more concerned with the cost of a teacher and with her personal conduct than her ideas.

If, in the feminization period, teachers' work was largely unregulated and autonomy was there for the taking, that is not the case today. Since the turn of the twentieth century and on into the twenty-first, the problem of teachers' autonomy or ability to act in/on the world must be filtered through the construct of school bureaucracies. Bureaucracies can be seen as neutral vehicles for organizing post-industrial society; as structures for reproducing class society; as a "dispersed apparatus of social control"; or as the manifestation of patriarchal power requiring conformity and withstanding the resistance of female workers.[16] Young teachers make disparate evaluations of work within a bureaucracy based on personal experiences that differ by school setting, and their views are shaped with respect to power by their own class, race, and social location. Some emerge after a few years discouraged by feelings of powerlessness: they have come up against the "system," the "district." Others, by contrast, find the routines of schooling comfortable and secure, continuous with their views of how children should be nurtured. And still others make a clear-eyed trade-off — limited autonomy for continued access to classrooms. These varied reactions and the contradictory reflections of observers raise the question of whether teaching is conserving or liberating work or both.

Evidence gathered by feminist analysts in the last few decades has been inconsistent. Some would argue, as does Madeleine Grumet in *Bitter Milk,* that "the degree to which schooling continues to imitate the spatial, temporal, and ritual order of industry and bureaucracy indicates the complicity of both men and women in support of the paternal authority."[17] To Grumet, teachers are socializing children to fit the needs of the male-dominated state for compliant workers. To others, that is precisely the point, but it is put in positive terms. Teachers have historically helped children adapt to American society; they have taught middle-class manners, speech, and thought patterns, skills for the workplace, and civics for democratic participation. They have been the authors of the American dream for immigrant families and for the poor, key agents of assimilation.

Other see teachers as agents of social change — as neither tools of the state nor socializers to middle-class values, but as advocates for social and economic equality and guides to the choices available to well-trained critical thinkers. Thought of this way, teachers make a difference to students as individuals; they can take leadership in schools and they can exercise autonomy and agency in their profession, whether through unions, teacher networks, or activism in their communities. Indeed, African American teachers place on themselves and have placed on them the responsibility for improving the prospects of all children in their communities. Their classrooms are, as the epigraph to this chapter says, "the shelter of hope for another generation." In *Women Teaching for Change: Gender, Class and Power* (1988), a study of high school teachers who define themselves as feminist, the data leads Kathleen Weiler to conclude that "teaching in public schools, although profoundly bounded by institutional constraints, also contains the possibility of transformative work"[18]

If teachers in the pre-bureaucracy period do not appreciatively note the freedom they enjoy in one-room schools, when that freedom is threatened they do speak up, perhaps realizing what has been lost. With the influx of immigrants into schools (immigration peaked in 1907), the widespread development of normal schools for training teachers, and the increasing bureaucratization of urban education systems, male psychologists, educators, and philosophers began to contend for power in decisions about curriculum and methods of teaching. The 1892 report of the National Education Association (NEA) Committee of Ten marked a turning point in the process of defining the field of education as the responsibility of elite men. Chaired by Charles Eliot, then president of Harvard University, the all-male group was assembled to address the purpose of the American high school and to agree on a standard curriculum. Their report called for a broadened core of academic subjects for students bound both for college and for work, and thus required major changes in the work of teachers. But teachers were included neither on this committee nor a subsequent NEA committee formed in 1918, which recommended that the academic core be substantially altered to sort students according to their academic talents and prospects. It was as if the Committee of Ten were oblivious to the power they were wresting away from women as well as from local communities. As David Angus and Jeffrey Mirel point out in *The Failed Promise of the American High School,* the report was "a crucial first step toward the professionalization of curriculum planning and as a direct assault on the control of high school curricula by lay boards of education."[19]

In *The Struggle for the American Curriculum, 1893–1958*, Herbert Kliebard argues that, in the 1890s, "the educational center of gravity . . . shifted from the tangible presence of the teacher to the remote knowledge and values incarnate in the curriculum."[20] In that odd phrase "tangible presence," he suggests that from a system in which the female teacher *was* the curriculum, the locus of control moved to a curriculum developed by males and dissociated from the knowing teacher. Indeed, Kliebard's book presents photographs of classrooms with students and their unnamed female teachers, side by side with portraits of the named male leaders in the curriculum development movement. Among the schoolmen, one of the few recorded gestures of discomfort in regard to the silencing of teachers is John Dewey's, who declared that if teachers "have not . . . authoritative positions in shaping the course of study, [it] is likely to remain an external thing to be externally applied to the child."[21] In short, in the twentieth century, the "what" and "how" of teaching were wrested away from teachers, as is often the case, as Geraldine Clifford puts it, in "sex segregated . . . occupations where women perform the services but men control policy and resources."[22]

To have voice within a mass profession, the exercise of agency and resistance to unfairness or disrespect requires more than individual acts. One positive result of bureaucratization was the rise of collective action among teachers. The selections in *Woman's "True" Profession* in chapter three concerning teaching in the urban schools at the turn of the twentieth century illustrate the simultaneous power and powerlessness of teachers — great power over their pupils, limited power over their own lives. These selections also illustrate why female teachers organized unions, how they interacted with the existing labor movement and the "woman movement" for several decades before teachers unions too became the province of men.

### "A thumping from within": The Teacher Constructs a Self

*When a child I was put into a school near home that professed to be normal and collegiate, i.e., to prepare teachers for colored youth, furnish candidates for the ministry, and offer collegiate training for those who should be ready for it. . . . I had devoured what was put before me, and, like Oliver Twist, was looking around to ask for more. I constantly felt (as I suppose many an ambitious girl has felt) a thumping from within unanswered by any beckoning from without. Class after class was organized for these ministerial candidates (many of them men who had been preaching before I was born) . . .*

*A boy, however meager his equipment and shallow his pretensions, had only to declare a floating intention to study theology and he could get all the support, encouragement and stimulus he needed, be absolved from work and invested beforehand with all the dignity of his far away office. While a self-supporting girl had to struggle on by teaching in the summer and working after school hours to keep up with her board bills, and actually to fight her way against positive discouragements to the higher education; till one such girl one day flared out and told the principal "the only mission opening before a girl in his school was to marry one of those candidates." He said he didn't know but it was . . .* [23]

Anna Julia Cooper, author of this stunning passage from *A Voice from the South by a Black Woman of the South*, exemplifies the construction of self within the emerging discourses of well-educated members of the "woman movement." Echoing other women of her generation, she argues against the gendered distribution of educational "goods" to favor boys and discourage girls even when they are superior in talent and ambition. In addition, she underscores a theme that pervades in a variety of guises the writing of and about women teachers in this book. The teacher wishes to be seen as a working person and in this case a thinker and intellectual; her male interlocutors see her first as a female sexual being. Indeed, by calling herself "one such girl," and "flaring out," Anna Julia Cooper puts herself in a category with other girls who do not want to hear the standard answer to the question that a young woman becomes associated with learning by marrying a learned man. (Ironically, Cooper did marry a minister, but he died two years after their marriage, leaving her able to pursue her career as an intellectual, teacher, scholar, and administrator — work to which she was entitled only because, as a widow, she had no one to support her.)

Why begin reflections about the teachers' construction of self with this discordant anecdote that puts cultivation of the female intellect, the desire to learn and teach against male expectation that woman's vocation is marriage? If there is one exceedingly complex issue that has plagued teaching as a profession for women, it is the entanglement of gender identity, sexuality, and worker identity. Indeed, the gender-related qualities that lead males and females alike to commend women for their superiority as teachers are precisely the qualities that suggest that women should pursue their destinies as wives and mothers. The contradiction inherent in public motherhood is that it is asexual; the teacher is mother without having conceived a child. Thus, evidence of female sexuality — physical allure, behavior that bespeaks sexual interest, or evidence of any sexual liaison — must be contained, repressed, or punished. Caught in this double bind, many women teachers attempted to define themselves through their work, to put before their male employers professional issues and questions, to hold gender and sexuality not only apart but in opposition to the work of teaching. One way then to read the writing of many of the teachers in this book is as an argument, sometimes buried and oblique, for an independent self, a self that transgresses the narrow confines of middle-class womanhood.

In each chapter of this book, the argument for independence appears variously. In the period of feminization, the assertion of a "worker" self appears in the numerous proud statements from young female teachers about their capacity to manage older male students, often in the face of skepticism from their male employers. Ellen Lee, one of Catherine Beecher's missionaries "at the West," claims that she defeated the prejudice against female teachers. She writes proudly that she "governs . . . a large number of young men between eighteen and twenty-one" when male teachers before "never had a school six weeks without trouble." Beneath what seems a simple worry about discipline lies a contest about gender, sexuality, and power. Should a young woman "govern" — the word often used to describe the exercise of authority in the classroom — male students her own age or older? Should young men spend days in the company of a female peer whose authority over them disrupts the possibility that she might be courted as a wife and put back into her proper sphere? Young Ellen cannot be a "mother made conscious," nor does she want to be. Such moments demonstrate what is necessarily the case: the teacher's vulnerability is written on her female body; she is always "a woman" in the classroom, thus she must construct an authoritative self against expectations — a challenge that young female high school teachers often struggle with today.

In Fuller's short story, "The Schoolmarm," the protagonist is engaged in a struggle for both her body and her mind. While the outcome is that the strong, defiant, smart Mary Pratt finally capitulates to the pressure of her family and her suitor not to "spile everything by [permanently] turning schoolmarm" (see p. 105), she struggles mightily to avoid the inevitable. Caught between the flattering invitation from an older woman to be her assistant teacher and a suitor who appears to find her even more attractive in her defiance of his courting — an older version of "she's beautiful when she's angry" — Mary gives in to marriage. She will become a ranch wife in the West, a fate that she despises. As Mary cries herself to sleep, the author winks at us as if to say, "read against this outcome."

In respect to African American teachers, the issue of teacher sexuality takes on an additional and heightened complexity that allows us to see more deeply into the perilous entanglement of gender, sexuality, and teaching. As Darlene Clark Hine observed, "because of the interplay of racial animosity, class tensions, gender role differentiation, and regional economic variations, African American women, as a rule, developed and adhered to a cult of secrecy, a culture of dissemblance, to protect the sanctity of inner aspects of their lives." She argues that the culture of dissemblance arose not only because of the threat of violence, but in response to "the negative social and sexual image of their womanhood."[24] African American women had to fend off the profoundly demeaning expectation from whites of their accessible sexuality, the expectation from within their own communities that they bear the burdens of improving the race while not threatening educated men, and the additional onus that educated African American women too should conform to the image of the "true woman." In addition, African American men often anticipated the white gaze, and thus imposed a standard of appropriate female behavior more constricted still than that of white sexism.

In her introduction to *A Voice from the South*, Mary Helen Washington gives the example of Lucy Ellen Moten, who was refused the position of principal of Washington's Minor Normal School because the all-male Board of Trustees felt that the tall, elegant mulatta "cut too fine a face and figure" for the job. Moten appealed to one of the trustees, the eminent Frederick Douglass, who told her he would intercede for her if she agreed to give up dancing, playing cards, going to the theater, entertaining gentlemen callers — and her fine clothes. She agreed to all conditions and got the job.

Similarly, Anna Julia Cooper was the subject of gratuitous critical rumors (likely true) that she was having an affair with John Love, a young man whom she had taken into her home as a foster child.[25]

Belying the "culture of dissemblance," a small group of African American women teachers educated at Oberlin, including Lucy Stanton (1831–1910), Sara Stanley (1836–1918), Fanny Jackson-Coppin (1837–1913), Anna Julia Cooper (1860–1964), and Mary Church Terrell (1863–1954), went beyond the assertion of their worker identities. Distinguished by their relative economic privilege, and fortified by the Quaker environment of Oberlin and their success in higher education, they not only asserted their professional identities but also spoke out about tabooed subjects such as race, racism, marital relations, and the limitations of males, African American and white. In constructing dangerous and challenging selves, these teachers are forerunners of today's strong African American women.

One might argue that just such struggles over the teacher's gender and sexuality were won by male school administrators in multi-classroom city schools as the nineteenth century came to a close. While one cannot generalize from a small sample of autobiographical writing, Marian Dogherty's 1889 account, "'Scusa Me Teacher," claims that a woman meeting her first class of students is like a man meeting his first love. In the romantic words, women's sexuality is erased and transformed into mother love — just what her male colleagues approved. One can argue as well that, affronted by such thinking, early twentieth-century women union organizers went beyond asserting their professional identities as "new women." They spoke with powerful and unified voices about the importance of their work, the changes required in their working conditions, and their own commitment to defy gender expectation as they took to the streets and the legislatures to speak loudly in their own self-interest.

### Has Teaching Served Women Well?

Is teaching a good profession for women? This book will probably leave the reader undecided. When women had few choices, the answer was undoubtedly yes. Even then, they labored under hardships — forty, fifty, sometimes sixty children in a classroom, and pay so meager as to have led one woman to testify in a National Education Association hearing, "I am so worn out from teaching sixty pupils that most of my money goes for medicine and trips for my health. . . . How few [of us] live to enjoy the pension."[26] There was petty tyranny to endure, no promise of status or power in the future, and a system that encouraged conformity. Charging in 1904 that no school in the United States submitted "questions of methods, discipline and teaching . . . to those actually engaged in the work of teaching," Margaret Haley, a teacher-organizer, quoted educator John Dewey: "How can the child learn to be a free and responsible citizen if the teacher is bound?"

In the bureaucratized urban schools at the turn of the century, and on into the present, women were often not treated differently from young children by patriarchal school administrators and school boards. Rather than helping women to break away from the traditional behavior of daughter, sister, mother, or wife in becoming members of the work force, teaching tended to institutionalize this behavior. Women found the pattern all too familiar, and some found it secure and acceptable. They saw male teachers at work in the high schools, in administration, and as policymakers. The structure of the school reinforced the notion that women were capable of teaching the ABCs and the virtues of cleanliness, obedience, and respect, while men taught about ideas and organized the profession. This division of labor has changed somewhat in recent years.

On the other hand, many women today, as in the past, feel themselves engaged in a socially significant activity. As teachers, they do in fact change lives. In letters, diaries, and essays, teachers write about exhilarating classroom experiences, about pleasure in their power to lead, about the gift of children's curiosity and resilience, about the honesty of teaching in a world hurrying to embrace material objects, a world with too many poor people and too many self-centered wealthy ones. And at some historical moments — the Civil War South, the turn of the twentieth century as unions were growing strong, the civil rights movement of the 1960s — teachers' work is embedded in larger social movements, and so can become intensely political. A white Boston teacher, fired in 1968 for walking out of her ghetto school with protesting African American pupils and their parents, saw herself as a civil rights activist intent on shifting some power from the rich and privileged to the disenfranchised poor. Her belief that teaching is compatible with working for social change is shared by many today.

Marion Moultrie, an African American woman who taught in a "run-of-the-mill" school in Philadelphia in the early 1970s, presented the advantages of her job in terms that are still common today: "When I finished college, I went right to the social workers school. Then I did social work for about three years. I came into teaching after I started raising a family. It gave me more time with my own children. I got out at two-thirty and had my summers off." Besides permitting her to integrate work and home life, teaching opened up social relationships with children. In her case, some students became "friend(s) for life." She separated herself from "missionary" teachers who only taught "black is beautiful" and neglected "moral and 'just living' issues." She made sure a student could fill out a job application, had mastered basic skills and concepts, and could imagine "the type of environment he wants all his life, and what he can do about it."[27]

Here the final words about teaching belong to two young women of color, one of Dominican parentage, the other of Puerto Rican descent. Recent graduates of a highly selective university, both returned to New York to teach in 2002, one in the high school from which she graduated. I was their professor, and I interviewed them together: "We see teaching as a way of empowering ourselves and empowering others like us. Our peers around the neighborhood never believed that they could go anywhere, because they didn't have anything. Teaching is our way of convincing them that they can do something, both as an example of ourselves coming from where they came from and through our teaching."[28]

CHAPTER ONE

Seminary for Social Power:
The Classroom Becomes Woman's Sphere

*E*ARLY IN THE 1840S, educator Catherine Beecher addressed a gathering of her countrywomen to arouse support for her favorite scheme — to send an army of "Christian female teachers" to start schools "at the West." The scheme had dual purposes: to save untutored children from ignorance, and to create an honored profession for women who had not yet married or who were to remain single. About the first purpose there was no argument, but Beecher had to convince her audience of the second. "Our sex" is depressed, Beecher claimed, because there is no road to "competence, influence, and honor" but marriage, no antidote to the "suffering that results from the *inactivity of cultivated intellect and feeling.* . . . This is not so because providence has not provided an ample place for . . . a profession for woman, but because custom or prejudice or a low estimate of its honorable character, prevents her from entering it. *The education of children, that* is the true and noble profession of a woman — *that* is what is worthy the noblest powers and affections of the noblest minds" (see pp. 75–76).

Some forty years later, Minerva Leland, a recent graduate of Colby College in Maine and a teacher in Brandon, Vermont, received a letter from her brother Sam back home in Massachusetts. As if he had taken to heart Catherine Beecher's plea that women needed intellectually challenging work before, or instead of, marriage, he wrote:

> *Dear Sister, we did enjoy your last letter very much. I am positively delighted that you are so enthusiastic about your schoolwork. There is no doubt that a new life has opened before you. Not that I am desirous that you be obliged to earn your own living and remain single, but I know that life can mean more if you are actively engaged in it than it can mean to you shut up at home.*

When June came, Minerva sent a letter and a check for her savings account home to her father. To him she wrote proudly, "I've earned a good, comfortable living for myself, and I'm truly thankful for that."[1]

In just a few decades, Catherine Beecher's dream of a profession for women had been fulfilled. Between 1840 and 1880, the number of female teachers tripled to make up 80 percent of the elementary school teaching force. In the 1880s, women were routinely trained as teachers in normal schools and in special postsecondary schools and classes, and were actively recruited for jobs in the new graded schools in cities and large towns. In Massachusetts where feminization happened earliest, between 1830 and 1880 a quarter of all native-born women who worked outside of the home were at one time teachers. Their tenure was on average two years. By 1900, there were about 450,000 teachers across the nation, three-fourths of them female, where three decades earlier there had been only 127,000. Of this group, about 21,000 were African American, about 60 percent of them female; a decade later 66 percent of African American teachers were female.[2] Like a multitude of young women of her generation, Minerva Leland had chosen work acceptable to her family, and she could be confident of her economic independence. The "custom" and "prejudice" that had once prevented woman from entering the profession, now held her to be more suited than man to the "sacred office." Where once marriage and children had been her sole appropriate profession, now teaching had become a reasonable prelude to or even substitute for marriage, an occupation for — as Louisa May Alcott called them — "women who stand alone in the world."[3]

This chapter tells the story of the transformation of common school teaching, from its pre-1840 status as stopgap or last-choice work for men to a profession for women. It tells another less happy story as well, typical in the history of women's work: a profession suffers when it is dominated by women and serves the needs of children. This story too emerges in Minerva Leland's correspondence.

In the same year that Minerva Leland was feeling so pleased with herself, she received a letter from a *male* college friend who had left New England for a teaching job in Mississippi. "When I arrived there," wrote the young man, "I found a community unappreciative of the fact that there are teachers and teachers. . . . There was another teacher there to underbid for the work, an old wreck of a man . . . so that, not being desirous of the school anyway, I ceased effort for it."[4] Minerva's friend added that he was now studying law. If "the old wreck of a man" represented Beecher's generation, Minerva's male friend represented the new. Common or public school teaching never became a first choice *career for a man*.[5] If men committed themselves to careers in education, they became administrators or wrote on the subject of education. Lacking male prestige and associated with children, teaching held special status more out of sentimentality than out of the power and significance that Catherine Beecher had claimed for it. By the 1880s, "custom" and "prejudice" had become forces that assigned women to a profession that could be characterized as "special, yet shadowed."[6] Special because it had the capacity to shape the lives of youth and the potential to set their course for the future; shadowed because it became and remained a poorly compensated semi-profession where women's "natural" dependence and lack of public power were exploited.

Beginning with the pioneering historical work of David Tyack, Richard Bernard and Maris Vinovskis, Geraldine Clifford, and Carl Kaestle, the story of the feminization of teaching is perhaps the most frequently told of the historical scholarship about the profession.[7] Yet so deeply embedded in our psyches is the picture of a female called up by the word "teacher" that it is useful for readers to attempt to "make the familiar strange" — to ask fresh questions about the conditions under which feminization took place. This chapter is framed in two ways: by recent historical analysis that places women's free labor in the context of the development of a market economy in republican America; and by the notion that the teacher, unlike other female wage laborers, could use her work as "a seminary for social power," in the phrase of one contemporaneous commentator.[8] Teaching gave women public standing and allowed them to enter public discourse. Neither of these frames of analyzing teaching has been much explored.

Historians concerned with women's participation in the market tend to focus on less professionalized forms of women's labor — factory work, millwork, and household service — that reveal the workings of emergent capitalism. With regard to social power, historians have tended to focus on more visible and high-profile platforms for women than teaching — preaching, abolitionist and suffragist activism, temperance, and the organization of women's benevolent associations. Indeed, although a very high proportion of female political and religious activists — African American and white — taught as young women, their teaching histories are presented as way stations that precede significant public work, rather than as consequential apprenticeships in which young women could practice speaking, leading, and managing. But there is much to learn in the analysis of teaching as a form of free labor; more than other work, teaching blurred the boundaries between the sexes and transferred some traits associated with men to the province of women.[9] And paradoxically, women's lived experience in the education labor market challenged assumptions about teaching as an extension of mothering just at the moment when such an analogy was most frequently used to justify women's work outside of the home. Teaching allowed women to gain their livelihoods, to further their educations in high schools and normal schools, to speak their minds (if only to children), and to have some public standing as they negotiated contracts and made agreements with men about the conditions of their employment. In their curricular demands and rigor, the early normal schools even explicitly worked against the deep-rooted assumptions that care is the greatest asset women bring to the profession, while disciplined thinking is the male contribution.

Acknowledging the shadow over teaching and its ambiguous status, a writer in *The National Teacher* (1872) nonetheless argued that teaching was the only way for a woman to become mature, realistic, and competent in the late nineteenth century. Much of his practical analysis might describe the impact of teaching on the teacher at least to the turn of the twentieth century, and on into the 1950s in small towns. First, the writer recognized that a well-educated young woman had really only two choices: to stay at home, or to teach. About the first choice, he agreed with Catherine Beecher — women waste their power, they languish without the purposefulness demanded by a career and a niche in public life. He criticized young women who left school "unable to lead their fellow beings, with no idea of responsibility to anybody for anything. . . . What an insecure position this is for any human being they sooner or later find out."

The writer also had a pragmatic grasp of the virtues of the classroom as a school for the female teacher. The teacher might "shape the soul and mould the character" of the young — the aspect of the job that earlier, more sentimental writers had emphasized — but she would only be successful if she learned the rules of work in the public world: "the homely virtues of punctuality, persistence, conformity to the imperative facts of daily life, regard for others, business accuracy, precision." She would mature as a leader under the discipline of "the pitiless frame-work of iron school law." He called the classroom a "seminary for social power" and urged women not to worry about society's prejudices against the woman who worked, but to teach. It was the best choice a nineteenth-century woman could make.[10]

## Teaching Before It Became Woman's Profession

"Civil society must be built on the four cornerstones of the church, the school-house, the militia, and the town-meeting," said John Adams, the second president of the United States.[11] Adams' word "cornerstone" suggests that simple but fundamental task of the school in pre–Civil War America. The red- or white-frame schoolhouse on the village green did its part to support civil society by making sure that young children were literate. In the typical twelve or fourteen weeks each winter that school "kept," boys and some girls, released from farm work, learned to read, to write, and to cipher by the method of rote recitation. Among agricultural people, parents assumed that generation would follow generation on the land. To want education for its own sake would have been thought odd, and certainly few would have approved schools that taught children more than their parents knew. As for values, there was a commonplace morality — obedience, respect, truthfulness, thrift — that appeared in the few current schoolbooks.

The teacher of the village school was usually a man, as were the teachers in urban areas. A student of the ministry or at college to learn a profession, he taught not for love but to earn money during his long winter vacation. Farther from the city, the teacher was often a college dropout or a fellow with some handicap that ill-suited him for farm life. Said one forthright commentator looking back in 1890, teaching was "a half-way house for those bound for the learned professions, and a hospital for the weak-minded of those who have already entered them."[12] Unpredictable in qualifications and frequently committed to no more than a single winter in a school, the rural teacher accurately reflected the low priority given to education in agricultural society. Carpenters, blacksmiths, carters, and other artisans critical to rural survival earned more money and respect.

Adult women and sometimes young girls also taught, though in small numbers, and rarely in winter school when travel was treacherous, at least in the Northeast. The older women, often widows in need of income, kept private "dame schools." For a small sum, a cord of wood, or a supply of eggs or milk, the dame would have three or four young children in her home to learn the ABCs and ciphering. Her instruction insured that the child could later participate in village civic and religious life, and keep track of simple financial transactions. These dame schools also apparently reflected the priorities of the village. There were numerous jokes at the expense of the dame, and stories of her cruelty. "These apologies for schools," wrote an anonymous author in *Harper's* in 1878, speaking of an earlier time, "are often kept by some Miss Hepzibah Pyncheon, who has a little shop with gingerbread and tape for sale; and in the window, by the side of these tempting wares, a sign is displayed announcing that 'a school is kept here.' . . . Young America, so scornful of all relics of the past, has forgotten that he . . . was pinned to an old woman's apron while he said his letters."[13] A less demeaning view is that the dame school provided basic education and child care for mothers who often gave birth at regular intervals and needed some provision for children who had finished nursing and were too young to work at domestic chores.

Of particular interest are schools run by female Quakers starting before the turn of the eighteenth century. In rural Pennsylvania, female Quaker ministers began to encourage young women to care for and teach the children of the poor. As the number of such young women increased, older women began to serve on school committees, to raise money for schools, and to promote more systematic schooling for the poor. Both Philadelphia and Wilmington, Delaware, had schools for "the Free Instruction of Female Children" staffed by young women. In the nineteenth century, Philadelphia Quakers established boarding schools and seminaries for girls where they could learn to be Quaker teachers.[14] Quakers also sponsored schools for African American youth. In the 1830s, for example, Sarah Mapps Douglas, an African American woman supported by Quakers, opened and led the first high school for African American girls. A second school, the famed Institute for Colored Youth, was founded under Philadelphia Quaker auspices in 1837. The Institute was led later in the century by Fanny Coppin-Jackson, author of *Reminiscences of School Life, and Hints on Teaching*, a selection from which appears here.[15]

The young New England girl who kept school often saw teaching as an escape from farm work, and her family was less likely to frown on her love of books than if she had been a boy. In accounts like those of Emma Hart Willard, Lucia Downing, and Mary Pratt included in this chapter, the young women seemed to be taken with the idea of teaching in an instant. All three had reveled in surpassing the achievements of their classmates and siblings in school, and teaching offered one of the rare chances for adventure, if only intellectual and social. In fact, the only acceptable way a young woman could "seek her fortune" as young men did with frequency was vicariously in books, and teaching allowed her to take a further step in making that "voyaging" public. Although Lucia Downing described herself deprecatingly as unable to sing and unskilled at drawing, at age fourteen, by her own account, she taught her four scholars "the entire realm of knowledge" (see p. 64) by means of "instructive Questions and Answers" (see p. 65) that she had composed herself. She was pleased to be rewarded with a school of fifteen children the following year. Sixteen-year-old Emma Hart, destined to become a pioneer educator of women, made her school a showplace, "the admiration of the neighborhood" (see p. 53). Unlike men who taught, both young women sought further schooling with the firm idea that teaching would be their life's work, their calling. In the informal rural school, each had discovered the pleasure of exerting her intellect and her will in public — pleasures usually reserved for men.

### The Teacher "Becomes" a Woman

While informal rural schools supported directly by parents survived in America late into the nineteenth century, the 1840s and 1850s marked the first attempts to create a state-supported system of common schools and to redefine the mission of schooling.[16] One might characterize the extremes of the old schooling and the new as follows. Through the first decades of the nineteenth century, schools had taught a few relatively basic skills to farm children. The crucial lessons — how to plant, to weave, to can, to milk, to sew — were learned "naturally" in the family, but now schools were explicitly to supplement the family as teacher. While in the past the village doctor or minister had examined, hired, and supervised teachers according to a local standard of his own, from their offices in state government, educated "schoolmen" were now to enforce *their* ideas of education. Where once the teacher had been the butt of humor — a laughable, absent-minded weakling; a crotchety old man — now the teacher was popularly portrayed as a thoroughly useful figure, a custodian of American character whose mission it was to discipline, instruct, and inspire the young. The teacher was also portrayed as a woman.

Three intertwined, massive social changes gave woman her new profession and education its new importance: industrialization, immigration, and urbanization. The first of these changes provides a backdrop for women's entrance into the paid labor market in any numbers. Throughout the nineteenth century, and with increasing volume at mid-century, opinion-makers cited the doctrine of separate spheres for women and men as necessary to the maintenance of a moral society in a world of exploding and largely unregulated capitalist expansion. In the typical formulation, they labeled the moral home the domain of women and the unruly market the domain of men. Not only did the separation of the spheres reinforce middleclass domesticity, the concept also introduced one of the most significant aspirations of the abolition of slavery. As imagined by abolitionists, the purpose of setting formerly enslaved men to wage labor was both the restoration of human dignity to males and the restoration of patriarchy within the family. Abolitionists argued that, if formerly enslaved men were able to earn a living wage, they would be able to situate their wives in the appropriate role as dependents — subordinated in marriage, relegated to the home, and able to promulgate the requisite pieties to protect the family from the exploitation of the market. Working males would sell their own labor, where in the antebellum system human beings were themselves commodities. Only some female abolitionists — Sojourner Truth and the Grimke sisters are preeminent — spoke explicitly against the commodification of women and claimed women's rights and contributions as laborers paid and unpaid.

In the 1960s, the emergent field of women's studies focused attention on the separation of the spheres using common nineteenth-century descriptive language uncritically, as if it represented the roles to which middle-class men and women were confined. In what Linda Kerber calls the current stage of understanding of the term *separate spheres*, historians see emergent capitalism as requiring renegotiation of gender relationships. As Amy Dru Stanley argues, there is substantial evidence that the match between the doctrine of separate spheres and material reality was "overly simple." From the turn of the eighteenth century on, women were increasing their participation in the market economy. The home became a more active site of production with women giving their labor cash value by selling wares in towns and villages. And as farming became more of a business, women took a role in managing money for and with their husbands, entering into trade agreements, producing crafts that sold on city streets. In the city, immigrants and poor women African American and white did "outwork" [factory piecework completed at home] and took in lodgers and boarders, and New England's young women flocked to the mills and factories in growing numbers. There is also evidence that prosperous women who led antebellum benevolent societies were often compensated for their work, and certainly carried out business-like practices in ministering to the poor — keeping accounts, investing, and raising money. And, finally, beginning in the 1830s, married women's property laws began to change — undercutting the traditional notion that women's identity was legally subsumed by that of their husbands. In short, market and home interpenetrated, and gender identities were far more fluid than the metaphor of separate spheres would lead one to imagine.[17]

Stanley argues that the doctrine of the spheres "did a great deal of ideological work," portraying "the home sphere of women" as the antidote to the "selfish materialism of the economic domain of men." But, she continues, not only was women's work changing, so too was the explanation of human psychology that "accompanied the triumph of the market economy":

> In the eighteenth century, to engage in speculative exchange relations, to be buffeted by fortune, was to be dependent — the fate of women. The emergence of a new "marketing psychology" entailed valorizing impulse, passion, fantasy, and appetite. That meant reconceiving as inherent in men's nature the very propensities that had been equated shamefully with female hysteria, slavish dependence, and social disorder.[18]

In other words, the characteristics of the self-sufficient, independent Republican farmer beholden to no one differed dramatically from the qualities of the capitalist who sold his labor, just as the dependent hireling had always done but with greater risk and reliance on chance. These capitalist qualities blurred the lines between the genders. If Stanley is correct, then the market arrangements that teaching engendered were like those experienced by men. To gain independence and agency, a teacher substituted for dependence on her family dependence on the market in which she sold her labor, but she was situated somewhere between the hireling and the capitalist — more autonomous than the mill worker or laundress, less free than the speculator or businessman.

These abstract assertions about gender and historical change are the fabric of a human drama that altered daily experience for most Americans in the course of three or four decades. Set as the changing landscape for an individual life, these abstractions become concrete. Because Catherine Beecher might be called the genius of woman's "true" profession, and because she came to adulthood just as the massive changes began, her life offers an illuminating example of the complex intersection of the individual actor and the historical moment.

In 1800, when Beecher was born, the United States was largely a society of small farmers. In southern New England, to which she moved with her family in 1810, two-thirds of the population lived in villages of fewer than 3,000 inhabitants. As the oldest daughter in the busy household of the sought-after minister Lyman Beecher, Catherine made or supervised the making of all daily necessities. These included the weaving of cloth and the sewing of garments, done by women in the household. By 1823, when Catherine and her sister Mary opened a girls' school in Hartford, Connecticut, other young women of their age were also leaving their families. The landscape of New England had begun to change. Factories where cloth was woven by machine hired, housed, and paid decent wages to Yankee mill girls. "Daughters are now emphatically a blessing to the farmer," wrote an observer in 1831.[19] Wages sent home gave woman economic value. They also gave her a taste for independence. In 1850, more than 59,000 Massachusetts women were employed in the cotton mills.[20] By 1869 there were so many laborers in Massachusetts that the General Court established a Bureau of Labor Statistics. The Bureau began the systematic collection of data about women workers. By 1883, so concerned had the Bureau become with the conditions of women's labor in Boston that Carroll Wright, the commissioner, ordered an in-depth study of 1,000 of the 20,000 working girls of Boston employed in nearly eighty occupations.[21]

During the 1830s, Catherine Beecher moved to Cincinnati with her father. There she began her campaign to train teachers for western children growing up beyond the reach of schools. As she traveled between the western cities, Beecher saw in the stream of westward migrants the results of overcrowding and competition for jobs in New England. Thousand upon thousand of immigrants, seven out of ten escaping persecution and famine in Ireland, were pouring into Boston, drawn by tales of lucrative factory jobs. The population of Beecher's Connecticut increased 31 percent in the ten years between 1840 and 1850, then an astonishing 42 percent between 1850 and 1860.[22]

As Beecher penned her popular *Treatise on Domestic Economy* (1841), its sequel *The Domestic Receipt Book* (1846), and *The Evils Suffered by American Women and American Children* (1846) (excerpted in this chapter), the housewife to whom she wrote needed all manner of advice. The young Yankee husband who was not inclined to farm now had an alternative to ministering and teaching. Leaving his wife to guard the hearth of their home near the city, the Yankee farmer's son responded to the lure of the business world. There were money, status, and excitement in trading cotton futures at the stock market, planning railroads, managing factories, and working out legal agreements, as Minerva Leland's friend planned to do. Man spends his life "in the collisions of the world," wrote Beecher, and desires "notoriety and the praise of men" — far different qualities than those valorized, for example, in the iconic *Letters from an American Farmer* by J. Hector St. John De Crevecoeur (1782), in which the land is personified as the source of plenty:

> *Bless the hour in which thou didst see my verdant fields, my fair navigable rivers, and my green mountains! If thou wilt work, I have bread for thee; if thou wilt be honest, sober, and industrious, I have greater rewards to confer on thee — ease and independence. I will give thee fields to feed and cloath thee; a comfortable fireside to sit by, and tell thy children by what means thou hast prospered; and a decent bed to repose on. I shall endow thee beside with the immunities of a freeman.*[23]

At the end of the Civil War in 1865, and thirteen years before

Beecher's death, the "collisions of the world" had resulted in a society dominated by industrial and business interests, a society more similar to that of the 1890s than to the world of Beecher's birth.

This radical transformation of society had its impact on education. First, there were simply more children, many in the city or nearby. Between 1840 and 1860, the school population doubled in Massachusetts. Nationally, in 1850 there were 3,350,000 common school students, and 5,000,000 ten years later.[24] In the industrial world they had to know much more than their parents had learned. And, second, thousands of teachers were needed just at the moment when the expanding economy provided unprecedented choices for men. Teachers were also needed at a moment when cities were designing schools and school systems that paralleled the hierarchical organization of factories and business enterprises. In the Northeast, where change was apparent by the mid-nineteenth century, educators began to declare that women, the "natural" teachers, should staff the graded schools. They received one third to one half of a man's pay, an inequality that went largely unquestioned until the first decades of the twentieth century, and was not universally resolved until mid-century.[25]

But the story is also more complex than the often-stated argument that cheapness and a dearth of qualified men inspired school boards to hire women regardless of their qualifications. Indeed, had school boards wished to hire well-educated women at the turn of the eighteenth century, they would have been unable to do so because women who could teach the "higher branches" were few. Indeed, in Massachusetts and Pennsylvania, states for which we have reasonable data, about 60 percent of females over twenty-one were still illiterate in 1775, but by 1820 almost all white native-born females were literate.[26] By mid-century, many young women had completed the same curriculum (writing, math, Latin) as young men, especially outside of the rural South.[27] Thus one might hypothesize that educated young women themselves may have been the heralds to school boards of their own availability and of their equal qualifications; they may have sought an education because they aspired to leave the family farm, to work for wages, and to use their minds.

That an education might enable a young woman to assume a public role became thinkable by mid-century. An interlocutor asks Christie, the impoverished antebellum heroine of Louisa May Alcott's novel *Work*, the identity of the speaker she has heard at church. Hardly disguising her envy of the free exercise of intellect, Christie replies:

> *A very young man who seemed to be airing his ideas and beliefs in the frank-*
> *est manner. He belabored everybody and every thing, upset church and state,*
> *called names, arranged heaven and earth to suit himself, and evidently*
> *meant every word he said... and though people smiled, they liked his*
> *courage, and seemed to think he would make a man when his spiritual wild*
> *oats were sown.*

Although Christie gets to marry the intellectual young man, not to "become" him, in later life she is enabled to read, to discuss, and to speak on behalf of working women. She becomes an advocate against the enforced idleness of women of means, urging a small circle to become reformers; and she sows the female version of her own wild oats by thinking, acting, and speaking controversially as she champions working women, both African American and white.[28]

Catherine Beecher, the early and eloquent spokesperson for woman's profession, used the doctrine of separate spheres to "do ideological work"; she reconceptualized the traits appropriate to women, putting useful work and independence in place of frivolity and dependence. From the time of the founding of Hartford Female Seminary, Beecher had been a tireless proselytizer for women's education. In her twenties she had already defined and exalted woman's work as teacher within the family circle. Women were more suited than men to the work of human development, she argued, because they were more "benevolent," more willing to "make sacrifices of personal enjoyment." Beecher thought that the mother's "curriculum" should consist of healthful habits, graceful manners, and above all, the formation of conscience.

By 1830, Beecher had identified a public arena for woman's power. "To enlighten the understanding and to gain the affections," she wrote to a friend, is "a teacher's business." (Note the use of the word "business.") For this work, woman is "best fitted." Always a public proponent of separate "spheres," Beecher distinguished teaching from improper intrusions of females into the male world of paid work: the school was an extension of or substitute for the domestic culture of the home. In her public addresses on the subject, Beecher reassured her audience that the female teacher remained truly feminine; she had no desire for notoriety and, like the ideal mother, worked "not for money, not for influence, nor for honour, nor for ease, but with the simple, single purpose of doing good."[29] If her highly visible public work, her fundraising, traveling, negotiating, and dependence on gaining the good will of others ever seemed an ironic contradiction to her own words, Beecher did not call attention to it.

Beecher had a second argument for promoting women as teachers: Women needed "a high and honorable profession to engage their time" (see p. 75). Troubled by woman's economic vulnerability, Beecher identified its cause as woman's limited choices of work. In the densely populated eastern states, Beecher saw women engaged in dangerous work "at prices that will not keep body and soul together." The clothing manufacturers "grow rich on the hard labors of our sex," she declared. "Tales there are to be told of the sufferings of American women in our eastern cities so shocking that they would scarcely be credited, and yet they are true beyond dispute" (see p. 72). Indeed, that teaching compared extremely favorably with factory work is a point not lost on young Mary Swift, a member of the first class at the first normal school in the country educating women to become teachers. In 1839, as a normalite, she visited factories for making cotton along the Charles River in Cambridge, Massachusetts. Wrote Mary in her journal:

*We entered the lower room which was [?] to Carding, the next above to Spinning, next to Weaving, and next to Dressing. — The noise of the Machinery was so great, that, at first, we were unable to hear each other speak.— The poor girls are now, more an object of my pity than ever before. — They generally looked very pale, & I should think, according to the principle of Physiology, must suffer much from lung complaints, on account of the particles of cotton constantly floating in the atmosphere.* (see p. 92)

Beecher also recognized that teaching, with its missionary ideology and its image as an extension of mothering, could be accepted as a *chosen* alternative to marriage for a woman of the educated classes. Marriage was, of course, the first choice, but Beecher asserted, "Woman ought never to be led to married life except under the promptings of pure affection. To marry for an establishment, for a position, or for something to do is a deplorable wrong. But how many women, for want of a high and honorable profession are led to this melancholy course." Only the teacher could "discern before her the road to honorable independence and extensive usefulness" where she need not out step the prescribed boundaries of feminine modesty. Like Beecher herself, a teacher could travel, live in the company of other women, spend money as she chose, and still remain a true woman.

Beecher's first two arguments were buttressed by a third that, in an extraordinarily modern way, encouraged women not to sacrifice, but to look out for themselves. Thinking perhaps of the many female complaints — hysteria among them — attributed to educated, idle, unmarried middle-class women, she saw the cause in the absence of serious work. Such women often became parlor ornaments, forced into rounds of superficial social obligations. Teaching, Beecher believed, no doubt from her own experience as an unmarried woman with a career, would end this debilitating and enforced idleness, end the consequent "diseases of the mind and body, that afflict females of the higher classes" (see p. 76).

Beecher's arguments and those of the schoolmen about moral decay fed the fears of public leaders. While the writings of the period are filled with testimonies to the thriving American economy, American inventiveness, practicality, and "admirable material progress," they are filled as well with earnest cautions. Urban industrial society, most old New Englanders believed, had a devastating effect on character. The "outward show" of the city destroyed inward strength and, furthermore, it encouraged envy and emulation (or competition). To get rich quickly now seemed more a matter of luck than of hard work, self-discipline, and conservatism. The school was to save the middle-class child from "the race for wealth, luxury, ambition and pride," and the immigrant child from "the inherited stupidity of centuries of ignorant ancestors."[30] Clearly, such an enterprise required more than instruction in the three Rs, and the reinforcement of the communal values of the pre-industrial village.

There were male idea-makers who, along with Beecher, caused Americans to shift their image of "teacher" from second-rate young man to exemplary woman. These men, however, were more interested in shaping the minds and moral values of untutored children than they were in developing education programs for women that would lead to paying work. Cyrus Peirce, Horace Mann, Henry Barnard,[31] and other New

England schoolmen represented educational reform so sweeping that they believed it would transform society. A common school system would be the "great equalizer"; it would create wealth; it would "perfect" the new republic. Most importantly, it would form character. Like Beecher, the schoolmen feared not only for the newly arrived immigrant child, but for the child of the new industrialist who would have qualities of the cosseted wife — indulged, undisciplined, and soft.

The schoolmen began with the teacher. If the common schools were to form character, the untrained, temporary male teacher was inadequate. Indeed, he was symbolic of the low status and lack of respect for the common school. And many established teachers were resistant to change. Institutions were needed to train a new teaching force to carry out the schoolmen's mission of shaping elementary-age children, especially in rural areas. Who would be the new teachers? Young women who loved books and sought dignified work. Designed on the model of European *école normale*, the first American normal school or teacher's college was soon on the drawing board. Although they had to pay their own fees for books and board, students were also promised reimbursement after a period of common-school teaching, an agreement that was attractive to many farm girls. Approved and funded in part privately, in part by the state legislature, Lexington Academy, the first of three state normal schools in Massachusetts, opened in 1839. The second girls-only school opened in Salem in 1854. Bridgewater and Barre opened co-ed schools in 1838 and in 1840, respectively. In 1869, just four years after her graduation from Oberlin College, Fanny Jackson-Coppin, then the principal of the private, Quaker-supported Institute for Coloured Youth in Philadelphia, created a coeducational normal course to supply African American teachers for the schools of the South. By 1870, the country could count thirty-eight state normal schools; by 1890, 102, including several all-white and all–African American institutions, among them one at Howard University.[32] While most elementary teachers, especially in rural areas, continued to be trained in their own village schools, the idea of professional training for teaching had taken hold. Indeed, there was even an American Normal School Association that had as its platform raising standards, requiring a high school diploma for matriculation, and educating not elementary teachers but high school teachers and administrators.[33]

## By Example and Precept: Normal School Education

On the morning of August 1, 1839, 17-year-old Mary Swift took her place in the Lexington Academy lecture hall for the first day at the first state normal school in America. Under the leadership of principal Cyrus Peirce, along with twenty-four other young women, Mary began to study the "common branches" or academic disciplines, a philosophy of forming character, and a pedagogy for succeeding at both. At Lexington Academy a profession for women was born.[34] In her new journal, purchased "agreeably to the wishes of our teacher," Mary began to record all that transpired in the creation of the new profession: its theory and practice; the themes of lectures given by a procession of distinguished visitors; the behavior of the young lady students. For Mary and her teachers, as the journal entries reprinted below make evident, the venture had great seriousness. Here young women were being educated as they had never been before — not to teach in private seminaries for the educated classes, not to go as Christian missionaries among "the heathens," but to take part in a public venture financed by the state on behalf of the populace. They were to be workers who would transform the inadequate rural schools and staff the new city institutions that would shape urban society. As Cyrus Peirce anxiously reminded them, all "friends of education" awaited their success.[35]

The themes of seriousness and professionalism were reinforced daily. On that first day, a visiting professor compared the young women to medical students, and suggested that they take lecture notes as future doctors did. In addition, he urged the future teachers to "think seriously upon the subject of [elevating the moral standards of the schools]." They would influence the pupils "both by example and precept." Two weeks later, in his weekly lecture, "Father Peirce" explicitly attacked the current image of teachers as "qualified for nothing else." This image, he declared, was historically inaccurate — the ancients employed only their wisest men as teachers. As if to encourage his teenage students to make their best efforts, he also stressed the teacher's significance to society. "Inadequacy in the common trades," he told the young women, "is felt only by the person himself, but in the teacher, its consequences are felt by the pupils, and their influence does not only extend to this moment or year, but is felt by succeeding generations. . . . It is better to make one thousand machines go wrong," said Peirce, using a striking trope from the new industrial age, "than to train up a child as he should not go."[36]

Despite the fact that most students attended only for a year or at most two, the first normal schools were a gift to studious girls who wanted to work and had not their brothers' option of enrolling in college. Like college, Lexington Academy required its students to study science, math, and philosophy. In addition, the first American theorists of education tried out radical new ideas on the young women. Against all current practice, they argued that rote recitations — the chant of the ABCs and the multiplication tables — should be exchanged for a pedagogy that engaged children's cooperation in learning to solve problems and seek information for themselves. Peirce compared the old and the new in the story of two boys "both eager to see all they can." One was carried to the summit of a hill by his parents, the second ascended alone, "by the use of much dexterity." At the next hill the first child was again carried, but the second ascended alone, and more easily. The parable illustrated that teaching a scholar to assist herself is better than assisting her in every difficulty.[37]

No narrow taskmaster, Peirce set an example of the new education for his students by fostering such a degree of speculation and critical inquiry that visitors remarked on it. Nor did he require conformity. In his own journal he wrote, "We have no block or mold by which all are cast, so that there may be uniformity of character in the Prepared Teacher." To illustrate the new mode of teaching and learning, Peirce established a model school for village children. Here the young women began an apprenticeship in their new profession. Usually taciturn about herself, according to the style of early nineteenth-century journal writers, Mary Swift was sufficiently inspired by the experience of teaching to write regretfully, "This day a new class of instructors go into the Model school, and I resign my place. . . . My attachment to the school is much greater than I could have anticipated from so short a connection with it."[38]

While Mary Swift may have been pleased with the new opportunities before her, as the first years unfolded, the schoolmen and Peirce himself became dissatisfied with the result. Too many young women, Peirce and his contemporaries complained, chose teaching "as an inexpensive way to resume their formal education to prepare themselves for desirable gainful employment" in the city. Their behavior belied the theory that women would sacrifice themselves to assume the work of "citizen-teachers" in rural schools more readily than men.[39] Peirce wrote critically in his diary of the limited intellectual capacities of his incoming students — missing the point that poorly educated and of meager means themselves, his young women students may have been motivated by finding paying work away from the farm rather than by the desire to fulfill a typically female charitable goal. This theory was further substantiated by the ease with which the city normal schools fulfilled their missions. Boston Girl's High School and Normal School, for example, had no difficulty attracting young women to prepare to take on elementary school classrooms when it added a normal course in 1852. (This unit separated in 1872 to become Boston Normal School, then Teachers College of the City of Boston, then Boston State Teachers College, and, finally, Boston State College, before merging with University of Massachusetts Boston in the late 1970s.[40])

There was a second important consequence of the failure of the original normal schools to attract women who wanted to work in rural elementary education: The heads of many "normals" responded by enlarging their mission — to provide more rigorous academic course work so that *male* graduates could teach in the expanding high schools and become administrators. But the male graduates remained few, and most disappeared into professions other than teaching.[41] Toward the end of the century, the city normal schools in many states became the training ground for female elementary teachers, and state normal schools increasingly defined their mission as the preparation of high school teachers, both female and male, the scientific study of pedagogy, and the preparation of administrators.[42]

As historian Jergen Herbst points out, citing as an example a Missouri report carried out by the Carnegie Foundation for the Advancement of Teaching, by the early decades of the twentieth century, despite their overwhelmingly female student population, "all references to teachers are to men. *He* not *she* would someday become a normal school professor or superintendent or would be professionally recognized as an elementary school teacher."[43] And so began the odd dissimulation: Although normal schools were always dominated by female students, professional educators who ran the schools sought prestige and reputation by depicting their students as men. As Geraldine Clifford argued in a provocative 1981 essay on teaching as a seedbed of feminism, most parents, teachers, and policy makers "unconsciously accept . . . the proposition that no occupation . . . can have status, appropriate compensation and public confidence unless it is significantly male." [44]

## Woman's "True" Profession: "Special, but Shadowed"[45]

By 1860, young women trained like Mary Swift had a profession of their own. The "sacred office" gave them public status, the claim to a decent income, freedom to marry only for "pure affection," and their own institutions of higher education. But like many victories for women, this one was contradictory and qualified. Both in resources and in reputation, normal schools suffered the fate of many women's institutions. Their work on behalf of women was obscured — the schools were silent about the degree to which they served women, or they actively sought males to gain prestige. Thus until recent reassessments by feminist historians of the significance of the normal schools movement, these schools were vastly under-appreciated and under-studied; indeed, their "real" histories were dated to when they shed the "normal" nomenclature and became higher-status state colleges. For example, one historian saw in them nothing more than the reflection of the bureaucratizing school systems, with their graded classrooms, prescribed curricula, and heavy-handed control from male administrators and school boards. He failed to understand the autonomy and enlargement they brought to young women who otherwise would have been unable to further their educations.[46]

The title of Christine Ogren's 2000 study announces the reassessment: "A Large Measure of Self-Control and Personal Power: Women Students at State Normal Schools During the Late-Nineteenth and Early Twentieth Century." Citing a phrase about Emma Willard's Troy Female Seminary established many years earlier — that it was "an important source of feminism and the incubator of a new style of female personality" — Ogren argues that in the "normals" "separate gender spheres faded into the background."[47] In these schools women from humble farm communities were taken seriously as scholars; they edited newspapers, ran and participated in drama and debating societies, gave public speeches, and even played basketball. In addition, because most "normals" supported campus or laboratory schools, women teacher candidates learned experientially, forming their own theories of learning, especially in the unexplored realm of educational psychology. While they did not by and large take part in the activist "woman" movement led by women who had taught, but were generally from more prosperous backgrounds, according to Ogren, "they wrote about women's rights . . . in their literary societies and publications." At a normal in Illinois, "the all-female Sapphonian Society . . . debated such resolutions as 'the maiden lady can do more to benefit humanity than the married lady' and 'woman should compete with man in all possible vocations.'"[48]

By the end of the nineteenth century, the profession of teaching had moved to the position that it would hold for the next century and beyond: less than equal in status to male professions, *and* a source of satisfaction and power for women. Teaching was to remain "shadowed," but it was also "special." This chapter ends with a reflection on that duality. It takes up once again the question of the degree to which teaching was, and is today, a seminary for social power, an incubator of a new kind of female personality.

A short story that appeared in 1865 in *Harper's New Monthly* demonstrates how the lofty calling defined by Beecher, Peirce, Mann, and others remained in the popular imagination as a burden assumed by women. Here, then, was the shadow. The key phrases in the following excerpt from the story, "Tom's Education," link "true woman" with "self-sacrifice," and oppose both to "stalwart man." Note that both the woman and the man disparage teaching. In the story, Tom has returned home after flunking out of college; his sister Milly, a teacher, urges him to "hear little Frank St. Clair's lessons" in order to "have something laid up against the fall." The following dialogue ensues:

> "Now, Milly, that's little too much," answered Tom, with quite an injured air. "Do you think I'm adapted to teaching stupid little brats? Do you think I could spend my time hammering ideas into a wooden-headed youngster! No, I thank you. I would rather measure ribbon, if you please; it is far more entertaining and easy."
>
> "And yet, Tom," I answered, with a throb of pain at my heart, "I have this to do. I have to retrace all the dusty and dry paths of elementary knowledge that you think so terrible."
>
> "Ah, yes!" answered Tom, conceitedly, "but you are a woman and women somehow adapt themselves so easily to circumstances. Now I have not the

*least adaptation to such things. I'd rather hang myself than be a school-teacher."*

*I was silent. I knew a better name than adaptation to apply to that readi-ness with which a true woman assumes burdens that a stalwart man would find intolerable. It was self-sacrifice."*

In the short story "The Schoolmarm," reproduced in this chapter, teaching is seen just as precisely as "special." For the story's central char-acter, Mary William Pratt, teaching in a village common school in the 1860s was not just an escape from household drudgery, but the beginning of an independent, self-confident womanhood. Against her grandmoth-er's warnings that she would end up an old maid, Mary took a job for $350 a year in the village school as an assistant:

> *She had never been so happy in her life as she was the day on which she stepped upon the platform at school and assumed the responsibilities of "schoolmarm." Mary William loved to teach, and she loved to rule — an art she understood to perfection. There were some pretty black sheep among her flock, but before she had had them a month they had learned a lesson in wholesome discipline. . . . By Christmas time Miss Pratt's name was men-tioned in connection with a $500 vacancy in the high school. Meanwhile Mary reveled in her independence, and if she thought of matrimony in con-nection with herself, it was as a state of bondage to be avoided at any cost."*

To return to Stanley's notion that gender traits allocated between males and females were blurred if not exchanged as the labor market grew, we might reflect on the words above about Mary Pratt — she loved to teach, she loved to rule; she opposed her independence to the bondage of matrimony. We might also reflect on the words of Sarah Dixon, an 1885 Bridgewater, Massachusetts, graduate writing about her model-school experience: "Few can estimate the value of this experience for after life. To mount the platform and brace feet, mind and heart for this difficult task called continually for a large measure of self-control and personal power." [49] And we might recall the male commentator who saw good in the requirement that teachers conform to "the homely virtues of punctuality, persistence, conformity to the imperative facts of daily life, regard for others, business accuracy, precision." He claimed that teachers would become leaders under the discipline of "the pitiless frame-work of iron school law." To what do these comments add up? If teaching was a seminary for social power, into what new kinds of work did women graduate? What was the quality of agency nineteenth-century teachers were able to exercise?

Writing in 1981, before feminist theory had provided many tools for analyzing such questions, Geraldine Clifford answers these questions in two ways that more recent analysis confirms: First, substantial numbers of women who spent their early years in classrooms became leaders in the abolitionist and suffrage movements as well as in pro-woman organizations like the Women's Christian Temperance Union, the National Women's Suffrage Association, the National Association of Colored Women, and women's club work. Second, "teaching . . . gave young, usually unsophisticated and parochial women a 'public' existence . . . [that enhanced] their capabilities and self-confidence."[50] The roll call of feminist and abolitionist teachers includes Elizabeth Cady Stanton, Lucretia Mott, Lucy Stone, Amelia Bloomer, Abbey Kelley Foster, Antoinette Brown, Clara Barton, and Dorothea Dix. It includes as well distinguished African American women: Myrtilla Miner, the founder (1851) of the Colored Girls School in Washington, D.C.; and Mary Ann Shadd Cary and Mary Bibb. Both became women's rights and anti-slavery activists, fled to Canada in 1850 to teach and establish newspapers — *The Provincial Freeman* and *Voice of the Fugitive*, respectively. Later African American leaders who began their public lives as teachers include Mary Church Terrell, the cofounder, with Josephine Ruffin, of the Association of Afro-American Women and the first president of the National Association of Colored Women (1896), and Mary McLeod Bethune, founder of Daytona Educational and Industrial Training School, later Bethune-Cookman College.

But for *this* social history that tells the story of teaching as a mass profession for women, it is the agency developed in teaching, not the later assumption of high-visibility public and politically radical work, that requires commentary. From this point of view, the classroom must be considered a different space than those that women occupied within the agrarian family, in the factory, or in the world of paid housework. The platform that most mounted at the front of the class; the lessons one organized, led and heard; the display of one's physical body in front of a group; the exercise of control over other humans, however youthful; the control over oneself in a culture that saw women as weak, prone to tears and unshielded emotions; the contracts in which young women negotiated terms of their employment; and the status one gained in earning a living and often sending some portion home — all of these suggest that the teacher had opportunities for power that contradicted gender conventions, combining rather than separating the characteristics associated with each sphere. Teachers were doing public work that, as Sarah Dixon claimed, engaged mind — and then "heart." Their work contributed to the slowly changing public notion of what women *could* do and might *choose* to do if given a chance.

# Pioneering the Education of Young Women

*Emma Hart Willard*

From Emma Hart Willard, *Educational Biographies, Memoirs of Teachers, Educators, and Promoters and Benefactors of Education, Literature, and Science, Part 1: Teachers and Educators*, 2nd ed. (New York: F. C. Brownell, 1861).

*Excerpted from an autobiographical sketch, the selection below by Emma Hart Willard (1787–1870) describes her first experiences as a teacher, at age seventeen. Willard's account exemplifies the challenge a young woman could set for herself in the village school before teaching became a woman's profession. The teachers a village might attract, however, varied widely in quality, as no training was required and there were no mandated school taxes, thus no commitment of citizens to pay for education. Emma Willard flourished in her schoolroom. First at Middlebury, Vermont, then at Troy Female Seminary, which she founded in 1821, Willard taught young girls subjects previously believed beyond their intellectual capacity. Science courses, for instance, were more rigorous than those at many men's colleges. Persistent in her mission to improve the education of females, she also challenged tradition by writing a treatise to the New York state legislature (women could not speak before a legislative body) advocating public support of female academies — a campaign that was ultimately successful.*

*In 1838 Willard relinquished Troy Seminary to her daughter-in-law and son, and she spent the rest of her years advocating woman's right to intellectual equality. She was briefly superintendent of schools in Hartford, Connecticut, under Henry Barnard.*

In my childhood I attended the district school, but mostly from causes already related, none of my teachers so understood me as to awaken my powers or gain much influence over me. My father, happily for his children, left to his own family, used to teach us of evenings, and read aloud to us; and in this way I became interested in books and a voracious reader. A village library supplied me with such books as Plutarch's Lives, Rollins' Ancient History, Gibbon's Rome, many books of travels, and the most celebrated of the British poets and essayists.

Near the close of my fifteenth year, a new academy was opened about three-quarters of a mile from my father's house, of which Thomas Miner, a graduate, and once a tutor of Yale College, was the Principal, afterwards well known as an eminent physician president of the State Medical Society, and one of the most learned men of our country. Before the opening of the Academy, my mother's children had each received a small dividend from the estate of a deceased brother. My sister Nancy determined, as our parents approved, to spend this in being taught at the new school; but having at that time a special desire to make a visit among my married brothers and sisters in Kensington, (whose children were of my own age), I stood one evening, candle in hand, and made to my parents, who had retired for the night, what they considered a most sensible oration, on the folly of people's seeking to be educated above their means and prescribed duties in life. So Nancy went to school, and I to Kensington. A fortnight after, one Friday evening, I returned. Nancy showed me her books and told me of her lessons. "Mother," said I, "I am going to school tomorrow." "Why, I thought that you made up your mind not to be educated, and besides, your clothes are not in order, and it will appear odd for you to enter school Saturday." But Saturday morning I went, and received my lessons in Webster's Grammar and Morse's Geography. Mr. Miner was to hear me recite by myself until I overtook the class, in which were a dozen fine girls, including my elder sister. Monday, Mr. Miner called on me to recite. He began with Webster's Grammar, went on and on, and still as he questioned received from me a ready answer, until he said, "I will hear the remainder of your lesson tomorrow." The same thing occurred with the Geography lesson. I was pleased, and thought, "you never shall get to the end of my lesson." That hard chapter on the planets, with their diameters, distances, and periodic revolutions, was among the first of Morse's Geography. The evening I wished to learn it, my sister Lydia had a party. The house was full of bustle, and above all rose the song-singing, which always fascinated me. The moon was at the full, and snow was on the ground. I wrapt my cloak around me and out of doors of a cold winter evening, seated on a horseblock, I learned that lesson. Lessons so learnt are not easily forgotten. The third day Mr. Miner admitted me to my sister's class. He used to require daily compositions. I never failed, the only one of my class who did not; but I also improved the opportunities which these afforded, to pay him off for any criticism by which he had (intentionally though indirectly) hit me, — with some parody or rhyme, at which, though sometimes pointed enough, Mr. Miner would heartily laugh — never forgetting, however, at some time or other, to retort with interest. Thus my mind was stimulated, and my progress rapid. For two successive years, 1802–3, I enjoyed the advantages of Dr. Miner's school, and I believe that no better instruction was given to girls in any school, at that time, in our country.

My life at this time was much influenced by an attachment I formed with Mrs. Peck, a lady of forty, although I was only fifteen. When we were first thrown together, it was for several days, and she treated me not as a child, but an equal — confiding to me much of that secret history which every heart sacredly cherishes; and I, on my part, opened to her my whole inner life, my secret feelings, anxieties and aspirations. Early in the spring of 1804 when I had just passed seventeen, Mrs. Peck proposed that a children's school in the village should be put into my hands.

The school-house was situated in Worthington street, on the great Hartford and New Haven turnpike; and was surrounded on the other three sides by a mulberry grove, towards which the windows were in summer kept open.

At nine o'clock, on that first morning, I seated myself among the children to begin a profession which I little thought was to last with slight interruption for forty years. That morning was the longest of my life. I began my work by trying to discover the several capacities and degrees of advancement of the children, so as to arrange them in classes; but they having been, under my predecessor, accustomed to the greatest license, would, at their option, go to the street door to look at a passing carriage, or stepping on to a bench in he rear, dash out of a window, and take a lively turn in the mulberry grove. Talking did no good. Reasoning and pathetic appeals were alike unavailing. Thus the morning slowly wore away. At noon I explained this first great perplexity of my teacher-life to my friend Mrs. Peck, who decidedly advised

*Emma Willard, founder of Troy Female Seminary (1821), devoted her life to educational equality for women.*

sound and summary chastisement. "I cannot," I replied, "I never struck a child in my life." "It is," she said, "the only way, and you must." I left her for the afternoon school with a heavy heart, still hoping I might find some way of avoiding what I could not deliberately resolve to do. I found the school a scene of uproar and confusion, which I vainly endeavored to quell. Just then, Jesse Peck, my friend's little son, entered with a bundle of five nice rods. As he laid them on the table before me, my courage rose; and, in the temporary silence which ensued, I laid down a few laws, the breaking of which would be followed with immediate chastisement. For a few moments the children were silent; but they had been used to threatening, and soon a boy rose from his seat, and as he was stepping to the door, I took one of the sticks and gave him a moderate flogging, then with a grip upon his arm which made him feel that I was in earnest, put him into seat. Hoping to make this chastisement answer for the whole school, I then told them in the most endearing manner I could command, that I was there to do them good — to make them such fine boys and girls that their parents and friends would be so delighted with them, and they be growing up happy and useful; but in order to [do] this I must and would have their obedience. If I had occasion to punish again it would be more and more severely, until they yielded, and were trying to be good. But the children still lacked faith in my words, and if my recollection serves me, I spent most of the afternoon in alternate whippings and exhortations, the former always increasing in intensity, until at last, finding the difference between capricious anger and steadfast determination, they submitted. This was the first and last of corporeal punishment in that school. The next morning and ever after, I had docile and orderly scholars. I was careful duly to send them out for recreation, to make their studies pleasant and interesting, and to praise them when they did well, and mention to their parents their good behavior.

Our school was soon the admiration of the neighborhood. Some of the literati of the region heard of the marvelous progress the children made, and of classes formed and instruction given in higher branches; and coming to visit us, they encouraged me in my school, and gave me valuable commendation.

*After several years of alternate teaching and studying, Emma Hart joined her old teacher Dr. Miner as an assistant. Then at age twenty-one she took over a female seminary in Middlebury, Vermont, and two years later married John Willard, a doctor there.*

When I began my boarding school in Middlebury, in 1814, my leading motive was to relieve my husband from financial difficulties. I had also the further object of keeping a better school than those about me; but it was not until a year or two after, that I formed the design of effecting an important change in education, by the introduction of a grade of schools for women, higher than any heretofore known. My neighborhood to Middlebury College, made me bitterly feel the disparity in educational facilities between the two sexes; and I hope that if the matter was once set before the men as legislators, they would be ready to correct the error. The idea that such a thing might possibly be effected by my means, seemed so presumptuous that I hesitated to entertain it, and for a short time concealed it even from my husband, although I knew that he sympathized in my general views. I began to write (because I could thus best arrange my ideas) "an address to the —— Legislature, proposing a plan for improving Female Education." It was not till two years after that I filled up the blank. No one knew of my writing it, except my husband, until a year after it was completed (1816), for I knew that I should be regarded as visionary, almost to insanity, should I utter the expectations which I secretly entertained in connection with it. But it was not merely on the strength of my arguments that I relied. I determined to inform myself, and increase my personal influence and fame as a teacher, calculating that in this way I might be sought for in other places, where influential men would carry my project before some legislature, for the sake of obtaining a good school.

My exertions meanwhile, became unremitted and intense. My school grew to seventy pupils. I spent from ten to twelve hours a day in teaching, and on extraordinary occasions, as preparing for examination, fifteen; besides, always having under investigation some new subject which, as I studied, I simultaneously taught to a class of my ablest pupils. Hence every new term some new study was introduced; and in all their studies, my pupils were very thoroughly trained. In classing my school for the term of study, which was then about three months, I gave to each her course, (being careful not to give too much) with the certain expectation, that she must be examined on it at the close of the term. Then I was wont to consider that my first duty as a teacher, required of me that I should labor to make my pupils by explanation and illustration *understand* their subject, and get them warmed into it, by making them see its beauties and its advantages. During this first part of the process, I talked much more than the pupils were required to do, keeping their attention awake by frequent questions, requiring short answers from the whole class — for it was ever my maxim, if attention fails, the teacher fails. Then in the *second* stage of my teaching, I made each scholar recite, in order that she might *remember* — paying special attention to the meaning of words, and to discern whether the subject was indeed understood without mistake. Then the third process was to make the pupil capable of *communicating*.[1] And doing this in a right manner, was to prepare her for examination. At this time I personally examined all my classes.

This thorough teaching added rapidly to my reputation. Another important feature of a system, thus requiring careful drill and correct enunciation, was manifested by the examinations. The pupils, there acquired character and confidence. Scholars thus instructed were soon capable of teaching; and here were now forming my future teachers; and some were soon capable of aiding me in arranging the new studies, which I was constantly engage in introducing.

Here I began a series of improvements in geography — separating and first teaching what could be learned from maps — then treating the various subjects of population, extent, length of rivers, &c., by comparing country with country, river with river, and city with city, — making out with the assistance of my pupils, those tables which afterwards appeared in Woodbridge and Willard's Geographies. Here also began improvements in educational history. Moral Philosophy came next, with Paley for the author, and Miss Hemingway for the first scholar, and then the Philosophy of the Mind — Locke the author, and the first scholars, Eliza Henshaw, Katharine Battey, and Minerva Shiperd.

The professors of the college attended my examinations; although I was by the President advised, that it would not be becoming in me, nor be a safe precedent, if I should attend theirs. So, as I had no teacher in learning my new studies, I had no model in teaching, or examining them. But I had full faith in the clear conclusions of my own mind. I knew that nothing could be truer than truth; and hence I fearlessly brought to examination, before the learned, the classes, to which had been taught the studies I had just acquired.

I soon began to have invitations to go from Middlebury. Gov. Van Ness, wishing me to go to Burlington, I opened my views to him. The college buildings were then nearly vacant, and some steps were taken towards using them for a Female Seminary, of which I was to be Principal, but the negotiations failed. In the spring of 1818, I had five pupils from Waterford, of the best families. On looking over the map of the United States, to see where would be the best geographical location for the projected institution, I had fixed my mind on the State of New York, and thought, that the best place would be somewhere in the vicinity of the head of navigation on the Hudson. Hence, the coming of the Waterford pupils I regarded as an important event. I presented my views to Gen. Van Schornhoven, the father (by adoption) of one of my pupils, — who was interested, and proposed to show my manuscript to

the Hon. J. Cramer, of Waterford, and to De Witt Clinton, then governor of New York; and if they approved it, then the "Plan" might go
before the legislature with some chance of success. Thereupon I copied
the manuscript with due regard to manner and chirography; having
already rewritten it some seven times, and thrown out about three
quarters of what it first contained — then sent it to Gov. Clinton with
the following letter.[2]

*To his Excellency, De Witt Clinton,—*

*Sir— Mr. Southwick will present to you a manuscript, containing a
plan for improving the education of females, by instituting public
seminaries for their use. Its authoress has presumed to offer it to your
Excellency, because she believed you would consider the subject as
worthy of your attention, and because she wished to submit her
scheme to those exalted characters, whose guide is reason, and whose
objects are the happiness and improvement of mankind; and among
these characters, where can plans to promote those objects hope for
countenance, if not from Mr. Clinton.*

*The manuscript is addressed to a legislature, although not intended
for present publication. The authoress believed she could communicate
her ideas with less circumlocution in this than in any other manner,
and besides, should the approbation of distinguished citizens, in any of
the larger and wealthier states, give hopes that such an application
would be attended with success, a publication might be proper, and the
manuscript would need less alteration.*

*Possibly your Excellency may consider this plan as better deserving
your attention, to know that its authoress is not a visionary enthusiast,
who has speculated in solitude without practical knowledge of her
subject. For ten years she has been intimately conversant with female
schools, and nearly all of that time she has herself been a preceptress.
Nor has she written for the sake of writing, but merely to communicate
a plan of which she fully believes that it is practicable; that, if realized,
it would form a new and happy era in the history of her sex, and if of
her sex, why not of her country, and of mankind. Nor would she
shrink from any trial of this faith; for such is her conviction of the
utility of her scheme, that could its execution be forwarded, by any
exertion or any sacrifice of her own, neither the love of domestic ease,
or the dread of responsibility, would prevent her embarking her
reputation on its success.*

*If Mr. Clinton should not view this plan as its authoress hopes he may, but should think the time devoted to its perusal was sacrificed, let him not consider its presentation to him as the intrusion of an individual ignorant of the worth of this time, and the importance of his high avocations, but as the enthusiasm of a projector, misjudging of her project, and overrating its value.*

*With sentiments of the deepest respect, I am, Sir,*

    *Your Obedient Servant,*
    *Emma Willard*
    *Middlebury, Vt., February 5, 1818*

The treatise is in reality the foundation of the Troy seminary. It will not be thought surprising that I waited with intense feeling Gov. Clinton's reply. It came before I expected it, expressing his accordance with my views in his happiest manner. His message to the legislature soon followed, in which referring to my "Plan" (though not by its title or author's name), he recommended legislative action in behalf of a cause heretofore wholly neglected. The Waterford gentlemen had made Gov. Clinton's opinion their guiding light. They were to present my "Plan" to the legislature; and advised that Mr. Willard and myself should spend a few weeks in Albany during the session, which we did. The Governor and many of his friends called on us; and I read my manuscript several times by special request to different influential members; and once to a considerable assemblage. The affair would have gone off by acclamation, could immediate action have been had. As it was, an act was passed incorporating the institution at Waterford; and another, to give to female academics a share of the literature fund. This law, the first whose sole object was to improve female education, is in force, and is the same by which female academics in the state now receive public money.

# Teaching in the Little Red Schoolhouse

―❧―

## Lucia B. Downing

From Lucia B. Downing,
"Teaching in the Keeler 'Deestrict' School,"
*Vermont Quarterly, A Magazine of History, n.s.,*
Vol. 19, No. 4 (October 1951), pp. 233–240.

*Lucia Downing (1868–1945), the author of this charming reminiscence written "nearly half a century" after her first teaching experience, began her career in 1882. Nearly eighty years after Emma Hart Willard began her career as a teenaged teacher, Downing faced similar conditions. In a farm village, a plucky 14-year-old could still be mistress of an entire school. Free to enforce discipline and design the curriculum, Lucia Downing evidently thrived under the responsibility entrusted her. There is a hint here, however, that Downing worked to avoid the pitfalls of young female teachers who were thought not capable of disciplining older boys: She managed to tie up her hair, dress to look more mature than her years, and to forbid an older boy from kissing the teacher. "Boarding out" (living with the family of a pupil) afforded her a welcome escape from the identity of "little sister" and gave her the experience of living with a sophisticated Yankee family. The work confirmed her wise choice of a career. She graduated from the University of Vermont Phi Beta Kappa in 1889, and taught in Vermont and Pennsylvania before her marriage.*

> Still sits the schoolhouse by the road,
> A ragged beggar sunning;
> Around it still the sumacs grow,
> And blackberry vines are running.

It is still standing — the little red schoolhouse where I, a little girl barely fourteen, began my career as a teacher; still standing, though with sunken roof and broken windows, a solitary reminder of the days of long ago. No longer does its door's worn sill resound to the clatter of copper-toed boots; no longer does its smoking box-stove drive pupils and teacher out into the frosty air; never again on a summer's day will the passer-by hear the droning sound of the ab-abs; or the singsong recital of the multiplication table. The children, if there are any now in the old "Keeler Deestrict," clamber into a bus and ride merrily away to a central seat of learning five miles distant. "Time rolls his ceaseless course!"

In the days of my adventure, Vermont had no law restricting the age or youth, of a teacher, but shortly after my experience, and possibly consequent thereto, the state passed a law making sixteen the earliest age at which one might begin what Thompson, who probably never taught a day in his life, calls

*Delightful task! To rear the tender thought,*
*To teach one young idea how to shoot.*

In our little town, the duties of school superintendent were not burdensome, nor the position lucrative, and for many years our superintendent was the village doctor (Dr. L. C. Butler), who was probably the best-educated man in town, not even excepting the minister! The doctor could easily combine the two occupations — I had almost said "kill two birds with one stone!" For instance, he could visit the school on Brigham Hill when he had a patient up there, and save a trip up a steep hill with narrow, rocky road, which even to a Ford presents difficulties to this day. The doctor lived about two miles out of the village (Page's Corners) in a lovely old colonial house, once used as an inn and a popular Mecca for horseback parties in the good old days. There was a schoolhouse — red, of course — just across the road, and the doctor could drop in there any time. But to the teachers in outlying districts it was a decided advantage to have a doctor for supervisor. The teacher always knew if any one in the neighborhood was sick, and she could keep watch of the road. When old white Dolly, drawing the easy low phaeton, hove in sight, there was time to furbish up a little, and call out a class of the brightest pupils!

The doctor had vaccinated me when a little girl came from Canada with symptoms of that dreaded disease, small pox, and all the parents were calling him in. And he had brought me through measles and chicken pox, and his wife was my Sunday School teacher, and I was not a bit afraid of him. So when my sister, already a teacher, went to take another examination, the spring I was thirteen, I went along too, and said to the doctor, who was only a superintendent that day, that, if he had enough papers, I should like to see how many questions I could answer. The doctor smiled at me, and gave me an arithmetic paper for a starter. It proved to be easy, for it brought in some favorite problems in percentage, which would be an advantage to a merchant, as they showed how to mark goods in such a way that one could sell below the marked price, and still make a profit. I guess all merchants must have studied Greenleaf's *Arithmetic!* There was either a problem under the old Vermont Annual Interest Rule, or we were asked to write the rule. As it covered a half page in the book, writing it out involved some labor. I felt quite well pleased with my paper, and then proudly started on Grammar. I knew I could do something with that, for I loved to parse and analyze and "diagram" according to Reed and Kellogg. In fact, my first knowledge, and for many years my only knowledge, of "Paradise Lost" was gleaned from a little blue parsing book, and I have always been puzzled to know whether "barbaric" modifies "kings" or "pearl and gold":

*High on a throne of royal state, which far*
*Outshone the wealth of Ormus and of Ind,*
*Or Where the gorgeous East with richest hand*
*Showers on her kings barbaric pearl and gold,*
*Satan exalted sat.*

Next came Geography. Though I had never traveled farther than Burlington, I knew, thanks to Mr. Guyot and his green geography, that Senegambia was "rich in gold, iron ore and gum-producing trees." (I always supposed it was "spruce gum," so popular before gutta-percha and licorices were combined and put up in slabs.) History and Civil Government were pretty hard for me, but next came Physiology, and I made the most of my bones and circulatory system, hoping to impress the physician. But it was in Theory and School Management that I did myself proud. I discoursed at length on ventilation and temperature, and, knowing that "good government" is a most desirable and necessary qualification for a teacher, I advocated a firm, but kind and gentle method, with dignity of bearing. In giving my views of corporal punishment, I related a story I had read of the Yankee teacher who was asked his views on the subject. He said, "Wal, moral suasion's my theory, but lickin's my practice!" When I reported at home that I had told that story, my Father laughed, but Mother expressed deep disgust.

When I compared notes with my sister, in regard to my answers, I began to feel that I did not know as much as I thought I did! An anxious week followed, and I haunted the post office. Finally, one morning, there was an envelope addressed in Dr. Butler's scholarly hand, but it bore my sister's name, and there was none for me. I was heartbroken — evidently my record was so poor that he was not going to tell me how I stood. But, as my sister opened her envelope, out fluttered two yellow slips — two certificates, entitling the recipients to teach in Vermont for one year. And one was in my name! I cannot recall any subsequent joy equal to what I felt at that moment — even a college diploma and a Phi Beta Kappa key, in later years, brought less of a thrill.

Of course, the eight or ten districts in town were already supplied with teachers, and no doubt that was why I was given a certificate, instead of a mere statement of standing. But one day my chum (Lena Brown) told me that in her Grandfather Keeler's district they planned to open up the old schoolhouse, unused for years because there were no children. Now there were at least four, of school age, and a school was demanded. She said the committeeman was Mr. Nichols (Charles Nichols), a friend of my father, and I insisted that he be interviewed. Thinking it was the "big girl" Father was talking about, Mr. Nichols talked very encouragingly, but when he found it was I who thus aspired, he laughed scornfully. Although Father told him I had a certificate, and was really bigger than the "big" one, the case looked hopeless. Sometime later he came to the house, and I happened to be the only member of the family at home. After various circumlocutions he told me that I might try it. He said they could not pay much, as there probably would be only four scholars, and said he would let me know when school would open and where I should board — "boarding around" was gone by at that time. I was the happiest person in town that night, but later I heard he had said to others that, with so few scholars, it didn't matter much anyway — and made up my mind to do or die.

Before the term opened I had a birthday and attained the mature age of fourteen, but, in spite of unusual height for my years, I really did not look very old, and my chief anxiety was to acquire the appearance that for many years now I have made every effort to avoid! My skirts were fearfully short, and though Mother let out the last tuck and hem, they only reached to the tops of my buttoned boots, and, unless I was careful in seating myself, there was a glimpse of my stockings that no modest young woman, especially a teacher, should permit! However,

Mother sewed a watch-pocket in my little dresses, and gave me her watch, a lovely little Swiss, with wide-open face, and there was a gorgeous long chain. You can't think how much dignity was added thereby! The next difficult was my hair, heavy and long, and the only way I could fix it was to make a long, thick, childish braid. But, after many experiments, I achieved a way of folding it up, under and under, tying it close to my head, and I thought it resembled a real pug.

It was to be a fall term, and it probably opened late in August. The morning dawned when I was to begin "the glorious adventure." Father harnessed old Diamond — he was just my age, but what is old age for a horse is youth to a human being — and I came out with a little black bag, borrowed from Mother, and wearing my blue gingham dress. I had insisted on wearing that one, because it was a half-inch longer than any other. I can visualize it now — rather tight at the waist, fortunately for the watch-pocket, with ruffles at the bottom.

I was supposed to board in the family of a Mr. Vespasian Leach, a former merchant, who, like many such, had retired to a farm. As we jogged along, we met Mr. Leach taking his milk to the cheese factory, and he told us that, owing to sickness, they could not take a boarder. My father expressed his regret, and, with fine old-fashioned courtesy, said he had counted on my being looked after by these old friends. Presently we met Mr. Nichols, and he said that I was to board in *his* family. Father said he was delighted to know that, and he would not worry about me at all. After we passed along I said, "Why, Father, you told Mr. Leach how sorry you are, and now you tell Mr. Nichols how glad you are." I do not recall his explanation, except that it sounded very reasonable, and that was my first lesson in diplomacy. I see now that there was no dishonesty in my father's mind or language.

Well, we journeyed on, passing the school house on the way to the Nichols farm. I don't know how I felt — that is one of the things I can't remember! I was to go home week-ends, though of course we called it "over Sunday," and it looked to me like a long, long, week. Mr. Nichols was a wealthy farmer, with a grown-up family; and one son, with his wife and two babies (only one baby the first week), lived at home. There were menservants and maidservants galore, and we all sat down to most marvelous meals at a long table in a big dining-room. And what wonderful food! Picture it, even if you have not had the experience, and have not the imagination, of an Ichabod Crane! We did not have exactly the things to eat that made the pedagogue's mouth water in anticipation, but in retrospection it seems that nothing could be so good again as what was daily set before us. We did not have a young roast pig, but we had delicious home-smoked ham and tender roasts, and milk-fed chickens and honey with biscuits rich with cream, and then all the fruits and vegetables that early fall makes possible on a rich "interval" farm, besides plenty of eggs and cream and butter.

Then, too, I was treated like an honored guest, and given the "spare room" with blue walls and curtains, and was always addressed as "Teacher" — much to my satisfaction. I had really worried over the matter, for to call me Miss B. was absurd, and I feared I might be addressed by a familiar nickname, or pet name, which was most undignified. But, with the new title, my self-respect increased amazingly, and also my *conceit*. After four o'clock I was free from school duties, and I enjoyed the family life, playing with the two babies, or listening to the little parlor organ, played by some member of the family, and often there was a song by the son. I remember how he sang "Finnegan's Wake," and the song about the man from India, who ate ice cream and could never get warm again.

From nine to twelve and from one to four I was supposed to spend in the schoolhouse, and I can't see how I ever managed to put in the time — six long hours every day — with four pupils! Most of the time there were only four (four — all named Leach — two families!), but one morning the number was increased. I was startled to see a young lady in trailing gown (how I envied her) approach and ask if she might come to school, adding that she loved me, just seeing me go by the house! She brought with her a little purple primer, which such lucid and inspiring sentences as, "Lo, I go! See me go up." She had learned to read out of that antiquated book before I was born, but in the intervening years reading had become a lost art, and she was ready to begin all over. It was a wonderful help to me in killing time, for each day we could go over and over the same thing, never too often to please her, as she stood by me and picked out the sentences, letter by letter.

But, I still wonder how I put in the time. I did not knit or crochet, for I had heard of teachers who had made trouble for themselves by so doing. I was not skilful at drawing, and I couldn't sing much, being like the old woman who knew just two tunes — "Old Hundred" and "Doxology"! and when each pupil had read and ciphered and spelled and passed the water and recessed and recessed and passed the water and spelled and had a lesson in geography and read and spelled, there was usually an hour before I dared dismiss them. I sometimes carried my watch key to school and turned the hands ahead, but that took me home to the committee-man's too early. Parents, what few there were, I suppose were glad to be relieved of the care of their offspring, and no one ever suggested a shortening of the hours. I had to earn my salary! We had few books, and my principal memorizing had been confined to the Westminster Catechism with its one hundred and seven long answers, but I knew a few poems, and I taught the children all I knew. I devised what I thought was a wonderful set of "Instructive Questions and Answers," suggested by a *New England Primer* that had come down in our family, but I did not limit the field of instruction to matters Biblical, attempting rather to cover the entire realm of knowledge in art, science, history, literature and what you will.

My pride suffered several falls. I did not have very good discipline, for one thing. Then, when I was proud of my success in teaching a boy to read by the word method, just coming into use, I ventured to suggest that words were made up of letters, and began to point them out. He said, "Yes, I knew my letters last year, and that's why I know how to read." Then there was one *big* boy who was *peeved* because I would not allow him the same privilege as the little ones who always wanted to kiss "Teacher" good night. And my oldest pupil took a dislike to her teacher, as sudden and as inexplicable as her erstwhile fondness.

The glorious autumn days flew by, and the ten weeks' term was drawing to a close. One of the most arduous tasks was "keeping the register," and the consequent figuring up of averages at the end of the term. There was the total number of days' attendance by all pupils; the average attendance per day, which would have been a fine record, except for the defection of the oldest pupil, and the number of days' attendance per pupil. My sister showed me how to do all those things, but there was a vital question that I was obliged to leave until the last moment, namely, the amount of salary received. Except that it would be a small salary, the subject had never been mentioned. I was worried; just suppose I did not get enough to pay my board! I really had eaten a great deal, and I knew Father would not want to pay my board, even if he had the money. Waiting until the last possible moment to finish my register, I approached Mr. Nichols after one of the fine dinners we always had. When I spoke of my difficulty in completing the register, he looked worried — maybe he had heard of those averages! But, as I told him my *real* difficulty, he looked relieved, and smiled, as he said, in his delightful, cultured Yankee drawl, that the *district calculated* they could afford to pay three dollars and a half a week, to cover salary and board, the proportion to be determined by the committeeman, and he had decided to give me two dollars a week for my work, and take only a dollar and a half for board, which, I may say, was a most generous arrangement, in view of everything!

But the last days of school were busy ones. I drilled the scholars on the pieces they were to speak — I can remember one of them now, "Little Dan" — and I told the children how important it was that they should behave well the last day, if never before or later. And school ended in a blaze of glory, a vast and terrifying audience having assembled — entirely out of proportion to the number of pupils. There were fond parents, and grandparents, and aunts and uncles and cousins thrice removed. I think there were twenty-five visitors and only four scholars, but the children did very well. They went through some specifically prepared lessons in the various subjects they had been studying, they spoke their pieces without prompting, and they went glibly through the "Instructive Questions and Answers," though if I had made a slip and asked the questions out of order, the results might have been disastrous. They might have said that Vermont is the largest state in the Union, or that George Washington had sailed the ocean blue in 1492, or that Rome was built by Julius Caesar, but I do not recall that any such contretemps occurred. I do fear, however, that "Teacher," herself, was at the time a bit uncertain as to whether the *I. Watts* who wrote hymns was the *J. Watt* whose mother had a teakettle. Everything went off well, and I presented the children with cards for which I had borrowed the money from my sister, and my pupils and their friends said goodbye, and I went proudly home with twenty dollars, the remuneration for ten weeks of toil. But never before or since has that sum of money gone so far. I went to Burlington the next week, and I bought blue flannel for a dress, a photograph album, a cage for my canary, a beaver hat, and numerous small things, besides paying up for my cards.

I went back to school, picking up my work at the Academy, and I felt rather superior to my classmates. When spring came, I was flattered to be asked to go back and teach another term. I was told that children had moved into the neighborhood, some had become of school age, and some had even been born, in the hope of going to school to me! I went back, and completed my second term as a teacher while I was fourteen. I had fifteen scholars, and probably more salary, though I do not remember. As a matter of fact, I do not recall much about that second term and the other terms I taught there and elsewhere during my school and college course. But the incidents of the first term are still vivid in my mind after nearly half a century. It was an unusual experience, and the events of each week were told over at home, and repeated to any one who would listen, as I did a "round, unvarnished tale deliver." In the telling I have not exaggerated or drawn upon my imagination, but as I call the old time back, memories rush upon mere, and I can visualize the scene, and it is all as fresh as if it had happened yesterday.

# Remedy for Wrongs to Women

—⁓⟨❧⟩⁓—

## Catherine Beecher

From Catherine Beecher, *The Evils Suffered by American Women and American Children: The Causes and the Remedy* (New York: Harper & Bros, 1846).

*Catherine Beecher's (1800–1878) "Address on the Evils Suffered by American Women and American Children" is an early (1846) and significant document proposing that teaching is woman's "true" profession. Stylistically florid by today's standards, the excerpts that follow convey the exuberance and drama Beecher brought to her subject. The sister of Harriet Beecher Stowe and daughter of the minister Lyman Beecher — the minister's calling was also followed by her seven brothers — Beecher assumed an exclusively Christian ethic. Her "Address" was not so much an argument as a series of assaults on the moral sensibilities of the Christian audience. Her intention was to promote her favorite scheme, that of sending women teachers to open schools "at the West" (that is, in Ohio, Illinois, Iowa, and Wisconsin). Beecher believed that "Christian female teachers" could save two million children growing up in ignorance, and at the same time remedy the depression of "our sex" by setting a model of "healthy and productive labor." Through the Board of National Popular Education, several thousand teachers did go west in the 1840s and 1850s, and normal schools for the education of teachers were founded in Wisconsin, Iowa, and Illinois.*

*For the history of women in teaching, however, the interest of this article lies not in the mission to the West but in Beecher's assertion that women, not men, should educate children, and that teaching should be regarded not as drudgery but as "the noblest of all professions." Despite her advocacy of self-sacrifice and her antisuffrage position, Beecher envisioned for women a domestic sphere that gave them, rather than men, power to shape society.*

## Address

Ladies and Friends:

The immediate object which has called us together, is an enterprise now in progress, the design of which is *to educate destitute American children, by the agency of American women.* It is an effort which has engaged the exertions of a large number of ladies of various sects, and of all sections in our country, and one which, though commencing in a humble way and on a small scale, we believe is eventually to exert a most extensive and saving influence through the nation.

Permit me first to present some facts in regard to the situation of an immense number of young children in this land, for whom your sympathies at this time are sought. Few are aware of the deplorable destitution of our country in regard to the education of the rising generation, or of the long train of wrongs and sufferings endured by multitudes of young children from this neglect.

The last twelve years I have resided chiefly at the West, and my attention has been directed to the various interests of education. In five of the largest western states I have spent from several weeks to several months — I have traveled extensively and have corresponded or conversed with well-informed gentlemen and ladies on this subject in most of the western states. And I now have materials for presenting the real situation of vast multitudes of American children, which would "cause the ear that heareth it to tingle." But I dare not do it. It would be so revolting — so disgraceful — so heart-rending — so incredible — that in the first place, I should not be believed; and in the next place, such an outcry of odium and indignation would be aroused as would impede efforts to remedy the evil. The only thing I can safely do is to present some statistics, which cannot be disputed, because they are obtained from *official documents* submitted by civil officers to our national or state legislatures. Look then at the census, and by its data we shall find that now there are nearly a million adults who cannot read and write, and more than *two million* children utterly illiterate, and entirely without schools. Look at individual states, and we shall find Ohio and

Kentucky, the two best supplied of our western states, demanding *five thousand* teachers each, to supply them in the same ration as Massachusetts is supplied. *Ten thousand* teachers are now needed in Ohio and Kentucky alone, to furnish schools for more than two hundred thousand children, who otherwise must grow up in utter ignorance.

To exhibit some faint idea of the results of such neglect, let me give an extract from a private letter of a friend of mine, on a journey of observation in regard to education in one of these states, which was addressed to his children.

Could you, my dear daughters, see what I in my journeys so often see, the poor of your own sex and age, limited in wardrobe to one sordid cotton garment, without education to read a word, without skill to make or mend a garment, without a sufficient variety of proper food to unfold their forms to any perfection, lank as greyhounds, and their clothes hanging upon them like dresses upon a broomstick, and yet possessed of all your native love of dress, your quick capacity and your sprightliness, I do think you would behave better, be more humble, study harder, and feel more kindly to the poor than you ever have done. And yet what is all this to having the mind darkened, the feelings hardened, and the interests of the soul neglected, as is the case with many thousands around me! My heart bleeds at the irreligion, abject poverty, filth, and wretched vice which everywhere prevail. But my Heavenly Father enables me to hold on, and I am tolerably well; yet I cannot say that I am cheerful; it is too intolerable, and my spirits sink. The Methodist circuit riders are doing something, and have pitched upon the very plan I had thought of, that of having *traveling schools* among the most sparsely settled districts. Oh that our Heavenly Father may bless my mission, and that light may enter here!

This presents only a glance at the forlorn and degraded state of large portions of our country where education is totally neglected. A picture almost as melancholy is presented when we examine into the shocking abuse of young children in some of those states which are doing the most for education. The state of New York, for a few years, has been making exemplary efforts to raise her common schools from the low state in which they were found. In every county of the state a salaried officer devotes his whole time to the improvement of the common

The youthful Catherine Beecher, practitioner and promoter of teaching as woman's "true" profession. Photograph by Black & Batchelder, Boston, ca. 1860.

schools in his county, and every year he sends an account of them, to be presented to the legislature by the state superintendent.

The following is extracted from the general report made up by the general superintendent from the reports of the county superintendents for the year 1844.

The nakedness and deformity of the great majority of the schools, the comfortless and dilapidated buildings, the unhung doors, broken sashes, absent panes, stilted benches, yawning roofs, and muddy moldering floors, are faithfully portrayed, and many of the self-styled teachers, who lash and dogmatize in these miserable tenements of humanity, are shown to be low, vulgar, obscene, intemperate, and utterly incompetent to teach anything good. Thousands of the young are repelled from improvement, and contract a durable horror for books, by ignorant, injudicious, and even cruel modes of instruction. When the piteous moans and tears of the little pupils supplicate for exemption from the cold drudgery or the more pungent suffering of the school, let the humane parent be careful to ascertain the true cause of grief and lamentation. . . . No subject connected with the cause of elementary education affords a source for such humiliating reflection, as that of the condition of a large portion of the school-houses visited. Only one-third of the whole number were found in good repair, another third in only comfortable circumstances; while *three thousand, three hundred and nineteen* were unfit for the reception of either man or beast. Seven thousand we found destitute of any playground, nearly six thousand destitute of convenient seats and desks, and nearly eight thousand destitute of any proper facilities for ventilation; while six thousand were destitute of outdoor facilities for securing modesty and decency!

And it is in these miserable abodes of filth and dirt, deprived of wholesome air or exposed to the assaults of the elements, with no facilities for exercise or relaxation, with no conveniences for prosecuting their studies, crowded on to comfortless benches, and driven by dire necessity to violate the most common rules of decency and modesty, that upward of *six hundred thousand* children of this state are compelled to spend an average of eight months each year of their pupilage! Here the first lessons of human life, the incipient principles of morality, and the rules of social intercourse, are to be impressed upon the plastic mind. The boy is here to receive the permanent model of his character, and imbibe the elements of his future career. Here the instinctive delicacy of the young female, the characteristic ornament of her sex, is to be expanded into maturity by precept and example. Such are the temples of science, such the ministers under whose care susceptible childhood is to receive its earliest impressions! Great God! Shall man dare to charge to *thy* dispensations the vices, the crimes, the sickness, the sorrows, the miseries and brevity of human life, who sends his little children to a pest-house fraught with the deadly malaria of both moral and physical disease? Instead of impious murmurs, let him lay his hand upon his mouth, and his mouth in the dust, and cry unclean! . . .

I wish now to point out that certain causes which have exerted a depressing influence upon our sex in this land; for we shall find that the very same effort, which aims to benefit the children of our country, will tend almost equally to benefit our own sex. The first cause that bears heavily on our sex is, the fact that in our country, the principle of *caste*, which is one of the strongest and most inveterate in our nature, is strongly arrayed against *healthful and productive labor*.

To understand the power of this principle, see what sacrifices men and women make, and what toils they endure, to save themselves from whatever sinks them in station and estimation. And this is a principle which is equally powerful in high and low, rich and poor. To observe how it bears against healthful and productive labor, let any woman, who esteems herself in the higher grades of society, put the case as her own, and imagine that her son, or brother, is about to marry a young lady, whose character and education are every way lovely and unexceptionable, but who, it appears, is a *seamstress*, or a *nurse*, or a *domestic*, and how few are there, who will not be conscious of the opposing principle of *caste*. But suppose the young lady to be one, who has been earning her livelihood by writing poetry and love stories, or who has lived all her days in utter idleness, and how suddenly the feelings are changed! Now, all the comfort and happiness of society depend upon having that work properly performed, which is done by nurses, seamstresses and chambermaids, and cooks; and so long as this kind of work is held to be degrading, and those who perform it are allowed to grow up ignorant and vulgar, and then are held down by the prejudices of caste, every woman will use the greatest efforts, and undergo the greatest privations, to escape from the degraded and discreditable position. And this state of society is now, by the natural course of things, bringing a just retribution on the classes who cherish it. Domestics are for-saking the kitchen, and thronging to the workshop and manufactory, and *mainly* under the influence of the principle of *caste*; while the fami-ly state suffers keenly from the loss. Meantime the daughters of wealth have their intellectual faculties and their sensibilities developed, while all the household labor, which would equally develop their physical powers, and save from ill-health, is turned off to hired domestics, or a slaving mother. The only remedy for this evil is, securing a proper edu-cation for all classes, and making productive labor honorable, by having all classes engage in it.

The next cause which bears severely on the welfare of our sex, is the *excess of female population* in the older states from the disproportionate emigration of the other sex. By the census we find in only three of the small older states, *twenty thousand* more women than men, and a similar disproportion is found in other states. The consequence is, that all branches of female employment in the older states are thronged, while in our new states, domestics, nurses, seamstresses, mantua-makers, and female teachers are in great demand. In consequence of this, women at the East become operatives in shops and mills, and at the West, men become teachers of little children, thus exchanging the appropriate labors of the sexes, in a manner injurious to all concerned.

Meantime, capitalists at the East avail themselves of this excess of female hands. Large establishments are set up in eastern cities to manu-facture clothing. Work of all kinds is got from poor women, at prices that will not keep soul and body together, and then the articles thus made are sold for prices that give monstrous profits to the capitalist, who thus grows rich on the hard labors of our sex. Tales there are to be told of the sufferings of American women in our eastern cities, so shocking that they would scarcely be credited, and yet they are true beyond all dispute.

The following extracts, from some statistics recently obtained in New York city, verify what has been stated.

There are now in this city, according to close estimates, *ten thou-sand* women who live by the earnings of the needle. On an average, these women, by working twelve or fourteen hours a-day, can earn only *twelve and a half cents*, with which they are to pay for rent, fuel, clothes, and food.

Here follow the prices paid for various articles of women's work at the clothing stores, and then the following —

A great multitude of women are employed in making men's and boy's caps. We are told by an old lady, who lives by this work, that when she begins at sunrise and works till midnight, she earns *fourteen cents a-day!* That is, *eighty-four cents* a week, for incessant toil every waking hour, and this her sole income for every want! A large majority of these women are American born; some have been rich, many have enjoyed the ease of competence; some are young girls without homes; some are widows; some the wives of drunken husbands. . . .

Let us now turn to another class of our country women — the *female operatives* in our shops and mills. Unfortunately, this subject cannot be freely discussed without danger of collision with the vast pecuniary and party interests connected with it. I therefore, shall simply *state facts,* without expressing the impressions of my own mind.

Last year, I spent several days in Lowell, for the sole purpose of investigating this subject. I conversed with agents, overseers, clergymen, physicians, editors, ladies resident in the place, and a large number of the operatives themselves. All seemed disposed to present the most favorable side of the picture; and nothing unfavorable was said except as drawn forth by my questions.

In favor of this situation it was urged, that none were forced to go, or to stay in the mills, and therefore all must believe themselves better off there than in any other situation at command; that owners and agents incur great pains and expense to secure the physical comfort and intellectual and moral improvement of the operatives; that much care is used to exclude vicious persons; that great pains are taken to secure respectable women to keep the boarding-houses; that the board and lodging provided are at least comfortable; that the state of society and morals is good, and is superior to what many enjoy at home; that the *esprit du corps* of the community guards its morals; that there is much good society among the operatives, as is manifest from the great number who have been school teachers; that the bills of mortality show that there are fewer deaths in proportion than in other country places; and finally, that the night schools, Sunday schools, and faithful labors of the clergy secure great advantages and most favorable results. . . .

Let me now present the facts I learned by observation or inquiry on the spot. I was there in mid-winter, and every morning I was wakened at *five*, by the bells calling to labor. The time allowed for dressing and breakfast was so short, as many told me, that both were performed hurriedly, and then the work at the mills was begun by lamp-light, and prosecuted without remission till twelve, and chiefly in a standing position. Then half an hour only allowed for dinner, from which the time for going and returning was deducted. Then back to the mills, to work till seven o'clock, the last part of the time by lamp-light. Then returning, washing, dressing, and supper occupied another hour. Thus ten hours only remained for recreation and sleep. . . .

As to the *wages*, the average is found to be $1.75 a week; but they are paid by *the job* so that all are thus stimulated to work as much as possible every day, while prizes are given to such overseers as get the most work out of those they superintend. Thus everything goes under the stimulus of rivalry, ambition, and the excitement of gain, leading multitudes to sacrifice health for money. Thus it is said that the hours of labor are not more than the majority of the operatives desire, while sometimes even the regular hours are exceeded, to the great discontent of the over-worked and feeble minority. As to the large sums deposited in the Savings' bank, it is found that, of six thousand women, less than one thousand have made such deposits, and the *average* of such deposits do not amount to but about $100 for each depositor for three years of such hazardous toils. . . .

Now, without expressing any opinion as to the influence, on health and morals, of taking women away from domestic habits and pursuits, to labor with men in shops and mills, I simply ask if it would not be *better* to put the thousands of men who are keeping school for young children into the mills, and employ the women to train the children?

Wherever education is most prosperous, there woman is employed more than man. In Massachusetts, where education is highest, five out of seven of the teachers are women; while in Kentucky, where education is so much lower, five out of six of the teachers are men.

Another cause of depression to our sex is found in the fact that there is no profession for women of education and high position, which, like law, medicine, and theology, opens the way to competence, influence, and honor, and presents motives for exertion. Woman ought never to be led to married life except under the promptings of pure affection. To marry for an establishment, for a position, or for something to do, is a deplorable wrong. But how many women, for want of a high and honorable profession to engage their time, are led to this melancholy course. This is not because Providence has not provided an ample place for such a profession for woman, but because custom or prejudice, or a low estimate of its honorable character, prevents her from entering it. *The educating of children, that* is the true and noble profession of a woman — *that* is what is worthy the noblest powers and affections of the noblest minds.

Another cause which deeply affects the best interests of our sex is the contempt, or utter neglect and indifference, which has befallen this only noble profession open to woman. There is no employment, however disagreeable or however wicked, which custom and fashion cannot render elegant, interesting, and enthusiastically sought. A striking proof of this is seen in the military profession. This is the profession of *killing our fellow creatures,* and is attended with everything low, brutal, unchristian, and disgusting; and yet what halos of glory have been hung around it, and how the young, the generous, and enthusiastic have been drawn into it! If one-half the poetry, fiction, oratory, and taste thus misemployed had been used to embellish and elevate the employment of training the mind of childhood, in what an altered position should we find this noblest of all professions!

As it is, the employment of teaching children is regarded as the most wearing drudgery, and few resort to it except from necessity; and one very reasonable cause of this aversion is the utter neglect of any arrangements for preparing teachers for this arduous and difficult profession. The mind of a young child is like a curious instrument, capable of exquisite harmony when touched by a skillful hand, but sending forth only annoying harshness when unskillfully addressed. To a teacher is committed a collection of these delicate contrivances; and, without experience, without instruction, it is required not only that each one should be tuned aright, but that all be combined in excellent harmony; as if a young girl were sent into a splendid orchestra, all ignorant and unskillful, and required to draw melody from each instrument, and then to combine the whole in faultless harmony. And in each case there are, here and there, individual minds, who, without instruction, are gifted by nature with aptness and skill in managing the music either of matter or of mind; but that does not lessen the folly, in either case, of expecting the whole profession, either of music or of teaching, to be pursued without preparatory training.

Look now into this small school-room, where are assembled a collection of children, with a teacher unskillful in her art. What noise and disorder! — what indolence, and discontent, and misrule! The children hate school and all that belongs to it, and the teacher regards the children as little better than incarnate imps!

Look, again, into another, where the teacher, fitted by nature or trained by instruction and experience, is qualified for her office. See the little happy group around their best-beloved friend — their *beau ideal* of all that is good, and wise, and lovely! How their bright eyes sparkle as she opens the casket of knowledge and deals out its treasures! How their young hearts throb with generous and good emotions, as she touches the thrilling chords she has learned so skillfully to play! What neatness and order in all her little dominion! What ready obedience, what loving submission, what contrite confession, what generous aspirations after all that is good and holy! She spends the pleasant hours of school in the exercise of the noblest powers of intellect and feeling. She goes to rest at night, reviewing with gratitude the results of her toils; and as she sends up her daily thanks and petitions for her little ones, how does the world of peace and purity open to her vision, where, by the river of life, she shall gather her happy flock, and look back to earth, and on through endless years, to trace the sublime and never-ending results of her labors. Oh, beautiful office! — sublime employment! When will it attain its true honors and esteem?

There is another class of evils, endured by a large class of well-educated, unmarried women of the more wealthy classes, little understood or appreciated, but yet real and severe. It is the suffering that results from the *inactivity of cultivated intellect and feeling.*

The more a mind has its powers of feeling and action enlarged by cultivation, the greater the demand for noble objects to excite interest and effort. It is the entire withdrawal of stimulus from the mind and brain that makes solitary confinement so intolerable that reason is often destroyed by it. Medical men point out this want of worthy objects to excite, as the true cause of a large class of diseases of mind and body, that afflicts females of the higher classes, who are not necessitated to exertion for a support, especially those who have no families. And the greater the capacity and the nobler the affections, the keener is this suffering. It is only small and ignoble minds that can live contentedly without noble objects of pursuit.

Now, Providence ordains that, in most cases, a woman is to perform the duties of a mother. Oh, sacred and beautiful name! How many cares and responsibilities are connected with it! And yet what noble anticipations, what sublime hopes, we are given to animate and cheer! She is to train young minds, whose plastic texture will receive and retain each impress for eternal ages, who will imitate her tastes, habits, feelings, and opinions; who will transmit what they receive to their children, to pass again to the next generation, and then to the next, until a *whole nation* will have received its character and destiny from her hands. No imperial queen ever stood in a more sublime and responsible position, than that which every mother must occupy, in the eye of Him who reads the end from the beginning, and who, foreseeing those eternal results, denominates those of our race who fulfill their high calling "kings and priests unto God." Kings, to rule the destiny of all their descendants — priests, by sacrifices and suffering to work out such sublime results!

Now every woman whose intellect and affections are properly developed is furnished for just such an illustrious work as this. And when such large capacities and affections are pent up and confined to the trifling pursuits that ordinarily engage our best educated young women between school life and marriage, suffering, and often keen suffering, is the inevitable result. There is a restless, anxious longing for they know not what; while exciting amusements are vainly sought to fill the aching void. A teacher, like myself, who for years has been training multitudes of such minds, and learning their private history and secret griefs, knows, as no others can, the great amount of suffering among some of the loveliest and best of the youthful portion of our sex from this cause. True, every young lady *might*, the moment she leaves the schoolroom, commence the exulted labor of molding young minds for eternity, who again would transmit her handiwork from spirit to spirit, till thousands and thousands receive honor and glory from her hands. But the customs and prejudices of society forbid; and instead of this, a little working of muslin and worsted, a little light reading, a little calling and shopping, and a great deal of the high stimulus of fashionable amusement, are all the ailment her starving spirit finds. And alas! Christian parents find no way to remedy this evil!

The next topic I wish to present, and which has been brought to my observation very often during my extensive travels, is the *superior character* of my countrywomen and the great amount of influence that is placed in their hands. . . .

It is the immediate object of this enterprise now presented, to engage American women to exert the great power and influence put into their hands, to remedy the evils which now oppress their countrywomen, and thus, at the same time, and by the same method, to secure a proper education to the vast multitude of neglected American Children all over out land.

The plan is, to begin on a small scale, and to take women already qualified intellectually to teach, and possessed of missionary zeal and benevolence, and, after some further training, to send them to the most ignorant portions of our land, to raise up schools, to instruct in morals and piety, and to teach the domestic arts and virtues. The commencement of this enterprise, until we gain confidence by experiment and experience, will be as the opening of a very small sluice. But so great is the number of educated and unemployed women at the East, and so great the necessity for teachers at the West, that as soon as the stream begins to move, it will grow wider and deeper and stronger, till it becomes as the river of life, carrying health and verdure to every part of our land.

If our success equals our hopes, soon, in all parts of our country, in each neglected village, or new settlement, the Christian female teacher will quietly take her station, collecting the ignorant children around her, teaching them habits of neatness, order, and thrift; opening the book of knowledge, inspiring the principles of morality, and awakening the hope of immortality. Soon her influence in the village will create a demand for new laborers, and then she will summon from among her friends at home, the nurse for the young and the sick, the seamstress and the mantuamaker, and these will prove her auxiliaries in good moral influences, and in sabbath school training. And often as the result of these labors, the Church will arise, and the minister of Christ be summoned to fill up the complement of domestic, moral, and religious blessing. Thus, the surplus of female population will gradually be drawn westward, and in consequence the value of female labor will rise at the East, so that capitalists can no longer use the power of wealth to oppress our sex. Thus, too, the profession of a teacher will gradually increase in honor and respectability, while endowed institutions will arise to qualify woman for her profession, as freely as they are provided for the other sex. Then it will be deemed honorable and praiseworthy for every young and well-educated woman, of whatever station, to enter this profession, and remain in it till pure affection leads her to another sphere. Then a woman of large affections and developed intellect will find full scope and happy exercise for all the cultivated energies conferred by heaven, alike for her own enjoyment and the good of others.

This will prove the true remedy for all those *wrongs of women* which her mistaken champions are seeking to cure by drawing her into professions and pursuits which belong to the other sex. . . .

# "Civilizing" the West: Letters from the Frontier

—❦—

## Ellen P. Lee and Mary S. Adams

From the National Board of Popular Education
Collection, Connecticut Historical Society, Hartford.

*Ellen P. Lee and Mary S. Adams were among 481 teachers sent west by the Board
of National Popular Education. The formation and mission of the Board originat-
ed with Catherine Beecher. She believed that women could find dignified and godly
work as Christian teachers away from the populous Eastern cities. With William
Slade, a former governor of Vermont, as its director, the Board raised funds, prepared teachers in four-week sessions in Hartford, Connecticut, then placed them "at
the West." Beecher clashed with Slade early in their collaboration, and left the
Board to establish normal schools for training teachers in western cities.*

*These two letters from young women teachers who went west under Board aus-
pices are among many preserved in the National Board collection along with the
brief autobiographical statements the women submitted with their applications.
Quotations from these statements appear in the headnotes. While the letters bear
witness to the teachers' loneliness, nostalgia for the more graceful and commodious
living quarters of New England, and ill health — twenty-one teachers died during the first decade of work — they also attest to the teachers' understanding of
the need for their services. Each letter makes clear the writer's firm belief that she
was doing God's work as an evangelical Christian, altering her community in the
ways Beecher and Slade had desired. There is, however, a striking contrast between
Beecher's ornamented, messianic rhetoric and the plain spoken practical language
of the teachers who were actually carrying out Beecher's mission.*

### Ellen P. Lee

*Ellen P. Lee was a member of the eleventh class (1851) of the Board of National
Popular Education. From Princeton, Massachusetts, she was one of eight children
in her family. After the death of a younger brother, Lee had a conversion experience*

*and joined the Baptist Church. She taught six-month school terms from age six-teen on, then decided to go west because she desired to do good: "In the school-room I feel perfectly at home"; by her own account, she governed men and young boys more forcefully than previous male teachers, thus forcing the community to relin-quish its prejudice against women teachers.*

Hamilton County, Indiana
January 6, 1852

Dear Friends,

It is with pleasure that I comply with your request to write to you. I have just commenced the second term of my school here, so that I am able to judge pretty correctly of my prospects in this place.

It is a new settlement here, it being only fifteen years since the first person settled here. But the settlement is quite large, and thickly settled.

Nearly all live in log-houses. The people are kind to me, very kind; they are peaceful, honest, intelligent naturally, but have not had an opportunity for improving their minds; so that they are very ignorant. I have not seen a well-educated person; many of the adults can neither read nor write, and some cannot tell one letter from another, and do not care if the children cannot. There are nine preachers here, and scarcely one can read a chapter in the Bible correctly; and I have heard most of them preach; they are not at all like New England ministers and it is often a cross to hear them preach; but I hope some of them are good Christian men who try to perform their duty, and not only preach, but practice what they preach. The religious societies here are United Brethren and New School or Antimason Methodist, the latter hold meetings in the house where I teach, and these I attend. They separated from the Episcopals on account of secret societies.

They have meetings every Sabbath, and preaching quite often; also meeting during the week evenings.

Just before I came here, a Sabbath School had been organized, and they had purchased a library of some more than 100 volumes; when I came they were on the point of giving it up. Those interested at first had got discouraged because they had failed to interest others. The school was conducted in a novel manner, no one here ever saw a school of the kind before, and considering this, and the qualifications of the teachers, they did well. I thought I could not get along without the

Sabbath School, and they consented to try it longer.

We have now divided it into two classes. I am obliged to take charge of all the females, there being no one else who can; and sometimes I have a great number, and of course can not do as I would: and beside they depend on me to assist the others, but I enjoy it much; in this way some can be taught, who can be taught in no other way. It now seems prosperous and the interest increasing; sometimes the house is nearly full of children. Some of the parents who at first felt no interest in it, say they would rather give up anything than the Sabbath School. I hope the interest will continue to increase, and that it will prove a blessing to the neighborhood.

I came here unexpected by the people, they not having heard from Gov. Slade, but I was received kindly. My school was not very large at first, but it has gradually increased, 'till I have now about 50[?] pupils most of whom are between the ages of 14 and 22. There has been no school here before for more than a year, and have never had a teacher who could do more than read, write and cipher a little; and these he did very imperfectly, so that my scholars are very backward but they are eager to learn, bright, active, attentive, and obedient, and learn very fast. I have a large number of young men between the ages of 18 and 21; they are very respectful, and obedient. I think I have gained the respect and affection of all my pupils, so that their obedience is cheerfully given. When I came here, there was a prejudice against female teachers; they had always employed men, and had never had a school six weeks without trouble, and they thought, of course, if a man could not govern their boys, a woman could not; but I was allowed to take my own course, and I gave them only one rule, that was — Do right. And by awakening their consciences to a sense of right and wrong, and other similar influences, I have succeeded much better than I expected, and have had to use no other influences than kindness. The parents have been interested to visit the school, and I find this the best way, and the surest way to interest them. I commence school with devotional exercises which I think have a good effect on the school during the day; this is something which has never been done here before. In my school I am content, and happy for I hope I am doing good, but I am entirely deprived of sympathy and good society. I have no human being here, in whom I can confide, or who possesses kindred feelings with mine. But there is one to whom I can go; were it not that I can cast all my care on God, and go to his Word for sympathy and consolation, I should be unhappy. I am also deprived of many New England comforts, and nearly all of its privileges, but when I think that I am giving a privilege to others, which they have never enjoyed I think I ought not to complain. But although I sometimes sigh, and long for Christian sympathy, and the privileges I once enjoyed, and feel lonely when I think of home, and friends, yet I am happy. I hope I have a friend who is always near and if I can in my way be useful I shall be happy. Pray for me, that my coming here may not be in vain. I should be pleased to hear from you.

Yours truly, Ellen P. Lee

## Mary S. Adams

*Mary S. Adams was a member of the fourteenth class (1853) of the Board. Her mother died when she was three, and her father remarried. She left home at age fourteen, and "depended upon [her] own exertions for livelihood and education." She was educated at Cherry Valley Academy near her home in Otsigo County, New York, and attended Mount Holyoke Female Seminary for a year and a half before going west. Founded by Mary Lyon in 1837, Mount Holyoke's mission was in Lyons' words, "to fit young women to be educators rather than mere teachers." In this letter, Adams voiced her objections to the traditional practice of having a teacher "board round"; evidently, she wanted a room to call her own. Obedient to the wishes of Beecher, Mary S. Adams started a Sabbath school where none had existed previously, although she claims that she has had "little religious experience" herself.*

Calhoun, Henry Co. Mo., June 28, 1853

My dear Miss Swift,*

I wish I could see you now for I feel somewhat troubled, and should like more of your valuable advice. When I first came to Calhoun I providentially met with Mr. Smith at the hotel where the stage left me, and he very kindly offered to bring me to this neighborhood, a distance of four miles.

He left me at the house of Mr. Knox, but said to them when he went away that he thought I had better board at Mr. Merritt's. They replied that they should like to have me remain with them, but expect-

---

*Nancy Swift, who directed the teacher-training program.

ed me to board with either of the three families of my employ that I might choose to. This was on Wednesday — Friday I called at Messrs. Merritt's and Bell's and decided to board with the former; as I could have a room with them, in a quiet, retired part of the house, that pleased me very well; and there was an air of comfort and neatness about them not observable at the other places. And besides Mr. M. has but four children while each of the others have eight. Accordingly on Monday following, I came here expecting to remain during the year. Last week, Mr. B. came to me and said he thought it time that writings were drawn between my employers and myself, and wished to know what my calculations were about boarding — said he expected me to "board around." I told him what had been said to me, and that it would be a disappointment for me to do otherwise, as I had just got settled and was feeling at home at Mr. Merritt's. Nothing more was said about it at this time — two or three days after, he came to the school house with Mr. Merritt to draw writings after these were completed, Mr. Bell turned to me and said that all was settled now excepting the matter of board. I repeated what I had before said and told him in addition that I did not feel under obligations to "board around" as it was well understood by them before the application for a teacher was made what your requirements were and that nothing was said about it in that. Yet not withstanding, I should be willing to accommodate him but did not feel able to walk so far, when teaching — he lives a mile from school, and would expect me to do my own washing, as he keeps no help — "Well" said he, "I want it understood now that I shall pay nothing for boarding when there is no reason why you should not board at my house. You look big and stout, and it seems like you might walk two miles well enough." He said much more that sounded about as kindly, but as I said nothing in reply, excepting that I thought I ought to be allowed to judge for myself concerning my own abilities, he got tired of talking alone and went away. . . . It would be very unpleasant for me to board at Mr. Bell's even if he lived nearer. He can not let me have what I consider a decent room. His four oldest children are over fifteen years old, and attract much company, especially on the Sabbath. . . .

Now I wish you to tell me what I ought to do. I do not feel as strong here as in N.E. — the climate is so warm that it overpowers me, and I need all the quiet and rest that I can have out of school. I have written you a long chapter about my trials, longer than I intended to. I will now say a few words about the pleasant things in my condition.

I commenced teaching the first Monday after I arrived, with fifteen scholars — the number has increased to twenty-one — and applications have been made for the admittance of six more. I am very much pleased with my school. I never before saw children so much interested in learning and so desirous to please me. The parents visit me every week, and seem to partake of the spirit of the children.

Mr. Bell told me the last time he was in that I was just such a lady as he wished to have teach his children — that they were learning mighty fast and "thought a heap of me." . . .

Our school house to be sure, might be a better one, for when it rains the water comes in quite freely, but then the floor furnishes numerous facilities for it to run out again soon. My oldest scholars are a son and daughter of Mr. B. one twenty, the other twenty-two. I do not find any difficulty in teaching the Latin that is required here. Two weeks after I commenced teaching a day school, I opened a S. School there had never been one in the place before. The first day I had eight scholars, since then our small house has been well filled. The parents and children in this neighborhood, and some young people from an adjoining one have come in so that we have had over thirty in all. . . . It seems rather hard that neither of the men are willing to open the School by prayer, but since they are not, I feel it is my duty to do so. They neither of them, have ever had family devotions. . . .

There seems to be a great opportunity for doing good here the people are so willing to receive instruction. But I do feel very incapable of giving it. I have had so little religious experience myself. Pray for me that I may be taught of God how to teach and that my feeble efforts to serve Christ may be blessed to this people. Miss Pratt spent a day with me last week. She is very much beloved here — is a very devoted Christian. She sends much love to you. I am sorry to add any to your numerous cares by telling you of my boarding trials, but I felt that I needed advise and knew of no other person whose counsel I should value so highly as yours. Don't forget to give my love to Helen. Please pardon the imperfections of this long letter and believe me,

Yours Affectionately
M.S. Adams

# Preparing to Teach: A Journal

## Mary Swift

From Arthur O. Norton, ed., *The First State Normal School in America: The Journals of Cyrus Peirce and Mary Swift* (Cambridge, Mass.: Harvard University Press, 1926).

*Only seventeen years old when she left Nantucket Island to join her former teacher Cyrus Peirce at the first state-financed normal school in America, Mary Swift (1822–1909) kept a daily journal of this historic experiment. Providing a first-rate record of lessons in the academic disciplines, lectures on pedagogy, and field trips, the journal rarely revealed her own thoughts — except to test a theory she had been taught. On March 14, for example, she discovered that ice cream made her feel cool, "contrary to the principles of Blackwell's philosophy." Innovative in its approach even today, the school activities attest to the seriousness of the profes-sional education: Distinguished visitors lectured, the young women attended a board of education meeting, and Peirce required them to hear one another's lessons and to teach in the model school.*

*Evidently, this new profession suited Swift. She became a pioneering teacher of blind, deaf mutes at the Perkins Institution in Boston, and wrote an influential book on her work entitled* Life and Education of Laura Bridgeman. *Helen Keller considered Swift, who attempted to teach her to speak, an inspiration, despite the fact that Swift did not succeed. After Swift married, she was a school committee member, and helped to found the Young Women's Christian Association in Boston. Until 1895, forty-six years after first meeting in Lexington, Massachusetts, the twenty-five women in Mary Swift's class met for a yearly reunion.*

### The First Term, August 1–October 1, 1839

Agreeably to the wishes of our teacher, Mr. Peirce, I have purchased this book, which is to contain an account of the business of the school, & of the studies in which we are engaged. . . .

After writing the above abstract (of the second Chapter of Combe's physiology) the remaining time on Saturday morning was occupied by Mr. P — in delivering a lecture to the pupils — The subject of which was Normal Schools, their origin & the expectations of the Board of Education & of the Friends of Education in general. When our forefathers first came to this country, (he said) they saw the necessity of schools, and established those which we call Grammar Schools. As the population became more numerous, the demand for public schools increased, and various kinds have been instituted, from the High Schools down to the Infant Schools. A better idea of the number of these schools, can be formed, by considering that nineteen-twentieths of the children of the United States, receive their Education from them — As our commerce increased, and the tide of emigration flowed more rapidly, the people found it necessary to do something for the support of the government, and knowing that it must devolve upon the rising generations, they turned their attention to the subject of Education. It was discussed freely, and Periodical Journals were established devoted to the subject — Finally, the Board of Education was formed. . . . The legislature of Massachusetts were awakened, and by the assistance of private munificence, the school, whose advantages we now enjoy, was established. To us, therefore, all the friends of Education turn, anxious for the success of the first effort to establish such schools. For this success, we shall depend, chiefly, on three particulars: 1st on interesting you in the studies to which you attend & in the daily remarks; 2nd on the course of lectures to be given & 3rd on the Model School.

*Thursday (8th).* The lessons for this morn were N. Philosophy, Physiology, N. History. The subjects of the first were Light & Refraction. Our teacher explained the rule, that the intensity of light diminished as the square of the distance increased, in such a manner as to make it much more clear than it has been before in my mind. — The lesson in Physiology was very practical, & he made some remarks in connection with it, upon tightness of dress, apparently, thinking that it was the fashion at the present time to dress tightly. He has not probably heard that the wisdom or some other good quality of the age has substituted the reverse fashion for the time present. . . .

*Saturday (10th).* After reading a portion in the Scriptures, Mr. Peirce proceeded to give a Second lecture to the pupils. — the object of the lecture was, to show what the teacher is to do. The two grand divisions of the teachers work, are 1st, the discipline of the faculties, 2nd, the communication of instruction. — These appear to be synonymous, but the difference between them may be made apparent by an example. Take the case of the lecturer, he understands his subject fully, and communicates facts to his hearers. — He, perhaps, carries most of the hearers along with him. They hear and understand, but it is without any exercise of the faculties of the mind. It is thus with the scholar the teacher may talk upon his studies, and impart knowledge, but his faculties will remain unimproved. . . . The next subject to be attended to is the trials & pleasures of a teacher's life. The teacher always has one consolation: that the work in which he is engaged, is useful: on account of the good he may do. The advantages of education are too numerous to enumerate. . . . School education is at the basis of every profession. The business of teaching is not only honest, but honorable: the ancients employed only their wisest men as teachers, for instance Aristotle, Plato, & Socrates. The wise of every age will honor the teacher. Females are peculiarly adapted to teaching; they possess more patience & perseverance, than the other sex & if the moral cultivation of the school be attended to, they will find little difficulty in governing.

*Wednesday (14th).* In the P.M. spent an hour in writing home & after mailing the letter met Mr. P. who gave us an invitation to attend the fair at the East Village. We accepted & had gone as far as the Monument House, when we met Mr. Morse the preceptor of the High School in Nantucket — He was intending to return to Boston in a short time & Mr. P. stopped to speak with him, promising to overtake us before we got to the Village. He did so, and accompanied us up to the scene of action — Upon the hill called Mt. Independence was a building which appears to have been erected for an observatory — It was prepared for the refreshment table, and hung with evergreens. To contain the articles for sale large tents were made covered with canvass — adjoining this was a tent at right angles in which a long table was set for the entertainment in the eve. — There were many people from the neighboring villages & all the tents were crowded — Groups were scattered among the trees and others were standing at the edge of the hill admiring the scenery around & below. — After viewing the fancy articles we entered the observatory & went into the upper part where Mr. P. named many of the hills around & showed us the state of New Hampshire, & the commencement of the White Mountains. We also saw the ocean, but it was at so great a distance that it appeared like mist over the land — When we had become wearied with standing we descended to the refreshment room, where Mr. P. treated us to ice-cream & cake — Contrary to the principles of Blakewell's Philosophy, we felt much cooler after eating the cream. — We sauntered through the grove & again through the tents, when it grew dark & we returned home, very well pleased with our afternoon excursion. — Went to tea with Mrs. Muzzy in company with Miss Stodder's sister who had just come out from Boston. —

*Friday (16th)*. This morn, Mr. Peirce wished to try the experiment of having one of the scholars hear the recitation in N. Philosophy. Accordingly he gave to me the charge of the recitation. The feeling caused by asking the first question tended rather to excite my risibles, but feeling the necessity of sobriety — I was enabled to play the teacher for a short time. I think that he can judge very little about our idea of teaching from the example which we give him in hearing a recitation for the manner in which it is carried on depends very much upon the interest felt by the teacher in the scholars & in their study. — To furnish a variety in conducting a recitation I think it will answer very well.

*Saturday (17th)*. This morn after the recitation in Orthography, & the solution of a few problems on the Globe, Mr. P. gave his weekly lecture. . . . There are certain qualities which are very desirable to a teacher — not that he intended to say they were indispensable, but that they were very great additions. The 1st is Health — some leave other occupations as too laborious and teach a school, thinking that the trials of the school room are much less than those of any other station. Health is essential to the teacher, not only on his own account but for the sake of his pupils. To the sick, every trial is doubled. — Some suffering bad health are better teachers, than those enjoying good, but if the same person were possessed with health, he would be probably a much better teacher. — Personal deformity would be an objection not but that a dwarf or cripple *may* keep a better school than one formed with the most perfect symmetry, but it would be better that the children should have the beauties of nature presented to them, than the deformities. 2nd a fair reputation and good standing in the community. If people speak slightly [sic] of you in the town in which you have a school, you will find your scholars will disrespect you. — 4th, a well balanced mind, free from eccentricities & from the infirmities of genius. – A person may have too much, as too little genius for a teacher. — 5th a

deep interest in children — she must feel an interest in whatever interests them; in their joys & their sorrows. Children readily perceive those
who are interested in them, & feel hurt by coldness. 6th Patience, mildness, firmness, & perfect self control, are essential properties to every
teacher. . . . Patience is requisite to meet the various trials which will
beset you. You may not make so much impression by mildness in one
instance, but in the end, much more will be accomplished. Mildness in
manner, measures, language, countenance & in everything else.

Firmness is especially necessary, be firm to your plans; let your
measures be the same each day — A teacher without these virtues, may
be compared to a city without walls; which the enemy enters without
opposition, & does what he chooses after entering. 7th nice moral discrimination, a high sense of moral responsibility, & accountability —
The knowledge that you are accountable to a being superior to man,
sustains you. — Teachers should be acquainted with their difficulties,
and know how to surmount them. The government should be just, uniform, & impartial. All rules should be made so that the pupils can see
they are for their good, & the reasons for making them should be
explained. Teachers should be well acquainted with the branches they
are to teach. — The next lecture will be upon the responsibilities of a
teacher & School order & government.

*Wednesday (21st).* This morn we recited the lesson in Philosophy & it
appeared to be better understood than it was yesterday. This took up
an hour & half & after recess we read our abstracts when there was a
half hour before school closed. Mr. P. gave us the questions, Can the
proper object of schools be secured without appeal to corporal punish-
ments & rewards or premiums? to discuss & we each in order proceeded to give our opinions upon the subject — Mine is that it is very seldom necessary to appeal to corporal punishment & that rewards should
not be given. — One or two agreed with me, & some approved of punishment & others not. — After conversing a while upon this subject it
was nearly 12 o'clock & school closed.

*Saturday (24th).* After some review, Mr. P. proceeded to give a lecture
upon the subject of the Responsibility of the Teacher. — To have some
conception of this, remember that you are to influence the character,
the future standing of the ten, fifty, or an hundred children who are
committed to your care. Imagine each in his course through the world,
& that your work will shape all their feelings, & the influence which

they will exert through life. This will be imparted to those who are placed under their care, & thus your influence, instead of being confined to the hundred under your eye, will extent to thousands. — The situation, by taking this view of it, assumes a high responsibility — It is responsible in every stage, but chiefly so at the beginning. It is like a building, if the foundation is laid uneven it totters to the base, but if the contrary it will stand for ages. It is the same with physical, mental & moral education. If you instill false principles into their minds, your successors will have to root them out, before they can begin to act. . . .

*Saturday 31st.* The last day of summer, & we have been here two months. 'Tis true that time waits for no man & it would appear that he had left us far behind but on taking a more favorable view of the subject we find that we have become initiated into the customs & rules of the school & thus have laid the foundation for future advancement. . . . After these remarks, [Peirce] proceeded to delivery his lecture, which was upon the subject of *School Order.* He commenced by calling our attention to the importance of the office of the teacher, with how many & various & invaluable interests it may connect us; if we are faithful how many will be rendered more happy by our instructions. — Follow each into life, notice his effect upon others & all his actions and after doing this we shall be able to answer the question "is not the relation of teacher one of unspeakable responsibility. — A good school must be orderly; whatever its object or title, or whoever its teacher may be. A school may be pleasant & forward, or even more than this, but order is necessary to make it a good one. The work of Education is a work of order. Order was Heaven's first law. The apostle directs that every thing should be done with order & the wise man associates the want of it with confusion. Look where you will, on celestial or terrestrial things; when you will in time past, present, or future & you will find it essential. If a man has failed, we hear, almost invariably, soon after, that his affairs were in a disorderly state. Death is put to all hopes of success without it. Oxygen is not more essential to vitality. — For your encouragement, I will add, that children, much as they like freedom, are fond of order & system. This is the cause of their admiration of regular figures, as the circles, & of their preference of such, when many are offered them. Consequently they are better suited by an orderly school, & if you would wish to please them, confine them to rules. . . .

*Friday 6th.* Political Economy — upon the division of labor. This is a very interesting study to me & I like the manner in which the author treats it very well. If he succeed as well in making every subject intelligible he must be an excellent teacher. — Will you, Mr. P. tell us about the school at Barre — something about its numbers & c? [illegible] It will be pleasant to hear of the success of those engaged in a similar undertaking. The next exercise was Orthoepy & after that Composition. The latter exercise consisted in reading aloud the pieces. Some seemed to feel very badly at being obliged to do it, but I think that it is about as easy to read one's ideas as to speak them as we do every day of our lives. It is only the associations connected with Composition that renders it so difficult to scholars as it almost invariably is. — After some comments upon the pieces in which Mr. P. expressed himself pleased with the attempt he proceeded to give his lecture. — The subject of the remarks was School Government. This is necessary to every school. Teachers or scholars must govern; it must be a Monarchy Democracy or Republic. It is the same with a family as with a school, if the reins of government be put into the hands of the pupils or children, failure must be the result. The most which can be done in a school is to admit the scholars to qualified participation. Let their opinion be asked & let them assist the teacher in devising means for improving the school as much as possible. But it is best to go no farther than this. After you are convinced that the teacher must be governor decide on what principles the government shall be based.

*Monday Sept. 16.* The school assembled again this morn, but two of our seats were vacant. After reading from the Scriptures Mr. P. spoke of the erroneous views that were pervading the state with regard to the conditions of entering the Normal School. Some believe that the pupils must bind themselves to instruct a certain number of years; while others, carry the story farther, and suppose that they are obliged to bind themselves to keep school for their life time. Some that they must teach a public school and others that the school must be in this commonwealth. — He told us these that we may be able when we meet with any person entertaining such opinions to contradict them & tell them the true conditions. — He also told us of his intentions concerning a Model school; that this would according to the plan marked out be included in the third year, but that as we should probably stay only one year he should interest himself immediately to procure one upon which some of the scholars might operate.

*Thursday December 26th.* A day which the present Normalites will probably have cause to remember for several *years,* at *least.* — This morn is very delightful, and all are collected waiting for the sleigh. — A few moments more, & we are seated & on our way to Mr. Dodge's to take a few in addition to the nineteen already there. — We were joined by Mrs. D——, Mrs. Trusk & Mr. D, & Mrs. P. — After a pleasant ride, got to Waltham & stopped at the door of the Central Tavern while the gentlemen made the necessary arrangements. Thence to the hall. . . . The first business transacted, was the reading of the Constitution. — Mr. Dodge said that it was customary to choose a committee, for the choice of subjects for debate. — Messrs. Peirce, Hyde, Keith were chosen. A short time in which there was no business, passed and then Mr. P. reported four resolutions, and fourteen questions or subjects for debate. — (My pencil & fingers refused to go fast enough to take these). — The report of the committee concerning the necessity of alteration in the common school system. . . . The committee appointed to choose officers, now being ready to report, a motion was made, & seconded, to lay the question upon the table, & listen to the nomination. — It was accepted & the meeting adjourned till two P.M. — Returned to the hotel and after waiting a half hour we were summoned to dinner, it being advisable, as the gentlemen of the party (and I presume some of the ladies) thought to attend to the physical as well as the intellectual wants. — From dinner we went to the Factories for making cotton, which are worked by the Charles River. We entered the lower room which was [?] to Carding, the next above to Spinning, next to Weaving, and next to Dressing. — The noise of the Machinery was so great, that, at first, we were unable to hear each other speak. — The poor girls are now, more an object of my pity than ever before. — They generally looked very pale, & I should think, according to the principle of Physiology, must suffer much from lung complaints, on account of the particles of cotton constantly floating in the atmosphere. — Leaving the upper room, we descended to the basement, to see the water wheel. — From there to the banks of the river & then back to the Hall. . . .

*Tuesday, December 31st.* The last day in the year, & the last day of the first six months, of my exile from home. On reflecting upon the pleasant connections formed here, it seems as if it will be nearly as difficult, to part with them as it was to leave our homes, — but we have six months more to enjoy their company, and we will not anticipate trouble. — The exercises were N. Philosophy, Combe, — Mental Philosophy & Book-keeping. In the P.M. Reading in the Dictionary, N. History, M. Philosophy. — In the P.M. Mrs. P. called & after a very short recitation in M. Philosophy, school was dismissed. —

And here is the end of the day, of the year, & of my journal, and I will close it with the hope, that when my next is completed it may show some slight improvement in the powers of Composition, and in Chirography.

# Reminiscences of School Life, and Hints on Teaching

—⚬◦⚭◦⚬—

*Fanny Jackson-Coppin*

From Fanny Jackson-Coppin,
*Reminiscences of School Life, and Hints on Teaching*
(Philadelphia: A. M. E. Book Concern, 1913), pp. 1–35.

*Best known for her leadership of the Institute for Coloured Youth, Fanny Jackson-Coppin (1837–1913) dedicates her book to the aunt who bought Fanny's freedom from slavery at age twelve and enabled her to become an educator. The "Autobiographical Sketch," selected from the* Reminiscences *and reproduced almost in its entirety here, is a moving and strangely contemporary story of a young woman's striving for an education both to satisfy her considerable intellect and to prepare to lead her people. Following the autobiographical sketch, Jackson-Coppin explains her approach to teaching, provides accounts of her travels in England and South Africa, and concludes the work with brief biographies from among the 668 students who graduated from the Institute during her tenure there. Particularly striking is Jackson-Coppin's formulation of her educational philosophy. Steeped in higher mathematics and Greek classics as a result of her Oberlin education,*

*Jackson-Coppin nonetheless argues that active students should not let book learning "crowd out the prosy process of thinking, comparing, [and] reasoning."*

*An outspoken activist against racism, as the Institute principal Jackson-Coppin fought to open careers for her students in trades previously closed to African Americans. She also took on the challenge of providing for elderly African Americans, women in particular. In 1881, well into her career as an educator, Fanny Jackson married Reverend Levi Jenkins Coppin, a minister of the African Methodist Episcopal Church. In 1902, Reverend Coppin was appointed Bishop of Cape Town, South Africa, and the couple lived there as missionaries for a decade. By then Jackson-Coppin had achieved considerable celebrity and many opportunities were open to her. South Africa connected her with "the original home of our people," and gave her the chance to contribute to their civil and religious development. Jackson-Coppin died in Philadelphia in 1913.*

*The legacy of the Institute and Jackson-Coppin are memorialized in two institutions: the Institute moved to Cheyney, Pennsylvania, in 1904 and eventually became Cheyney State College, and in 1926 the Fanny Jackson-Coppin Normal School was established in Baltimore. Like many normal schools, this school grew from a one-year course to educate African American elementary school teachers at Douglass High School to a two-year Normal Department, before becoming an autonomous institution, Coppin State College.*

THIS BOOK IS INSCRIBED TO MY BELOVED AUNT SARAH ORR CLARK WHO, WORKING AT SIX DOLLARS A MONTH SAVED ONE HUNDRED AND TWENTY-FIVE DOLLARS, AND BOUGHT MY FREEDOM

We used to call our grandmother "mammy," and one of my earliest recollections — I must have been about three years old — is, I was sent to keep my mammy company. It was in a little one-room cabin. We used to go up a ladder to the loft where we slept.

Mammy used to make a long prayer every night before going to bed; but not one word of all she said do I remember except the one word "offspring." She would ask God to bless her offspring. This word remained with me, for, I wondered what offspring meant.

Mammy had six children, three boys and three girls. One of these, Lucy, was my mother. Another one of them, Sarah, was purchased by my grandfather, who first saved money and bought himself, then four of his children. Sarah went to work at six dollars a month, saved one hundred and twenty-five dollars, and bought little Frances, having taken a great liking to her, for on account of my birth, my grandfather refused to buy my mother; and so I was left a slave in the District of Columbia, where I was born. . . . When my aunt had finally saved up the hundred and twenty-five dollars, she bought me and sent me to New Bedford, Mass., where another aunt lived, who promised to get me a place to work for my board, and get a little education if I could. She put me out to work, at a place where I was allowed to go to school when I was not at work. But I could not go on wash day, nor ironing day, nor cleaning day, and this interfered with my progress. . . . Finally, I found a chance to go to Newport with Mrs. Elizabeth Orr, an aunt by marriage, who offered me a home with her and a better chance at school. I went with her, but I was not satisfied to be a burden on her small resources. I was now fourteen years old, and felt that I ought to take care of myself. So I found a permanent place in the family of Mr. George H. Calvert, a great grandson of Lord Baltimore, who settled Maryland. His wife was Elizabeth Stuart, a descendant of Mary, Queen of Scots. Here I had one hour every other afternoon in the week to take some private lessons, which I did of Mrs. Little. After that, attended for a few months the public colored school which was taught by Mrs. Gavitt. I thus prepared myself to enter the examination for the Rhode Island State Normal School, under Dana P. Colburn; the school was then located at Bristol, R. I. Here, my eyes were first opened on the subject of teaching. I said to myself, is it possible that teaching can be made so interesting as this! But, having finished the course of study there, I felt that I had just begun to learn; and, hearing of Oberlin College, I made up my mind to try and get there. I had learned a little music while at Newport, and had mastered the elementary studies of the piano and guitar. My aunt in Washington still helped me, and I was able to pay my way to Oberlin, the course of study there being the same as that at Harvard College. Oberlin was then the only College in the United States where colored students were permitted to study.

The faculty did not forbid a woman to take the gentleman's course, but they did not advise it. There was plenty of Latin and Greek in it, and as much mathematics as one could shoulder. Now, I took a long breath and prepared for a delightful contest. All went smoothly until I was in the junior year in College. Then, one day, the Faculty sent for me — ominous request — and I was not slow in obeying it. It was a custom in Oberlin that forty students from the junior and senior class-es were employed to teach the preparatory classes. As it was now time for the juniors to begin their work, the Faculty informed me that it was their purpose to give me a class, but I was to distinctly understand that if the pupils rebelled against my teaching, they did not intend to force it. Fortunately for my training at the normal school, and my own dear love of teaching, tho there was a little surprise on the faces of some when they came into the class, and saw the teacher, there were no signs of rebellion. The class went on increasing in numbers until it had to be divided, and I was given both divisions. One of the divisions ran up again, but the Faculty decided that I had as much as I could do, and it would not allow me to take any more work.

When I was within a year of graduation, an application came from a Friends' school in Philadelphia for a colored woman who could teach Greek, Latin, and higher mathematics. The answer returned was: "We have the woman, but you must wait a year for her." Then began a correspondence with Alfred Cope, a saintly character, who, having found out what my work in college was, teaching my classes in college, besides sixteen private music scholars, and keeping up my work in the senior class, immediately sent me a check for eighty dollars, which wonderfully lightened my burden as a poor student.

When I first went to Oberlin I boarded in what was known as the Ladies' Hall, and altho the food was good, yet, I think, that for lack of variety I began to run down in health. About this time I was invited to spend a few weeks in the family of Professor H. E. Peck, which ended in my staying a few years, until the independence of the Republic of Hayti was recognized, under President Lincoln, and Professor Peck was sent as the first U. S. Minister to that interesting country; then the family was broken up, and I was invited by Professor and Mrs. Charles H. Churchill to spend the remainder of my time, about six months, in their family. The influence upon my life in these two Christian homes, where I was regarded as an honored member of the family circle, was a potent factor in forming the character which was to stand the test of the new and strange conditions of my life in Philadelphia. I had been so long in Oberlin that I had forgotten about my color, but I was sharply reminded of it when, in a storm of rain, a Philadelphia street car conductor forbid my entering a car that did not have on it "for colored people," so I had to wait in the storm until one came in which colored people could ride. This was my first unpleasant experience in Philadelphia. Visiting Oberlin not long after my work began in Philadelphia, President Finney asked me how I was growing in grace; I told him that I was growing as fast as the American people would let me. When told of some of the conditions which were meeting me, he seemed to think it unspeakable.

At one time, at Mrs. Peck's, when we girls were sitting on the floor getting out our Greek, Miss Sutherland, from Maine, suddenly stopped, and, looking at me, said: "Fanny Jackson, were you ever a slave?" I said yes; and she burst into tears. Not another word was spoken by us. But those tears seemed to wipe out a little of what was wrong.

I never rose to recite in my classes at Oberlin but I felt that I had the honor of the whole African race upon my shoulders. I felt that, should I fail, it would be ascribed to the fact that I was colored. At one time, when I had quite a signal triumph in Greek, the Professor of Greek concluded to visit the class in mathematics and see how we were getting along. I was particularly anxious to show him that I was as safe in mathematics as in Greek.

I, indeed, was more anxious, for I had always heard that my race was good in the languages, but stumbled when they came to mathematics. Now, I was always fond of a demonstration, and happened to get in the examination the very proposition that I was well acquainted with; and so went that day out of the class with flying colors.

I was elected class poet for the Class Day exercises, and have the kindest remembrance of the dear ones who were my classmates. I never can forget the courtesies of the three Wright brothers; of Professor Pond, of Dr. Lucien C. Warner, of Doctor Kincaid, the Chamberland girls, and others, who seemed determined that I should carry away from Oberlin nothing but most pleasant memories of my life there. . . .

Being very fond of music, my aunt gave me permission to hire a piano and have it at her house, and I used to go there and take lessons. But, in the course of time, it became noticeable to Mrs. Calvert [with whom Fanny lived in Newport, R.I.] that I was absent on Wednesdays at a certain hour, and that without permission. So, on one occasion, when I was absent, Mrs. Calvert inquired of the cook as to my whereabouts, and directed her to send me to her upon my return that I might give an explanation. When the cook informed me of what had transpired, I was very much afraid that something quite unpleasant awaited me. Upon being questioned, I told her the whole truth about the matter. I told Mrs. Calvert that I had been taking lessons for some time, and that I had already advanced far enough to play the little organ in the Union Church. Instead of being terribly scolded, as I had feared, Mrs. Calvert said: "Well, Fanny, when people will go ahead, they cannot be kept back; but, if you had asked me, you might have had the piano here." Mrs. Calvert taught me to sew beautifully and to darn, and to take care of laces. My life there was most happy, and I never would have left her, but it was in me to get an education and to teach my people. This idea was deep in my soul. Where it came from I cannot tell, for I had never had any exhortations, nor any lectures which influenced me to take this course. It must have been born in me. At Mrs. Calvert's, I was in contact with people of refinement and education. Mr. Calvert was a perfect gentleman, and a writer of no mean ability. They had no children, and this gave me an opportunity to come very near to Mrs. Calvert, doing for her many things which otherwise a daughter would have done. I loved her and she loved me. When I was about to leave her to go to the Normal School, she said to me: "Fanny, will money keep you?" But that deep-seated purpose to get an education and become a teacher to my people, yielded to no inducement of comfort or temporary gain. During the time that I attended the Normal School in Rhode Island, I got a chance to take some private lessons in French, and eagerly availed myself of the opportunity. French was not in the Oberlin curriculum, but there was a professor there who taught it privately, and I continued my studies under him, and so was able to complete the course and graduate with a French essay. Freedmen now began to pour into Ohio from the South, and some of them settled in the township of Oberlin. During my last year at the college, I formed an evening class for them, where they might be taught to read and write. It was deeply touching to me to see old men painfully following the simple words of spelling; so intensely eager to learn. I felt that for such people to have been kept in the darkness of ignorance was an unpardonable sin, and I rejoiced that even then I could enter measurably upon the course in life which I had long ago chosen. Mr. John M. Langston, who afterwards became Minister to Hayti, was then practicing law at Oberlin. His comfortable home was always open with a warm welcome to colored students, or to any who cared to share his hospitality.

I went to Oberlin in 1860, and was graduated in August, 1865, after having spent five and a half years.

The years 1860 and 1865 were years of unusual historic importance and activity. In '60 the immortal Lincoln was elected, and in '65 the terrible war came to a close, but not until freedom for all the slaves in America had been proclaimed, and that proclamation made valid by the victorious arms of the Union party. In the year 1863 a very bitter feeling was exhibited against the colored people of the country, because they were held responsible for the fratricidal war then going on. The riots in New York especially gave evidence of this ill feeling. It was in this year that the faculty put me to teaching.

Of the thousands then coming to Oberlin for an education, a very few were colored. I knew that, with the exception of one here or there, all my pupils would be white; and so they were. It took a little moral courage on the part of the faculty to put me in my place against the old custom of giving classes only to white students. But, as I have said elsewhere, the matter was soon settled and became an overwhelming success. How well do I remember the delighted look on the face of Principal Fairchild when he came into the room to divide my class, which then numbered over eighty. How easily a colored teacher might be put into some of the public schools. It would only take a little bravery, and might cause a little surprise, but wouldn't be even a nine days' wonder.

And now came the time for me to leave Oberlin, and start in upon my work at Philadelphia. In the year 1837, the Friends of Philadelphia had established a school for the education of colored youth in higher learning. To make a test whether or not the Negro was capable of acquiring any considerable degree of education. For it was one of the strongest arguments in the defense of slavery, that the Negro was an inferior creation; formed by the Almighty for just the work he was doing. It is said that John C. Calhoun made the remark, that if there could be found a Negro that could conjugate a Greek verb, he would give up all his preconceived ideas of the inferiority of the Negro. Well, let's try him, and see, said the fair-minded Quaker people. And for years this institution, known as the Institute for Colored Youth, was visited by interested persons from different parts of the United States and Europe. Here I was given the delightful task of teaching my own people, and how delighted I was to see them mastering Caesar, Virgil, Cicero, Horace and Xenophon's Anabasis. We also taught New Testament Greek. It was customary to have public examinations once a year, and when the teachers were thru examining their classes, any interested person in the audience was requested to take it up, and ask questions. At one of such examinations, when I asked a titled Englishman to take the class and examine it, he said: "They are more capable of examining me, their proficiency is simply wonderful."

One visiting friend was so pleased with the work of the students in the difficult metres in Horace that he afterwards sent me, as a present, the Horace which he used in college. A learned Friend from Germantown, coming into a class in Greek, the first aorist, passive and middle, being so neatly and correctly written at one board, while I, at the same time, was hearing a class recite, exclaimed: "Fanny, I find thee driving a coach and six." As it is much more difficult to drive a coach and six, than a coach and one, I took it as a compliment. But I was especially glad to know that the students were doing their work so well as to justify Quakers in their fair-minded opinion of them. General O. C. Howard, who was brought in at one time by one of the managers to hear an examination in Virgil, remarked that Negroes in trigonometry and the classics might well share in the triumphs of their brothers on the battlefield.

When I came to the School, the Principal of the Institute was Ebenezer D. Bassett, who for fourteen years had charge of the work. He was a graduate of the State Normal School of Connecticut, and was a man of unusual natural and acquired ability, and an accurate and ripe scholar; and, withal, a man of great modesty of character. Many are the reminiscences he used to give of the visits of interested persons to the school: among these was a man who had written a book to prove that the Negro was not a man. And, having heard of the wonderful achievements of this Negro school, he determined to come and see for himself what was being accomplished. He brought a friend with him, better versed in algebra than himself, and asked Mr. Bassett to bring out his highest class. There was in the class at that time Jesse Glasgow, a very black boy. All he asked was a chance. Just as fast as they gave the problems, Jesse put them on the board with the greatest ease. This decided the fate of the book, then in manuscript form, which, so far as we know, was never published. Jesse Glasgow afterwards found his way to the University of Edinburgh, Scotland.

In the year 1869, Mr. Bassett was appointed United States Minister to Hayti by President Grant; leaving the principalship of the Institute vacant. Now, Octavius V. Catto, a professor in the school, and myself, had an opportunity to keep the school up to the same degree of proficiency that it attained under its former Principal and to carry it forward as much as possible.

About this time we were visited by a delegation of school commissioners, seeking teachers for schools in Delaware, Maryland and New Jersey. These teachers were not required to know and teach the classics, but they were expected to come into an examination upon the English branches, and to have at their tongue's end the solution of any abstruse problem in the three R's which their examiners might be inclined to ask them. And now, it seemed best to give up the time spent in teaching Greek and devote it to the English studies.

As our young people were now about to find a ready field in teaching, it was thought well to introduce some text books on school management, and methods of teaching, and thoroughly prepare our students for normal work. At this time our faculty was increased by the addition of Richard T. Greener, a graduate of Harvard College, who took charge of the English Department, and Edward Bouchet, a graduate of Yale College, and also of the Sheffield Scientific School, who took charge of the scientific department. Both of these young men were admirably fitted for their work. And, with Octavius V. Catto in charge of the boys' department, and myself in charge of the girls — in connection with the principalship of the school — we had a strong working force.

I now instituted a course in normal training, which at first consisted only of a review of English studies, with the theory of teaching, school management and methods. But the inadequacy of this course was so apparent that when it became necessary to reorganize the Preparatory Departments, it was decided to put this work into the hands of the normal students, who would thus have ample practice in teaching and governing under daily direction and correction. These students became so efficient in their work that they were sought for and engaged to teach long before they finished their course of study.

Richard Humphreys, the Friend — Quaker — who gave the first endowment with which to found the school, stipulated that it should not only teach higher literary studies, but that a Mechanical and Industrial Department, including Agriculture, should come within the scope of its work. The wisdom of this thoughtful and far-seeing founder has since been amply demonstrated. At the Centennial Exhibition in 1876, the foreign exhibits of work done in trade schools opened the eyes of the directors of public education in America as to the great lack existing in our own system of education. If this deficiency was apparent as it related to the white youth of the country, it was far more so as it related to the colored.

In Philadelphia, the only place at the time where a colored boy could learn a trade, was in the House of Refuge, or the Penitentiary!

And now began an eager and intensely earnest crusade to supply this deficiency in the work of the Institute for Colored Youth.

The teachers of the Institute now vigorously applied their energies in collecting funds for the establishment of an Industrial Department, and in this work they had the encouragement of the managers of the school, who were as anxious as we that the greatly needed department should be established.

In instituting this department, a temporary organization was formed, with Mr. Theodore Starr as President, Miss Anna Hallowell as Treasurer, and myself as Field Agent.

The Academic Department of the Institute had been so splendidly successful in proving that the Negro youth was equally capable as others in mastering a higher education, that no argument was necessary to establish its need, but the broad ground of education by which the masses must become self-supporting was, to me, a matter of painful anxiety. Frederick Douglass once said, it was easier to get a colored boy into a lawyer's office than into a blacksmith shop; and on account of the inflexibility of the Trades Unions, this condition of affairs still continues, making it necessary for us to have our own "blacksmith shop."

The minds of our people had to be enlightened upon the necessity of industrial education.

Before all the literary societies and churches where they would hear me; in Philadelphia and the suburban towns; in New York, Washington and everywhere, when invited to speak, I made that one subject my theme. To equip an industrial plant is an expensive thing, and knowing that much money would be needed, I made it a rule to take up a collection wheresoever I spoke. But I did not urge anyone to give more than a dollar, for the reason I wanted the masses to have an opportunity to contribute their small offerings, before going to those who were able to give larger sums. Never shall I forget the encouragement given me when a colored man, whom I did not know, met me and said: "I have heard of your Industrial School project, come to me for twenty-five dollars." That man was Walter P. Hall; all honor to him.

In preparing for the industrial needs of the boys, the girls were not neglected. It was not difficult to find competent teachers of sewing and cooking for the girls. Dressmaking on the Taylor system was introduced with great success, and cooking was taught by the most improved methods. As the work advanced, other trades were added, and those already undertaken were expanded and perfected. When the Industrial Department was fully established, the following trades were being taught: For boys: bricklaying, plastering, carpentry, shoemaking, printing and tailoring. For the girls: dressmaking, millinery, typewriting, stenography and classes in cooking, including both boys and girls. Stenography and typewriting were also taught the boys, as well as the girls. . . .

We carried on an industrial crusade which never ended until we saw a building devoted to the purpose of teaching trades. For the managers of the Institute, seeing the need of the work, threw themselves into this new business, after their thirty previous years working for the colored youth. Our money in the end amounted to nearly three thousand dollars, and of this we have always been justly very glad. We could have had twenty times as much more, except for my backwardness and unwillingness to press poor people beyond what I thought they could give. Three thousand dollars was a mere drop in the bucket, but it was a great deal to us, who had seen it collected in small sums — quarters, dollars, etc. It was a delightful scene to us to pass thru that school where ten trades were being taught, altho in primitive fashion, the limited means of the Institute precluding the use of machinery. The managers always refused to take any money from the State, altho it was frequently offered.

Many were the ejaculations of satisfaction at this busy hive of industry. "Ah," said some, "this is the way the school should have begun, the good Quaker people began at the wrong end." Not so, for when they began this school, the whole South was a great industrial plant where the fathers taught the sons and the mothers taught the daughters, but the mind was left in darkness. . . .

# The Schoolmarm

## Anna Fuller

From Anna Fuller, "The Schoolmarm,"
*Pratt Portraits, Sketched in a New England Suburb*
(New York: G. P. Putnam's Sons, 1892).

*Taken from a late-nineteenth-century collection, this story turns on woman's classic question — should she sacrifice work for love? The spirited heroine, Mary Pratt, turns the question on her suitor: "Would you give up your ranch and come and teach school with me?" His reply, "That's not a fair question," has a thoroughly modern ring. Well into the twentieth century, in most states female teachers — not male — were forbidden to marry, presumably because, as moral exemplars to the young, they had to demonstrate that a married woman's sphere was the home. Thus, many women faced Mary Pratt's dilemma.*

*This story touches indirectly on a second social injustice encountered by women: The woman who chose teaching and a life of "single blessedness" was often pitied and punished. A "mother" to children to whom she did not give birth, and with no man of her own, in the popular imagination she was expected to grow into a jealous, intolerant "old maid."*

*No biographical information is available about Anna Fuller, the author of the story, except that she lived from 1853 to 1916 and published a number of books, including:* A Literary Courtship *(1893);* A Venetian June *(1896);* One of the Pilgrims *(1898); and* Later Pratt Portraits, Sketched in a New England Suburb *(1911).*

A disagreeable sensation was caused throughout the entire Pratt family when Mary William announced her intention of "keeping school." Old Lady Pratt, who knew the history of the family ever since she came into it some sixty years before, could testify that no daughter of that highly respectable house had ever "worked for a living." An unprejudiced observer might have thought that Old Lady Pratt herself had worked for a living, and worked harder than any school-teacher, all through the childhood of her six boys and girls. But that, of course, was a different matter, as anybody must understand. A woman toiling early and late for husband and children was but fulfilling the chief end and aim of her being, but a woman who set out to wrest a living from the world, when she "need want for nothing at home," was clearly flying in the fact of Providence.

"Well, Mary," she said to her grand-daughter, "you must not expect me to countenance any such step."

"Why not, Grandma?"

"Why not! Because I don't approve of young women getting' dissatisfied with the sphere to which they've been called. That's why not."

"But I haven't been called to any sphere. Now that Bessie and Willie are almost as grown up as I am, mother doesn't need me any more, and I don't see why I'm not entitled to a change if I want one."

"If you want a change," said Grandma, promptly, "you'd better get married."

"Now, Grandma! You know well enough that I never had an offer. If

I had, you'd have heard of it fast enough."

"And you don't deserve to have one," cried the old lady, with asperity, "if you go and spile everything by turning schoolmarm."

This was a sore subject with Old Lady Pratt. She who was the sworn foe to single blessedness,[3] had constantly to hear that her own granddaughters had "never had an offer." It was not that they were less sought than other girls of their age, but early marriages had almost gone out of fashion since Grandma's day, and many a handsome girl might get to be well on in the twenties before a serious suitor made his appearance.

Mary William — so called to distinguish her from her Uncle Anson's daughter, who went by the name of Mary Anson — Mary William was at this time twenty-one years of age. Her father, the hero of the family, had been killed at the first battle of Bull Run, six years previous. He had left his affairs, what there was of them, in such perfect order that his widow knew precisely what she had to depend upon — a fact on which all the Pratts laid great emphasis. But to know one's financial status, if that status chance to be extremely low, is scarcely compensation for hardships and privations, and Mrs. William Pratt used fervently to wish that there had been just sufficient inaccuracy in her husband's accounts to leave a margin of possibility that a windfall might yet occur.

Mrs. William Pratt was not a woman of much energy or resource. She had a few fixed ideas, one of them being that she could not consent to "come down in the world." Coming down in the world meant to her comprehension renting or selling the commodious, well-built house in which her husband had installed her during the days of her prosperity, and moving into smaller quarters. Her house was Edna Pratt's special pride. It was large and rambling, with a front hall which did not confine itself to the manifest mission of furnishing a landing-place from the stairs, but spread itself out into an octagonal space, wherein pillars stood supporting arches; a dim ancestral-looking hall, which could not fail to impress a stranger. But as strangers rarely visited Mrs. William Pratt, and as nearly all the frequenters of the house distinctly remembered its erection a dozen or more years previous, the hall did not make quite the baronial impression which might have been expected. Mary William, especially when performing the arduous duties of maid-of-all-work minus the wages, used to murmur within herself against all the spacious rooms, which seemed to have taken their cue from it. For she reflected that every superfluous square yard of floor meant just so much more carpet to sweep; that every inch of wood-work offered just so much more of a resting-place for dust. Mary William was of the opinion that her youth had been deliberately sacrificed to the house, and pre-eminently to the pillared hall, and she secretly rebelled against it with all her might and main. Not work for her living, indeed? How many a time had the one "girl" of the establishment been dismissed on some slight pretext! How many a time had her "place" remained vacant, and while Mrs. William Pratt sat in the parlor or lingered among the baronial pillars, complaining to visitors of the inferiority and scarcity of servants, the unfortunate Mary William had stood scorching her face over the kitchen stove, or cleaning the set of elaborate repoussé silver, which lent such an air of distinction to their sideboard.

But Mary William was a young person of much determination and rather unusual intelligence, and while her hands grew rough and her temper just a little sharpened in the drudgery of her daily life, she saw to it that no rust should gather upon her excellent facilities. She had graduated from the high-school at the head of her class, and after her education was thus "completed," she managed with the aid of the public library, to do a good deal of solid reading and some studying. Mary William was not intended for a book worm, but she turned to books as being the most congenial and the least exacting society within her reach. She was not able to dress well and tastefully. She was not able to entertain her friends at home, being far too poor for such luxuries. Neither was she the girl to enjoy playing a subordinate part in life, and she felt keenly the social disabilities which her poverty imposed upon her. She had never been of a complaining disposition, and no one suspected her of any discontent with her lot. But in her own mind she had long contemplated a declaration of independence, to be made when she should come of age. This was to occur in July, but she had no intention of hurrying matters. When she came down to breakfast, however, on the very morning of her twenty-first birthday, she suddenly found it impossible to refrain from making known her plans.

"Teach school" cried her mother, in a tone of ineffectual protest.

"Be a schoolmarm!" cried Bessie; while Willie, who was still subject to the redoubtable race of schoolmarms, gazed upon her with a mixture of awe and incredulity.

"I never heard of such a ridiculous idea," said Mrs. William Pratt.

"I don't see anything ridiculous about it," Mary retorted, giving vent to her feelings with unprecedented freedom. "I've been scrimping

THE SCHOOLMISTRESS.

*"The Schoolmistress," an 1853 engraving. In the early popular consciousness, the teacher was often a dour-faced "old maid" with a switch; the stereotype persists today.*

and pinching and slaving all my life, and now I want to try how it feels to have a few dollars of my own."

"A few dollars of your own," cried her mother. "Why, Mary, what an ungrateful girl you are! Doesn't your Aunt Harriet give you twenty-five dollars every single birthday?"

"Yes, Aunt Harriet is very kind; but twenty-five dollars isn't what you would call an ample income."

"But you have more than that to spend, and your living not costing you a cent either!"

"No, neither does her living cost Bridget a cent"; and then Mary William stopped, and did not pursue the comparison, an act of forbearance which should be recorded to her credit.

Now Mrs. William Pratt, though a weak woman, and both vain and selfish, was much respected in her husband's family. All were grateful to her for having kept up appearances on so small an income, and the fact that this had been done at her daughter Mary's expense was not wholly understood, even by her sharp-eyed mother-in-law. Hence, when she raised a cry of indignation at Mary's revolutionary behavior, she was sustained by a full chorus of disapproval from the whole clan.

Nevertheless Mary carried her point. Her venture was successful beyond her hopes. She had not led her class in the high school for nothing. No sooner had she made known her intentions than she was offered the position of assistant in the grammar-school of her own district, with the munificent salary of $350.

Singularly enough, her actual engagement as a teacher wrought an entire change in the feelings of the family. It was like the first plunge into cold water. The family pride had shrunk from it, but a reaction set in almost immediately, and that same family pride experienced a glow of gratification that one of their number should be so capable and so well thought of. . . .

Old Lady Pratt alone withheld her approval. The fact that Mary's having a little more money seemed to her to be of small consequence in comparison with the girl's "prospects." She was made of sterner stuff than her descendants; she knew deprivation and hard work by heart, and she was not in the least afraid of them for herself or for anybody else. Even when Mrs. William Pratt told her that Mary had offered to pay three dollars a week for the "girls" wages, Old Lady Pratt remained obdurate.

"Nonsense, Edna!" she said, sharply. "It wouldn't hurt you a mite to do your own work. You'd a sight better do it than to have Mary turn out an old maid. There's Eliza Pelham, now. She acted jest so when she was Mary's age, and she'll teach school to the end of the chapter. She got so set in her ways and so high-flyin' in her notions that the Gov'nor himself wouldn't have suited her. You mark my words, Mary'll be an old maid, jest like Eliza. You see 'f she ain't."

And if Mary herself had been asked, she would have been the first to admit the reasonableness of her grandmother's predictions. She had never been so happy in her life as she was the day on which she stepped upon the platform at school and assumed the responsibilities of "schoolmarm." Mary William loved to teach, and she loved also to rule — an art which she understood to perfection. There were some pretty black sheep among her flock, but before she had had them a month they had learned a lesson in wholesome discipline which seemed to them much more incontrovertible than anything Murray had to say against alliances between plural subjects and singular verbs, or any of Greenleaf's arithmetical theories. The new teacher's success made so strong an impression upon the school committee that by Christmas-time Miss Pratt's name was mentioned in connection with a $500 vacancy to occur the coming year in the high school. Meanwhile Mary reveled in her independence; and if she thought of matrimony in connection with herself, it was as a state of bondage to be avoided at any cost.

One pleasant day in April the young teacher had just dismissed a class in compound fractions, and sat looking down upon the motley collection of boys and girls arranged with geometrical symmetry over the large room. She was aware of a spirit of restlessness among them. There were more boys than usual engaged in the time-honored custom of twisting their legs in intricate patterns about the legs of their chairs, more girls gazing dreamily at the budding tree-tops just visible through high windows. Mary knew by her own uneven pulse that the seeds were sprouting in the ground outside, and that the spring trouble was stirring in the veins of all that youthful concourse. Mary William was in some respects wise beyond her years, and she did not reprove the vagaries of boyish legs and girlish eyes. But she kept a careful watch upon them during the study hour which preceded the long noon recess.

Just before twelve o'clock she was surprised by the entrance of two well-dressed ladies who did not look quite like products of Dunbridge soil. As she went forward to meet them they called her by name, the more stately of the two introducing herself as Mrs. Beardsley, of Stanton. Mary William, though somewhat mystified, bade her guests welcome with a very good grace saying that she was on the point of dismissing the school.

The dispersion of the fifty or more boys and girls was a matter of some ceremony — a ceremony regulated by a succession of strokes on

the teacher's bell, and usually very strictly observed. At a certain critical point in the proceedings to-day, of all days of the year, the boys
broke loose, and made a stampede for the door, the girls remaining in
the aisles, with their arms crossed behind them — models of propriety
before company. Mary William's face flushed brightly, and she struck
the shrill bell three times in rapid succession. Instantly the rabble of
unruly boys stood transfixed. Two or three of them who had already
escaped into the sunshine came sneaking back at the peremptory sum-
mons, while Mary William's voice, with a bell-like ring in it, said
"Boys, return to your seats!"

When all the boys' seats were filled with more or less contrite occu-
pants, the order of exercises was resumed on the part of the girls, who
filed quietly out of the room. Then Mary turned to her guests in a disengaged manner, with the assurance that she was quite at their service.
A momentous conversation ensued.

Mrs. Beardsley stated that she was the Mrs. Beardsley whose school
for young ladies had so long maintained its reputation as the leading
school for young ladies in the state. Miss Pratt had doubtless heard of
Mrs. Beardsley's school for young ladies. Miss Pratt was very sorry, but
she was totally ignorant of any young ladies' school whatever outside
her own town.

Mary had the discrimination to perceive that Mrs. Beardsley was a
thorough woman of the world, and that she thought extremely well of
herself. Nevertheless, she listened with entire self-possession to the
revelations which followed.

Mrs. Beardsley was in search of a teacher to fill the place in the coming year of a valued assistant about to retire. She had heard Miss Pratt
well spoken of by her cousin, the Rev, Mr. Ingraham, of Dunbridge,
and she had come, with her sister, Miss Ingraham, to interview Miss
Pratt. Miss Pratt signified her willingness to be interviewed, asking permission at the same time to dismiss the culprits, whose durance she
considered to have been sufficiently long. This time the dispersion was
performed with a precision which an army sergeant might have envied.
As the door closed behind the last round jacket, Mrs. Beardsley
resumed the thread of her discourse:

"My requirements, Miss Pratt, are somewhat severe. My school has
a reputation to sustain, which necessitates rather exceptional qualifications in my assistants. The sort of discipline, for instance, which you
have just carried out so successfully with those rough boys, would be
entirely out of place in a school whose members are young ladies from

the first families in the state. Tact and worldly wisdom ware essential in the government of such a body. Having no doubt of your acquirements as a mere teacher of the branches desired — namely, Latin and mathematics — I am disposed to dwell more especially upon my exactions of a social nature. A teacher in my school must have the good-breeding and the equanimity of a lady, and pardon my suggestion, she must dress in perfect taste."

Mary flushed slightly, being conscious of the ugliness of her gown, which had descended to her from a cousin whose means exceeded her discretion in matters of taste.

Mrs. Beardsley, having paused a moment, that the full weight of her words might take effect, asked, "Do you feel, Miss Pratt, that you are fitted in every particular to fill such a position?"

The flush of Mary's face had subsided, and to her own surprise she did not flinch. She raised her clear hazel eyes to those of her catechist, and with a direct gaze, in which there was unmistakable power, she said, quietly, "Yes, Mrs. Beardsley, I do."

Mrs. Beardsley returned the girl's look with an accession of interest. The "woman of the world" was not a creature of impulse, but she was a student of character, and without a moment's hesitation, she said, "I engage you."

"Thank you," said the new assistant, as though the conversation were ended.

Mrs. Beardsley and Miss Ingraham exchanged glances, and waited for Mary's next remark; but it was not forthcoming. Mary seemed for the moment to have forgotten herself. She was looking about the homely room where she had served her short apprenticeship, lost in wonder over her sudden good fortune. Mary William was deeply impressed by Mrs. Beardsley's personality. She had always wanted to have a taste of the "great world" She loved the amenities of life, she loved the power which social training gives, and to her unsophisticated mind it seemed as though a school presided over by Mrs. Beardsley — a school where were gathered the daughters of the "first families in the state" — must offer an opening through which she might get at least a peep into that same great world.

Finding her future assistant disinclined to take the initiative, Mrs. Beardsley said, "You have asked me nothing about terms, Miss Pratt."

"Oh yes! Terms!" answered Mary William, recalled to practical affairs, in which she felt no sentimental lack of interest.

"That is, of course, in a certain sense, my affair," Mrs. Beardsley resumed; "but I should be curious to know your ideas on the subject."

Mary looked at her shrewdly, "I suppose the salary would be proportionate to the requirements," she said.

"A very reasonable supposition," Mrs. Beardsley admitted. "then we will come to the point. As only a small number of my pupils live in my family, I shall not require your services there. You will, therefore, be at some expense for your living, and I had thought of offering you" — she paused a moment to notice whether the girl looked eager, but Mary William gave no sign — "twelve hundred and fifty dollars. Should you think that a fair compensation?"

Mary's eyes sparkled. Touched by the generosity of such an offer to a mere grammar-school teacher, she cried, impulsively, "I ought to be a better teacher than I am, to be worth all that to you."

Mrs. Beardsley was gratified, but she only said, "If you are not worth that, you are worth nothing to me."

Mrs. Beardsley had gone out in search of a "treasure," and she had found one. . . .

All summer long Mary spent much of her time in fashioning tasteful garments, wherein to meet one, at least, of Mrs. Beardsley's requirements, and her needle went in and out as gaily as though set to music.

One day she stood before her mirror, arrayed in a claret-colored cashmere, which was to be her "Sunday gown" in the coming winter. There was a trimming of velvet ribbon which was highly effective, and the broad tatting collar was very becoming to the round white throat within it. Mary studied the dress with some satisfaction, and then she inadvertently looked up at her reflected face. For the first time in her life she was struck with her own good looks, and her eyes danced with pleasure. Mrs. Beardsley would be more likely to approve her, the school-girls would perhaps like her, if she looked like that. She smiled at herself, and the pretty teeth thus revealed added greatly to the favorable impression.

The first week in September — for schools began earlier in Mary William's day than in ours — Mrs. Beardsley's "treasure" arrived upon the scene, and took all hearts by storm. It would be difficult to say whether the exhilaration of her spirits made the new teacher charming, or whether her almost instant popularity was the secret of that same exhilaration. Such things go hand in hand. Certain it is that Mary William lived in a round of pleasures far more stimulating, and far more satisfying too, than the pleasures usually thus designated. She loved her work so thoroughly that its very difficulties but lent it zest. She liked the girls, and she regarded Mrs. Beardsley with the enthusiastic devotion felt by a subaltern for his superior officer.

And so the first school term went by only too swiftly, and the long Christmas vacation came as an unwelcome interruption. How much more unwelcome would it have been had Mary William known what it held in store for her! Nothing could have been more unlooked for, nothing could have been to Mary more unwished for, than the events which followed upon the arrival from his Western ranch of the minister's son, Fred Ingraham. When Mary returned home for the holidays, he had been in Dunbridge scarcely a week, and had not yet ceased to be the sensation of the hour.

Fred Ingraham came into her life with all the freshness and insistency of a prairie breeze, which goes sweeping across level leagues unhindered by any obstacle, unabashed by any contrary currents. This minister's son, with his high-bread features and his air of conscious power, belonged to the finest type of ranchman. In him many of the best qualities springing from the old civilization existed side by side with the spirit and vigor which animate the pioneer. There was not lacking a touch of the absolute monarch, such as your genuine ranchman was five-and-twenty years ago. Being, then, a young man of ready decision and of hitherto unalterable determination, no sooner did he behold the little girl whom he had patronized in big-boy fashion a few years previous, transformed into a surprising likeness to his secretly-cherished ideal of a woman, than he fell precipitately in love with her. There was no time to be lost in preliminaries, and Fred pressed his suit with the courage and persistency which might have been expected of an absolute monarch — to say nothing of a Yankee boy accustomed to deal with rough cowboys and pitching broncos.

Mary was at first thrown off her guard by the very suddenness of the assault. She had been predisposed in this favor by all she knew of the daring and independence of his course in breaking loose from family traditions and choosing his own rough path in life. She looked upon him as a kindred spirit, and they had many a long talk and more than one walk together in the sparkling Christmas weather before she took the alarm.

He had often talked to her of ranch life — so new and interesting a theme in those early days, before the cowboy had been tamed into print.

They were walking home together from the skating pond one afternoon, their two pairs of skates rattling gaily together in her companion's hand, making a pleasant metallic accompaniment to his narration.

Suddenly he interrupted himself to say: "Mary, you would like ranch life immensely. I am sure of it. Don't you think you would?"

His words were harmless enough, but the sudden pleading urgency of his manner, and something new and intensely personal in his tone, startled her, and she instantly bristled.

"Oh, yes!" she said, "I've no doubt I should like it if I were a man. But it must be a hideous life for a woman."

Fred bore the rebuff manfully, though it felt as grating and as blinding as a sudden prairie sandstorm. He turned and looked at her as she walked erect and strong by his side. A more defiant-looking young person he had never seen, nor a more altogether desirable one. Good heavens! The very curve of her chin was worth dying for, and Fred drew a deep breath and swore within himself that she should yet be vanquished.The rest of that day Mary tried vainly to believe that her panic had been foolish and uncalled for. But she knew better. She feared that it was unmaidenly and conceited; that she was deserving of all the worst epithets usually applied to a forward girl; but she knew as positively as though Fred had told her so in plain English that this remarkable strong-willed young man was planning to overturn her whole scheme of life, to wrest from her her precious independence, to make her life subordinate to his.

He, meanwhile, saw his opportunity slipping away with the fleeting vacation days; he knew that in a cruelly short time Mary would be once more entrenched in her beloved work under the protection of that much-respected dragon Mrs. Beardsley. But he also knew that her mind, if not her heart, was set against his suit, and he did not dare defy her openly. They met less frequently now, Mary having developed a talent for eluding him which was most baffling. . . .

All through those tedious days of wasted opportunity he never for a moment questioned his inalienable right in the woman of his choice.

Mary meanwhile did not consciously yield an inch. . . .

"Summer after next," she would say to herself, "I shall go abroad," and she marshaled all the wonders and delights of Europe to the support of her resolution.

The last night of the old year — which was also the last night of her visit at home — was to be celebrated with a "social gathering" at the Rev. Mr. Ingraham's house. Mary was arrayed for the occasion in her claret-colored cashmere, intending to accompany her family to the very stronghold of the enemy, when a sudden misgiving seized her, and she decided not to go.

"You may say I have a headache, if you like," she told her mother.

"But, Mary, it will never do to leave you alone in the house. You know Bridget is going out, and we've let the furnace fire go down, and you'll take cold."

"I can light a fire in the hall grate," said Mary. "That will make the house warmer when you come in. Besides, I shall go to bed early."

She watched the blue flames dancing on top of the bed of coals, and the little rows of sparks running along the soot at the back of the chimney — "folks going to meeting," she had been taught to call them. Somehow the suggestion of a string of people all bound for the same place made her feel cross.

"Everybody's always doing just the same thing as everybody else. It is so tiresome! If nobody else had ever got married, Fred would never thought of anything so foolish"; and then she laughed at her own childishness. She would have like to cry just as well as to laugh, but she usually drew the line at tears.

It must have been about nine o'clock when there was a sharp ring at the door-bell. Mary shuddered. Was it some midnight marauder? Alas! Her forebodings were worse than that. Thieves and murderers she might perhaps know how to deal with, but there was an enemy more to be dreaded than they. The bell rang a second time reverberating loudly through the empty house before she answered it. Her worst fears were realized.

"Why, Fred, is that you?" she said, holding the door half open in a gingerly manner. "did mother want anything?"

"No. It's I that want something. Aren't you going to invite me in?"

"Oh, yes! Come in. I was so surprised! How could you leave your party?"

"That was easy enough. I just walked out of the room. . . . May I get a chair?"

Mary had never known him to be so voluble, but she was not in the least reassured by his flow of words.

"What are you reading?" he asked, as he sat down on the other side of the fireplace.

Her fingers still clasped the red book, though she had not opened it for an hour past. At mention of it, she recovered herself.

"It is Murray's guide-book of Switzerland. Have I never told you that I am going abroad summer after next?"

"Really? How enterprising you are!"

"Oh, it can be easily managed. You know I have quite a princely income."

"Mary," he cried, abruptly, "give up your income, give up Europe, give up all those plans. Come with me! Not now — of course you couldn't — but next summer."

She shut her lips firmly together, and stared at the fire.

"See!" he went on. "I put it in the baldest words. I concede everything from the very beginning. I know you would be giving up everything you care for; I know I am asking a perfectly tremendous sacrifice."

"Would you make such a sacrifice for me?" she asked, in a hard, dry tone. "I love my way of life just as well as you do yours. Would you give up your ranch and come and teach school with me?"

"That's not a fair question, Mary. You might as well ask if I would wear girl's clothes to please you. You wouldn't respect me if I did."

"I don't agree with you at all," she said, sharply and argumentatively. It did not sound like her pleasantly-modulated voice. "I don't see that the sacrifice would be any greater for you than for me. My work and my ambitions are just as necessary to me as yours are to you. And you would never think of sacrificing yours for my sake."

"I'm not so sure that there is anything under heaven that I wouldn't do for you, Mary," he cried, impetuously. "But that is something you would never ask. You wouldn't be yourself if you did. Men sacrifice their lives for women, not their careers. It would not be in the nature of things for you to ask of me what I am asking of you."

He paused a moment, and then he was sorry he had done so. Her face was set and repellant. But she spoke before he could stop her.

"No, Fred, I can't do it," she said; "and please don't talk to me any more. Didn't mother say I had a headache?"

"As though I believed that! I don't believe you ever had a headache in your life. And supposing you have? What is a headache, I should like to know, compared to a heartache? If I can bear to hear you say no in that horrid cold voice, you can bear to hear me talk as long as I ever choose. Mary, you shall hear me, and I am going to tell you something that will make you think you hate me. You know that I love you with all my heart and soul. But it seems foolish to talk about that. Of course I love you. Who could help it? Cousin Letitia adores you, though she may not tell you so. Everybody adores you, simply because you are the most perfectly adorable woman that ever lived. But, Mary," and his voice sank to a lower key — "Mary, there is one thing you don't know, and that I am going to tell you — you love me."

"How dare you say such a thing to me, Fred Ingraham?' cried Mary, springing to her feet, white with anger, her eyes flashing, her breath coming fast.

"I suppose it does sound like a brutal thing to say," he admitted, "here in the house, where everything is conventional."

He was also standing now, leaning back in the shadow against the chimney, watching Mary's face with the uncertain firelight on it. The lamp was behind her. She had not got her breath sufficiently to speak again. The red book had dropped to the floor, and her hands were clinched. As he looked at her a sudden pity came over him. . . .

Then she lifted her face in the firelight. "Fred Ingraham" she cried, in a despairing tone, "I believe I do hate you — you are — so — cruel."

Fred looked at the tragic face, and an exultant light came into his own.

"It's a kind of hate I'm not afraid of, Mary," he said, and he held out his arms.

The shadows among the baronial pillars seemed to be swaying and wavering before he eyes and her own step faltered. But she went to him, because she could not help it. He kissed her, rather cautiously, and she made no resistance. A strange, delicious, poignant happiness overwhelmed her.

That night Mary cried herself to sleep for the first time since she was a little child. But in that beneficent storm of grief her last tottering defenses were swept away. When, but a few hours later, the time of parting came, her valiant lover knew that her surrender was complete.

Mrs. Beardsley generously forgave her young cousin for robbing her of her "treasure," though, as her short period of possession went by, she learned still better to measure her impending loss. She permitted herself but one form of revenge, which, however, she always clung to. As often as she had occasion to write to him in after years, she never failed to address him as her "dear bandit."

As for Old Lady Pratt, though Mary had gone contrary to all prognostications, she was too much relieved to resent being put in the wrong. Her unfailing comment when the event was discussed in the family was: "Mary William's got more sense, after all, than I giv' her credit for."

CHAPTER TWO

A Noble Work Done Earnestly:
Missionary Teachers in the Civil War South

*A*T THE OUTBREAK OF the Civil War, as the Union army moved into the South to suppress the rebellious Confederacy, news of the victory at Fort Sumter, South Carolina, quickened the passion of anti-slavery Northerners of every persuasion. In the most feverish spirit, Henry Stanton wrote to his wife, Elizabeth Cady Stanton, some days after Sumter, "I hear old John Brown knocking on the lid of his coffin and shouting, 'let me out, let me out!' The doom of slavery is at hand. It is to be wiped out in blood. Amen."[1] Weary of years of discussions and demonstrations, many abolitionists were eager to act on their belief that once the yoke of oppression was lifted, with proper aid, the freed people could take their place as full citizens of democracy. For an abolitionist man, there was a soldier's uniform and the test of battle; for a woman, there was relief work — bandage-making, collecting clothing, and raising funds to provide for four million African Americans, many of them in flight toward the advancing Union Army, others living on plantations and farms from which their former masters had fled.

As the first months of the terrible and bloody war stretched on into a year, another choice developed — to go south to help the freedpersons or "contraband" (the term meant "property confiscated in war") in their transition to freedom. Women and men commissioned by the Army congregated along the coastal islands of Virginia, the Carolinas, and Georgia, where land was distributed, a labor system put in place, and the newly freed people invited for the first time in their lives to sit legally in school rooms in the light of day. By all accounts, the newly freed people's most fervent hope was to learn to read and write, a hope consonant with the talents and aspirations of anti-slavery missionaries. By far the most numerous participants in the effort to help the ex-slaves toward freedom were teachers, the majority of them young women educated in the North. They established "freedmen's schools" wherever the Union Army had control — in churches, in abandoned buildings, in the open air. Most schools were new, but some were the former clandestine schools that had been led by educated free Southern African Americans during the dark days of slavery.

By 1870, five years after the end of the Civil War, some five thousand teachers were instructing about 150,000 students, a modest proportion of the former slave population. The majority were white Northern women, but about one-third were African Americans from the North and South, with African American males dominating.[2] The passions and needs that motivated them varied considerably — from doing God's work, to retribution for the death of a loved one in the Civil War, to zeal to prove the equality of African Americans, to the need to earn an independent living, to adventurousness, opportunism, and escape from gender constraints at home.

Whatever their motivation, the circumstances demanded more than the conventions of gender had prepared teachers for: hardiness, both social and physical risk-taking, inventiveness, leadership in the face of danger and deprivation, and a willingness to break race and gender taboos. The work also revealed teachers' prejudices as they lived out cross-race and class relationships that they had previously only theoretically considered. They came with varying degrees of religiosity: from liberal Quakers with secular goals to evangelical Christians wanting to make new converts. In some cases, their Protestant evangelical beliefs came head on against African religious practices; others found deep emotional satisfaction in African American prayer meetings. And their estimations of what African American students could achieve laid the seeds of debates later in the century about industrial versus liberal education. Whatever the contradictions of this movement, it was unified by the notion that education was a tool of liberation, a route to agency and choice. And all agreed that success could be measured by the students' ability to help themselves. For the most progressive teachers, the best result was that the graduates of freedmen's schools went on to study in, staff, and lead black schools and colleges of the South and to become political and spiritual leaders and activists.

For the newly freed individuals, schooling was the secular religion of freedom, the act signifying liberation from oppression. Teacher after teacher described children and adults flocking to schools, challenging them to manage huge schoolrooms without desks, benches, books, slates, or writing implements in buildings that the previous day had been empty sheds or rudimentary churches. Mary Peake, a free African American woman considered the first freedmen's teacher, started freedmen's classes at Fortress Monroe on September 17, 1861, only a few months after the outbreak of war. She began her week with six students and ended with more than fifty.[3] The 14-year-old newly freed Susie King Taylor was also among the earliest teachers of the freedmen. In *Reminiscences of My Life in Camp*, she described fleeing from Savannah, Georgia, with her uncle to a Union ship that had just taken Fort Pulaski. Asked by the ship's captain about her skills, she revealed that she had gone to a clandestine school in Savannah and could read and write. Settled with six hundred newly freed people on St. Simon's Island, the young Susie agreed to hold a school in exchange for some books. She recounted, "I had about 40 children to teach, besides a number of adults who came to me nights, all of them so eager to learn to read, to read above anything else" (see p. 145).

Mary Peake and Susie King Taylor may have been among the first women to take up teaching freedmen, but theirs is not the central story of the freedmen's schools. This teaching movement began and gained a public face not in the South, but in the North, with the formation of societies in Boston, New York, and Philadelphia to support the work of abolitionist missionaries. These societies, sponsored by town committees or church organizations — the American Missionary Association (AMA) was the most active abolitionist organization — raised funds, sent barrels of supplies south, and recruited and funded teachers of the freedmen. Teachers' efforts were coordinated and their lives protected first by the Union army, then by the Bureau of Refugees, Freedmen, and Abandoned Lands, commonly called the Freedmen's Bureau. In the 1870s, funds donated to support the freedmen's schools began to dwindle, and, as the army withdrew, racist violence reasserted itself in the South. Some northern teachers, African American and white, remained in the South to the end of their days in independent schools, black colleges, and public schools, but most returned home to the lives from which they had come. Their work had launched the battle for equal educational opportunity, but it was the challenge of local African American communities to establish a decent public school system — a struggle that continues today.

For white women, the choice to go south was often inspired by a speech extolling the African Americans' thirst for learning. The challenge of educating the race was presented in terms both religious and secular: expiation of the collective sin of slavery and participation in a momentous social experiment. There had never been an attempt at mass education of African Americans in the country. African American women applicants, fewer in number than whites, often put their decisions in terms of racial identity. In her application to the American Missionary Association, Sara Stanley, one of a number of African Americans to go south from Oberlin College, wrote:

*My reasons for seeking to engage in the work of instructing the freed people are few and simple. I am myself a colored woman, bound to that ignorant, degraded, long enslaved race, by the ties of love and consanguinity; they are socially and politically, "my people," and I have an earnest and abiding conviction that the Almighty Father, whose loving kindness gave to me advantages which his divine wisdom withheld from them, requires me to devote every power with which he has endowed me to the work of ameliorating their condition, to advancing the civilization of a people, who though, through long years have been victims of oppression and brutality, are yet susceptible of high cultivation, and for whom, I feel assured, that an inscrutable providence has appointed a destiny far greater and more glorious than any political charlatan or statesman has yet conceived of, such a testimony as Christian men and women rejoice to contemplate — of intellectual power and spiritual greatness, of holiness perfected in the fear of God.* (see p. 195)*

Both African American and white women, true to the conventions of gender, used the lofty language of self-sacrifice, divine calling, and service to the oppressed and to God in justifying their decisions to teach. But some screening committees asked applicants hard and practical questions, articulating an understanding of what these young women might face and simultaneously conceptualizing the work as having momentous consequences for the nation. One Massachusetts official described the appropriate qualifications: "No mere youthful enthusiasm, love of adventure, or desire of change, will sustain a teacher through the labors and hardships of her work." She had to have "good health," "religious faith," "patriotism," and a superior education, for she was to form "the people who are to influence very largely [this country's] future for good or for evil." Found wanting in the requisite qualities, the teacher would be told sternly, "one may labor for the freedmen as truly in Massachusetts as in the South Carolina." Found worthy, with very short notice, the young woman would be steaming down the coast on a boat filled with soldiers, or, as in the case of Maria Waterbury, given directions by a missionary society: "Go South about 800 miles, until you find the plantation school waiting for you."[4]

Young Mary Ames and her friend Emily Bliss were typical missionary teachers who went south in 1865, just as the war was ending. After hearing Harriet Ware,[5] a returned teacher, tell of her experiences, they went straight to Boston to see the chief of the Freedmen's Bureau, and were enrolled. Although their families ridiculed their going and tried to stop them, ten days after leaving Boston an army wagon deposited them on a desolate piazza of a plantation abandoned by its white owners on the South Carolina Sea Island of Edisto. The only whites for miles around, they were taken in by Sarah, a former slave who lived at the back of the "big house" with her husband and six children. She found them a dry place to sleep on the floor, shared her tin teacup with them, and helped secure them against rattlesnakes and Confederate spies. Thus began their careers as Yankee schoolmarms. One month after their arrival, Mary Ames wrote proudly in her diary, "Our books number a hundred and forty scholars, and from sixty to seventy are in daily attendance. Our evening school [for adults] on the piazza is well attended, and we enjoy our labors. All are respectful and eager to learn." Eighteen months later, Mary made her final diary entry: "The owner of the house we had lived in . . . wanted to come back. There was no place for us, and in the last week of September 1866, we said goodbye to our Negro friends" (see p. 170).

These few personal voices hint at a history of heroism, self-sacrifice, and self-fulfillment carried out by young women with grand aspirations to "help," to do important work in a world that often denied them opportunity. They left their "dear ones at home" to live out political and religious beliefs, to take physical risks, and to earn a living independently rather than remain, as one recruiting pamphlet frankly put it, "ornaments in their fathers' parlors, dreaming, restless, hoping, til some fortunate mating shall give them a home and a sphere."[6] In a time of dramatic social upheaval, they rarely acknowledged the leadership they provided from their unique position — outcasts among local whites of comparable education, and exotic others to the African American community. Most modestly said that the African American community was their ready "field of work," teaching "a labor of love," and success a "harvest" so gratifying that modest cultural dislocation, physical hardship, and threats against their lives by white Southerners were put in perspective.

Teachers write little about their lives in classrooms — today and in the past. Writing is not an obligatory aspect of their work, and teaching is so ordinary an act that there seems little remarkable to record. The schoolmarms, however, were compelled to leave a record, and like many people thrust onto the stage in strange and challenging circumstances, they wrote to help themselves and others make sense of their experiences. As members of a social change and missionary movement, the teachers had to justify their work for their families, for northern skeptics, and for benefactors whose financial support they sought. Isolated from family and friends, they kept diaries and wrote constantly to their dear ones. Many of their letters were published and saved, allowing the reader an unusual entrée into these women's work lives. The American Missionary Association Archive, housed at the Amistad Research Center at Tulane University, for example, contains over 350,000 items, many of them letters and reports that state AMA offices required on a regular basis and frequently published in their newsletters. The Freedmen's Bureau is a second major source of documents. A War Department agency operational in March 1865, it had relief responsibilities and helped to launch 3,000 schools for African Americans in the South, until its activities were curtailed about 1872. The teachers were also the subjects of articles in *The Nation, Atlantic Monthly,* and other national magazines, and inspired fiction by Albion Tourgee (1838–1905), Charles Chesnutt (1858–1932) and W. E. B. DuBois (1868–1963). As they retired toward the turn of the twentieth century, the teachers published at least a dozen books of reminiscence and autobiography, which enjoyed a short-lived vogue.[7]

The teachers' work and writing were all but forgotten until the civil rights movement of the 1960s generated a new interest in African American history. When rediscovered by scholars in this field, the teachers' writing was used to document the values, thoughts, and actions of newly freed people. Then, in the 1970s and 1980s, as interest in women's history grew, the work and writing of the Yankee schoolmarms became consequential in its own right — for what it revealed about their extraordinary work lives, their views on education, their attitudes about race, gender, and class, and their authentic accomplishments. Key work from the 1980s incorporating the perspectives of women's and African

American history includes Jacqueline Jones' *Soldiers of Light and Love: Northern Teachers and Georgia Blacks 1865–1873,* Robert C. Morris' *Reading, 'Riting, and Reconstruction: The Education of Freedmen in the South, 1861–1870,* and a brief but important article by Linda Perkins, "The Black Female American Missionary Association Teacher in the South, 1861–1870." Since the 1980s, however, little has been published about or by the missionary and abolitionist teachers. A recent exception is *Beloved Sisters and Loving Friends: Letters from Rebecca Primus of Royal Oak, Maryland, and Addie Brown of Hartford, Connecticut, 1854–1868.* Rebecca Primus, the better educated of these two African American friends, taught in a Maryland freedpersons' school from 1865 to 1869, and like other teachers wrote reports and letters to friends and family. As is typical of the teachers' correspondence, few records remain to fill in the remainder of either Rebecca's or Addie Brown's lives or work, beyond the time when, separated by thousands of miles, they supported and sustained each other by constant communication.[8]

## *Fashioning Relationships: Across the Gulf of Race and Class*

"We have come to do anti-slavery work, and we think it noble work, and we mean to do it earnestly," wrote the Unitarian teacher and physician Laura Towne in her diary a few days after her arrival on the South Carolina Sea Islands, in March 1862, as part of the Port Royal Experiment.[9] In quite another tone, an AMA teacher wrote home, "I have always been taught to abhor slavery, but never, until I came among its victims, did I know anything of the blasting effects of that system; and the more I became acquainted with these people, the more do I realize the great work that is to be accomplished before their souls are brought from natural darkness into the marvelous light of God's truth."[10] These statements by Laura Towne and her anonymous sister, the former plainspoken and secular, the latter evangelical, share an emphasis on the word "work," but their similar word choice belies a difference in meaning and a difference in the orientations of the various organizations sponsoring teachers. For Towne and the secular minority of teachers, work meant preparing the freedpersons for life in a democracy, for social and political equality: helping them to become decision-makers, teachers, landowners, office-holders, voters,[11] and friends. For the evangelicals, work meant first ensuring that freedpersons became or were Christian, and were able to live by Christian principles. Under slavery, church marriage between slaves was a rare occurrence; African American women bore children as a result of their masters' crimes of rape and adultery, and the opportunity to read Scripture was at odds with legally enforced illiteracy. Secular and evangelical teachers alike saw the Puritan Protestant virtues of piety, self-reliance, industriousness, sobriety, and thrift as the foundations of freedpersons' education.

Whether the teachers' primary goals were secular or religious education, their statements were often framed in terms of a transition to full personhood. Using the metaphor of progress from childhood to adulthood or from barbarism to civilization, most believed African Americans would arrive at what they considered intellectual and moral equality with whites and asserted that their capacity for learning was equal to that of whites. One teacher's words are representative: "The freedman compared with the educated white man is a child needing instruction and guidance. He needs to be protected for a time against the unscrupulous and designing. But it will not be well for him to be treated like a hothouse plant, the wider fields of competition as well as toil shut out from him." Charlotte Forten, a Northern African American teacher and colleague of Laura Towne, wrote that the African American people's "shouts" were "the barbarous expression of religion, handed down to them from their African ancestors." These shouts, she thought, were "destined to pass away under the influence of Christian teachings" (see p. 176). While such words as "barbarous" call up now-outmoded distinctions between "primitive" and "civilized" and may offend the contemporary reader, it is important to evaluate the teachers' attitudes against other possible formulations of the period that raised doubts about African Americans' capacities or held firmly to beliefs in their inferiority, and to note as well that Forten's views changed dramatically over the course of her service. Within a year or two, she was writing to her journal about the deep inspiration and beauty of the shouts she attended.

Social equality — meaning the mixing of races in friendship, in worship, on the street — was a complex and fraught matter, more so than intellectual equality. Only a small number of white teachers and school officials advocated or even accepted openly interracial friendship, marriage, and the like. Here metaphors of progress tell us much less than do accounts of the teachers' daily activities. While many white and African American teachers of similar social class and education seem to have entered into informal and respectful relationships with each other, there is also evidence of hurtful prejudice and discrimination in the interaction between whites and African Americans.

Given the gulf of culture, class, and — for the majority — race that separated them from the newly freed people, the teachers turned to each other for strength to carry on. In general, in the nineteenth century, by virtue of having paid work and social permission to live independently, female teachers were set apart from other women and formed a sisterhood. For the teachers of freedpersons, sisterhood and teamwork were more than social; they were tools of survival. Almost no one went south alone, and some, like Ellen Murray, Laura Towne, Sallie Holley, and Caroline Putnam, lived and worked together for as long as forty years. Even those who stayed the typical two or three years formed close bonds — they tended each other in sickness, strategized together during rebel attacks, taught and prayed together, and socialized — gossiping about the "rebs," the Union officers, politics, and fashion; went boating and strolling on summer days, and even discussed issues of race.

Usually relationships between teachers were negotiated in the first few weeks of work as living arrangements — sharing of rooms, dining space — were sorted out. The outspoken African American Oberlin teacher, Sara Stanley, wrote to the AMA superintendent of schools in Norfolk, Virginia, in 1864 to complain that a Mr. Coan took "especial pleasure in advocating the inferiority of 'negroes' and the necessity of social distinctions, with special application to colored missionary teachers." He had forbidden Sara's friend Edmonia Highgate to room with a white teacher when they were "chosen friends." She argued for a standard of behavior higher than that in New England, where "Mr. Coan would have an incontrovertible right to select his own circle of acquaintances. . . . Here in the missionary field . . . he has no right to pursue any course that will militate in the slightest degree against the Cause he professes to serve" (see p. 198 ff). Similarly, Sara Stanley castigated a Miss Gleason for her insistence that she would not live in the teachers' residence "if all the colored teachers are not removed." Stanley considered this position a violation of "the union of all beings created in the divine likeness." It is important that Sara Stanley persisted in her complaints and got partial satisfaction — Mr. Coan was removed to another post; Miss Gleason stayed on. And Rebecca Primus, the African American Hartford teacher posted to Royal Oak, Maryland, writes easily about cross-racial socializing of teachers, noting that, in Washington, D.C., a white teacher was living with an African American family, an arrangement that would have carried serious dangers in the rural deep South. There is also evidence that teachers of color had a more difficult time finding work in freedpersons' schools than did white teachers, despite the African American community's stated preference for a less educated African American teacher over a better educated white one.[12]

The relationships between teachers and newly freed adults can be gleaned from diary entries and letters describing daily work and social activities outside of the schoolhouse. Usually, in the first days after arrival, teachers and freedpersons began constructing tacit rules of behavior. Clear that they were not to replicate slave and master, the Northerners had little to go on. More self-conscious about race than other white teachers and unusually introspective, Laura Towne wrote home ten days after her arrival that she had stopped a young girl from whipping two children: " I told them I had come here to stop whipping, not to inflict it." And she describes a bold exercise at the supply house: she had African American workers order her around in order for all to experience turned tables. Similarly, another anti-slavery worker insisted that an old Auntie take a seat in the carriage while he rode on the back. Some teachers also report explicit acts to transgress an especially profound Southern racial taboo — breaking bread formally in interracial groups.

Elizabeth Hyde Botume, a white teacher, tells of a Thanksgiving meal at which the twelve oldest contrabands of the village took seats at a dining table for the first time, instead of eating around the cooking fire as they had under slavery. Identifying unselfconsciously with the African American guests, she wrote, "We had peace if not plenty, and were contented, if not comfortable. By we I mean the black people."[13] Laura Towne told her family how "natural" it was to dine with African American friends, and there were even more deeply symbolic acts. In 1870, Laura Towne and her life-long companion and co-worker, Ellen Murray, adopted Puss, a neglected African American child. Laura wrote the "grand news" home, describing Puss as "bright as a dollar. She has been my

scholar for years" (see p. 215). Young Mary Ames writes about being challenged by Ben, a favorite African American child with whose family Mary
lives. Mary remembers Ben asking, "Is the reason you don't kiss me
'cause I'm black?" In reply, Mary takes Ben in her arms and holds him
until he sleeps.[14] There are also numerous instances of African American
children and adults returning to the North with teachers to work as servants, go to school, or enter a trade or profession. No wonder one white
Southerner said that these "Yankee bitches" were engaged in a fight for
control of African American minds, and that their most potent weapon
was acting on their convictions.[15]

Many teachers took a pragmatic view of equality — it was an end and
they were the means, the vehicle for a long journey, the difficulties of
which should not be exaggerated. The sophisticated Quaker sisters Sarah
and Lucy Chase criticized "enthusiastic philanthropists" who over-praised
African American achievement as "giving undue praise to the barbarous
teachings of slavery."[16] They meant that since slavery actively denied
African Americans opportunity for intellectual development, to praise
African Americans' intellectual attainment prematurely was disingenuous
and patronizing. Under the best of circumstances, time would be
required for African Americans to match white educational achievement.
The behavior of missionary Austa French on her arrival at Hilton Head,
South Carolina, was a standing joke among the teachers. According to
one account, this misguided person had rushed from the boat upon a startled African American woman who happened to be passing by. Embracing
and kissing her, she had sobbed, "Oh my sister."[17] Far more typical was
the straight talk of Elizabeth Hyde Botume, thirty years a teacher in
South Carolina. When counseled by an enthusiastic philanthropist that
she would insult old house servants if she asked them to wash clothes for
her, she answered that "laundry work had not been my business: I came
to teach the freed people to help themselves. Whatever they could do
better than I, in so far, they were my superior. In consideration of their
previous 'condition' I gave them my time and instruction, whilst I should
pay regular wages for their labor. But I should expect good work, and no
make-believe."[18]

## The Schoolroom

If white teachers needed to negotiate the new rules for enjoying social time with African American children and adults, in the schoolroom such negotiations were unnecessary. The universal inequality of power between young student and adult teacher was a familiar structure with which both races were comfortable. And even if we assume some exaggeration by the teachers about their students' brilliance — Charlotte Forten first confided to her diary that "most of the children are crude little specimens," and a year or so later, in an article for *Atlantic Monthly*, enthused about her pupils' astonishing progress — there is ample evidence that students learned quickly, motivated by the sacred status afforded the act of reading itself, and a curriculum that put the rights and responsibilities of freedom at its center.

A white schoolmarm might arrive with questions about the intellectual capacity of the race, but the moment of discovering the African Americans' insatiable thirst for learning amounted to a conversion experience. The secular teacher Elizabeth Hyde Botume chose to teach the Gullah-speaking Combahee people because they were considered the connecting link between "human being" and the "brute" creation. The response to her arrival converted her to an attitude of reverence for her students:

> When I first came in sight of the house, the piazza was filled with men, women and children. I heard many exclamations of the "Dar, da him," "Missus comes fur larn we . . ." The men and women had only come to "get their names put down," as fieldwork was not done. Each one regarded it as an honor to be enrolled as a scholar. They all left with a new consciousness of their own individuality and personal dignity. I use this term advisedly. The poorest and most downtrodden of these people are self-respecting.

Botume continued, "Before Christmas the field work was done. . . . Now children and parents, even old gray-headed people, hurried to the schoolroom . . . 'Us want book-larning too, bad,' they said over and over again."[19]

Given the makeshift schoolrooms, the lack of materials, the uneven preparation of teachers, and the rapid expansion of classes, what can we make of the learning that went on? How did teachers imagine and carry out a curriculum? One teachers' committee official said the goal was "to spread New England education" of so high a standard that "no local government will be able to overthrow it."[20] That meant inculcating traits of morality and good citizenship along with the three Rs, using McGuffey's reader and Noah Webster's spelling book. Sara Stanley, well-educated, self-critical, and more reflective than most about the results of her teaching, wrote a series of particularly interesting letters in 1866 from her school in Louisville, Kentucky. She describes streets full of "hundreds of filthy, squalid untaught children" for whom no effort had been made to remove from them "the brutalizing influence of slavery." Of those in her own classroom, she saw "little of that quickness of learning, that ready comprehension of ideas, that facility of acquisition" that she had found elsewhere. Yet by July, in the end of the school year examinations, she asserted that "the classes in history, grammar, geography and arithmetic passed examination creditably, responding to questions not found in the textbooks with . . . that easy confidence which evinces of a familiarity with general principles, as well as the letter of the books."[21]

There is also surprisingly strong evidence that secular and evangelical teachers designed their lessons so that the lines between teaching about civics and teaching for political activism were blurred.[22] From hanging pictures of Abraham Lincoln, William Lloyd Garrison, John Brown, and Toussaint L'Ouverture on classroom walls, to reading lessons using as texts the Emancipation Proclamation, the Fourteenth Amendment, and the Constitution, to studying Africa, and using a wide selection of "freedmen's" books — a series of readers published by the American Tract Society (ATS) for freedpersons' schools — teachers politicized their lessons. Indeed, the ATS published its first freedpersons' book in 1862, described by the *Chicago Tribune* as follows:

> On the title page, a neat vignette presents a colored child and a white teacher. . . . This book is the initial volume of a reform that turns a new page in history. It is the first book ever printed for the elevation and education of the black race — the American slave. It is designed for the use of the contrabands at Fortress Monroe and Port Royal and Kansas. In its general aspects, it is just such a stepping-stone to knowledge as you would throw down before the feet of your pet child, — neat and bold in typography,

*ornate with wood cuts, elegant in embossed muslin. But, in its purpose and*
*intent, it is eloquent with suggestions of the era now opened.*[23]

Lucy Chase taught history and contemporary thought from the most famous of those texts, *The Freedmen's Book*, compiled by the feminist abolitionist Lydia Maria Child, which included among its authors Frances E. W. Harper, Harriet Jacobs, Frederick Douglass, and Phillis [sic] Wheatley. African American authors' names were marked with an asterisk to identify them for readers from white writers like Lydia Sigourney, William Lloyd Garrison, and John Greenleaf Whittier.

There are many accounts of year-end school exhibitions — celebrations of progress for the entire African American community. Parents often received written invitations and expressed themselves "proud for mad" when neat copy books were passed around, or children went to the blackboard to "calculate the price of two bales of cotton sold here at the market price per pound" and compared the price of the same two bales at New York, "deducting expenses [and] commissions." Besides exercises in grammar, math, geography, and reading, students recited poems about freedom, little girls and boys demonstrated — no doubt, to teach parents — cooking, cleaning, and animal care skills, and older students performed comic satires.[24] Singing was almost always part of school, and Southerners passing by schoolrooms were infuriated when they heard songs like "John Brown's Body" sung in rousing tones along with "Auld Lang Syne."

Indeed, many Southerners were angered at what they called the political indoctrination carried out by freedpersons' teachers, especially with regard to that forbidden subject — social equality of African Americans and whites. The following exchange between Anna Gardner, a Nantucket teacher in Charlottesville, Virginia, and the editor of the *Charlottesville Chronicle,* represents the sentiments on both sides. Gardner asked the editor, a man with a professed "deep interest in the welfare of the Negro race," to print diplomas for her school. He replied in the negative: "Your instruction of the colored people . . . contemplates something more than the communication of ordinary knowledge implied in teaching them to read, write, cipher, etc. The idea prevails that you instruct them in politics and sociology, that you come among us . . . as a political missionary, that you communicate to the colored people by precept and example, ideas of social equality with the whites." To which Anna Gardner retorted with New England firmness, "I teach in school and out so far as my influence extends, the fundamental principles of 'Politics, and sociology' viz. — 'Whatsoever ye would that men should do to you, do you even so unto them.' Yours in behalf of truth and Justice."[25] When asked by a group of visiting journalists and benefactors for a message to take north, Elizabeth Botume's students say simply, "Tell 'em we is rising." But there is also some evidence that, caught between Southern racial fears and Northern radicalism, the largely white male school administrators from the Freedmen's Bureau counseled their teachers to avoid antagonizing Southerners and Northern moderates.

## Staying On

For about a decade, Northern schoolteachers continued to come south for an average stay of about three years. But by the early 1870s, the picture of African American Southern education was changing. Northern aid societies had not intended to build a permanent system of private education for African Americans, and some were beginning to lose the ability to raise funds for their cause. In addition, many schools were absorbed into the segregated public school system where young African American women and men, graduates of freedpersons' schools, formed the faculties. A new group of institutions — high schools, normal schools, and colleges to educate an African American leadership — had been developing under the guidance of the American Missionary Association and the African American church. By 1871 there were sixty-one private normal schools and eleven black colleges and universities, among them Howard, Rust, Atlanta University, Wilberforce, Hampton Institute, Shaw, Morehouse, Fisk, and Tougaloo. Some sought Northern women teachers, but many Northern white women felt their work was over and that it was appropriate for Southern African Americans trained as teachers to take over African American education. Five years after the end of the war, in his final report as general superintendent of education for the Freedmen's Bureau, John Alvord reported, "Many hundreds of teachers and leading minds have already been sent forth from [the black colleges] to commence a life work, and will make their mark upon the coming generation. These hundreds will be followed by thousands."[26]

Anna Gardner, the outspoken sociologist who taught on behalf of truth and justice, had a typical career for a secular white Northern teacher. A Nantucket Quaker, her home had been a station on the Underground Railroad. By the age of eighteen she was a militant abolitionist. In 1841, at age twenty-five, she had been instrumental in calling an anti-slavery convention on her island. At age forty-six, she traveled south with nineteen other teachers to establish a freedpersons' school in New Berne, North Carolina. From 1865 to 1870 she taught in a second freedpersons' school in Charlottesville, Virginia, then, after a brief stint as a normal school teacher educating African American teachers, she returned to Nantucket. There she took up a cause she had relinquished reluctantly during her teaching years — the advancement of women's suffrage.[27]

Other patterns emerged in the careers of African American teachers and a small group of white schoolmarms who stayed in the South. The careers of many African American women teachers look like those of teachers today. That is, many did marry, and they followed their husbands throughout the South and elsewhere. Their careers were intermittent — teaching coupled with farming, childrearing, and other community activity. And, like teachers today, they left very little record, having no public audience and few benefactors for whom to write. Even the full career of Sara Stanley, the Oberlin graduate whose anti-slavery writings were much quoted, is lost to view. We know only that she taught in and led freedpersons' schools in Norfolk, Virginia; St. Louis, Missouri; and Mobile, Alabama — the latter after her controversial marriage to a white man. (We do have, of course, a historical record of the development of the system of African American schooling in the South, but that is a different matter from having autobiographical writing from individual teachers.) A small group of African American and white women became administrators in public schools and served in the rapidly growing black colleges. A particularly powerful group including Anna Julia Cooper, Charlotte Forten, and Mary Church Terrell taught and administered in Washington, D.C., at the legendary Washington Preparatory High School for Colored Youth (later M Street School and Dunbar High School). A second group led by Fanny Jackson-Coppin taught in Philadelphia at the Institute for Colored Youth, which in 1869 established a normal school to educate teachers, a number of whom staffed Southern black schools. A selection from Jackson-Coppin's book, *Reminiscences of School Life, and Hints on Teaching*, appears in Chapter One of this book.

Another group of white women who stayed on continued to raise money privately in order to carry on their schools as of old. Those we know most about include Sallie Holley (1818–1893) and Caroline Putnam (1818–1893), both Oberlin graduates who had a school in Lottsburgh, Virginia, from 1868 to 1893, when both died; Martha Schofield (1839–1916) who taught first on the Sea Islands (1865), then in Aiken, South Carolina, from 1868 to her death in 1916. Elizabeth Hyde Botume (?–1895) taught in Beaufort, South Carolina, from 1861 to 1891; Cornelia Hancock (1840–1927) was first a nurse at Gettysburg, then taught briefly with Laura Towne, and finally in Charleston, South Carolina, from 1866 to 1875. She was succeeded by Abby Munro (?–1905). Sara Ann Dickey (?–1904) taught at Mt. Hermon Female Seminary in Jackson, Mississippi, from 1875 to her death in 1904, and was succeeded by Rossa B. Cooley (1873–1949), a Vassar graduate who taught until her death in 1949. These women constructed an unusual place for themselves in Southern life and culture, one they would never have imagined had they stayed at home, continuing what one teacher called "that selfish way of half living that used to be 'jist tolable' to me"[28]

Unlike the male anti-slavery worker, these Yankee schoolmarms had not abandoned budding careers in the North to pursue abolitionist work, and often they had already made the crucial decision of a woman's life — not to marry. Teacher Maria Waterbury reported that Sarah Mahoney, a college graduate from Michigan, used to say "the freedmen work was her husband and children," a phrase repeated through all the years teachers were not permitted to marry and remain employed.[29] Thus, free of family and without paid work at home, they had liberty to stay in the South long past the time when young white men had returned to college, the law, or business. Furthermore, these proper middle-class women had been taught to shun worldly achievement for its own sake. In the South, one could be modest and achieving as well.

Those women who grew to status with their schools often refused praise for their success. Independent female educators, they were graduating African American students from their private schools on into the twentieth century, and their letters to friends, family, and benefactors continued to flow north, testifying to their satisfaction in their work. The histories of their independent schools suggest that the pairs of women who ran them became more than teachers. They carved enclaves of power for themselves.[30] They were partisans of African American political leadership as well as activists and organizers who had come to enjoy the fray of the battle for civil rights and to identify themselves with the African American Southern cause. Historical circumstance allowed a group of independent women to use their capacities to solve problems, endure physical dangers, speak boldly in public, and manage all spheres of human existence.

As Reconstruction collapsed and Ku Klux Klan activity heightened in the 1870s, the old hierarchy of authority revived — white men, then white women, African American men, and finally African American women, whose franchise many white women and some African American men refused to support. But in the African American community, the teachers continued to advise and defend the African American men whose new franchise was threatened. Sallie Holley wrote in 1872 to a Northern friend from her school in Lottsburgh, Virginia, "Although the old rebels are earnestly trying to get our coloured men to vote for Greeley, I hold monthly Republican meetings in our schoolhouse, and don't mean a single man shall vote for Horace Greely."[31] In 1876, Laura Towne saw that the South Carolinians intended to put an end to African American education and participation in politics. After several African American male political activists were dragged from their homes nearby and beaten, she used her national reputation as an anti-slavery worker to champion the African Americans' cause in a letter to the liberal journal, The Nation. With her African American male allies, she would fight to control "this yankinized region." Towne's letters and diary also tell a story of her local political activism — lobbying at the state level to permit African Americans to pay taxes to fund their own schools (they were already taxed for white schools), the passing of key school resolutions in St. Helena that she had written, and support and counsel for Robert Smalls, an African American South Carolina congressman and Civil War hero. She also continued to do much of the legal work to help African Americans claim land for themselves. "I want to agitate, even as I am agitated," Laura Towne wrote.[32]

The record of the schoolmarms' activity continues on for decades, in a stable, regularized pattern. In the surviving schools, rituals such as the annual school district meeting, year's end exercises, the celebration of emancipation, the teachers' summering in the North and their autumn return marked the habits established and maintained year after year. Those Northern benefactors committed to long-term support corresponded with Laura Towne or Sallie Holley over routine matters — the whereabouts of thirty-six dollars for teachers' salaries, the building of a new school house, marriages, a student honored by an invitation to attend Hampton Institute. From the *Lyons Republican* came a description of the Holley School: "This is the centre around which everything else revolves; and whatever else may fail, this goes on uninterruptedly from year's end to year's end, an ever active centre of influence constantly operating upon this community in the diffusion of intellectual light." For Holley and Towne, personal satisfaction seemed just as important as public influence. In May 1871, just a week after her forty-sixth birthday, and after nearly a decade on the Sea Islands, Laura Towne declared, "I do never intend to leave the 'heathen country.' I intend to end my days here and I wish to."[33] She died in 1901 at Frogmore, her home, at age seventy-six.

The final words about the schoolmarms belong to the African American writers W. E. B. DuBois and Charles Chesnutt — Chesnutt's short story ironically titled "The March of Progress" ends the selections for this chapter. Acute and critical observers of the South and of race relations in general, both fall prey to gender stereotypes and sentimentality when writing about freedpersons' teachers. Published in 1900, the Chesnutt story turns on the competition for a teaching job between a frail white teacher of fifteen years seniority in a small town freedpersons' school and one of her former male pupils, "a 'bright' mulatto . . . [who has] familiarity with the dead and living languages and the higher mathematics" (see p. 221). The story reflects accurately the economic and racial situation in the South in the 1880s and 1890s — the lack of employment for educated African Americans, barriers to exercising the franchise, continuing poverty and racial violence. But, like most fiction about the schoolmarms and much about teachers in general, Chesnutt heartily over-simplifies who they were, how and why they went about their work, and what they accomplished. For example, he described the eponymous Miss Noble as "thin, homely, and short-sighted," a figure of "true womanhood," self-abnegating in the extreme (see p. 225). Needing work after the death of her parents and the departure for the war of "a certain captain . . . who had paid her some attention" (see p. 218), Miss Noble sacrifices herself to help the poor African American community. She lives a lonely life, socially isolated from whites, teaching, in the words of a school committee member, "manners an' religion an' book-l'arnin'" and ministering to the sick "like an angel" (see p. 225). After fifteen years, she is a pathetic figure who deserves pity and alms herself. DuBois' schoolmarm is simply womanly perfection: "the best of all" to come from the Freedmen's Bureau. "This was the gift of New England to the freed Negro; not alms, but a friend; not cash, but character . . . love and sympathy . . . which these once saintly souls brought to their favored children in the crusade of the sixties; that finest thing in American history, and one of the few things untainted by sordid greed and cheap vainglory."[34]

In truth, the teachers were neither angels nor saintly souls, but women pushing against the boundaries of the possible in regard to race and class arrangements, in physical, intellectual and spiritual endurance, and by taking on the sheer hard work of teaching. They did not prevent the years of deprivation and neglect of African American public schooling that followed their short burst of activity — the legacy African American students deal with today in many public schools. Historian Michael Fultz, citing DuBois' comment in *The Souls of Black Folk* that there was work the Freedmen's Bureau "did not do because it could not," describes the systematic underdevelopment of African American education — and the powerlessness of African American communities and their teachers in the South from the post-civil war period through the 1940s. Fultz argues that African American teachers were caught in "an ideologically charged middle." Without proper support and education, they were the focus of racist white Southerners wanting to prove their incapacity and African American intellectuals blaming them in order to highlight the deplorable condition of Southern African American schooling, and thus protest injustice and inequality.[35]

In sum, most teachers changed their own lives for the better and the lives of many of their students, but they faced racism woven too deeply into the fabric of Southern society for any teaching movement to overthrow. For teachers to gain power for themselves and for the education of children, they needed collective action, and that story is part of the history of women teaching in the cities in the first decades of the twentieth century.

# Teaching During the Civil War: A Fourteen-Year-Old's Story

--❦--

## Susie King Taylor

From Susie King Taylor,
*Reminiscences of My Life in Camp with the
33rd United States Colored Troops Late 1st B. C. Volunteers*
(1902; reprinted Princeton, N.J.:
Markus Wiener Publishers, 1988).

*In early April 1862, Susie King Taylor (1848–1912), a 14-year-old African American slave, fled behind Union lines with her uncle and his family. Taken aboard a Federal gunboat that had successfully attacked Fort Pulaski in the Savannah harbor, she demonstrated her reading, writing, and sewing skills for an inquiring and surprised white officer. Likely the first African American woman to teach newly freed people, she wrote an unusual memoir of that experience and of her subsequent work as a laundress, nurse, teacher, and aide in what was to become the First South Carolina Volunteers commanded by the antislavery leader, Colonel Thomas Wentworth Higginson. It is he who wrote the original introduction to Taylor's memoir. According to Willie Lee Rose, the historian who introduces the current edition of the* Reminiscences, *Taylor was among the first slaves actually freed by the Union Army. During the first year of the war, Lincoln had permitted slaves who had escaped behind the Union lines to be labeled "contraband of war"; contraband, or confiscated property, did not have to be returned under the rules of war. But it was Major General David Hunter at Fort Pulaski whom Lincoln permitted to declare families like Susie Taylor's free people.*

*In the excerpt below, Taylor describes her life under slavery, how she learned to read and write in a clandestine school, and how she arrived on St. Simon's Island,*

Georgia. Taylor worked unpaid among the 33rd U.S. Colored Troops for four years and married Edward King, one of the soldiers. At the end of the war, Susie King Taylor returned to Savannah, opened a school, and taught in the state for three years. After her husband was killed in an accident, she moved north to Boston with her young son, where she worked as a household servant until she married Russell L. Taylor in 1879. In 1889, Taylor made a trip south to Shreveport, Louisiana, encountered lynch mobs and hangings, and felt her own safety threatened. Reminiscences ends with Taylor's plea: "Justice we ask, — to be citizens of these United States . . ."

## CHAPTER II
## MY CHILDHOOD

I was born under the slave law in Georgia, in 1848, and was brought up by my grandmother in Savannah. There were three of us with her, my younger sister and brother. My brother and I being the two eldest, we were sent to a friend of my grandmother, Mrs. Woodhouse, a widow, to learn to read and write. She was a free woman and lived on Bay Lane, between Habersham and Price streets, about half a mile from my house. We went every day about nine o'clock, with our books wrapped in paper to prevent the police or white persons from seeing them. We went in, one at a time, through the gate, into the yard to the L [sic] kitchen, which was the schoolroom. She had twenty-five or thirty children whom she taught, assisted by her daughter, Mary Jane. The neighbors would see us going in sometimes, but they supposed we were there learning trades, as it was the custom to give children a trade of some kind. After school we left the same way we entered, one by one, when we would go to a square, about a block from the school, and wait for each other. We would gather laurel leaves and pop them on our hands, on our way home. I remained at her school for two years or more, when I was sent to a Mrs. Mary Beasley, where I continued until May, 1860, when she told my grandmother she had taught me all she knew, and grandmother had better get some one else who could teach me more, so I stopped my studies for a while.

I had a white playmate about this time, named Katie O'Connor, who lived on the next corner of the street from my house, and who attended a convent. One day she told me, if I would promise not to tell her father, she would give me some lessons. On my promise not to do so, and getting her mother's consent, she gave me lessons about four months, every evening. At the end of this time she was put into the convent permanently, and I have never seen her since.

A month after this, James Blouis, our landlord's son, was attending the High School, and was very fond of grandmother, so she asked him to give me a few lessons, which he did until the middle of 1861, when the Savannah Volunteer Guards, to which he and his brother belonged, were ordered to the front under General Barton. In the first battle of Manassas, his brother Eugene was killed, and James deserted over to the Union side, and at the close of the war went to Washington, D.C., where he has since resided.

I often wrote passes for my grandmother, for all colored persons, free or slaves, were compelled to have a pass; free colored people having a guardian in place of a master. These passes were good until 10 to 10.30 P.M. for one night or every night for one month. The pass read as follows: —

SAVANNAH, GA., MARCH 1ST, 1860
Pass the bearer _____ from 9 to 10.30 P.M.
Valentine Grest.

Every person had to have this pass, for at nine o'clock each night a bell was rung, and any colored persons found on the street after this hour were arrested by the watchman, and put in the guard-house until next morning, when their owners would pay their fines and release them. I knew a number of persons who went out at any time at night and were never arrested, as the watchman knew them so well he never stopped them, and seldom asked to see their passes, only stopping them long enough, sometimes, to say "Howdy," and then telling them to go along.

About this time I had been reading so much about the "Yankees" I was very anxious to see them. The whites would tell their colored people not to go to the Yankees, for they would harness them to carts and make them pull the carts around, in place of horses. I asked grandmother, one day, if this was true. She replied, "Certainly not!" that the white people did not want slaves to go over to the Yankees, and told them these things to frighten them. "Don't you see those signs pasted about the streets? One reading, 'I am a wildcat! Beware,' etc. These are warnings to the North; so don't mind what the white people say." I wanted to see these wonderful "Yankees" so much, as I heard my parents say the Yankee was going to set all the slaves free. Oh, how those people prayed for freedom! I remember, one night, my grandmother went out into the suburbs of the city to a church meeting, and they were fervently singing this old hymn, —

*"Yes, we all shall be free,*
*Yes, we all shall be free,*
*Yes, we all shall be free,*
*When the Lord shall appear,"* —

When the police came in and arrested all who were there, saying they were planning freedom, and sang, "the Lord," in place of "Yankee," to blind any one who might be listening. Grandmother never forgot that night, although she did not stay in the guard-house, as she sent to her guardian, who came at once for her; but this was the last meeting she ever attended out of the city proper.

On April 1, 1862, about the time the Union soldiers were firing on Fort Pulaski, I was sent out into the country to my mother. I remember what a roar and din the guns made. They jarred the earth for miles. The fort was at last taken by them. Two days after the taking of Fort Pulaski, my uncle took his family of seven and myself to St. Catherine Island. We landed under the protection of the Union fleet, and remained there two weeks, when about thirty of us were taken aboard the gunboat P_____, to be transferred to St. Simon's Island; and at last, to my unbounded joy, I saw the "Yankee."

After we were all settled aboard and started on our journey, Captain Whitmore, commanding the boat, asked me where I was from. I told him Savannah, Ga. He asked if I could read; I said, "Yes!" "Can you write?" he next asked. "Yes, I can do that also," I replied, and as if he had some doubts of my answers he handed me a book and a pencil and told me to write my name and where I was from. I did this; when he wanted to know if I could sew. On hearing I could, he asked me to hem some napkins for him. He was surprised at my accomplishments (for they were such in those days), for he said he did not know there were any negroes in the South able to read or write. He said, "You seem to be so different from the other colored people who came from the same place you did." "No!" I replied, "the only difference is, they were reared in the country and I in the city, as was a man from Darien, Ga., named Edward King." That seemed to satisfy him, and we had no further conversation that day on the subject.

In the afternoon the captain spied a boat in the distance, and as it drew nearer he noticed it had a white flag hoisted, but before it had reached the Putumoka he ordered all passengers between decks, so we could not be seen, for he thought they might be spies. The boat finally drew alongside of our boat, and had Mr. Edward Donegall on board, who wanted his two servants, Nick and Judith. He wanted these, as they were his own children. Our captain told him he knew nothing of them, which was true, for at the time they were on St. Simon's, and not, as their father supposed, on our boat. After the boat left, we were allowed to come up on deck again.

## III
## ON ST. SIMON'S ISLAND
### 1862

Next morning we arrived at St. Simon's, and the captain told Commodore Goldsborough about this affair, and his reply was, "Captain Whitmore, you should not have allowed them to return, you should have kept them." After I had been on St. Simon's about three days, Commodore Goldsborough heard of me, and came to Gaston Bluff to see me. I found him very cordial. He said Captain Whitmore had spoken to him of me, and that he was pleased to hear of my being so capable, etc., and wished me to take charge of a school for the children on the island. I told him I would gladly do so, if I could have some books. He said I should have them, and in a week or two I received two large boxes of books and testaments from the North. I had about forty children to teach, besides a number of adults who came to me nights, all of them so eager to learn to read, to read above anything else. Chaplain French, of Boston, would come to the school, sometimes, and lecture to the pupils on Boston and the North.

About the first of June we were told that there was going to be a settlement of the war. Those who were on the Union side would remain free, and those in bondage were to work three days for their masters and three for themselves. It was a gloomy time for us all, and we were to be sent to Liberia. Chaplain French asked me would I rather go back to Savannah or go to Liberia. I told him the latter place by all means. We did not know when this would be, but we were prepared in case this settlement should be reached. However, the Confederates would not agree to the arrangement, or else it was one of the many rumors flying about at the time, as we heard nothing further of the matter. There were a number of settlements on this island of St. Simon's, just like little villages, and we would go from one to the other on business, to call, or only for a walk. . . .

# Missionary Maidens

## Mary Clemmer Ames

From Linda Warfel Slaughter, ed.,
*The Freedmen of the South*
(Cincinnati, Ohio: Elm Street Printing Co., 1869).

*As one of the most disrupting events in American history, the Civil War broke apart traditional class, gender, and racial constructions and challenged Americans to rethink their relationship to their fellow countrymen. During the war many women, like the Northern teachers who traveled south, undertook new public roles and responsibilities. The teachers who taught in the South found themselves in the center of a national debate over slavery and race relations. Not surprisingly, few of the articles written about women teachers portrayed them as the independent and politically savvy women they were. A good example is this vignette, written just after the end of the Civil War, when teachers were arriving in the South in large numbers. Its author, Mary Clemmer Ames, gives a wildly romantic account of a group of young schoolteachers. These "nigger teachers"— an epithet used through-out the South — emerge as quintessential martyrs, embodying all the popular female virtues: grace, elegance, Christian piety, and refined intelligence. As later selections in the chapter reveal, Ames' characterization of Northern teachers is more telling of society's efforts to restore the post–Civil War notions of gender during reconstruction than it is of the true character of these women.*

*This piece was included in a book of essays and letters from teachers. The editor, Linda Warfel Slaughter, was an author and poet with writings published in Godey's Lady's Book. Slaughter (1843–1911) taught in Kentucky and Tennessee for two years after her graduation from Oberlin College, worked as a missionary in India, and upon her return led an active life of civic engagement in the Dakota territory, including advocating for temperance and woman suffrage. Slaughter was the first woman school superintendent, the first woman postmaster, the first woman to hold elective office, and the first woman to vote in a national political party convention for a presidential candidate. A friend of Susan B. Anthony, she was active in the suffrage movement. She was admitted to the bar in Washington, D.C., in 1895, among the first women to be so.*

Harper's Ferry, West. Va.,
December, 1866

Yesterday, looking from my window, I caught a glimpse of "animated nature," which quickened with new life the repose caught from the blending here of ruins, rocks, and rivers. What was it? It was a small procession of Yankee girls, just from the cars, coming into Harper's Ferry, to scatter through the valley of Virginia, as teachers of the freed-people. *That* was a sight you would have to come all the way to the old slave-lands to appreciate! There they were — "the teachers!" The teachers! For whom Virginians had the most chivalric contempt, and the few Northern hearts here the warmest greeting.

A troop of maidens, who, in some undefinable way, suggest Tennyson's "sweet girl graduates with their golden hair," although I am very sure that their tresses are not all of the hue of the sun. I see jaunty hats and natty jackets, gay scarfs and graceful robes. I see elegance, beauty and youth; all come to brighten the lot of the lowly, to deliver from ignorance and vice that victim race which our brothers with their blood delivered from chains.

Opposite my window they encounter a Virginian belle, arrayed in the splendor of a purple dress, a scarlet shawl, a green hat, and a blue vail [sic]. Her scornful eyes behold the object which of all others she despises most — "a nigger teacher." What is worse, she beholds more than a dozen "nigger teachers" all together. It is a dreadful, unbearable sight, is it not, my dear? I suppose I ought to be very sorry for you; but I am not sorry a bit. It is an affliction of great magnitude, to be sure, that your whilom servants should be taught by better and prettier teachers than you ever had in your life; but it is a humiliation which you will have to bear, and the only way that you can lessen it is to improve yourself.

This old house, once occupied by the superintendent of the armories is now used as the temporary abode of the superintendent of the freed-people's schools in the valley of the Shenandoah, the Rev. Mr. Brackett, of Maine. In a grand old room, defaced by war, yet brightened with pictures and books from home, overlooking the prospect which I just inadequately sketched, I saw yesterday a scene not to be forgotten. That lovely Sabbath afternoon no church-doors opened to the teachers! With their books in their hands, they surrounded this wide room, holding a simple service of their own. A room full of youthful women, far from home and all its loves, sang the Lord's song in a strange land. Those old walls, which within the last five years had resounded so often to the oath and jest of dissolute men, now sent back the echoes of sweet womanly voices, though which loving hearts trembled as they sang,

> *Nearer, my God, to Thee,*
> *Nearer to Thee.*

Here was the red-lipped school-girl, just from school; here the young widow, holding in tearful love the memory of buried husband and child; here were women in the prime of matured power, with their rare beauty of sumptuous womanhood — women whose elegance and grace and fine mentality would have lent luster to the highest sphere. Such were the teachers of the freed slaves, who sat and knelt together, whose soft eyes dimmed with tears as they sang the hymns of home, and prayed for the blessing of God upon their work. After making due allowance for all superficial enthusiasm and the romance which may be inseparable from the womanly nature and missionary labor, who can measure the significance of the fact that hundreds of young, gifted and cultivated women from the North are now scattered through the South as teachers of its former slaves; and though much against their will, and almost contrary to their knowledge, teachers as well of the old-time masters?

All unconsciously to themselves, in their mere presence, these women are educators.

# From Northern Home
# to Southern Dangers

## Maria S. Waterbury

From Maria S. Waterbury,
*Seven Years Among the Freedmen*
(Chicago: T. B. Arnold, 1891).

*This hair-raising account from Maria Waterbury's* Seven Years Among the
Freedmen *establishes the two worlds of the Northern teacher — the white world
in which she is a hunted enemy and the potential victim of a lynch mob; and the
African American world in which she is the friend to be protected and guarded
because she brings access to formal education. Indeed, for Northern teachers and
Southern students alike, the opening of schools was a visible sign of God's favor,
and the teacher was often perceived as the agent of connection. The emotion of the
education journey is well expressed in the tender prayer that Jesus keep the school
in "de holler ob his han'."*

*Like many teachers, Waterbury spent her summers in the North, away from dan-
ger and the disease rampant in the swampy Southern countryside. She then repeated the journey south each fall. The journey recounted here — most likely her first
— is harrowing in the extreme, and demonstrates that once a white woman associated with African Americans as a social equal, she lost her rights to the respect
afforded Southern ladyhood.*

*Waterbury appears to have spent seven years in Tennessee and Mississippi dur-
ing the 1870s. There is no biographical information available.*

## Journeying

"*In perils by mine own countrymen.*" — 2 Cor. xi. 26.

The instructions of the missionary society, are, "go south about eight
hundred miles, until you find the plantation school waiting for you."
The last week of November two of us start from near Chicago. Our

Saratoga trunks are heavy with books. Our friends in the northern churches, have sent us with many prayers and blessings, and our gray-haired pastor has given us letters of introduction to churches at the South, wherever we may find a home. We are to teach our first Freedmen's school, on a plantation, twenty-five miles from a railroad. From Cairo, Illinois, we go down the Mississippi, and across to Paducah, Kentucky. The marks of the bomb-shelling the town received in war time, are still visible. The houses are unpainted, gloomy-looking habitations, some of them with ball holes in them.

From the large steamer we have crossed the river in, we ascend the bluffs, and take the cars on the M. & O. railroad. All day we have been traveling with a party of southern ladies, who have been north to attend a wedding; one of them walks with crutches. We have been through the train in Illinois, distributing tracts, and the sweet-faced lady on crutches, says to us:

"Oh! You have tracts. Yes, I'll take some tracts, and I'll join your company too. I'm a preacher's wife, and I do that kind of work sometimes."

"Indeed! Do you work among black and white both?"

"Yes' I tell 'em they're all bound for the same place. The grave'll soon hold us all."

Directly one of the southern ladies, two or three seats distant, says in a loud voice, "You'll soon see some nigger teachers. My husband says they all wear spectacles, and read newspapers."

We laugh in our sleeves to think the high-toned southerners sought our society, and don't dream they are traveling with hated nigger teachers; but we say nothing . . .

We reach the end of our railroad ride at midnight, and find at the shed-like depot only a white man with a lantern, and a dozen half-grown boys dressed in cotton sacks and cast-off clothes of Union soldiers. . . .

*After a night at a country hotel, the women were sent off on a mule cart. The driver, discovering that he had been cheated by the stable keeper, abandoned the women in the woods. They were rescued and taken to their destination, but there relatives of their to-be host refused the "nigger teachers" entry. Finally they arrived on foot at the planter's, spent the night, and the next day journeyed another six miles to their school site.*

Arriving at the plantation, we find a store, a shop or two, a white school, and an immense building, used in slave times for a white boys' school. We are to have living rooms in the upper story of the large building, and school rooms in the lower. A colored woman is employed as cook for us; and at our first Sunday-school, the next morning over a hundred black people, men and women, join in singing so grandly, that it brings tears to our eyes to hear the wonderful pathos of their music. The white planter believes the school will please the blacks, and be a means of helping him keep the better class of them to do his work. At the first Sunday-school, he brings his newspaper, and sits in the chapel near us to hear our instruction. They tell us he is a class-leader, and we ask him to open the school with prayer. He peers at us over his spectacles and says, "That's your business, ma'am," and we two teachers go on with the school, giving oral instruction, as not ten of the hundred before us can read.

In the afternoon we go to the first colored meeting we have ever attended. Five ministers are in the pulpit. The church building is far inferior to the barns at home. A young preacher, very black, reads from Revelation vi, of "an angel with a pair of banisters in his hand." The ignorant sermon is done, and the praying! Oh! That is enough to pay us for our journey of eight hundred miles, mule rides, poor whites, and all. We are lifted on those prayers heavenward, and the songs reach to the depths of our souls. As the benediction is pronounced, the only white man in the large audience, wearing lemon-colored kid gloves, rises and says he has heard of a school to be opened for the people, that he has thought of teaching a school himself, and will begin in the morning.

The young preacher of the day, says, "We has got our teachers here, from de norf, with much trouble, an' de good book says, ef we put our hand to de plow, an' look back, we aint fit fur de kingdom. An' we is goin' tu stick tu our teachers."

But the war against us has begun, and we are threatened with many things. "The building will be burnt I fear," says the planter. "You all can come to my house for awhile."

In the upper story of the plantation house, we are guarded by freedmen, not daring to begin our school. Here we pass the Christmas holidays, cared for by the planter's family, and guarded at night by colored people, who build great bonfires, and we hear them in their night watches, talking and sometimes singing. They are paying dear for their first attempt at starting a school. On Christmas morning before breakfast, a colored woman, bearing two glasses of egg-nog, comes up stairs, saying "Mrs. S. sends her compliments, and wishes you a merry Christmas." We thank her and say, "Tell the lady we never drink anything of the kind."

The astonished girl goes down, and again returns, saying, "The missus wants to know if you will take some wine." We tell her we never drank a glass in our lives, and ask her to excuse us, saying, "Our church at home has the temperance pledge, as a part of the creed."

We pass the day writing, and towards evening, to down to chat a little with the family. The planter rises and begins telling us we needn't fear, as he has his gun loaded, and dogs ready, and if there is any fuss, he can stop it. We notice his gun standing in the corner of the room, and soon he begins to stagger towards it, so drunk he nearly falls down. Alas! This is our protection! We hope it is better with the freedmen, but find many of them too, have been drinking. The planter has a wine cellar, and to cheer them up in their trouble, has taken one or two favorite ex-slaves into it, and dealt out liquors to them, and they have given to others, until many on the place are drunk.

We retire to our room, realizing that our "weapons are not carnal." Before the holidays are over, we see children drunk, for the first time in our lives. In a week we begin school, and immediately start a temperance society. Before the five months of school are closed, there are over a hundred members to our Band of Hope, and over thirty are hopefully converted. . . .

## "At Home" and Safer

A large brick house with a lovely garden in the rear, walks bordered with box, fig trees and green and ripe figs on them, tall pines down the walk, lovely roses, and climbing vines — one of the homes of aristocracy in slave times. The planter who lived here owned several hundred slaves. Now a family from the North reside here, and we two "nigger teachers" board with them. The family have been visiting twenty miles away for a day or two, and we teachers are keeping house for them, with a colored family of six persons living in the kitchens . . . and doing all the work for us. We are in charge of two colored schools a mile away. We have heard of the Ku-Klux being on their night raids of late, and this morning as the clock struck two, we heard a low whistle outside the gate, and Miss C—— and the writer woke the same moment, each saying to the other, "Did you hear that?" We stuck a light, pulled down the shades of the windows, and hastily dressed, but not before we heard the tramp of heavy feet on the porch outside. Our room opened into another room kept for storage purposes, where was a large box of shelled corn. 'Twas the work of a moment for us to slip a package containing a large sum of money, that had been left by an officer under government, in care of the lady of the house, into the box of corn, and drag our Saratoga trunks against the door. The money was left in our care in the absence of the family, and for a moment we supposed the night riders had found it out; but afterwards learned they knew nothing of it, but were trying to impress upon the teachers, and northern family, the fact that "this is a white man's government."

Tramp, tamp went the feet, first on the north porch, then on the south, and ever and anon a whistle, and we expected them to enter, but God heard our prayers for safety. We sat, one on each side of our little table, with our lamp lighted, and our Bibles in our hands, and read aloud the promises of our God, so mighty to save.

"As the mountains are round about Jerusalem, so the Lord is round about his people from henceforth even forever." — Psa. cxxv. 2.

"If two of you shall agree on earth, as touching any thing that they shall ask, it shall be done for them of my Father which is in heaven." — Matt. xviii. 19.

We said, "Lord, we *do agree*, and we ask that the intruders may not enter this room."

Together we repeated the same prayer, over and over, and soon one of us said, "I have the assurance that they *will not* enter." Tramp, tramp went the feet on the porch, and we heard them try the locks of the doors, and whistle to each other, and thus for over two hours we watched and waited, and only until the morning began to dawn, did they go to their carriages and ride away.

In the morning, we saw the tracks of horses, and of many people. The next night a guard from the town, a mile away, came and staid on the plantation.

We afterwards heard there were two wagon loads of Ku-Klux, but they dared not enter to molest us, as they feared we were armed, and so we were, and guarded, too, for "the angel of the Lord encampeth round about them that fear him, and delivereth them." We had only proved God's faithfulness.

"How d'ye, ma'am! I cum tree mile dis mornin', tu tell ye de Lawd stood by me last night, an' he tell me you all is *safe!* He ain't gwine tu let ye get 'sturbed by de white 'uns, honey. You jes go on teechin' de skule, and de good Massa tote you in his bosom.

I got shoutin' happy last night, an' my old man says, Peggy, what ails ye? I says, 'Ole man, wake up! de Lawd is yer! He done jes filled me, an' he ain't gwine tu let dat are skule be broke up' Honey, de Lawd jes showed me how he shet de lions' mouths, an' he got ye all in de holler ob his hand; dey can't touch a hair o' you heads. Hallelujah! Massar Jesus got sumthin' tu do wid dis skule. You jes go on teechin' honey. De Lawd dun sent de angles, tu stan' by ye. He cover ye wid his feathers."

A prayer-meeting — fifty black people — some gray-headed, who were stolen from Africa when they were infants; some whose mothers had been sold and run off to the sugar plantations, before they were a year old. Ah! how such had learned to pray. Now the school had been threatened by Ku Klux. A letter had been written to a teacher, with the picture of a white girl tied to a tree, and a man standing on each side, with an overseer's whip, laying strokes on her back. "On the side of their oppressors there was power." Under the picture was written, "This is the way we serve northern *'nigger teachers.'* Beware lest you shere the same fate." This is not a fancy picture, reader, but an actual fact.

Old Aunt Emeline begins the prayer-meeting by singing in the old slavery wail, trotting her foot to keep time, and all join in singing, swaying their bodies from side to side, as if over-whelmed with grief:

> *'Rastlin' Jacob! an' I will not let thee go!*
> *'Rastlin' Jacob! an' I will not let thee go!*

Still wailing out the song, they fall upon their knees, and with sobs and prayers, tell Jesus about "dem people who's trying tu brake up de skule."

"Masser Jesus, put dy hand ober our teachers. Jesus, ain't you de same God as took Jonah out ob de belly ob de whale? Shine in our hearts, Masser Jesus, and help us tu lub our enemies. Ain't you de same God as 'livered Dan'l from de den ob lions? 'Liver us, good Lawd, an' tote us in yo' bosom, and 'hedge us 'bout, an' plant us out anew fur de

*Formal group portrait in a classroom of the Holley School, ca. 1897.*

kingdum. Masser Jesus, set down de right foot ob dy power *hea'!* an'
keep dis skule in de holler ob you' hand. Cum dis way, Masser, an' bind
us all in de bundle ob life." . . .

## Going Home

Our first year of school is over. We have taught two hundred colored
people, only two lady teachers, of all ages, sizes, and colors, from jet
black to pure white-looking, and many of the class called by the jet-
black ones "yaller ones." We have lived in the old school building, used
for a white school in slave times, now a harbor for rats by day, and dogs
by night. . . .

Now the school is done, and the people have come to say good-bye's. We are to start at four o'clock in the morning, for a twenty-five mile ride. . . .

Next in order is a prayer-meeting, to pray for our safe journey home. They pray for everything we shall ever need, if we live a thousand years. They remind Masser Jesus of all his promises.

"Lawd, don't ye say you'll stan' by dem as trusts in ye? Cum right down yer now, Masser Jesus, an' take a walk troo dis country, an' see what de debbil's duin' in de kingdom."

"Lawd, place blessings by de wayside fur our teachers."

"Tote 'em safe down de stream o' time, Masser Jesus, an' let de old ship o' Zion lan' 'em high up in heaven, an' crown 'em dine." . . .

"The carriage is ready, ma'am." The children are giving us great bouquets, and some give us cakes and candy, and the blacks almost push each other, for the privilege of stowing our luggage. The good-bye's come between sobs and tears. Some reach up to touch our hands, after we are seated in the carriage, and one calls out, "My God, is they gone?" . . .

Three miles on our journey, and a halloo announces to us that we are followed by one of our young men scholars — Robert, a young Methodist Episcopal preacher, has determined to go North with us to get an education. Some of the white people have found it out, and all night he has been hunted by those who have threatened to kill him. He rides a mule, has lost his hat, and left all his books and most of his clothing behind. One of the teachers pays his fare, and he comes on with us.

Jackson, Tennessee — the end of our first day's railroad travel. No trains have passed out of this place for three days. There is a strike on the road. Many passengers and trains are waiting. The workmen claim they haven't had their pay for two years, and as our train nears the depot, a committee of three or four men loosen the engine, and run it into an engine house near by. Two or three hundred of excited people are on the platform, and all is confusion.

We go to the nearest hotel, and to another, and another, but everywhere are refused a night's lodging, or a meal of victuals. We go back to the train. Evening: Lamps lighted in the cars. Passengers, all but us, seem to have found some place for the night. Soon we hear the familiar title, *"nigger teachers!"* hissed out near us. The conductor tells us there are soldiers on board the train, who have come to guard the engines. He brings the head officer of the staff to us; we show him the commissions of the American Missionary Association recommending us to the protection of the government, and immediately we are under guard. Enter the postmaster on the train — a northern gentleman. He tells us the people of this place say *they have never surrendered.* Instantly he comprehends the situation. Some outside are calling out our names. Pounding on the cars, some one calls out.

"Miss W———, Miss T———, you'd better come out. There's goin' to be a nigger killed!"

The soldiers raise the window, and threaten to shoot the next man who moves his tongue against us. The postmaster, with his arms full of velvet cushions off the seats, followed by one or two colored helpers, proceeds to fit up the postal car, and soon orders our trunks into it, and we follow him out of doors, and around to the end of the car. The mob by this time has increased; but one soldier is behind us, another near by, and the brave postmaster is fully armed. He makes a way through the crowd, and we are locked into our quarters among the mail bags, and could sleep if we knew what had become of Robert, and if the mercury was not up to 90°, and the *fleas would keep still.* . . .

Just at dark, the fifth day of our imprisonment, a lady comes on board the train, guarded by a soldier. She has heard of our situation, and comes to invite us to spend the night with her, out in a house, half fallen down, where she lives alone. She is a teacher of freedmen; has a pass from Governor Brownlow, to go where she pleases, and pleases to stay in this place, because her only son, all she has left since the war, is a soldier, and quartered here.

We thought we had seen poverty before, but here is *abject poverty;* no comforts in her room, no Bible. Her education is so poor she can hardly talk correctly. She tells us she has never studied grammar; wants us to spend the night with her, and help her teach the school on the morrow. The woman, in her endeavors to have us enjoy our prison life, fairly outdoes herself; gives us her small couch, suitable only for one person, finds a blanket or two among the freedmen, brings a lamp and a few sticks, lights a fire, and asks us to read our Bibles and have family worship. Together we read, and draw water from the wells of salvation. God seems so near we don't either fear or feel lonely. The new-found friend rolls herself up in a blanket, lays her loaded revolver by her pillow, and lies on the floor at night, saying, "I've often done it since that war," and gives us two teachers her bed. Morning: Our food is provided by some of the freedmen — a few biscuits, coffee, and milk. We eat in singleness of heart, and are thankful. We have at least found

Christian companionship, and we go into the school and teach for an hour or two; but soon a colored man comes to inform us we are being followed and are unsafe, and we go back to our car and remain another day under guard.

In the evening, a lady closely veiled, and guarded by a soldier, comes on the train to see us — a northern woman, bound for New York — a sympathizer with us. She proposes a walk around the fortifications. The next day, we three ladies, with a soldier following not far from us, go out to view the earth works and rifle-pits; not as much to see the lions, as to get fresh air. We are returning to our train, but on the way, stop at the hotel where the lady boards, and for a few moments, rest in her room. The proprietor of the hotel, very soon knocks at the door, calls the lady into the hall, and tells her he will not have us in his house, and if she associates with *nigger teachers,* she must also leave his house. He says we ought to marry niggers, and quite a little more of that kind of talk.

We are now *three* ladies on the train, under guard. For nine successive days and nights we have endured the tropical heat, but our courage holds out. Many have been on the train to see us, much as we have seen animals exhibited in a menagerie. Men and women have come in and passed through the cars, looking at us, as if we were there for show. To all who would accept them, we have given tracts, and most of them go away reading. . . .

As all things come to an end in time, on the tenth day the strike is over. The train is about to pull out, when our colored young preacher makes his appearance. Some of the people have offered him twenty-five dollars to leave the teachers and stay with them; but he prefers to continue his journey northward, and is allowed to ride in the smoking car. Several hundred people are on the platform; and the train is to move on, some attempt to open the door, and find it locked. The soldiers are on duty, and safely we leave the Jackson friends, to meet them, perhaps, in another world. Who shall say where? "Inasmuch as ye have done it unto one of the least of these my brethren, ye have done it unto me.". . .

# Sisters in the Service

―∘∾⊚∾∘―

## Sarah Chase, Lucy Chase, Julia Rutledge

From Henry L. Swint, ed.,
*Dear Ones at Home* (Nashville, Tenn.:
Vanderbilt University Press, 1966).

*Quaker sisters from a prosperous Worcester, Massachusetts, family, Sarah (1836–1911) and Lucy (1822–1909) Chase journeyed to the South in 1863 as teachers appointed by the Boston Educational Commission. They first taught in refugee camps on Craney Island, Virginia, and then throughout the South. Like many of their contemporaries, Sarah and Lucy Chase found that wartime America offered many new opportunities for independent women, allowing them to take on — without criticism — public leadership roles not available during the early 1800s. These letters to "dear ones at home" not only reveal the experiences of two skilled educators, but also illuminate the variety of roles teachers were asked to take on. With little help from the Boston Commission, these women set up massive school systems, distributed supplies, and established labor systems throughout the South. What emerges from their narrative is the role of Northern teachers in working with African Americans to create stable, productive communities. The last letters in this selection, letters to Sarah from Julia Rutledge, a freedmen's school graduate, also show these sisters' roles as mentors to a new generation of teachers.*

*Richmond*
*April 18th [1865]*

Hurray!! The peace — thank God![1]
Though much exhausted with my morning task of governing and teaching (oral and with the black board) my *little* school of *one thousand and twenty-five* children, who but a few days ago were slaves — I will try to give you a few hints of my work since I last wrote. It is useless to wait longer for leisure and freshness for writing. . . .
Although the officers and newspapers say truly that no one can get to Richmond, unless ordered — and such multitudes are waiting in

Washington-Norfolk and at Fortress Monroe for passes — our party . . . through intimate acquaintance with the leading officers here, got passes to come at once, to organize the work in the beginning of the new regime — and constantly and diligently have we labored through the day; and in the night I have *thought* for coming time. Government can only give us leave to *work*, but by ourselves we have got the field and labor organized in less than ten days, in a manner that gratifies and surprises us.

Never have I attended committee meeting more dignified and to the point than the many we have appointed with the leading men in the colored churches. At our first meeting a noble looking and most intelligent deacon started up suddenly saying, "I felt frightened for a moment seeing more than five colored people together" — it being the law here that more than five must never assemble without a white man was authorized to sit with them. Not long ago, the white man they employed to sit in one of their Sunday Schools stepped out on an errand and was detained a little, and the whole school with its teachers was carried to jail. . . .

We have already enrolled over two thousand pupils and expect to nearly double the number before long. As soon as our teachers come up and the schools are turned over to them, I shall open employment offices and get manufactures under way — it is too soon yet — and most too soon for schools. The officers sent their wives passes to come up and had to telegraph them *not* to come. So of course the teachers cannot come for it is not yet safe. I have heard many threats, and these impetuous people are every day shooting or stabbing someone, so I want no one to come until these people are convinced they are under Govt. The delay is not disadvantage to the little ones, who can be taught to sit still & how to give attention, en masse — their brains can be roused and put in working order by general instructions and exercises, so that when they have their books and teachers they can make a better beginning and I feel that these mental gymnastics I give them will always make study easier for them. I have talked with them in all the churches and met them outside where they weep over me, call down blessings on my head, shake my poor hands so they keep lame so I can hardly hold my pen — as I pass some caressingly take hold of my raiment while some push back the crowd — All this I well know is not for me but for "de good Norf people." And how much I wish these same good North people who have prayed and worked for the people here could join with them in their songs of joy and thanksgiving, as it has been my privilege in this, their day of jubilee. I have opened books in the different churches with headings of occupations where I register names — and soon expect to find very advantageous in getting work.

The colored people will need little help except in helping themselves. We are not going to make beggars of them. Will you please consult with your Society in regard to getting a box of straw & materials for braiding — and yarn & needles & other materials for manufacture . . .

*Savannah Wharf on "a stack" of boxes barrels & trunks*
*Dec. 1st 1865.*

Dear Mrs. May;[2]

Since I saw you, I have been almost like a bag of the wind; at no time sufficiently settled to report on "Winter plans."

The last six weeks of our vacation were to have been given to pleasant recreation, and farewell glances into beloved households in the northern cities, but a crying need for someone who knew the lay of the land, to found a family[3] in Norfolk made us turn our steps that way, instead; where we took a large empty old house (but two doors from the one we occupied last season) and fitted it up for the teachers. The day after we arrived, we reopened all the schools belonging to our family, and held them in a large church three weeks till other members came, teaching regularly and faithfully all who were ready to come to school. The schools are never full till Winter — all working, who are able, as long as they can get "jobs"; many selling cakes and candies about the streets. Each day the stragglers came in — and all took hold, with a good will, to learn. Mr. Banfield[4] was the young man sent out by the society to be gentleman of the house, and we three worked together in converting the dismal, deserted old place, into a pleasant home.

As soon as the family came, we gave over the schools, and opened two large schools at the Rope Walk, (the Refugee Camp) — of which we had general supervision. I wish you could have seen our grotesque, wild, lawless menagerie of a school, the first few days, when it seemed as if the little "fliberty gibbets" had arms and legs by the dozens; and all seemed to have more than the lawful number of tongues — the third day, saw an orderly and most interesting school; and I could hardly believe it had any relationship to the first days gathering. These schools we held while we remained; taking care of the old women's home, in addition; — and fitting them up for Winter — visiting the families of the sick and needy; and attending to the wants of all old & extremely destitute people, in the time not given to the school. The enthusiastic welcomings of the people on our return, were most touching as well as gratifying. They told us they knew we were coming back; though we had told them we certainly should not — when we left. "Wese been a praying for yer, — and prayin you might come back to us; for you knowd our ways and trials, as if you was of us, always; and peared like we could tell you, and you could understand & do for us, as no one else could" said they.

"Teachers are wanted in Georgia — only men — it not being agreeable, proper, or safe for ladies — Who'll go?" We reported ourselves as ready to start any time at a days notice & Nov. 20th Mr. Banfield, Miss Ellen B. Haven (of Portsmouth N.H. one of our family and a particular friend of ours) Lucy & I took the overland route for Savannah. Nine toilsome tedious days of tortuous terrible traveling brought us to this lovely (all but the dirt) city.

I marvel much that we are here alive — traveling as we did, day and night — the wheels' getting on fire — axles breaking, frequent fording and occasional collisions — the roads, engines and cars, so much out of order. Most grateful too am I to be thus far on the road. Our final destination I know not, the agent of the State being in the interior and not answering our telegram (wh. probably do not reach [him?]).

Savannah is ravishingly lovely: all the streets are very wide — running entirely across the city, dividing it in squares, like Phila. A broad strip of green, with trees on both sides, runs though the centre of the streets — which also have shade tees over the sidewalk. High in the gardens hang the golden oranges, sending their sweet perfume afar, and drooping over the full blooming Camilla [sic], which gladdens the eyes through the Winter. . . .

*Normal School Va.*
*Oct. 4th 1868*

Dear Miss Chase

I will venture to send you another letter hoping you will may get it I have not heard a word from you for the last year which keeps me in an anxious state Dear Miss Chase I cannot tell you how very anxious I am to hear from you — if you get this letter I will send my picture as I promise it and would like you to have one please if we are fortunate enough to take up our corresponds again I would like very much to have a picture of you and Miss Lucy. I will give you an account of my self. I am here in Virginia at school the school you wrote to tell me about paying my own way by working the girls work in doors and the boys on the farm the girls all have all the domestic affairs wash for the boys sow all the scrubbing to do

There are about 14 girls and 22 boys five from Charleston Mr. Jefferson are one of the number I like it very much indeed we are very comfortably fix our chambers are neatly furnish cottage setts and every convienientcy we have water pipes in the house a baithing room.

I will tell you the rules the bell ring at half pass five allowing us half our to dress then it ring at six for breakfast tha allow five minutes if you are not there in time you are mark the bell ring at eleven for the boys to stop work and fix for dinner and school we dine at 12 clear up our dineing room and get in school by one we have school from one to five and then we recrute about a half our and the bell ring for evening prayers after prayers we go in to supper at half pass seven the bell ring for us to study we study untill half pass 8 the bell ring for us to get ready for bed at nine it ring for us to out the lights, and the best of it were have such a very kind Matron She tries in every way to make us happy each schollar love her and would not be happy without her She is a Miss Breck from Massachusetts. I hear from home pretty often Sarah did not come she is at home My sisters did not think wise for both of us to leave home the rebs have taken Mr. Sumners school building at the corner of Morris and Jasper Court where we spent those delightful ours in the afternoon trying to gain kowledge tha have it for the Colored Children the picture you gave I had it very neatly frame in a guild fram I have sent to have it here with me

Louissia Elliott expect to come on very soon Louissia are one of your schollrs dear Miss Chase I am very anxious to see you I often wish you were here to teach I trust I will have the pleausure of seeing you once more. Should we not meet on earth may we meet in heaven where parting is no more give my best love to Miss Lucy tell her I will write her next —

Good bye with a double portion of love.

Yours truly,

Julia A. Rutledge

NOTE: The above letter to Sarah Chase is reproduced with the errors uncorrected.

*Julia Rutledge, the author, is a young African American woman who had just learned to read and write and now is working in a school.*

Gordonsville, Virginia
Decr 14th '69

Miss Lowell,[5]
 My kind, generous frd:
 Excuses are said to be "lame"; but surely mine halt not; they are indeed sure footed, I am still alone! . . .
 In the meantime, although my duties are onerous, I am delighted with my school. As I am alone, of course, the school is ungraded, and my classes are many; but I keep school until half past three; and, very often until four o'clock, and so I am able to add what I will call intellectual exercises to the ordinary exercises. I oblige every class to learn the meaning of all the important words in every-days reading-lessons; and I am daily gratified by their promptness and accuracy in defining the words, when they stand in class. I appoint, every morning, one from each class as interlocutor, and I oblige the whole school to listen to all the definitions; while all who can write, put upon their slates the words in their own lessons, with the definitions thereof. Time is demanded for that exercise, but it is indeed well spent. The children, all of them enjoy it. Most of them have one class in the Fr'dm'ns Book which offers an amazing store of valuable words.[6] I frequently call the attention of the whole school to illustrations of the meaning of familiar words. I spend a good deal of time in teaching Arithmetic both Mental and Written. Many of the children add, almost without halting, long columns of figures which I place upon the black-board, and many of them can mentally add, subtract, multiply and divide, units tens, and even hundreds with readiness. I spend so much time upon these exercises that I can mark the improvement, which is rapid. I have three classes in Geography, and I give, daily, lessons to the whole school on Maps. All the children can navigate the Gulfs and Bays of the Globe, and they are now journeying with pleasure through the U.S., halting at the capital cities and sailing on the pleasant rivers. In addition to the defining exercise, of which I have told you, I hear the spelling and defining of the words above the reading lessons, and I also hear the whole school spell daily from a speller. . . .
 Alone, too, I keep a night school. For awhile, I kept it five nights in the week, but generally I have but three night sessions. What little time

these labors leave me is industriously seized hold of by the needy and sociable, who, having no love for the rebels about them, would fain seek help from me; and give me the reverence they love to bestow on a white skin.

Sincerely,
Lucy Chase

# Hard Work Every Day: A New England Woman's Diary in Dixie

## Mary Ames

From Mary Ames,
*From a New England Woman's Diary in Dixie in 1865*
(Springfield, Mass.: Plimpton Press, 1906).

*Perhaps more than any other writings, these simple diary entries of Mary Ames (1831–1903) (not the Mary Clemmer Ames of the earlier selection) typify the flavor of daily life for an average teacher. Ames and her friend Emily Bliss, natives of Springfield, Massachusetts, spent fifteen months on the South Carolina Sea Islands at the end of the war, when supplies were scarce, sickness and death stalked everyone, and Yankee teachers, isolated from and ostracized by Southern white communities, depended on the African American community for survival. These excerpts illustrate, among other themes, the closeness that grew between the freedmen and their Northern teachers.*

*Ames' Diary, written in 1865 and 1866, was published in 1906 in memory of her sister, and to provide a scholarship for an African American student to Hampton Institute, a historically black college founded in 1868 for the education of the freedmen.*

*May 17 [1865].* A very warm morning. We find our half-mile walk to school tiresome. A large school, sixty-six scholars, and rather unruly. Poor Emily is not adapted to deal with such rough boys. I am obliged to go to her aid and stamping my feet and shouting my commands, bring them to order. We are teaching the children the days of the week, the months, and also to count.

Six new scholars. A woman came with a prayer-book, asking to be taught to read it. We told her we would teach her willingly, but it would be some time before she could read that. She was satisfied, and as she was leaving, put her hand under her apron and brought out two eggs — one she put in Emily's lap, the other in mine.

*May 18.* The evening was delightfully cool. We had our first evening school for men and women on our piazza. It was well attended, all sitting on the floor and steps. One woman, who was much bent with rheumatism, and seemed very old, said she was "Mighty anxious to know something."

*June 2.* Mr. Everett is quite sick. We sent to the commissary for the Government doctor, who had gone to Beaufort. Then we sent to headquarters for Dr. Mason. He says Mr. Everett has typhoid symptoms.

At school there were seventy scholars, who behaved pretty well. A girl came just recovering from smallpox. She was indignant when we sent her away, but we pacified her by telling her she could come back in a few weeks. Going up to our bedroom we met on the stairs a rattlesnake. We screamed lustily, and Uncle Jack, Jim, George, and Zack[7] appeared. I jumped over it, and it fell through the balusters to the hall, where the men killed it. We find in our room many holes where it could have come up in the walls from the cellar. To-morrow we shall paper our walls with newspapers.

*Sunday, June 4.* No church going — too warm, and the walk too long for Sundays, as we are obliged to take it every week-day. We seated ourselves on the piazza to write letters. Soon a crowd of children were around us, all wanting books, and before we knew it we were teaching school. George and Zack came with the others. George is patient and promising. We are surprised at the ease with which he acquires the sound of words. He teaches his father after leaving us.

*Sunday, June 11.* Hottest morning we have had — not a breath of air. Dr. Mason advises us to leave the island as soon as possible — not safe for us to stay much longer. A woman who brought some cucumbers said she would make any sacrifice to serve us, who were doing so much to teach her children, who knew nothing but how to handle a hoe. George killed another rattlesnake under the plum tree, — they are after the figs — horrid creatures!

*June 13 and 14.* Intolerably hot days — rather cooler at night. Had a very large school, one hundred and one scholars — too many — cannot keep order with so many. I am well worn out before noon with shouting and stamping, for I am obliged to help Emily when she gets into difficulty. We stayed after school closed with three unruly boys, rough and tough customers, who confessed that they liked to tease us; but they were ashamed and promised to do better in the future.

Captain Storrs called. He told us there were five guerillas at camp; they had been caught on the island, but there is no evidence to convict them and they will probably be set at liberty.

*June 15.* Hot, hotter, hottest! Impossible to go up to the church for school. The children came down to see why we did not appear. We kept them and had school on the piazza; Emily there, and I down in the yard.

Mr. Blake brought whisky and remedies for Mr. Everett. He went to Beaufort for them, and nearly lost his life coming back. A storm arose, and the high wind blew their little boat thirty miles out to sea; if he had not had a small compass, he could not have got back. Mr. Blake gave us liberty to stop teaching when we like, and we have decided, as it is so fearfully hot and Emily's head troubles her so much, to have school in our house until we can go to the bay for our vacation.

*June 16.* Jim and Uncle Jerry have cleared out our big front room and arranged some boards on blocks for seats for the older children. The little ones can sit on the floor. Fifty came this morning. They are to bring stools — as many as have them — so we shall get on well.

Mr. Everett bade us farewell, riding off on his white beast; he seemed pretty weak. Mr. Redpath writes that we are to report to Mr. Pillsbury, as he himself goes North on the next steamer, and advises us to close our school. All the Charleston schools are closed, as there is much sickness; one northern teacher having died. He thinks we had better go North for our vacation. We cannot do that, for we should never return.

If our friends at home could only see our flowers! Cloth of gold roses and lovely Cape Jessamines. The evening was pleasant; the children sang to us and we told them stories, — Red Riding Hood, etc. They had never listened before to stories of any kind, and were most attentive.

*June 19.* We like the new school arrangement, for we do not get so warm, can wear loose sacks, and can spare our lungs.

When we feel tired, we sing, which they all enjoy. They particularly delight in singing "Hang Jeff Davis to a sour apple tree."

The children told us some of their experiences in slave life. One boy, Tom, showed us deep scars on his arms; said they were from severe whippings. When about eight years old, he rode a horse to a distant place, and lost the colt that was following; and of course was whipped.

*Sunday, June 25.* The sun came out and we had Sunday school in the school-room. I do the preaching and Emily attends to the singing. She is highly amused at my teachings. What surprises me is that they know so little of the life of Christ; not knowing even of his birth, but they all are familiar with his sayings. They all believe in a hell! I asked the children whom they love best. Some answered "God", Zack said, "Ma, she loves me and feeds me." . . .

*[Fall 1865.]* When we made our the school report to send to Boston, we were surprised that out of the hundred, only three children knew their age, nor had they the slightest idea of it, one large boy told me he was "Three months old." The next day many of them brought pieces of wood or bits of paper with straight marks made on them to show how many years they had lived. One boy brought a family record written in a small book. . . .

We had been inconvenienced by the lack of a chimney in the school-house. One day when, choking with smoke, we asked the children if some of their fathers could not come and fix the stove, they began, "I haven't any father" — "I live with Aunty," and so on. We were surprised to learn how orphaned our school was. Eight of Captain Bacheller's men built a chimney for us. In return we gave each of them a book, which pleased them. They were fine-looking fellows and all of them could read. . . .

*[Winter 1866.]* A [government] horse was sent to Emily; we had the carry all and a buggy which came from home. We were altogether so comfortable that we invited my sister, Elizabeth, my friend Mrs.

French, and Emily's sister and her husband to visit us. They came in February; helped us with our school and criticized our housekeeping.

Robert and Rhoda had come with us from the bay, Rhoda was not the best of cooks, and now that she was "Striving for religion," she and Robert had to go to so many "Shouts" and dances that we moved them into the basement, so that they might not disturb us by their late hours.

Perhaps this "Striving" was the cause of her erratic cooking. We ate in silence the dried beef which she fried for breakfast, only wondering why the bacon was so queer.

Our friends, knowing that Emily was unusually fastidious, were surprised that we could live "in such a shiftless way." They said they "Would have things decent and the food properly cooked." We offered them the privilege of employing their New England energy in keeping house for us. One day was enough. At the end of it, I asked my friend where she had been all day? "In the kitchen, holding up the stovepipe so that Lizzie could bake!"

They taught the alphabet to the little children who had forgotten it during the smallpox vacation, and they clothed the other ones, who went from the school to the house in squads of four or five, coming back completely metamorphosed, their mouths stretched from ear to ear with delight. . . .

In May we moved to the bay with our school benches and books, and had a large school there, but a month later the Freedmen's Bureau was dissolved and we were notified that our services were no longer needed. As we were so well established, we obtained permission from the Superintendent of Schools in Charleston to continue, although our large salary of twenty dollars a month was stopped. My salary had always been paid through the Bureau by Mr. Charles Hubbard, of Boston, whose pleasure it was to be responsible for one teacher. . . . We closed the school in July, but the heat was so intense that we did not wish to travel until it was cooler.

In September we returned the "union" horse and confiscated carry-all, which had served us and the small pox patients, and sent to Governor Aiken his furniture which we had bought from the negroes; one piece was the armchair given him by his mother when he was elected governor of South Carolina.

The houses all about us were occupied by Edisto families, who had taken possession of their own. Mr. Edings, the owner of the house we had lived in both summers, wrote that he too wanted to come back.

There was no place for us, and in the last week of September, 1866, we said goodbye to Edisto and our negro friends.

# An African American Teacher in South Carolina

—◦⟨❧⟩◦—

## Charlotte L. Forten

From Ray A. Billington, ed.,
*The Journal of Charlotte L. Forten*
(New York: Dryden Press, 1953), and
Charlotte L. Forten, "Life on the Sea Islands,"
*Atlantic Monthly* (May 1864), pp. 67–86.

*Charlotte Forten (1837–1914) was among a small group of African American women and men who went south to teach in freedmen's schools. She left a reveal-ing record of her experiences: a very personal, private journal, and a lengthy "pub-lic" essay that appeared in the* Atlantic Monthly. *The two pieces of writing —which are not always in agreement — are interspersed, below, for contrast. It is not the essay, but the journal, that reveals Forten's struggles with racial prejudice and racial identity, along with her feminist concerns. These issues often deflected her attention from the literary and cultural pursuits that she loved.*

*The granddaughter of a prosperous Philadelphia sailmaker, Forten joined in the abolitionist work of her family. Forten's family educated her at home, so that she could avoid the segregated Philadelphia schools. She completed her education at Salem State Normal School in Massachusetts, and was the first African American to teach white children there. A deeply intellectual, reflective woman who flour-ished in literary and abolitionist circles, Charlotte Forten went south in 1862 to join Laura Towne (see reference in Towne selection that follows) and take part in the Port Royal Experiment on the South Carolina Sea Islands. Teaching there tried her professional competence, gave her little of the privacy that she needed, and accentuated her sense of racial isolation; after a year and a half of service, she returned to Philadelphia. In 1878 she married Francis Grimké, a former slave, and the son of Henry Grimké, a white man and brother of Sarah and Angelina Grimké,* noted proponents of abolition and women's rights.

## From the Journal, 1854–1862

*Salem, Massachusetts. Monday, Oct. 23 1854.* At last I have received the long expected letter, which to my great joy contains the eagerly desired permission to remain. I thank father very much for his kindness, and am determined that so far as I am concerned, he shall never have cause to regret it. I will spare no effort to become what he desires that I should be; to prepare myself well for the responsible duties of a teacher, and to live for the good that I can do my oppressed and suffering fellow-creatures. . . .

*Sunday, Jan. 18 1856.* Dined with Mr. and Mrs. P[utnam]. We talked of the wrongs and sufferings of our race. Mr. P[utnam] thought me too sensitive. — But, oh, how inexpressibly bitter and agonizing it is to feel oneself an outcast from the rest of mankind, as we are in this country! To me it is *dreadful, dreadful.* Were I to indulge in the thought I fear I should become insane. But I do not *despair.* I will not *despair;* though very often I can hardly help doing so. God help us! We are indeed a wretched condition. I will do *all,* all the *very little* that lies in my power, while life and strength last! . . .

*Monday, Nov. 15 1858.* . . . I am *lonely* to-night. I long for one earnest sympathizing soul to be in close communion with my own. I long for the pressure of a loving hand in mine, and touch of loving lips upon my aching brow. I long to lay my weary head upon an earnest heart, which beats for me, — to which I am dearer far than all the world beside. There is none, for me, and never will be. I could only love one whom I could look up to, and reverence, and the *one* would never think of such a poor little ignoramus as I. But what a selfish creature I am. This is a forlorn old maid's reverie, and yet I am only twenty-one. But I am weary of life, and would gladly lay me down and rest in the quiet grave. There, alone, is peace, peace! . . .

*Friday, Nov. 19.* Went to town with Aunt H[arriet] . . . This eve. Went to hear Mr. Curtis. I have rarely been so delighted with any lecture as I have been to-night with "Fair Play for Women." It is as much Anti-Slavery as Woman's Rights. The magnificent voice of the orator — the finest voice I have ever heard, his youth, beauty and eloquence, and the fearlessness with which he avowed his noble and radical sentiments before that immense, fashionable, and doubtless mostly pro-slavery audience, — all these impressed me greatly, and awakened all my enthusiasm. I *will not* despair when such noble souls as he devote the glory of their genius and their youth to the holy cause of Truth and Freedom. . . .

*Salem, June 22, 1862.* More penitent than ever I come to thee again, old Journal, long neglected friend. More than two years have elapsed since I last talked to thee — two years full of changes. A little while ago a friend read to me Miss Mullock's "Life for a Life." The Journal letters, which I liked so much, — were as first addressed to an unknown friend. So shall mine be. What name shall I give to thee, oh, *ami inconnu?* It will be safer to give merely an initial — A. And so, dear A, I will tell you a little of my life for the past two years. When I wrote to you last, — on a bright, lovely New Year's Day, I was here in old Salem, and in this very house. What a busy winter that was for me, I was assisting my dear Miss S[hepard] with one of her classes, and at the same time studying, and reciting at the Normal, Latin, French and a little Algebra. Besides I was taking German lessons. Now was I not busy, dear A? Yet is seems to me I was never so happy. I enjoyed life perfectly, and all the winter was strong and well. But when Spring came my health gave way. First my eyesight failed me, and the German which I liked better than anything else, which it was a real luxury to study had to be given up, and then all my other studies. My health continuing to fail, I was obliged to stop teaching, and go away. . . .

Week before last I had a letter from Mary S[hepard] asking me to come on and take charge of S.C.'s[?] classes during the summer, so she was obliged to go away. How gladly I accepted, you, dear A, may imagine. I had been *longing* so for a breath of N[ew] E[ngland] air, for a glimpse of the sea, for a walk over our good hills. . . . We left P[hilidephia] on Tuesday, the 10th; stopped a little while in N[ew] Y[ork]. . . . Then took the evening boat, and reached here Wed[nesday] morn. Mrs. I[ves][8] gave us a most cordial welcome; and we immediately felt quite at home. . . .

*Sunday, July 6.* Let me see? How did I spend last week? In teaching, as usual, until Friday, on which, being the "glorious Fourth," we had no school, and I went to Framingham to the Grove Meeting.[9]

Ah, friend of mine, I must not forget to tell you about a little adventure I met with to-day. I was boarding with Mrs. R[?] a very good anti-slavery woman, and kind and pleasant as can be. Well, when I appeared at the dinner-table to-day, it seems that a *gentlemen* took umbrage at sitting at the same table with one whose skin chanced to be "not colored like his own," and rose and left the table. Poor man! He feared contamination. But the charming part of the affair is that I, with eyes intent upon my dinner, and mind entirely engrossed (by Mr. Phillips' glorious words, which were still sounding in my soul), did not notice this person's presence nor disappearance. So his proceedings were quite lost upon me, and I sh'ld have been in a state of blissful ignorance as to his very existence had not the hostess afterward spoken to me about it, expressing the wish, good woman — that my "feelings were not hurt." I told her the truth, and begged her to set her mind perfectly at ease, for even had I have noticed the simpleton's behavior it w'ld not have troubled me. I felt no thorough a contempt for such people to allow myself to be wounded by them. . . .

### From "Life on the Sea Islands," 1864

It was on the afternoon of a warm, murky day late in October that our steamer, the United States, touched the landing at Hilton Head. A motley assemblage had collected on the wharf — officers, soldiers, and "contrabands" of every size and hue: black was, however, the prevailing color. . . .

From Hilton Head to Beaufort the same long, low line of sandy coast, bordered by trees; formidable gunboats in the distance, and the gray ruins of an old fort, said to have been built by the Huguenots more than two hundred years ago. Arrived at Beaufort, we found that we had not yet reached our journey's end. While waiting for the boat which was to take us to our island of St. Helena, we had a little time to observe the ancient town. . . .

Little colored children of every hue were playing about the streets, looking as merry and happy as children ought to look, — now that the evil shadow of Slavery no longer hangs over them. Some of the officers we met did not impress us favorably. They talked flippantly, and sneeringly of the negroes, whom they found we had come down to teach, using an epithet more offensive than gentlemanly. They assured us that there was great danger of Rebel attacks, that the yellow fever prevailed to an alarming extent, and that, indeed, the manufacture of coffins was the only business that was at all flourishing at present. Although by no means daunted by these alarming stories, we were glad when the announcement of our boat relieved us from their edifying conversation.

We rowed across to Ladies Island, which adjoins St. Helena, through the splendors of a grand Southern sunset. The gorgeous clouds of crimson and gold were reflected as in a mirror in the smooth, clear waters below. As we glided along, the rich tones of the negro boatmen broke upon the evening stillness, — sweet, strange, and solemn: —

> *Jesus make de blind to see,*
> *Jesus make de cripple walk,*
> *Jesus make de deaf to hear.*
> *Walk, in kind Jesus!*
> *No man can hender me. . . .*

Arrived at the headquarters of the general superintendent, Mr. S., we were kindly received by him and the ladies, and shown into a large parlor, where a cheerful wood-fire glowed in the grate. It had a home-like look; but still there was a sense of unreality about everything, and I felt that nothing less than a vigorous "shaking-up," such as Grandfather Smallweed daily experienced, would arouse me throughly to the fact that I was in South Carolina.

The next morning L. and I were awakened by the cheerful voices of men and women, children and chickens, in the yard below. We ran to the window, and looked out. Women in bright-colored handkerchiefs, some carrying pails on their heads, were crossing the yard, busy with their morning work; children were playing and tumbling around them. On every face there was a look of serenity and cheerfulness. My heart gave a great throb of happiness as I looked at them, and thought, "They are free! So long down-trodden, so long crushed to the earth, but now in their old homes, forever free!" And I thanked God that I had lived to see this day.

After breakfast Miss T.[10] drove us to Oaklands, our future home. The road leading to the house was nearly choked with weeds. The house itself was in a dilapidated condition, and the yard and garden had a sadly neglected look. But there were roses in bloom; we plucked handfuls of feathery, fragrant acacia-blossoms; ivy crept along the ground and under the house. The freed people on the place seemed glad to see us. After talking with them, and giving some directions for cleaning the house, we drove to the school, in which I was to teach. It is kept in the Baptist church, — a brick building, beautifully situated in a grove of live-oaks. These trees are the first objects that attract one's attention here; not that they are finer than our Northern oaks, but because of the singular gray moss with which every branch is heavily draped. This hanging moss grows on nearly all the trees, but on none so luxuriantly as on the live-oak. The pendants are often four or five feet long, very graceful and beautiful, but giving the trees a solemn, almost funeral look. The school was opened in September. Many of the children had, however, received instruction during the summer. It was evident that they had made very rapid improvement, and we noticed with pleasure how bright and eager to learn many of them seemed. . . .

The first day at school was rather trying. Most of my children were very small, and consequently restless. Some were too young to learn the alphabet. These little ones were brought to school because the older children — in whose care their parents leave them while at work — could not come without them. We were therefore willing to have them come; although they seemed to have discovered the secret of perpetual motion, and tried one's patience sadly. But after some days of positive, though not severe treatment, order was brought out of chaos, and I found but little difficulty in managing and quieting the tiniest and most restless spirits. I never before saw children so eager to learn, although I had had several years' experience in New England schools. Coming to school is a constant delight and recreation to them. They come here as other children go to play. The older ones, during the summer, work in the fields from early morning until eleven or twelve o'clock, and then come into school, after their hard toil in the hot sun, as bright and as anxious to learn as ever.

Of course there are some stupid ones, but these are the minority. The majority learn with wonderful rapidity. Many of the grown people are desirous of learning to read. It is wonderful how a people who have been so long crushed to the earth, so imbruted as these have been, — and they are said to be among the most degraded negroes of the South, — can have so great a desire for knowledge, and such a capability for attain it. One cannot believe that the haughty Anglo-Saxon race, after centuries of such an experience as these people have had, would be very much superior to them. And one's indignation increases against inferiority while they themselves use every means in their power to crush and degrade them, denying them every right and privilege, closing against them every avenue of elevation and improvement. Were they, under such circumstances, intellectual and refined, they would certainly be vastly superior to any other race that ever existed.

After the lessons, we used to talk freely to the children, often giving them slight sketches of some of the great and good men. Before teaching them the "John Brown" song, which they learned to sing with great spirit, Miss T. told them the story of the brave old man who had dies for them.[11] I told them about Toussaint,[12] thinking it well they should know what one of their own color had done for his race. They listened attentively, and seemed to understand. We found it rather hard to keep their attention in school. It is not strange, as they have been so entirely unused to intellectual concentration. It is necessary to interest them every moment, in order to keep their thoughts from wandering. Teaching here is consequently far more fatiguing than at the North. In the church, we had of course but one room in which to hear all the children; and to make one's self heard, when there were often as many as a hundred and forty reciting at once, it was necessary to tax the lungs very severely. . . .

In the evenings, the children frequently came in to sing and shout for us. These "shouts" were very strange, — in truth, almost indescribable. It is necessary to hear and see in order to have any clear idea of them. The children form a ring, and move around in a kind of shuffling dance, singing all the time. Four or five stand apart, and sing very energetically, clapping their hands, stamping their feet, and rocking their bodies to and fro. These are the musicians, to whose performance the shouters keep perfect time. The grown people on this plantation did not shout, but they do on some of the other plantations. It is very comical to see little children, not more than three or four years old, entering into the performance with all their might. But the shouting of the grown people is rather solemn and impressive than otherwise. We cannot determine whether it has a religious character or not. Some of the people tell us that it has, others that it has not. But as the shouts of the grown people are always in connection with their religious meetings, it is probable that they are the barbarous expression of religion, handed down to them from their African ancestors, and destined to pass away under the influence of Christian teachings. The people on this island have no songs. . . .

Christmas night, the children came in and had several grand shouts. They were too happy to keep still.

"Oh, Miss, all I want to do is to sing and shout!" said our little pet, Amaretta. And sing and shout she did, to her heart's content.

She read nicely, and was very fond of books. The tiniest children are delighted to get a book in their hands. Many of them already know their letters. The parents are eager to have them learn. They sometimes said to me, —

"Do, Miss, let de chil'en learn eberyting dey can. *We* nebber hab no chance to learn nuttin', but we wants de chil'en to learn."

They were willing to make many sacrifices that their children may attend school. One old woman, who had a large family of children and grandchildren, came regularly to school in the winter, and took her seat among the little ones. She was at least sixty years old. Another woman — who had one of the best faces I ever saw — came daily, and brought her baby in her arms. It happened to be one of the best babies in the world, a perfect little "model of deportment," and allowed its mother to pursue her studies without interruption. . . .

Daily the long-oppressed people of these islands are demonstrating their capacity for improvement in learning and labor. What they have accomplished in one short year exceeds our utmost expectations. Still the sky is dark; but through the darkness we can discern a brighter future. We cannot but feel that the day of final and entire deliverance, so long and often so hopelessly prayed for, has at length begun to dawn upon this much-enduring race. An old freedman said to me one day, "De Lord make me suffer long time, Miss. 'Peared like we nebber was gwine to git troo. But now we's free. He bring us all out right at las'." In their darkest hours they have clung to Him, and we know He will not forsake them.

> *The poor among men shall rejoice,*
> *For the terrible one is brought to nought.*

While writing these pages I am once more nearing Port Royal.[13] The Fortunate Isles of Freedom are before me. I shall again tread the flower-skirted woodpaths of St. Helena, and the sombre pines and bearded oaks shall whisper in the sea-wind their grave welcome. I shall dwell again among "mine own people." I shall gather my scholars about me, and see smiles of greeting break over their dusky faces. My heart sings a song of thanksgiving at the thought that even I am permitted to do something for a long-abused race, and aid in promoting a higher, holier, and happier life on the Sea Islands.

## From the Journal, 1862–1863

*Friday, Oct. 31, 1862.* Miss T[owne] went to B[eaufort] to-day, and I taught for her. I enjoyed it much. The children were well-behaved and eager to learn. It will be a happiness to teach them.

I like Miss Murray so much.[14] She is of English parentage, born in the Provinces. She is one of the most whole-souled warm-hearted women I ever met. I felt drawn to her from the first (before I knew she was English) and of course I like her none the less for that.

Miss Towne also is a delightful person. "A charming lady" Gen. Saxton calls her and my heart echoes the words. She is housekeeper, physician, everything, here. The most indispensable person on the place, and the people are devoted to her. . . . And indeed she is quite a remarkable young lady. She is one of the earliest comers, and has done much good in teaching and superintending the negroes. She is quite young; not more than twenty-two or three[15] I sh'ld think, and is superintendent of two plantations. I like her energy and decision of character. Her appearance too is very interesting. . . .

*Wednesday, Nov. 5.* Had my first regular teaching experience, and to you and you only friend beloved, will acknowledge that it was not a very pleasant one. Part of my scholars are very tiny, — babies, I call them — and it is hard to keep them quiet and interested while I am hearing the larger ones. They are too young even for the alphabet, it seems to me. I think I must write home and ask somebody to send me picture-books and toys to amuse them with. I fancied Miss T[owne] looked annoyed when, at one time the little ones were unusually restless. Perhaps it was only my fancy. Dear Miss M[urray] was kind and considerate as usual. She is very lovable. Well I *must* not be discouraged. Perhaps things will go on better to-morrow. . . .

We've established our household on — as we hope — a firm basis. We have *Rose* for our little maid-of-all-work, *Amaretta* for cook, washer, and ironer, and *Cupid*, yes Cupid himself, for clerk, oysterman[16] and future coachman. I must also inform you dear A., that we have made ourselves a bed, whereon we hope to rest to-night, for rest I certainly did not last night, despite innumerable blankets designed to conceal and render inactive the bones of the bed. But said bones did so protrude that sleep was almost an impossibility to our poor little body.

Everything is still very, very strange. I am not at all homesick. But it does seem so long since I saw some who are very dear, and I believe I am quite sick for want of a letter. But patience! patience! *That* is a luxury which cannot possibly be enjoyed before the last of next week. . . .

Talked to the children a little while to-day about the noble Toussaint

[L'Ouverture]. They listened very attentively. It is well that they sh'ld know what one of their own color c'ld do for his race. I long to inspire them with courage and ambition (of a noble sort,) and high purpose.

It is noticeable how very few mulattos there are here. Indeed in our school, with one or two exceptions, the children are all black. A little mulatto child strayed into the school house yesterday — a pretty little thing, with large beautiful black eyes and lovely long lashes. But so dirty! I longed to seize and thoroughly cleanse her. The mother is a good-looking woman, but quite black. "Thereby," I doubt not, "hangs a tale.". . .

*Monday Nov. 17.* Had a dreadfully wearying day in school, of which the less said the better. Afterward drove with the ladies to "The Corner," a collection of negro houses, whither Miss T[owne] went on a doctoring expedition. The people there are very pleasant. Saw a little baby, just borne [sic] today — and another — old Venus' great grand-child for whom I made the little pink frock. These people are very gratiful [sic]. The least kindness that you do them they insist on repaying in some way. We have had a quantity of eggs and potatoes brought us despite our remonstrances. Today one of the women gave me some Tanias. Tania is a queer looking root. After it is boiled it looks a little like potato, but is much larger. I don't like the taste.

*Sunday, Dec. 14.* There were several new arrivals at church to-day. Among them Miss T[owne]'s sister — Miss Rosa T[owne]. She does not look at all like Miss Laura. Is very fair, and has light hair; an English looking person, as I told her sister. A Miss Ware was also there. . . . A lovely but good face. . . .

Nearly everybody was looking gay and happy; and yet I came home with the blues. Threw myself on the bed, and for the first time since I have been here, felt very lonely and pitied myself. But I have reasoned myself into a more sensible mood and am better now. Let me not forget again that I came not here for friendly sympathy or for anything else but to work, and to work hard. Let me do that faithfully and well. To-night answered Mr. McK[im]'s letter, and commenced one to my dear A[nnie] about whom I feel very anxious. . . .

*Thursday March 24 1863.* With Miss T[owne] came the latest arrival — Mr. Pierce — the former *pioneer* down here. His manners are exceedingly pleasant — I can't help acknowledging that, though I had a preconceived dislike for him, because I had heard that he said he "wanted no colored missionaries nor teachers down here." His conversation at table to-night was most entertaining and genial. But I shall take an early opportunity of asking an explanation for the speech. If he said that, of course there's no possibility of my liking him. . . .

*Sunday, July 26.* A few week since I stopped going to the church finding it impossible to drive there longer through the heat of the day, and opened a small school for some of the children from Frogmore, in a carriage house on out place. Most of the children are crude little specimens. I asked them once what their ears were for. One bright-eyed little girl answered promptly "To put rings in." When Mrs. H[unn] asked some of them the same question. They said "To put cotton in." One day I had been telling them about metals; how they were dug from the ground, and afterward, in review, I asked "Where is iron obtained from?" "From the ground" was the prompt reply. "And gold?" "From the sky!" shouted a little boy.

I have found it very interesting to give them a kind of object lessons with the picture cards. They listen with eager attention, and seem to understand and remember very well what I tell them. But although this has been easier for me than teaching at the church — where, in addition to driving through the hot sun to get there, I was obliged to exert my lungs far above their strength to make myself heard when more than a hundred children were reciting at the same time in the same room — yet I have found my strength steadily decreasing, and have been every day tortured by a severe head ache. I take my good Dr.'s advice, therefore, and shall go North on a furlough — to stay until the unhealthiest season is over.

*At Sea — Friday, July 31.* Said farewell to Seaside and its kind household, white and black, and very early this morn Lieut. W[alton]'s boy drove me to Land's End, whence we were to take the steamboat which was to convey us to the steamer at Hilton Head.

And here we are, homeward bound.

# Emancipation's Primer:
## *The Freedmen's Book*

—⁘—

## *Lydia Maria Child*

From Lydia Maria Child, *The Freedmen's Book*
(Boston: Ticknor and Fields, 1865).

The Freedmen's Book, *compiled and edited by Lydia Maria Child (1802–
1880), is an anthology of works written by African Americans and white abolitionists. Used in freedmen's schools, it introduced former slaves (mainly adults) to
the written African American cultural tradition and encouraged racial pride.*

*Child was a distinguished woman of letters, the author of novels, political
essays on the rights of African Americans and Native Americans, and, for two years,
the editor of* The National Anti-Slavery Standard.

To the Freedmen

I have prepared this book expressly for you, with the hope that
those of you who can read will read it aloud to others, and that all of
you will derive fresh strength and courage from this true record of
what colored men have accomplished, under great disadvantages.

I have written all the biographies over again, in order to give you as
much information as possible in the fewest words. I take nothing for
my services; and the book is sold to you at the cost of paper, printing,
and binding. Whatever money you pay for any of the volumes will be
immediately invested in other volumes to be sent to freedmen in various parts of the country, on the same terms; and whatever money
remains in my hands, when the book ceases to sell, will be given to the
Freedmen's Aid Association, to be expended in schools for you and
your children.

Your old friend,
L. Maria Child

# Contents

| | | |
|---|---|---|
| IGNATIUS SANCHO | L. Maria Child | 1 |
| EXTRACT FROM THE TENTH PSALM | | 12 |
| PREJUDICE REPROVED | Lydia H. Sigourney | 13 |
| BENJAMIN BANNEKER | L. Maria Child | 14 |
| ETHIOPIA | Frances E.W. Harper* | 24 |
| THE HOUR OF FREEDOM | William Lloyd Garrison | 25 |
| WILLIAM BOEN | L. Maria Child | 26 |
| ANECDOTE OF GENERAL WASHINGTON | | 31 |
| PRAYER OF THE SLAVE | Bernard Barton | 32 |
| TOUSSAINT L'OUVERTURE | L. Maria Child | 33 |
| THE ASPIRATIONS OF MINGO | Mingo, a Slave* | 84 |
| BURY ME IN A FREE LAND | Frances E.W. Harper* | 85 |
| PHILLIS WHEATLEY | L. Maria Child | 86 |
| A PERTINENT QUESTION | Frederick Douglass* | 93 |
| THE WORKS OF PROVIDENCE | Phillis Wheatley* | 94 |
| THE DYING CHRISTIAN | Francis E.W. Harper* | 96 |
| KINDNESS TO ANIMALS | L. Maria Child | 97 |
| JAMES FORTEN | L. Maria Child | 101 |
| THE MEETING IN THE SWAMP | L. Maria Child | 104 |
| A REASONABLE REQUEST | Peter Williams* | 110 |
| THE SLAVE POET | George Horten, a Slave* | 111 |
| RATIE | Mattie Griffith | 114 |
| THE KINGDOM OF CHRIST | James Montgomery | 123 |
| PROGRESS OF EMANCIPATION IN THE BRITISH WEST INDIES | L. Maria Child | 124 |
| THE LAST NIGHT OF SLAVERY | James Montgomery | 146 |
| MADISON WASHINGTON | L. Maria Child | 147 |
| EXTRACT FROM THE VIRGINIA BILL OF RIGHTS | | 154 |
| PRAISE OF CREATION | George Horton* | 155 |
| FREDERICK DOUGLASS | L. Maria Child | 156 |
| HOW THE GOOD WORK GOES ON | | 176 |
| DEDICATION HYMN | J.M. Whitefield* | 177 |
| A PRAYER | John G. Whittier | 178 |
| WILLIAM AND ELLEN CRAFTS | L. Maria Child | 179 |
| SPRING | George Horton* | 205 |
| THE GOOD GRANDMOTHER | Harriet Jacobs* | 206 |
| THE COLORED MOTHER'S PRAYER | | 219 |
| WILLIAM COSTIN | | 220 |

| EDUCATION OF CHILDREN | L. Maria Child | 221 |
| THANK GOD FOR LITTLE CHILDREN | Frances E.W. Harper* | 226 |
| SAM AND ANDY | Harriet Beecher Stowe | 227 |
| JOHN BROWN | L. Maria Child | 241 |
| THE AIR OF FREEDOM | Frances E.W. Harper* | 243 |
| EMANCIPATION IN THE DISTRICT OF COLUMBIA | James Madison Bell* | 244 |
| THE LAWS OF HEALTH | L. Maria Child | 246 |
| PRESIDENT LINCOLN'S PROCLAMATION OF EMANCIPATION | Frances E.W. Harper* | 250 |
| NEW-YEARS DAY ON THE ISLANDS OF SOUTH CAROLINA | Charlotte L. Forten* | 251 |
| SONG OF THE NEGRO BOATMEN AT PORT ROYAL, S.C. | John G. Whittier | 257 |
| EXTRACT FROM SPEECH TO COLORED PEOPLE IN CHARLESTON | Hon. Henry Wilson | 259 |
| EXTRACT FROM SPEECH TO COLORED PEOPLE IN CHARLESTON | Hon. Judge Kelly | 261 |
| BLACK TOM | A Yankee Soldier | 263 |
| LETTER FROM A FREEDMAN | Jourdan Anderson* | 265 |
| COLONEL ROBERT C. SHAW | Eliza B. Sedgwick | 268 |
| ADVICE FROM AN OLD FRIEND | L. Maria Child | 269 |
| DAY OF JUBILEE | A.G. Duncan | 277 |

*The names of the colored authors are marked with an asterisk [Lydia Maria Child's note].

## The Aspirations of Mingo

*A slave in one of our Southern States, named Mingo, was endowed with uncommon abilities. If he had been a white man, his talents would have secured him an honorable position; but being colored, his great intelligence only served to make him an object of suspicion. He was thrown into prison, to be sold. He wrote the following lines on the walls, which were afterward found and copied. A Southern gentleman sent them to a friend in Boston, as a curiosity, and they were published in the Boston Journal, many years ago. The night after Mingo wrote them, he escaped* from the slave-prison; but he was tracked and caught by bloodhounds, who tore him in such a shocking manner that he died. By that dreadful process his great soul was released from his enslaved body. His wife lived to be an aged woman, and was said to have many of his poems in her possession. Here are the lines he wrote in his agony while in prison:

Good God! and must I leave them now,
My wife, my children, in their woe?
'Tis mockery to say I'm sold!
But I forget these chains so cold,
Which goad my bleeding limbs; though high
My reasons mounts above the sky.
Dear wife, they cannot sell the rose
Of love that in my bosom glows.
Remember, as your tears may start,
They cannot sell the immortal part.
Thou Sun, which lightest bond and free,
Tell em, I pray, is liberty
The lot of those who noblest feel,
And oftest to Jehovah kneel?
Then I may say, but not with pride,
I feel the rushings of the tide
Of reason and of eloquence,
Which strive and yearn for eminence.
I feel high manhood on me now,
A spirit-glory on my brow;
I feel a thrill of music roll,
Like angel-harpings, through my soul;
While poesy, with rustling wings,
Upon my spirit rests and sings.
He sweeps my heart's deep throbbing lyre,
Who touched Isaiah's lips with fire.

May God forgive his oppressors.

# New Rules for African American and White

—◦◦◦◦—

## Elizabeth Hyde Botume

From Elizabeth Hyde Botume,
*First Days Amongst the Contrabands* (1893; reprinted
New York: Arno Press and the *New York Times*, 1968).

*Turning her practiced and critical eye to the state of race relations after the Civil War, Elizabeth Hyde Botume analyzed her experiences living for three decades in the South in her work,* First Days Amongst the Contrabands *(1893). Her remark that African American's respect for "a white skin sometimes made us ashamed of our own race" suggests a sensibility that goes far beyond noblesse oblige. The memoir counterposes the teachers' lofty ideals and trials against the small satisfactions of the classroom. Botume believes that "nothing in the history of the world has ever equaled the magnitude and thrilling importance" of educating African Americans, but she spends her time as most of the freedmen's teachers did — finding seats for the students who crowd into her schoolroom, helping young girls mind babies and go to school, and welcoming her new assistant, Miss Lizzie, fresh from a teacher education program.*

*Originally from the Boston area, Botume was active nationally on behalf of African Americans — her name shows up frequently in the abolitionist conferences and publications. Her few extant letters indicate that she also took an active interest in the women's rights movement.*

## Slavery

People at the North knew but little of slavery as it existed in the United States seventy-five or even fifty years ago. It was a terra incognita to them. When brought fact to face with the slaves, as they were during the war, it was like the discovery of a new race. I do not mean political-ly. Everybody knows something of the politics of the times. History gives us the facts. What was known of the slaves themselves? Had they any individuality? Were they, as we were often told, only animals with certain brute force, but no capacity for self-government? Or were they reasoning beings?

"I do assure you," once said a Southern woman to me, "you might as well try to teach your horse or mule to read, as to teach these niggers. They *can't* learn."

"Then," said I, "will you be so kind as to tell me why they made stringent laws at the South against doing *what could not be done?*" . . .

The negro mind had never been cultivated; it was like an empty reservoir, waiting to be filled. Under their calm exterior was always a smouldering volcano ready to burst forth. . . .

Not long ago I heard some negro women talking of old times over their sewing. One said, —

"My father and the other boys used to crawl under the house an' lie on the ground to hear massa read the newspaper to missis when they first began to talk about the war."

"See that big oak-tree there?" said another. "Our boys used to climb into that tree an' hide under the long moss while massa was at supper, so as to hear him an' his company talk about the war when they come out in the piazza to smoke."

"I couldn't read, but my uncle could," said a third. "I was waiting-maid, an' used to help missis to dress in the morning. If massa wanted to tell her something he didn't want me to know, he used to spell it out. I could remember the letters, an' as soon as I got away I ran to uncle an' spelled them over to him, an' he told me what they meant."

I was attracted by this, and asked if she could do this now.

"Try me, missis; try me, an' see!" she exclaimed. So I spelled a long sentence as rapidly as possible, without stopping between the words. She immediately repeated it after me, without missing a letter.

The children of this woman were amongst the first to enter a freed-man's school during the war. They took to books as ducks take to water. The youngest, a boy, was really entered when a baby in his sister's arms, and was only allowed to remain because his nurse could not come without him. As soon as he could walk his mother complained he did not know anything. When he was three years old she was bitterly disappointed that he could not read.

"Why, if I had his chance," she exclaimed, rolling up her eyes and stretching out her hands, "do you think I would not learn!"

It goes without saying, that her children became good scholars. This youngest boy is now a leader amongst his own people. . . .

## Northern Friends

During this time my Northern friends, individually and collectively, were doing their utmost to help on the work "amongst the freedmen." . . .

The best gift of all was "Miss Fannie," who was forwarded to me just after New Year's, ostensibly to be my assistant. But I halt at the word, for she was everything to me, and to the poor people around me. Young, active, and enthusiastic, fresh from school, with all the new methods of study and teaching, she inspired an admiration and enthusiasm which fell little short of hero worship. . . . The first I saw of her she was standing in the schoolroom door radiant with delight. The children began to buzz, so I gave an extra recess; but they only gathered around the door on the piazza and gazed at us.

"Who da him?" I heard them say.

"Him's Miss Fonnie," said one girl, with superior knowledge, having heard me speak the name.

"Oh, but him's prime!" they declared. . . .

## Miss Lizzie

Now that field-work was over, all the contrabands flocked to the school, until the room was over-crowded. It took most of my time to enroll and place the newcomers. They appeared irregularly, and at all times and seasons.

"Please read me quick, ma'am; I'se hasty. I'se got a baby at home," said a big black woman. This is but a specimen of many other days. In vain did we struggle to bring order out of this confusion. In this dilemma, Miss Fannie signaled to her sister, "come over and help us;" and in due time, Miss Lizzie arrived.

That was a day of jubilee to the contrabands. The children, laughing and shouting, surrounded the house, and peeped into the windows. Miss Lizzie had to go out and be formally introduced before they dispersed. "Oh, but him jes' like Miss Fonnie," said Sally, a sometimes waitress.

In times of trouble the contrabands always came to their teachers for help and advice. Sometimes we were much embarrassed to know what to say or do. When I saw their implicit confidence in our knowledge and sympathy, I found it very hard to tell them I could do nothing.

A sick woman came to me one day, who was suffering from a serious organic trouble. After listening to her story, and getting all the facts, I said, "Auntie, this is beyond me. I really do not know what to do for you."

Her look of astonishment and dismay was really startling as she exclaimed, "O missis! You'na can read books, an in course you knows more'na we."

Yes, I could read books, but they did not tell me everything. In fact, I soon discovered they told me very little of what I needed to know most.

### The New Bell

I had expressed a wish for a bell for my schoolhouse, hoping to bring about a more regular attendance, with less delay. Immediately a Boston friend, who had been in the department, responded by sending me just what I needed. Oh, what a delight was this bell to the whole neighborhood! The children would collect around the house very early, and lie on the ground waiting and watching for it to ring. For a long time this was a mystery incomprehensible to them. They talked often to each other about "we bell," and seemed to feel as if each one had a kind of right of possession in it.

"Oh, but him can talk loud!" said the boys with delight. I told them all what the bell was for, where it came from and who sent it. Without consulting me they immediately named the school for our generous friends, "Hooper School, A No. 1."

The children were allowed to take turns in ringing the bell; but this was a privilege only granted as a reward for good behavior. . . .

A man and his wife stood together in a class to read. They were great stalwart creatures, black as ink. Their three children were in the class above them, having conquered words of one syllable.

As soon as the parents began to read, the children simultaneously darted to their sides to prompt them.

"Boy! Daddy, boy! Him don't know nothing." Laughingly said Dick, prompting him.

"Shut you mouf, boy! I only want to catch dat word, sure," the pleased father answered, scratching his head.

"Dem chillen too smart. I ain't know what to do wid' dem," declared the proud mother. . . .

Quite different from them was a "Combee"[17] woman, who came to school daily with a baby in her arms and two boys by her side. They all stood up to read together.

These families were refugees. They have all returned to their old homes on the "mainland." Primus, one of the boys, has become a teacher and a preacher, and is the wise man of that neighborhood. His mother comes to see me once a year, and tells with pride of her boy's position, always speaking of him as an "A No. 1 scholar."

### "Min' Chile"

Babies! There was a host of them, and it was not easy to keep them away from school. Even the tiniest creatures were brought along. Each child had its own nurse, and all wanted to be in school. So it was arranged that one girl should come in the morning and get a lesson, and then run home to mind child, and let the nurse come. But usually the one left behind would come on with the baby and wait around the house until relieved. She always brought with her a tin can with hominy for the child when hungry. It was not unusual for the little nurse to appear in her class as soon as it was called, having passed her baby along to any friend who was disengaged. There must have been some signal from the window, for a girl would ask "to step out for a minute," when the baby-tender would return in her place.

These babies needed but little care; even the youngest would eat hominy when hungry, and then go to sleep. I have seen eight and ten of these little black creatures asleep on the piazza at a time. Usually the nurse would take off her apron and spread it down for baby to lie on; that was all. But, at the best, babies were very confusing to the school. Finally, I engaged an old mamma to mind them during school hours. Now the little girls were happy. Each one brought her charge to Aunt Clara's house, and left it on her way to school. It was pleasant to look upon this primitive nursery and see these pickaninnies sitting upon the well-sanded floors, or asleep in the corner. . . .

About this time two little white girls presented themselves and asked to be taken into school. They belonged to a good old Southern family, but were out of the reach of any other school. The children of their mother's cook had told them what we were doing, and they were eager to be enrolled. They came regularly, and were very happy, and made good progress. The youngest was in the same class with her little black playfellow, both learning to read; but the black girl started first, and so was ahead.

It was touching to see her zeal in trying to help on her white com-

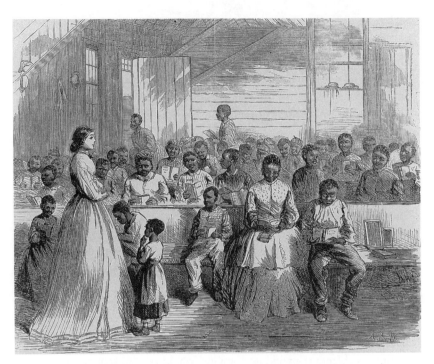

*View of primary classroom at the School for Freedmen, in the charge of Miss Green, at Vicksburg, Mississippi. Mechanical engraving published in* Harper's Weekly, *June 23, 1866.*

panion, and her manifest delight when her friend said anything particularly good.

But at the end of two months the little maidens told me with evident reluctance and regret, that they could not come any longer, "they were needed at home."

I suspected there were other reasons, so I called upon the mother, a most intelligent and refined woman. She confessed the Southern white people had "made so much fuss" because she allowed the children to go to a "*nigger school*," she felt obliged to take them way. She regretted this, for the children played all the time with their colored companions. They had been brought up with them, but must grow up in ignorance rather than be allowed to study with them.

"I would not care myself, but the young men laugh at my husband. They tell him he must be pretty far gone and low down when he sends his children to a '*nigger school*.' That makes him mad, and he is vexed with me," said the mother sadly.

We all greatly regretted that these bright young girls should be removed, and so lose the opportunity for study; but I could well understand the odium was too great to be resisted.

Nothing in the history of the world has ever equaled the magnitude and thrilling importance of the events then transpiring. Here were more than four millions of human beings just born into freedom; one day held in the most abject slavery, the next, "de Lord's free men." Free to come and to go according to the best lights given them. Every movement of their white friends was to them full of significance, and often regarded with distrust. Well might they sometimes exclaim, when groping from darkness into light, "Save me from my friend, and I will look out for my enemy."

Whilst the Union people were asking, "Those negroes! what is to be done with them?" they, in their ignorance and helplessness, were crying out in agony, "What will become of us?" They were literally saying, "I believe, O Lord! Help thou mine unbelief."

They were constantly coming to us to ask what peace meant for them? Would it be peace indeed? or oppression, hostility, and servile subjugation? This was what they feared, for they knew the temper of the baffled rebels as did no others.

"And this is what we fight for?" asked the young soldiers.

The hatred of some white people for the colored race amounted almost to frenzy. It was by no means confined to the old Southerners, but was largely shared by Northern adventurers, a host of whom had followed the army.

It took time for the freed people to find out who were their true friends. But they gradually learned to discriminate. Their respect, however, for a white skin was amazing and sometimes made us ashamed of our own race.

One of our colored men, who had been deceived, and grossly cheated, and ill-treated by one who was known as a missionary, recounted his troubles to me, exclaimed, —

"I declar', ma'am, he don't desarve to be a white man. He'll shuck han's wid hi right han', an' fling a brick-bat at you wid his lef'."

# An African American
# Oberlin Student Goes South

───❧───

## *Sara Stanley*

From the Amistad Research Center
at Tulane University,
New Orleans, Louisiana

*The granddaughter of a prosperous, slave-owning African American family in New Bern, North Carolina, Sara Stanley (1836–1918) was privately educated in the Stanley School run by her father. Her mother was a teacher in the school. The fourth of six siblings, she was light-skinned enough to be able to "pass," although she was disdainful of New Bern mulattos who set themselves apart from "colored" people. In 1852, at the age of sixteen, Stanley went north to Oberlin College, probably with an African American friend, and entered the "Literary Degree" program as one of the earliest African American students.*

*Throughout her documented career, Stanley spoke out against racism and for the equality of African Americans. A forceful and eloquent writer, Stanley received approbation for an antislavery speech of 1856 and a Civil War essay, both of which were widely circulated. In 1864 Stanley applied to become an American Missionary Association teacher of the freedmen. She was sent first to recently freed Norfolk, Virginia, where she spoke out against the racist attitudes of some white teachers, and found support from others. She also taught in St. Louis, Missouri, and Mobile, Alabama, where, in 1868, she met and married a white man, a highly risky and controversial act. Because of her light skin, this interracial marriage caused later confusion about which partner was white, which African American, but also protected her somewhat from Southern racist violence. We know little of the later years of her life except that she died in Philadelphia after living there some years on a widow's pension of eight dollars a month.*

*This selection of letters and documents is unusual in their forthright revelation of Sara Stanley's emotions — especially her self-criticism and her open anger at* injustice. In addition, the selections give a glimpse into the long and problematic transfer of responsibility for African American education from the Freedman's Bureau and the AMA to local white authorities for whom the education of African Americans remained anathema. One among a number of letters in the selections included here exemplifies the way in which teachers entered the marketplace — negotiating for salaries, travel expenses, and schoolroom supplies.

* This note draws on the research of Ellen NicKenzie Lawson and Marlene D. Merrill in The Three Sarahs: Documents of Antebellum Black College Women (New York: Edwin Mellen Press, 1984).

### Application to Teach Freedmen: Sara G. Stanley to American Missionary Association, 19 January 1864.

Cleveland, Ohio
Dear Sir (George Whipple):

I take the liberty of addressing you these lines, with the prayerful hope that you may spare one moment from the multitudinous and important affairs which engage your attention, to listen to my simple appeal.

I am a colored woman; having a slight admixture of negro blood in my veins; and have been for several years a teacher in the public schools of Ohio. Since the providence of God has opened in the South, so vast a field for earnest and self abnegating missionary labor, I have felt a strong conviction of duty, an irresistible desire to engage in teaching the freed people; to aid to the extent of what ability God has given me, in bringing these poor outcasts from the pale of humanity, into the family of man.

Possessing no wealth and having nothing to give but my life to the work, I therefore make this application to you. Can I become a teacher under the auspices of the American Missionary Association? I should be very glad and happy if it might be so, for my warmest and deepest feelings are enlisted in the cause.

"This is the way, walk ye on it," speaks a voice within my heart, and I know that no thought of suffering and privation, nor even death, should deter me from making every effort possible for the moral and intellectual salvation of these ignorant, and degraded people; children of a beneficent Father, and heirs of the kingdom of Heaven. And I feel moreover how much greater my own spiritual advancement will be, for while laboring for them, while living a life of daily toil, self sacrifice and denial, I can dwell nearer to God and my Savior and become constantly, by divine aid, richer in faith, richer in love, richer in all the graces of the Holy Spirit.

I am counseled to make this application to you by that noble Christian and philanthropist Rev. James A. Thome of this city. He further suggests that I request you, if you can not give me an appointment, to be so kind as to direct me to whom I might apply with the greater probability of success.

I shall be very grateful if you will send me word in reply to this. I know that the efforts of a single individual seem small and insignificant, but to me this is of the most vital importance.

Hoping that you will kindly bestow upon me a moment's attention. I remain

Very Respectfully Yours,
Sara G. Stanley

### Further Application to Teach Freedmen: Sara G. Stanley to American Missionary Association, 4 March 1864.

Cleveland, Ohio
Dear Sir (George Whipple):

I addressed a brief letter, bearing date Jan. 19th to you, and received a reply from Rev. S. S. Jocelyn; also a circular containing a summary of the general principles of your Association and methods of operation. In compliance with the regulation of the Executive Committee requiring all applicants for positions as teachers under your auspices to make a brief statement of name, age, occupation, etc. etc. I respectfully submit the following: —

Name, Sara G. Stanley; age, twenty five years; occupation, nominally a teacher, i.e. have taught at intervals during eight years, and have abstained from devoting myself exclusively to that vocation to which my inclination and temperament lead me, only because my usefulness has been greater by the domestic hearth and in the family circle. I am unmarried. My power of endurance is perhaps more than ordinary. I have good health; have not been seriously ill, since my childhood, and therefore conclude that my physical stamina must be equal to the best. Of education, and religious advantages I will say, I have received a common school education, and subsequently spent three years in study at Oberlin College in this state; was in the third year of the Ladies Course when I left. I have been carefully instructed in the fundamental principles of the Christian religion from my childhood by pious and exemplary parents; and am a member of the Presbyterian church in this city.

My reasons for seeking to engage in the work of instructing the Freed people of the South are few and simple. I am myself a colored woman, bound to that ignorant, degraded, long enslaved race, by the ties of love and consanguinity; they are socially and politically, "my people," and I have an earnest and abiding conviction that the Almighty Father, whose loving kindness gave me to advantages which his divine wisdom withheld from them, requires me to devote every power with which he has endowed me to the work of ameliorating their condition, to advancing the civilization of a people, who though, through long years have been victims of oppression and brutality, are yet susceptible of high cultivation, and for whom, I feel assured, that an inscrutable providence has appointed a destiny far greater and more glorious than any political charlatan or statesman has yet conceived of, such a testimony as Christian men and women rejoice to contemplate — of intellectual power and spiritual greatness, of holiness perfected in the fear of God.

As to pay, location and surroundings, I do not know that I have any special expectation or preference. The salary you are accustomed to give I would be compelled to ask for, my friends not being in sufficient affluent circumstances to enable me to teach gratuitously.

The time for which I wish to engage, I cannot specify. I would be glad if it might be so long as I may be found worthy and efficient. I will (submit) with regard to location, that perhaps Eastern Virginia or any portion of the Department of N. Carolina would be most acceptable; the climate is less enervating than in some other localities, and I might be enabled, in consequence, to labor more advantageously and better endure fatigue.

Hoping that the accompanying testimonials will speak in my favor, I am
For Truth and Humanity
Respectfully Yours
Sara G. Stanley

### First Report from Norfolk, Va.: Sara G. Stanley to American Missionary Association, 28 April 1864.

Norfolk, VA
Dear Sir (George Whipple):

I reached Norfolk after a very pleasant and uneventful journey, on Saturday April 9th and entered school on Monday morning following. I have 60 pupils enrolled in my division, all eager to learn, and far more docile and tractable than I supposed possible for such illiterate and undisciplined children to be. Through their affectionate nature I find that they are very easily governed; kind words and gentle tones possessing far more potency and producing a more permanent effect, than a stern deportment of rigid discipline. . . .

I am much surprised and gratified to find among the people with whom I have talked, an almost universal comprehension of the fact, that only by great faithfulness, industry and perseverance in attending to their duties, can they testify their love and gratitude to the kind of friends at the north who have sent them teachers and are doing so much for them. Untaught and oppressed as they have been, they yet have very clear and well defined ideas of their great obligation to the noble hearted Christians and philanthropists who are opening to their darkened intellects the light of knowledge. From many a wretched hovel, from many a broken and fireless hearthstone, ascend to God the prayers of his poor but beloved children for blessings upon your heads. Simple and illiterate in language, but pure and beautiful to him who searcheth the heart; the effectual, fervent prayer of the righteous which availeth much

I had not intended sending you such a lengthy epistle, (knowing) from the cursory glance I have had, that time at the Missionary Room is too valuable to be given to non-essentials, but I have filled this sheet undesignedly. Another time brevity shall receive due regard.

I am with great respect
Very Truly Yours
Sara G. Stanley

### Protest of Racism of Associates: Sara G. Stanley and Edmonia Highgate to Superintendent of Norfolk American Missionary Association Schools, 21 July 1864.

Norfolk, Va.
Dear Friend:

I am perhaps assuming an unwarrantable liberty in this trespassing upon your time and attention, but my [patient?] impulse is to write you. "He approacheth nearest to the Gods," says Cato, "who knows how to be silent even though he is right." When great principles are involved I deem silence criminal.

Your absence from this field of missionary labor is very deeply felt; there is a hiatus which, to the discerning, nothing but your presence can supply. If your presence here had never effected any good beside serving to keep Mr. W. S. Coan's peculiar secession, pro-Slavery and Christian negro-hating principles and malign prejudices in abeyance or preventing the expression of them, I think your services to the cause will have been sufficiently great, and meriting the highest mode of praise — Since your departure he seems to have set aside whatever restraint he may have taught proper to assume, and does not hesitate, or rather I should say, takes an especial pleasure in advocating the inferiority of "negroes" and the necessity of social distinctions, with special application to colored missionary teachers. You have been informed of his conversation with one of our teachers, when it was her deliberate choice to occupy a room with Miss Highgate whom she esteemed not only for her talents but as a personal friend, and so expressed to him. Was it not an assumption of authority for him to attempt forcing an individual's private preferences — on the ground of her accordance with his own views? By whom is he invested with power to dictate who shall and shall not be the chosen friends of any teacher in this Department? He said further more to the young lady who committed the heinous offense referred to, that had she been in his house he would never have permitted it, but would have slept on the floor himself, and caused his wife to sleep on a sofa, and given their bed for her occupancy, if no separate room could have been provided for her.

Mr. Coan is, I think, doing an incalculable injury to the cause. Being identified by the ties of love and consanguinity with these people for whom we are all laboring, I am convinced that I can perceive more clearly than others the deleterious efforts of his influence upon this work of elevating God's poor oppressed and outraged children. Already is the contagion of his example upon the teachers evident. The mission to which he has recently devoted the energies of his mind is apparently to revive and perpetuate prejudice and Caste which is the very spirit and essence of slavery.

As I have understood the religion of Christ, the brotherhood of man is its fundamental and elementary constituent — "Whatsoever ye would" — "God has created of one blood" — "Let us love one another. He that loveth not his brother whom he hath seen, how can he love God whom he hath not seen?" etc. etc. the propagandist then of a religion which denies the first principle of the Gospel, viz. "The

Fatherhood of God and the Brotherhood of Christ," not only dissemi-
nating his views to those who legitimately belong to his own household, but endeavoring to make them universal among all engaged in
promoting the moral, mental and spiritual welfare of the Freed people,
is irretragally [sic] laboring for the advancement of the kingdom of
Satan. As that martyr saint of Harper's Ferry remarked of a Southern
clergyman who visited him while imprisoned "He needs to learn the
A.B.C. of Christianity."

You will please understand Professor, that I am not advocating a
social unity of the races in New York or New England. I fully appre-
hend the distinctions of Society, and at the North Mr. Coan would
have a incontrovertible right to select his own circle of acquaintances,
and without any detriment to any persons of any things; but here, in
the missionary field, it is different. He has no right to pursue any
course that will militate in the slightest degree against the Cause he
professes to serve. For the success of our efforts there should be a
Christian unity and sociality among the laborers – Hitherto there has
been in a large degree, but if Mr. Coan is to administer affairs, the
kindness; forbearance love which you have so carefully cultivated
among us, will soon be dissipated. We will be no more as one family,
but resolved into discordant and irreconcilable elements.

I am rejoiced to know that the gentlemen is removed from this
point —, but I sincerely commiserate the people over whom he is
appointed. He will of course carry his opinions wherever he goes and
they must inevitably find expression. "By they words shall thou be justified, and by thy words shalt thou be condemned."

I have written you, Professor, of this matter for but one reason, with
but one motive — viz, to do what one individual, however insignificant, can do toward demonstrating the deep, the vital importance of
your returning to this work in which God has signally blessed your
efforts. Such as you only can do it effectually — men of stamina moral-
ly, men of exalted principles, men who do not practically pronounce
the sublime truth proclaimed by Paul upon Mars' hill, "God hath made
of one blood all nations of men," *a lie*. And my motive is to serve these
people, to utter a plea for those who have no voice to plead for themselves.

I am with Great Respect,
Very Truly Yours,
Sara G. Stanley

Prof. Woodbury — I fully and heartily concur with my gifted friend. Do not think either of us aroused to a spirit of merciless denunciation by mere galling manifestations of the Spirit of Caste. No sir! It is the deep underlying principle — For the sake of God's suffering long outraged do not mistake your life purpose. Edmonia G. Highgate.

P.S. Brother Walker wished me to say that he received your letter today, and will reply immediately.
    S.G.S.

## *"This prejudice against color!": Sara G. Stanley to American Missionary Association, 6 October 1864.*

Norfolk, Va.
Dear Friend (George Whipple):
    It is a commonplace and familiar subject of which I have to speak — the old, old subject of human brotherhood, the equal rights, and the unity of all beings created in the divine likeness; in denying which we "commit sin and are convinced of the law as transgressors." It is an old subject, and a hackneyed one, yet nevertheless of vital importance to those who have their manhood insulted and the God-like principle within them denied and contemned [sic] by fellow creatures of equal origin and equal mortality

    I spoke to you in a former note — regarding Miss Gleason, who has emphatically affirmed to the wife of one of the military officers at this post, that "If all colored teachers are not removed from Mission house No. 80 Main Street — she will not return to it." I am what is called a colored teacher, of the Mission house referred to, and consider the remark as having direct application to myself.

    I am much pained by this manifestation of hostile feeling by a person placed in the responsible position she is to assume. I have never, under any former rule of the household, when Prof. Woodbury's presence gave tone and character to the family circle, received the slightest intimation that my presence nor that of any other colored teacher, was obnoxious, or that I was defective in any quality which entitled me to be regarded and treated with the deference due any other lady. And as for the mere matter of complexion, I might say by way of illustration, that Capt. Brown, our Army Quartermaster, addressed me a few days since as Mrs. Walker (an acknowledged white woman I believe), introduced his wife, and did not discover the mistake until I informed him.

Oh the profound wisdom of this prejudice against color! When one half shade difference is to determine whether an individual is to be respected or despised.

These exhibitions of prejudice on the part of Missionary teachers supposed to be in the work because the love of Christ constrained them, is to me very sad to contemplate. I think it must prove a very serious obstacle in the way of the advancement of the work, and most lamentably shows how little in sympathy with the cause of human elevation some of our teachers are. And it seems too, to be disregarding and treating with contempt or indifference, the divine truth "All the love is fulfilled in one work even in this; Thou shalt love they neighbor as thyself" — thrusting the cornerstone from the whole system of Christian faith in worship. Oh! That you and our dear Professor with his earnest soul, and strong deep sympathy with humanity, however oppressed or insulted could find some potent spell by which to exorcise this demon, whose machinations threaten to destroy the spirit of love and harmony which should permeate our hearts and find expression in our words and deeds.

As for Miss Gleason, she has unfortunately, for some time past, been under a tutelage somewhat opposed to the culture of the pure and catholic spirit of love which is an integral element of the character of all true followers of Christ Jesus; whose perfect *essence is Love*. If we could entirely set aside the fact of individual responsibility, we might, in consideration of her former surroundings, and the fact that her intellectual training has not perhaps been as thorough and extended as some others of us, pass by this expression of her feelings with indifference. But as the character of nations, communities, societies depends upon the character of individuals composing them, there can be Truth, Honesty, Equity, in the whole, only as these qualities inhere in individuals. Oh! Mr. Whipple if we could have in this work only earnest, humble, true hearted Christians — regarding all mankind as brothers, God's children, Christ's redeemed, feeling not that the great desire of all hearts should be to near a Saxon complexion, but to be "clothed upon with righteousness" how blessed it would be, and what an outpouring of God's love, and the inexhaustible riches of his grace, it would receive.

Truly Yours,
Sara G. Stanley

*Informal Report: Sara G. Stanley to American Missionary Association, 25 March 1865.*

St. Louis, Mo.
Dear Friend (George Whipple),

I am rather favorably impressed with the aspect of things here, or rather the material with which an improved condition of educational affairs can be effected. I have been received with great cordiality of the colored Board, who appear to be devoting themselves earnestly with singleness of purpose to the work in hand, — have had a lengthy conference with several of the most intelligent members, respecting their plan of organization, and the changes in their crude arrangements which are absolutely essential to their success of the schools. They all are [men?] of acquiescence and hearty cooperation in whatever measures may be proposed for the promotion of the general welfare, and are disposed to impose more confidence in my judgment and ability than it is probable I shall ever be able to justify. . . .

I am quite sure Mr. Whipple, that you will be surprised when I tell you that the people here have bestowed upon me their fullest approbation already. They are brim full of gratitude and affection, and regard me with a tender interest which touches me deeply. One good old patriarch of the School Board attributes my coming here to a direct interposition of Providence, and says "This child is just what we want, she is the *very* one we have been praying for this long time." I wonder if you will commend me a little for having made a good impression upon somebody in the vast universe. I certainly take great credit to myself for the achievement and consider it decidedly a matter for self-gratification. You know I have been so unfortunate, since teaching among the Freedmen, in displeasing so many people, that I may indulge in a little pardonable vanity now. I have remembered your kind reproof of what you thought haughtiness in my manner, and strive to cultivate a different deportment, — I could not do otherwise than remember it, for the pain of finding that you had been displeased with me from the beginning, was too acute to be easily forgotten. . . .

In glancing over these pages I find that I have written you with a sort of informality which perhaps is not strictly admissible. Please permit it for this time. In my present state of feeling, a "Report," according to any prescribed rule, would be very irksome, and it is so much pleasanter to address you as a friend and Christian brother. Another time, my language shall be more carefully chosen, and with direct reference to the work assigned me.

    I am with Respect
    Very Truly Yours
    Sara G. Stanley

Orange St. 2nd Door West of 15th
I would like very much to ask you to write to me when you are quite at
leisure, but am afraid of trespassing too much upon your attention.

**Formal Report from St. Louis: Sara G. Stanley to American
Missionary Association, May 1865.**

St. Louis, Mo.
Sir:
    The day after my arrival here, I found my way to the school to
which I had been assigned. It was in the basement of one of the colored churches, and perhaps not more disagreeable and unattractive in
its surroundings and appointments than might have been expected
from its subterranean locations; yet when I first beheld it, I recoiled
with a shiver that could not be repressed. It was a raw bleak day early
in March, the sky was dark with clouds and the atmosphere damp and
heavy. Cheerless enough it was out of doors, but within the school
room, "chaos and old night" prevailed universally. On opening the
door nothing was immediately perceptible, but as the eye gradually
became accustomed to the darkness, I was enabled to discern a long
low room, furnished with ungainly, movable seats, and containing
perhaps one hundred fifty children. It was bare and dreary, the
smoked and darkened walls unrelieved by a single map, tables, or
blackboard. Through the dusty windows the dim light struggled for
admission and the chill March wind found entrance through number-
less broken panels.
    I looked about me with a feeling akin to despair, as the question
presented itself, with all the difficulties of its solution. How can I ever
counteract the influence of this room? which must rest like an incubus
upon the minds and hearts of the children. An airy, cheerful, attractive
schoolroom I have always considered essential to the success of a
school, and to the proper moral and intellectual culture, as well as the
physical well being of the pupils. Its importance cannot be overrated.
Children grow readily unto the likeness and Spirit of their surroundings; their characters take hue from the objects with which they come

into contact; more than we think. My experience in the schoolroom has taught me the subtile [sic], moral influence of material objects. Maps, globes, pictures, are disciplinary; the vase of fragrant flowers on the teachers desk, the green foliage visible at the open window through which the sunshine pours its golden flood and the air comes purely and freshly, are more efficacious in preserving order, in calming turbulent spirits and keeping them attuned to the sweeter harmony of love, gentleness and truth, than any instrument of corporal punishment I have ever seen.

I am glad to be able to report that the aspect of our room has somewhat improved. I have succeeded in procuring a blackboard, which I have ornamented with bits of landscape, figures of animals, diagrams of the planets, geometrical figures, etc. explanations of which are an unfailing source of interest to the children. By marvelous good fortune, I have obtained a number of discarded, obsolete outline maps, upon which I have sketched with crayon, the present geographical boundaries, — their appearance is not much improved by this addition but the children learn something from them and they serve the important purpose of partially concealing and unsightly walls. More than these the beautiful Spring has come to us, God's pure sunshine falls from heaven, and our poor schoolroom, like other desolate places of earth, becomes radiant with its glory.

I commenced school with fifty four scholars, which in two weeks increased to seventy five. The whole number at present is one hundred and the average attendance nearly eighty. All the pupils can read using McGuffey's series of readers from the First to the Fifth. I have organized classes in Geography, Grammar, and Mental Arithmetic; they have entered upon these studies, which are entirely new to them, with great avidity. The progress already made by one of the classes in Geography is highly commendable. I can assume no merit for this advancement, it is owing almost wholly to their own efforts, the large daily attendance rendering it impossible for me to bestow as much attention upon individual classes as I desire. Having no school apparatus and no facilities whatever for teaching, I find my inventive faculties called into frequent requisition; for example, I illustrate the rotation of the earth on its axis and the succession of day and night, with a ball borrowed of one of the pupils poised between thumb and finger and whirled from left to right; proceeding on the hypothesis that some convenient sunbeam is the centre of our solar system.

I must not fail to refer to the general cleanliness and appearance of most of my scholars. The girls come daily to school attired in neat print dresses and shaker hoods; the boys in garments, if patched, yet scrupulously clean. Now and then there are innocent little attempts at elegance too — polished boot and a fragment of a ribbon encircling a white shirt collar. May of them, whose parents became *free* previous to the rebellion, are as well clad as any children of the north. I have had but one occasion to administer reproof for untidiness and neglect of proper ablution. I spoke to the child, a flaxen-haired rosy-cheeked little boy, privately and as tenderly as possible, understanding that little children have sensitive hearts as well as those of "larger growth." The little one's face flushed painfully and turning his sad blue eyes filled with tears to my face he said simply, "My mother is dead, and I never had any father." I think my own eyes filled then, and my heart yearned inexpressibly over this poor neglected orphan, whose Saxon face was sufficient evidence that he had said truly, "I never had any father." There are many such as he in the school; the great preponderance of the mulattos over the blacks immediately arrests the attention of the spectator. Of the whole number (one hundred) there are not I think twenty blacks. The caucasian element is largely ascendant, many of the children have blond and red hair and the peculiarly white transparent complexion which is their usual accompaniment. A woeful commentary on the hideous iniquity of Slavery. . . .

Yours Truly,
Sara G. Stanley

### Finances: Sara G. Stanley to American Missionary Association, 10 July 1865.

St. Louis, Mo.
Dear Sir,

Yours of July 1st containing check for thirty dollars is on hand. The amount of indebtedness of the A.M. Association to me was $60 (sixty dollars) a salary of $15 per month being due me for four months, viz. March, April, May and June.

As your books show I was in receipt of my salary to January 1st. During a portion of the months of Jan. and Feb. I was at Cleveland, Ohio and consequently received nothing. In March I began labors in St. Louis and have received no money since coming here.

The check for $30 sent me by Mr. Whipple was designed for my traveling expenses from Cleveland to St. Louis, Mo. The expenses of that journey I find by reference to my memorandum, were as follows; Railroad fare $23, Hack and luggage $3, Parts of meals by the way $2, — total $28. The overplus of two dollars I retained, as my traveling expenses from N. York overran by some five or six dollars the amount I had received for discharging them.

I am this particular in stating these items that you may perceive how the check, which you understood to be the payment of my salary, was appropriate.

You spoke of $10 per month; I did not know that there had been any reduction of the sum previously paid. I have received $15 per month since Oct. 1st 1864, and having had no information to the contrary, very naturally supposed it was continued. My pecuniary affairs are such that it will cause me serious embarrassment if I have falsely supposed that I was receiving more than the actual amount. I will be glad to hear from you at your earliest convenience.

With Great Respect I remain,
Very Truly Yours,
Sara G. Stanley

### No Need for A.M.A Schools in St. Louis: Sara G. Stanley to American Missionary Association, 19 July 1865.

St. Louis, Mo.
Dear Friend,

I wish to state that on Sept. 1st — free schools are to be opened in this city, by legislative enactment, for colored children. There will therefore be no further necessity for the assistance of benevolent associations to be extended to the Freedmen of this city or state. During the month of June and July I have been teaching a school (as stated in my report) in which the pupils are assessed a sum sufficient to pay the expenses of the school, — rent of room $12 per month, and my board of $25. Their payment has been very prompt and the school in all respects an interesting and excellent one receiving the generous and unqualified praise of white and colored citizens who have visited it. It has become a good school, not because of any special qualification of mine or aptitude for the duties which devolve upon me, but because the elements with which I had to work, were superior in quality, and so flexible that any person of ordinary discrimination and acquirements might have wrought them into a model school.

My object in writing is to say that I wish to close the school on the

1st of August; not that my interest or the interest of my pupils have for a moment flagged, but I have worked so constantly and rested so little since coming here that my health is not sufficiently robust to endure the confinement of teaching in the month of August. If you do not desire otherwise, I will return home (Cleveland, Ohio) at the close of school. I can not remain here after the school is discontinued from the fact that my expenses can be met only by what accrues from the tuition of the pupils, and beside, it would be useless to do so even if practicable, as teachers will be provided in the fall by the Board of Directors (white) of Public School, whose preference, it is presumed, will be for indigent females of their own state, whom the rebellion has impoverished.

Please let me hear from you as early as may be convenient.
Yours Very Truly,
Sara G. Stanley

### Appointed Principal: Sara G. Stanley to American Missionary Association, 4 May 1866.

Louisville, Ky.

The chief event of the month has been my appointment to the principalship of the school in which I have hitherto acted as assistant. This change has necessitated much additional labor on my part, especially as my assistants are young ladies of very limited experience as teachers, and of consequent inefficiency. I have thoroughly reorganized the school and have been much more successful in effecting a classification of pupils than our undisciplined material at first promised. We have a Primary, Secondary, and Intermediate grade; Grammar and History being among the studies of the intermediate department. We have been supplied with maps, globes, charts and other school apparatus, which are indispensable to a schoolroom, and without which there can be no effective teaching.

I am happy to report that the school has increased in numbers since it has been under my control; more than fifty have been added to it. Of the interest manifested by the pupils, and of their advancement in study, I can speak in the most commendatory manner. . . .

I am unable to make any report of visits to colored families. Six hours labor in the schoolroom, with the number of hours spent in performing work pertaining to the same, leaves me no leisure for other duties. The moral and religious instruction of my pupils, with their intellectual training, engross me to the exclusion of all things else.

Sara G. Stanley

## Observations on Freedmen in Louisville: Sara G. Stanley to American Missionary Association, 18 July 1866.

Louisville, KY.

The month has been one of pleasure and profit to myself and my pupils. At no previous time has there been such close application of study and continuous effort to gain the mastery over difficulties encountered, as have been exhibited during the month. Instead of employing the closing weeks of school in preparing for a public exhibition, as is the custom in the schools of Louisville, we omitted all attempt at rhetorical display or private theatricals, and spent the last four weeks in reviewing the studies of the term. The result was highly satisfying, — there was manifested a power of continuity and concentrativeness which I did not suppose was a pardonable vanity I experienced in the closing day of school when the classes in history, grammar, geography and arithmetic passed examination creditably, responding to questions not found in the textbooks with correctness and that easy confidence which evinces of a familiarity with general principles, as well as the letter of books. The severe training of this month of hard study has been of incalculable benefit to them. They became so thoroughly familiar with the branches pursued as to cause the knowledge acquired to seem a part of themselves, and capable of practical application in everyday life; they have learned to have confidence in their own powers and properly to estimate their capability for improvement. Summarily, the work in Louisville for the first and half months I was engaged here, abundantly repaid the effort made. Considering it in a character merely intellectual it was decidedly a success. – For thoroughness in the rudiments taught, — for accuracy and precision in recitation, cheerful submission to government, and propriety of demeanor, the school was unsurpassed. What was to me most extraordinary, in the ready adaptation of the children to new regulation and strict discipline, was the fact that they had been for the most part under the charge of inexperience[d] teachers, who being deficient in the governing faculty permitted their pupils to govern themselves, and consequently to establish a most liberal and irresponsible democracy. . . .

Sara G. Stanley

*Objections to Her Marriage: Sara G. Stanley to American Missionary Association, 6 April 1868.*

Mobile, (Alabama).

Dear Friend,

Mr. Putnam has informed you of my engagement with Mr. Woodward and of our intention of being married in Mobile. He has stated to me that we "cannot be married at this house" (as I very innocently supposed it to be the only proper place here, where a teacher should be married) and "that if such marriage is allowed to take place he will immediately resign." Surprised, indignant and grieved by this manifestation of a spirit of caste and prejudice, my dignity and self-respect forbid my ever holding any further communication with Mr. Putnam on the subject. If I had anticipated any objection to my marriage being solemnized at the Home I would have addressed you in the first instance. As an officer of an Association established upon the principle of human Brotherhood, God being no respecter of persons, you see the matter in the light of simple right and justice, rather than that of unchristian prejudice. I had designed stating to you the objection which Mr. Putnam has urged, and showing how futile and untenable his argument is, but failing strength admonishes me to be brief. I do deny that our quiet and unostentatious marriage here, will "create a talk," as it asserted, among any class of people or do injury to anyone. The injury Mr. Putnam purposes doing me would be far greater than any injury caused to others by a contrary course. Something is due me in the matter as a woman simply. Your delicacy of perception will at once show you how my character would be compromised by a refusal to be allowed to be married in the house where I have lived, and to be required to skulk away as if I were committing a crime. It is well perhaps to say that I do not wish to remain here one moment after the marriage is solemnized. It will not be required. Mr. Woodward will make such arrangement as to obviate any necessity for remaining. We had appointed the time for the marriage after the close of school, but my illness has changed that somewhat. I was taken seriously ill on the day of my conversation with Mr. Putnam. The physician pronounces the difficulty heart-disease, caused principally by over-taxation of strength in school, and precipitation by the mental excitement of that day. The physician has informed Miss Cooley that even if I should recover from this attack any attempts to teach again will be attended with great danger. In this sad state of things we prefer being married

when I recover (if I ever do) and I beg of you to write me without
delay. My anxiety to communicate with you has led me to violate my
physician's order, to be kept entirely free from all exertion, or mental
exertion, and write this letter in bed.

My marriage at this house I consider as an act of common justice,
and willingly leave the matter now to your sense of honor and right,
not doubting that your decision as a Christian gentlemen will be such
as I feel myself justified in expecting.

I remain, Very Truly Yours,

Sara G. Stanley

# A Good Life, Staying On

—◦◦◦◦◦—

## *Laura M. Towne*

From Rupert Sargent Holland, ed.,
*Letters and Diary of Laura M. Towne* (1912; reprinted
New York: Negro Universities Press, 1969).

*One of the first teachers to go south, Laura Towne helped to establish The Port
Royal Experiment. The project, which established schools and promoted agricultural experiments in land ownership and management in the African American
communities of the South Carolina Sea Islands, served as the proving ground for
Northern abolitionists' views of African American emancipation. A physician and
accomplished administrator, teacher, and devoted abolitionist, Towne served as a
leader and mentor to the various teachers with whom she worked. These selections
from her diaries clearly illustrate how Towne built a full and rich life for herself
among the African American island community. Central to Towne's life was the support of her friend Ellen Murray. The two women worked together, lived together,
and parented an adopted African American child, "Puss." Lifelong partnerships
between women were not unusual in the mid 1800s, and in fact were widely
accepted. The Civil War altered the expectations of a generation of women who
often found themselves widowed at a young age, or without marriage prospects. As*

Towne's account demonstrates, teaching provided these women with the means to make an independent life for themselves; for some, it enabled them to live in female couples and to avoid the expectation that they should marry.

St. Helena's, August 20, 1862

It is too bad that I have had lately so little time to write. But you may guess how hard it is by the sketch of a day that I will give you.

I get up about six and hurry down so as to have breakfast by seven for Captain Hooper to set out to the ferry for Beaufort. After that I generally have three or four patients, feed my birds, and am ready by nine for driving out to see my patients on five plantations — only one plantation or two a day, though. The roads are horrible and the horses ditto, so I have a weary time getting along, but it is enlivened by a little reading aloud, Ellen and I taking turns at driving and reading. We come hurrying home by two o'clock or a little before, using mental force enough to propel the whole concern — horse, carriage, and ourselves. We snatch a lunch and begin school. I have the middle class, Ellen the oldest and youngest. At four, school is out for the children. Ellen then takes the adults while I go doctoring down to the "nigger houses," or street of cabins. As soon as I get home (generally with six or seven little negro girls and boys — or babies — tugging at my dress and saying, "my missus" — the little things that can scarcely speak each having chosen a favorite "missus"), I run up the flag and the men come for their guns. This is about six o'clock. They drill an hour or so, and then I take the guns again. They are kept in the room next to mine, under lock and key. Then I dress for dinner, and order it, or see to its coming upon the table in some presentable shape. Dinner takes till eight or half-past, or even, if Captain H. is detained, till half-past nine. I generally have several patients to attend to in the evening, and the rest of the time Ellen and I are kept busy folding papers for the medicines. We go upstairs so as to begin to undress at ten, and we are so sleepy that I often get sound asleep just as soon as my head touches the pillow. We both keep hearty and strong. The negroes say I am strong "too much" . . . I am not sorry that I did not accept the superintendency of the place, for it would be too much care of a kind that I do not like — accounts, pay-rolls, rations to be measured exactly, complaints to hear and satisfy, authority to exert. I like my position as volunteer and would not willingly give it up.

*Aunt Rachel's Village*
*St. Helena, February 7, 1864*

Your nice long letter reached me only to-day. That is the worst of our living here, letters are very long getting to us and come by very uncertain hands, and we never know when a mail is going out. I have to trust to chance for getting our mail to Beaufort. So do not be alarmed if a vessel sails with no word from me, the next one will probably bring double. . . .

I suppose you thought me unconscionable in sending for carpets and household things, but this is my home probably for the rest of my days, and I want to be comfortable in it. I have lived now for two years in the midst of makeshift and discomfort, and have often thought this winter that even servants at home were more nicely provided with domestic conveniences and things to save time and trouble. So, I sent for a few things of my own; that is, I wanted them taken from our house, and in the sale of division of our household goods charged to my account — such as the carpet. Our room is nearly as ill-built and open as a rough country stable. H.'s[18] stable is a palace to it, and, our only bit of carpet being on our parlor floor, we have bare boards in our rooms with the air rushing through every crack, and sunlight along every board plainly visible where the sun shines under the house. This is comfortless and cold as you cannot imagine, who have not had uncarpeted floors since you can remember. When we first came here, and for a time, these things were endurable, but year after year it is hard to live so. Besides, now that things are taking a more permanent form here, everybody's style of living is improving and we do as others do. You know what South Carolina fare is. We are just in the oyster hole again, and have nothing else till we are sick of the sight of them. I was going to send home for butter, for we have had neither butter nor milk for some time — so much less than last year; but Mr. Ruggles says he will supply us. We had a cow sent to us and were happy, but she was a jumper — and our fence such as you might expect — and she jumped and ran, after our feeding her for three days and getting just one quart of milk. Her feed, too, was a heartbreak — we are not sure of it from day to day — none to be begged, borrowed or bought, so her escape was a relief. . . .

*December 18, 1864*
Merry Christmas to all.

Our new school-house is now being hurried forward pretty fast, and

*Laura Towne, with pupils Dick Washington ("my right hand man"), Maria Wyne, and Amoretta ("bright and sharp as a needle"), 1866. Among the first teachers in "freedmen's schools," Towne and her friend Ellen Murray continued teaching in South Carolina for the remainder of their lives.*

we hope to get in by the first of the year. How happy we shall be, nobody can tell who has not taught in a school where he or she had to make herself heard over three other classes reciting in concert, and to discover talkers among fifty scholars while one hundred fifty more are shouting lessons, and three other teachers bawling admonitions, instructions, and reproofs. Generally two or more of the babies are squalling from disinclination to remain five hours foodless on very small and tippy laps — their nurses being on benches too high for them and rather careless of infant comfort in their zeal for knowledge. . . .

I went to-day to see Maum Katie, an old African woman, who remembers worshipping her own gods in Africa, but who has been nearly a century in this country. She is very bright and talkative, and is a great "spiritual mother," a fortune-teller, or rather prophetess, and a woman of tremendous influence over her spiritual children. I am going to cultivate her acquaintance. I have been sending her medicine for a year nearly, and she "hangs upon top me," refusing all medicine but mine. I never saw her till to-day, and she lives not a stone's throw off, so you may guess how hurried I am.

*March 9, 1866*
I send the enclosed picture of me with three of my pets. The big boy is Dick Washington, my right-hand man, who is full of importance, but has traveled and feels as if he had seen the world. He is incorrigibly slow and stupid about learning but reads bunglingly in the Testament, does multiplication sums on the slate, and can write a letter after a fashion. The little girl with the handkerchief on her head is Amoretta — bright and sharp as a needle. She reads fluently in the Testament, spells hard and easy words in four syllables, and ciphers as far as nine times twelve on the slate. The other child is Maria Wyne, who is very bright in arithmetic, but very dull and slow in learning to read. My face is burnt out so as to do justice to them. Amoretta's head kerchief is put on as the candidates for baptism wear them. . . .

*June 1, 1867*
The people are just now in a state of great excitement over their rights to vote, and are busy forming a Republican Party on the island. At their first meeting they had an informal time, at the second there was some business done. Our school was invited to sing at this/one, and it seemed the main attraction. But two or three white men — one of them Mr. Wells — got up and said women and children ought to stay at home on such occasions. He afterwards sent us an apology, saying he had no idea of including us or our school, but only outsiders who were making some noise. Nevertheless, the idea took. To-day in church Mr.

Hunn announced another meeting next Saturday. "The females must stay at home?" asked Demas from the pulpit. "The females can come or not as they choose," said Mr. Hunn, "but the meeting is for men voters." Demas immediately announced that "the womens will stay at home and cut grass," that is, hoe the corn and cotton fields — clear them of grass! It is too funny to see how much more jealous the men are of one kind of liberty they have achieved than of the other! Political freedom they are rather shy of, and ignorant of; but domestic freedom — the right, just found, to have their own way in their families and rule their wives — that is an inestimable privilege! In slavery the woman was far more important, and was in every way held higher than the man. It was the woman's house, the children were entirely hers, etc., etc. Several speakers have been here who have advised the people to get the women into their proper place — never to tell them anything of their concerns, etc., etc.; and the notion of being bigger than woman generally, is just now inflating the conceit of the males to an amazing degree. When women get the vote, too, no people will be more indignant that these, I suppose.

*May 29, 1870*
We have had our little upset. A rabbit spring across the road just in front of Saxton's nose, and he shied. We were a no-top buggy that had no railing even, and Ellen, who had the reins and was driving, was slung out under the wheel, which went over her waist. When I saw myself and the big, heavy old fashioned wheel upon top of her, I screamed; and her fall and the scream made Saxton give two more great jumps into the woods. I had not the reins, of course, and could not guide him, so the second jump brought the wheel against the trunk of a felled tree, and the buggy turned a complete summerset with me under it. Saxton's old harness gave way and he trotted a little way, and then came back, anxious to find his "aunties." By that time Ellen and I were both up again, I caught Saxton, who came at my call, and Ellen picked up the ruins of our lunch-basket — her splendid lunch basket! — and various other things. Ellen had a pain in her side that was so severe at first that I feared internal injury, but it is almost well now, I was only a little bruised here and there, and not hurt seriously at all. . . .

Something far more important has happened to us. We have taken a little child to live with us — perhaps to bring up. She is Miss Puss — about the worst little monkey that ever was. Topsy was nothing to her. She wrote to Rosie a short time ago. That poor child has been undergoing all sorts of ill treatment all winter from her father. She is a dwarf already, and he starved and beat her every day. She is one of the best scholars in my class, as bright as a dollar, always noticed by strangers for her intelligence, good reading, etc., but under her father's management and direction, just as smart at lying and stealing. She often ran away to escape a beating, and almost lived in the woods. At last they locked up her clothes and made her go almost naked to keep her from coming to school, or going to some neighbors. One day this week she did not do the field work her father set her, so he told her to follow him home to be tied up and beaten. She dodged into the woods and came to me with a ragged little petticoat and an apron tied over her back. I told her she much go home and face the beating, and took her into the buggy, for she was exhausted with crying and starvation. We left her near home and she promised to go there, but she dodged again, her heart failing her when she saw the family searching for her. She spent the stormy night no one knows where, and meantime Ellen and I concluded to take her for poultry-minder at half a dollar a month and food, but not clothing. The father did not feel willing to let her come, but the mother would have it, so the next day as we went to school and saw her in a field eating blackberries, we hailed her and told her she was to come to Frogmore to live. You never saw such a delighted little creature. So far she is good as gold, but the time will come when we shall have our trials. She has been my scholar for years. . . .

Our school exists on charity, and charity that is weary. If turned over to the state, no Northern colored person has a chance of being appointed teacher of a state school. There are too many here who want the places and the school trustees are not men capable of appointing by qualification.

*May 7, 1871*
Just think, forty-six years of age! Almost half a century and with so much history in it, too! United States free; Italy free; France where she must be, and Prussia where she ought to be. Russia free, too, from serfs. I have seen a good deal in my half-century.

*May 14, 1871*
I do never intend to leave this "heathen country." I intend to end my days here and I wish to. . . . Next year is to be positively the last [for Northern support], but I shall not give up teaching; I couldn't live without it now.

*September 27, 1874*

I think stormy times are always best near the sea — for beauty. None of you bathe, I suppose. I go in sturdily nearly every day with my dogs, and I find great invigoration from it. My swimming improves a little, but I tire very soon, and I am very careful not to do too much and spoil my fun by getting to be afraid of doing anything. It is my arms that get tired, and back. I can swim with the tide a good distance, but against it cannot hold my own. But the best swimmers, indeed the best rowers, cannot contend with the strong currents we have here. My Bruno and Tim are great company for me and stick close by my side all day, of course, but I never think of such a thing as being lonely, I am so busy. For three weeks now, and for a long time in the evening too, I have been mending school-books. W. helped me,[19] and indeed was so skilful at binding that he did most of it for two weeks; but now he is away, and I am patching torn leaves. Sometimes I put nearly a hundred patches in one book, so you may know the labor. I use thin paper and paste over the print. These books have been put away as worn out, but now that the fund is so nearly exhausted, we cannot afford new books, and must have some, so I have undertaken a heavy, tiresome job. . . .

I have written to Mr. Cope[20] to say that as the Fund is nearly at an end, and my brother has so liberally provided for me, I will not take a salary any longer, but reserve it for the other teachers, so that the school may go on as it is for one or two years longer. He answered, saying that he had no doubt I took great pleasure in this arrangement, as I enjoyed before being a volunteer teacher so much, and apparently he was very glad to have the Fund spun out longer. Ellen is, of course, pleased at the prospect of continuance, and I thank Henry more for this than for any other thing I could get with his money — that is, for being able to live here, keep up this home, to feel sure of Ellen's staying and of the school not being turned over to some teacher I could not agree with, or to some set of trustees who would do with it exactly what we wouldn't like.

*November 11, 1877*

We are in the midst of preparation for exhibition, and I have begun to teach "Pinafore,"[21] but oh! What an attempt! I am going to have "We Sail," and "I am the Captain," with the salutations before it, — "I am Monarch" and "Cousins and His Aunts"; also "Buttercup." This will fill out my time. Another of my exercises will be "Political Economy," — just a little of what relates to capital labor, and money, — the uses of rich and poor men; and that piece will wind up with Burns' "A man's a man for a' that."

# The March of Progress

—◦⦓⦔◦—

*Charles W. Chesnutt*

From Charles W. Chesnutt, "The March of Progress,"
*The Century Illustrated Monthly Magazine,* Vol. 39
(Nov. 1900–April 1901), pp. 422–428.

*A fitting epilogue to the history of the "Yankee Schoolmarms," this short story by the African American writer Charles Chesnutt (1858–1932) chronicles the competition for a teaching position between an experienced white Northern teacher and one of her former African American pupils who has returned home from college. While Chesnutt's account is fictional, it is worth noting his portrayal of an African American community's struggle to come to terms with its beliefs about race and education. The young African American teacher in the story represents the future of the African American race and the finest legacy of the freedmen's school while the established teacher, Miss Noble, represents the African American community's indebtedness to the efforts of Northern teachers. At this point in his career, Chesnutt was writing openly about racial prejudice, and the story's protective view of Miss Noble speaks volumes about how many African Americans viewed their Northern teachers. Chesnutt is best known for his works* The Wife of His Youth, and Other Stories of the Color Line *(1899),* The Conjure Woman *(1899), and* The Colonel's Dream *(1905).*

The colored people of Patesville had at length gained the object they had for a long time been seeking — the appointment of a committee of themselves to manage the colored schools of the town. They had argued, with some show of reason, that they were most interested in the education of their own children, and in a position to know, better than any committee of white men could, what was best for their children's needs. The appointments had been made by the county commissioners during the latter part of the summer, and a week later a meeting was called for the purpose of electing a teacher to take charge of the grammar school at the beginning of the fall term.

The committee consisted of Frank Gillespie, or "Glaspy," a barber, who took an active part in local politics; Bob Cotten, a blacksmith, who owned several houses and was looked upon as a substantial citizen; and Abe Johnson, commonly called "Ole Abe" or "Uncle Abe," who had a large family, and drove a dray, and did odd jobs of hauling; he was also a class-leader in the Methodist church. The committee had been chosen from among a number of candidates — Gillespie on account of his political standing, Cotten as representing the solid element of the colored population, and Old Abe, with democratic impartiality, as likely to satisfy the humbler class of a humble people. While the choice had not pleased everybody, — for instance, some of the other applicants, — it was acquiesced in with general satisfaction. The first meeting of the new committee was of great public interest, partly by reason of its novelty, but chiefly because there were two candidates for the position of teacher of the grammar school.

The former teacher, Miss Henrietta Noble, had applied for the school. She had taught the colored children of Patesville for fifteen years. When the Freedmen's Bureau, after the military occupation of North Carolina, had called for volunteers to teach the children of the freedmen, Henrietta Noble had offered her services. Brought up in a New England household by parents who taught her to fear God and love her fellowmen, she had seen her father's body brought home from a Southern battle-field and laid to rest in the village cemetery; and a short six months later she had buried her mother by his side. Henrietta had no brothers or sisters, and her nearest relatives were cousins living in the far West. The only human being in whom she felt any special personal interest was a certain captain in her father's regiment, who had paid her some attention. She had loved this man deeply, in a maidenly, modest way; but he had gone away without speaking, and had not since written. He had escaped the fate of many other, and at the close of the war was alive and well, stationed in some Southern garrison.

When her mother died, Henrietta had found herself possessed only of the house where she lived and the furniture it contained, neither being of much value, and she was thrown upon her own resources for a livelihood. She had a fair education and had read many good books. It was not easy to find employment such as she desired. She wrote to her

Western cousins, and they advised her to come to them, as they thought they could do something for her if she went there. She had almost decided to accept their offer, when the demand arose for teachers in the South. Whether impelled by some strain of adventurous blood from a Pilgrim ancestry, or by a sensitive pride that shrank from dependence, or by some dim and unacknowledged hope that she might sometime, somewhere, somehow meet Captain Carey — whether from one of these motives or a combination of them all, joined to something of the missionary spirit, she decided to go South, and wrote to her cousins declining their friendly offer.

She had come to Patesville when the children were mostly a mob of dirty little beggars. She had distributed among them the cast-off clothing that came from their friends in the North; she had taught them to wash their faces and to comb their hair, and patiently, year after year, she had labored to instruct them in the rudiments of learning and the first principles of religion and morality. And she had not wrought in vain. Other agencies, it is true, had in time cooperated with her efforts, but any one who had watched the current of events must have been compelled to admit that the very fair progress of the colored people of Patesville in the fifteen years following emancipation had been due chiefly to the unselfish labors of Henrietta Noble, and that her nature did not belie her name.

Fifteen years is a long time. Miss Noble had never met Captain Carey; and when she learned later that he had married a Southern girl in the neighborhood of his post, she had shed her tears in secret and banished his image from her heart. She had lived a lonely life. The white people of the town, though they learned in time to respect her and to value her work, had never recognized her existence by more than the mere external courtesy shown by any community to one who lives in the midst of it. The situation was at first, of course, so strained that she did not expect sympathy from the white people; and later when time had smoothed over some of the asperities of war, her work had so engaged her that she had not had time to pine over her social exclusion. Once or twice nature had asserted itself, and she had longed for her own kind, and had visited her New England home. But her circle of friends was broken up, and she did not find much pleasure in boarding-house life; and on her last visit to the North but one, she had felt so lonely that she had longed for the dark faces of her pupils, and had welcomed with pleasure the hour when her task should be resumed.

But for several reasons the school at Patesville was of more importance to Miss Noble at this particular time than it ever had been before. During the last few years her health had not been good. An affection of the heart similar to that from which her mother had died, while not interfering perceptibly with her work, had grown from bad to worse, aggravated by close application to her duties, until it had caused her grave alarm. She did not have perfect confidence in the skill of the Patesville physicians, and to obtain the best medical advice had gone to New York during the summer, remaining there a month under the treatment of an eminent specialist. This, of course, had been expensive and had absorbed the savings of years from a small salary; and when the time came for her to return to Patesville, she was reduced, after paying her traveling expenses, to her last ten-dollar note.

"It is very fortunate," the great man had said at her last visit, "that circumstances permit you to live in the South, for I am afraid you could not endure a Northern winter. You are getting along very well now, and if you will take care of yourself and avoid excitement, you will be better." He said to himself as she went away: "It's only a matter of time, but that is true about us all; and a wise physician does as much good by what he withholds as by what he tells."

Miss Nobel had not anticipated any trouble about the school. When she went away the same committee of white men was in charge that had controlled the school since it had become part of the public-school system of the State on the withdrawal of support from the Freedmen's Bureau. While there had been no formal engagement made for the next year, when she had last seen the chairman before she went away, he had remarked that she was looking rather fagged out, had bidden her good-by, and had hoped to see her much improved when she returned. She had left her house in the care of the colored woman who lived with her and did her housework, assuming, of course, that she would take up her work again in autumn.

She was much surprised at first, and later alarmed, to find a rival for her position as a teacher of the grammar school. Many of her friends and pupils had called on her since her return, and she had met a number of the people at the colored Methodist church, where she taught in the Sunday-school. She had many friends and supporters, but she soon found out that her opponent had considerable strength. There had been a time when she would have withdrawn and left him a clear field, but at the present moment it was almost a matter of life and death to her — certainly the matter of earning a living — to secure the appointment.

The other candidate was a young man who in former years had been one of Miss Noble's brightest pupils. When he had finished his course in the grammar school, his parents, with considerable sacrifice, had sent him to a college for colored youth. He had studied diligently, had worked industriously during his vacations, sometimes at manual labor, sometimes teaching a country school, and in due time had been graduated from his college with honors. He had come home at the end of his school life, and was very naturally seeking the employment for which he had fitted himself. He was a "bright" mulatto, with straight hair, an intelligent face, and a well-set figure. He had acquired some of the marks of culture, wore a frock-coat and a high collar, parted his hair in the middle, and showed by his manner that he thought a good deal of himself. He was the popular candidate among the progressive element of his people, and rather confidently expected the appointment.

The meeting of the committee was held in the Methodist church, where, in fact, the grammar school was taught, for want of a separate school-house. After the preliminary steps to effect an organization, Mr. Gilliespie, who had been elected chairman, took the floor.

"The principal business to be brought befo' the meet'n this evenin'," he said, "is the selection of a teacher for our grammar school for the ensuin' year. Two candidates have filed applications, which, if there is no objection, I will read to the committee. The first is from Miss Noble, who has been the teacher ever since the grammar school was started."

He then read Miss Noble's letter, in which she called attention to her long years of service, to her need of the position, and to her affection for the pupils, and made formal application for the school for the next year. She did not, from motives of self-respect, make known the extremity of her need; nor did she mention the condition of her health, as it might have been used as an argument against her retention.

Mr. Gillespie then read the application of the other candidate, Andrew J. Williams. Mr. Williams set out in detail his qualifications for the position: his degree from Riddle University, his familiarity with the dead and living languages and the higher mathematics; his views of discipline; and a peroration in which he expressed the desire to devote himself to the elevation of his race and assist the march of progress through the medium of the Patesville grammar school.

The letter was well written in a bold, round hand, with many flourishes, and looked very aggressive and overbearing as it lay on the table by the side of the sheet of small note-paper in Miss Noble's faint and somewhat cramped handwriting.

"You have heard the readin' of the applications," said the chairman. "Gentlemen, what is yo' pleasure?"

There being no immediate response, the chairman continued:

"As this is a matter of consid'able importance, involvin' not only the welfare of our schools, but the progress of our race, an' as our action is liable to be criticized, whatever we decide, perhaps we had better discuss the subjec' befo' we act. If nobody else has anything to obse've, I will make a few remarks."

Mr. Gillespie cleared his throat, and assuming an oratorical attitude, proceeded:

"The time has come in the history of our people when we should stand together. In this age of organization the march of progress requires that we help ourselves, or be left forever behind. Ever since the war we have been sendin' our child'n to school an' educatin' 'em; an' now the time has come when they are leavin' the schools an' colleges, an' are ready to go to work. An' what are they going to do? The white people won't hire 'em as clerks in their sto's an' factories an' mills, an' we have no sto's or factories or mills of our own. They can't be lawyers or doctors yet, because we haven't got the money to send 'em to medical colleges an' law schools. We can't elect many of 'em to office, for various reasons. There's just two things they can find to do — to preach in our own pulpits, an' teach in our own schools. If it wasn't for that, they'd have to go on forever waitin' on white folks, like their fo'-fathers have done, because they couldn't help it. If we expect our race to progress, we must educate our young men an' women. If we want to encourage 'em to get education, we must find 'em employment when they are educated. We have now an opportunity to do this in the case of our young friend an' fellow-citizen, Mr. Williams, whose eloquent an' fine-lookin' letter ought to make us feel proud of him an' of our race.

"Of co'se there are two sides to the question. We have got to consider the claims of Miss Noble. She has been with us a long time an' has done much good for our people, an' we'll never forget her work an' friendship. But, after all, she has been paid for it; she has got her salary regularly an' for a long time, an' she has probably saved somethin', for we all know she hasn't lived high; an', for all we know, she may have had somethin' left by her parents. An' then again, she's white, an' has got her own people to look after her, they've got all the money an' all the offices an' all the everythin', — all that they've made an' all that we've made for fo' hundred years, — an' they sho'ly would look out for her. If she don't get this school, there's probably a dozen others she can get at the North. An' another thing: She is getting' rather feeble, an' it 'pears to me she's hardly able to stand teachin' so many child'n, an' a long rest might be the best thing in the world for her.

"Now, gentlemen, that's the situation. Shall we keep Miss Noble, or shall we stand by our own people? It seems to me there can hardly be but one answer. Self-preservation is the first law of nature. Are there any other remarks?"

Old Abe was moving restlessly in his seat. He did not say anything, however, and the chairman turned to the other member.

"Brother Cotton, what is yo' opinion of the question befo' the board?"

Mr. Cotton rose with the slowness and dignity becoming a substantial citizen, and observed:

"I think the remarks of the chairman have great weight. We all have nothin' but kind feelin's fer Miss Noble, an' I came here to-night somewhat undecided how to vote on this question. But after listenin' to the just an' forcible arguments of Brother Glaspy, it 'pears to me that, after all, the question befo' us is not a matter of feelin', but of business. As a business man, I am inclined to think Brother Glaspy is right. If we don't help ourselves when we get a chance, who is goin' to help us?"

"That bein' the case," said the chairman, "shall we proceed to a vote? All who favor the election of Brother Williams — "

At this point Old Abe, with much preliminary shuffling, stood up in his place and interrupted the speaker.

"Mr. Chuhman," he said, "I s'pose I has a right ter speak in dis meet'n? I *s'pose* I is a member er dis committee?"

"Certainly, Brother Johnson, certainly; we shall be glad to hear from you."

"I s'pose I's got a right ter speak my min' ef I is po' an' black an' don' weah as good clo's as some other members er de committee?'

"Most assuredly, Brother Johnson," answered the chairman, with a barber's suavity, "you have as much right to be heard as any one else. There was no intention of cuttin' you off."

"I s'pose," continued Abe, "dat a man wid fo'teen child'n kin be 'lowed ter hab somethin' ter ay 'bout de schools er dis town?"

"I am sorry, Brother Johnson, that you should feel slighted, but there was no intention to igno' yo' rights. The committee will be please' to have you ventilate yo' views."

"Ef it's all be'n an' done reco'nized an' 'cided dat I's got de right ter be heared in dis meet'n, I'll say w'at I has ter say, an' it won't take me long ter say it. Ef I should try ter tell all de things dat Miss Noble has done fer de niggers er dis town, it'd take me till ter-morrer mawnin'. Fer fifteen long yeahs I has watched her incomin's an' her outgoin's. Her daddy was a Yankee kunnel, who died fighting fer ou' freedom. She come heah when we — yas, Mr. Chuhman, when you an' Br'er Cotten — was jest sot free, an' when none er us did n' have a rag ter ou' backs. She come heah, an' she tuk yo' child'n an' my child'n, an' she teached 'em sense an' manners an' religion an' book-l'arnin'. When she come heah we did n' hab no chu'ch. Who writ up No'th an' got a preacher sent to us, an' de fun's ter buil' dis same chu'ch-house we're settin' in ter-night? Who got de money f'm de Bureau to s'port the school? An' when dat was stop', who got de money f'm de Peabody Fun'? Talk about Miss Noble gittin' a sal'ry! Who paid dat sal'ry up to five years ago? Not one dollah of it come outer ou' pockets!

"An' den, w'at did she git fer de yuther things she done! Who paid fer teachin' de Sunday-school? Who paid her fer de gals she kep' f'm thrown' deyse'ves away? Who paid her fer de boys she kep' outer jail? I had a son dat seemed to hab made up his min' ter go straight ter hell. I made him go ter Sunday-school, an' somethin' dat woman said teched his heart, an' he behaved hisse'f, an' I ain' got no reason fer ter be 'shame' er 'im. An' I can 'member, Br'er Cotten, when you did n'own fo' houses an' a fahm. An' when yo' fus wife was sick, who sot by her bedside an' read de Good Book ter 'er, w'en day wuz n'nobody else knowed how ter read it, an' comforted her on her way across de col', dahk ribber? An' dat ain' all I kin 'member, Mr. Chuhman! When yo' gal Fanny was a baby, an' sick, an' nobody knowed what was de matter wid'er, who sent fer a doctor, an' paid 'im fer comin', an' who he'ped nuss dat chile, an' tol' yo' wife w'at ter do, an' save' dat chile's life, jes as sho' as de Lawd had save' my soul?

"An' now, aftuh fifteen yeahs o'slavin' fer us, who ain't got no claim on her, aftuh fifteen years dat she has libbed 'mongs' us an' made her-self one of us, an' endyoed havin' her own people look down on her, aftuh she has growed ole an' gray wukkin' fer us an' our child'n, we talk erbout turnin' 'er out like a' ole hoss ter die! It 'pears ter me some folks has po' mem'ries! What would we 'a' be'n ef her folks at de No'th had n' membered us no bettuh? An' we had n' done nothin', fer dem to 'member us fer. De man dat kin fergit w'at Miss Noble has done fer dis town is unworthy de name er nigger! He oughter die an' make room fer some 'spectacle dog!

"Br'er Glaspy says we got a' educated young man, an' we mus' gib him sump'in ter do. Let him wait; ef I reads de signs right he won't hab ter wait long fer dis job. Let him teach in de primary schools, er in de country; an' ef he can't do dat, let 'im work while. It don't hahm a' educated man ter work a little; his fo'fathers has worked fer hund'eds of years, an' we's worked, an' we're heah yet, an' we're free, an'we's get-ting' ou' own houses an lots an' hosses an' cows – an' ou' educated young men. But don't let de fus thing we do as a committee be some-thing' we ought ter be 'shamed of as long as we lib. I votes fer Miss Noble, fus, las' an' all de time!"

When Old Abe sat down the chairman's face bore a troubled look. He remembered how his baby girl, the first of his children that he could really call his own, that no master could hold a prior claim upon, lay dying in the arms of his distracted young wife, and how the thin, homely, and short-sighted white teacher had some like an angel into his cabin, and had brought back the little one from the verge of the grave. The child was a young woman now, and Gillespie had well-founded hopes of securing the superior young Williams for a son-in-law; and he realized with something of shame that this later ambition had so daz-zled his eyes for a moment as to obscure the memory of earlier days.

Mr. Cotten, too, had not been unmoved, and there were tears in his eyes as he recalled how his first wife, Nancy, who had borne with him the privations of slavery, had passed away, with the teacher's hand in hers, before she had been able to enjoy the fruits of liberty. For they had loved one another much, and her death had been to them both a hard and bitter thing. And, as Old Abe spoke, he could remember, as distinctly as though they had been spoken but an hour before, the words of comfort that the teacher had whispered to Nancy in her dying hour and to him in his bereavement.

"On consideration, Mr. Chairman," he said, with an effort to hide a suspicious tremor in his voice and to speak with the dignity consistent with his character as a substantial citizen, "I wish to record my vote fer Miss Noble."

"The chair," said Gillespie, yielding gracefully to the majority, and greatly relieved that the responsibility of his candidate's defeat lay else-where, "will make the vote unanimous, and will appoint Brother Cotten and Brother Johnson a committee to step round the corner to Miss Noble's and notify her of her election."

The two committeemen put on their hats, and, accompanied by sev-eral people who had been waiting at the door to hear the result of the meeting, went around the corner to Miss Noble's house, a distance of a block or two away. The house was lighted, so they knew she had not gone to bed. They went in at the gate, and Cotton knocked at the door.

The colored maid opened it.

"Is Miss Noble home?" said Cotten.

"Yes; come in. She's waitin' ter hear from the committee."

The woman showed them into the parlor. Miss Noble rose from her seat by the table, where she had been reading, and came forward to meet them. They did not for a moment observe, as she took a step toward them, that her footsteps wavered. In her agitation she was scarcely aware of it herself.

"Miss Noble," announced Cotten, "we have come to let you know that you have be'n 'lected teacher of the grammar school fer the next year."

"Thank you; oh, thank you so much!" she said. "I am very glad. Mary" — she put her hand to her side suddenly and tottered — "Mary, will you —"

A spasm of pain contracted her face and cut short her speech. She would have fallen had Old Abe not caught her and, with Mary's help, laid her on a couch.

The remedies applied by Mary, and by the physician who was hastily summoned, proved unavailing. The teacher did not regain consciousness.

If it be given to those whose eyes have closed in death to linger regretfully for a while about their earthly tenement, or from some higher vantage-ground to look down upon it, then Henrietta Noble's tolerant spirit must have felt, mingling with its regret, a compensating thrill of pleasure; for not only those for whom she had labored sorrowed for her, but the people of her own race, many of whom, in the blindness of their pride, would not admit during her life that she served them also, saw so much clearer now that they took charge of her poor clay, and did it gentle reverence, and laid it tenderly away amid the dust of their own loved and honored dead.

Two weeks after Miss Noble's funeral the other candidate took charge of the grammar school, which went on without any further obstacles to the march of progress.

## CHAPTER THREE

# Teaching in the Big City:
# Women, the Education Bureaucracy,
# and Teacher Organizing

"EXCEPT FOR PROBLEMS IN simple arithmetic, how to read and how to write . . . I have forgotten everything the schools ever taught me," wrote Catherine Brody of her New York childhood. "But the glamour of the lady teachers, shining on the East Side World, I shall never forget. I see them now, all fused and molded into one symbolic figure, in dresses that seemed always delicate and gracefully silhouetted, in great puffed sleeves, with a neck that always seemed long and arched, with a pompadour that always seemed to make the forehead lofty and noble. The symbol sits enthroned on the dais-platform before a desk. . . . I see her with the record book, stumbling over the syllables of awkward foreign names, repeated over and over for her benefit by suffering, red-faced little girls."[1]

"But even more than the music of the hurdy-gurdy was the inspiring sight of the *teacher* as she passed the street," wrote Anzia Yezierska in her novel *Bread Givers*. "How thrilled I felt if I could brush by Teacher's skirt and look up into her face as she passed me. If I was lucky enough to win a glance or a smile from that superior creature, how happy I felt for the rest of the day! I had it ingrained in me from my father, this exalted reverence for the teacher."[2]

In this not uncommon turn of the twentieth century portrait, the teacher sat enthroned on the classroom platform. She stood out on the ghetto street. She touched and transformed the lives of individual children by her personal care and instruction. She was the link between the old world and the new, the intermediary who interpreted to children the language and culture of their adoptive country. These were the mythologized images of the teacher of immigrant children, and, like most myths, they had their grounding partially in reality, partially in wishfulness. For as much as she embodied the family's hopes — that the young would escape their parents' destiny: the bent backs, "the swollen veins in our legs, in our work-stained hands"[3] from the sweatshop, the factory, and domestic labor — she also exposed their children's deficiencies, their perhaps intractable difference from what true American schoolchildren should be.

Like her sister teachers of nineteenth-century rural New England, the teacher of immigrants was expected to shape character, impart the rudiments of good citizenship, and prepare her charges for vocations. But her job differed in two key ways from earlier teaching in the United States — the composition of her classes and her own status as an employee.

The city teacher worked with immigrants, but also with small numbers of African American students whose families had arrived in the cities with skills learned on the land or in small Southern towns. Many lived in urban poverty. Of the newly arrived immigrants, most did not speak English; many could not read or write in their home languages, and any number came from cultures of which the teacher herself was ignorant. Without special approaches to teaching non-English speakers a second language, the teacher forged ahead in English with a curriculum modified only slightly from the work of the New England schoolmen.[4] Her students' first English words were her words; their first American ideas, her interpretation of American morals, manners, and culture. Thus, the teacher's personal power had an enhanced significance and was of a more intense quality than that she had exercised in earlier days when she was more a part of her students' communities. As the selections in this chapter suggest, she could use her American accomplishments as weapons and as tools.

The power the teacher exercised over the children "beneath" her was more than matched by the power of school administrators over the teacher herself. At the turn of the century, big-city school systems were in the process of transformation: from decentralized organizations that gave out patronage jobs and were tied to locally organized political machines, to professionally managed centralized systems controlled by professional schoolmen, business leaders, and other civic elites. While many teachers resisted the move to centralization, neither the old system nor the new gave teachers power or permitted collaboration in setting policy. In the eyes of the men above them, teachers were dutiful daughters helping out their families until marriage. In 1841, the Boston School Committee *commended* women teachers because they were unambitious and "less intent on scheming for future honors or emoluments."[5] That attitude about women employees held on into the twentieth century. Women were ideal for centralized schools, which were structured on the hierarchical model of the factory, with levels of male managers and a flat female work force. Like the manager of the cotton mill, the school superintendent could regulate the performance of the "hands" (or teachers) and keep the "product" (educated children) of good quality. Lost to the city teacher were the autonomy and agency that were hers for the taking in the ungraded rural school.[6]

This chapter explores the teacher's personal relationship to and impact on the children she was to Americanize — in other words, her power. But it explores her powerlessness as well, the extent to which she tolerated a hierarchy that rewarded not initiative and creativity, but obedience to authority. This chapter also explores the story of the few African American teachers who worked in the schools of northeastern cities, and the paradoxical relation between desegregation and gaining a livelihood as a teacher of color. Finally, this chapter defines the end of the teacher's tolerance of powerlessness, the point at which she began to think of herself as exploited and to organize on her own behalf. In the cities, especially Chicago and New York, in the first decades of the twentieth century, women formed organizations and used political power with considerable success to improve their working conditions. Much of the material in this chapter describes teaching in Boston, metropolitan New York, and Chicago. Insofar as the chapter describes the building of big-city school systems, the cases have similarities. But the differences in these cities also emerge in regard to the specific immigrant groups they attracted, the pace and extent of African American migration, and the timetable and details of centralization plans.

The writing in this chapter includes previously published sketches, oral history, journalism, and essays, but unfortunately no personal diaries or letters by teachers about their experiences in the turn-of-the-century urban classroom. One among an army of teachers numbering nearly 15,000 in New York City in 1910, for example, and often still living with her family in the city of her birth, the urban teacher may have felt her daily routines too commonplace to record, or, if she did record them, not worth preserving. And, as several selections suggest, she may have been too exhausted from her labors to write. Luckily, her students memorialized her — for her love, for her ability to humiliate, and in remembrance of the youthful triumph conferred by her approval. Journalists and teachers turned writers judged her ability and criticized her. When legendary teachers died, friends and colleagues memorialized them in testimonials and biographical sketches. Beginning in the 1970s in the developing fields of African American history and women's history, interviewers captured teachers' memories of the early years of the century. Two notable projects that supply teachers' voices are the *Black Women Oral History Project* (1991) and the interviews with New York teachers carried out by historian Kate Rousmaniere for her book *City Teachers* (1997).[7]

## The Teacher's Power: "God's delegates on earth"[8]

"It was quarter past nine and Miss Bailey was calling the roll, an undertaking which, after months of daily practice, was still formidable. Beginning with Abraham Abrahamowski and continuing throughout the alphabet to Solomon Zaracheck, the roll call of the First-Reader Class was full of stumbling blocks and pitfalls." So wrote Myra Kelly, a New York schoolteacher, in a 1904 volume called *Little Citizens*,[9] excerpted in this chapter. Although Miss Bailey spoke humorously of her navigation through the roll call, she did not obscure the most striking challenge to the big-city school system — assimilating immigrants. Between the Eastern European Jewish names beginning with "A" and "Z" were others that reflected their Italian, Spanish, German, Russian, Irish, or Scotch origins. As New York school superintendent William Maxwell reported in 1908:

> There are more Jews in New York than in Palestine, more Italians than in Rome, and enough foreigners of other nationalities to make a city as big as St. Louis. Of the 75,000 new pupils who enter the New York schools every year, probably two-thirds cannot speak a word of English. In one school I counted children of twenty-nine different nationalities who spoke twenty-nine different languages or dialects.[10]

By the turn of the century in New York City, native-born Americans, including a growing number of African American students immigrating from the South, had become a minority of the population.

From the 1820s on, Irish immigrants escaping political persecution and repeated famine had flooded East Coast seaport cities. There they settled into crowded tenements, the best they could manage on their wages as unskilled workers on roads, as carters, teamsters, drivers, laundresses, cooks, and maids. By 1900 they controlled local politics in

Boston, New York, and Philadelphia, and had given pause to the old leadership of the city. Their most academically adept daughters had become teachers, their sons administrators. (Note the selections in this chapter by Kelly and Dogherty and references to male administrators named Quincy and O'Shea, likely first-generation Irish school employees.) But nothing compared in its power to transform urban life and institutions to the wave of non-English-speaking immigrants who arrived from the Mediterranean world and Eastern Europe at the turn of the twentieth century. In 1900, 449,000 arrived; by 1903, over 850,000; and in 1907, immigration reached a peak with 1,285,000 immigrant entries recorded.[11] Those patricians who had grown rich on immigrant labor now saw the proliferation of social and political problems so profound that they feared that their way of life and their children's would be utterly changed. "The dangerous classes" were alleged to have brought with them or developed in their overcrowded ghettos a long list of vices: their family structure was weak, their women and children immoral, their men drunks; they carried smallpox, tuberculosis, vermin; they ignored the health and safety ordinances of the city, and many clung to "the old ways." Most were not Protestants, but Jews, Catholics, or worse — atheists. Then there was the imported political radicalism of the Eastern European Jews, including enthusiasm for socialism, anarchism, "free love," birth control, labor organizing, and other anti-authoritarian causes.

Even those Americans who appreciated the new arrivals' culture as "immigrant gifts" agreed in one respect with those who saw them only as "un-American": that the immigrants must be assimilated into American society, "melted" into approximations of Protestant Americans. There was general agreement, too, that the American public school was the institution destined to carry out the task. The "cornerstone of democracy" had a legal claim on immigrant youth: however fitfully implemented, compulsory education laws obliged young people to attend school from ages eight to fourteen in most states. School could substitute for family, church, and cultural center by teaching malleable children (and through them, their parents) American history and values. Education could impart the legacy of hard work and self-reliance of the country's founders.[12] Thus, the cities would gradually be restored, if not to a comfortable homogeneity, to civic order.

In an address to the National Education Association, Julia Richman, herself a prospering Jewish immigrant and school administrator, made the classic statement about the function of the school so common in the literature of the period: "Ours is a nation of immigrants. The citizen voter of today was yesterday an immigrant child. Tomorrow he may be a political leader. Between the alien of today and the citizen of tomorrow stands the school, and upon the influence exerted by the school depends the kind of citizen the immigrant will become."[13] There is little evidence that either old-line citizens or the immigrants themselves questioned the power of the school to solve social problems and promote active citizenship, any more than we do today. A New York high school principal made this ominous and apparently acceptable claim: "Education will solve every problem of our national life, even that of assimilating our foreign element. . . . Ignorance is the mother of anarchy, poverty, and crime. The nation has a right to demand intelligence and virtue of every citizen, and to obtain these by force if necessary."[14]

The burden of transforming children fell on the teacher who, even under the best of conditions, had an overwhelming charge. Eight hours a day in a dark, uncomfortable classroom, sometimes with seventy or eighty children, two to a desk, some hungry and ill, she was not only to teach school subjects but, as the journalist Adele Marie Shaw observed in an article excerpted here, "make self-supporting men of probable paupers, good men and women of probable criminals, and good American citizens of thousands and thousands of children whose parents speak no English, and learn loyalty to government only by seeing what it does for their offspring" (see p. 257). Then, after hours, for her meager $650 a year,[15] she was to "go into the children's homes to teach the mothers," said Julia Richman. Echoing Catherine Beecher and a long line of women educators, Richman asserted: "The wives and mothers who nurture children [and] influence men [have] the destiny of the nation in their keeping." The day had passed, Richman said, "when ability to teach the studies of the school course is regarded as the whole service required of the ideal teacher."[16]

When this lofty charge was reduced to actual practice, evidence suggests that many teachers did perform according to Julia Richman's ideal. Fiction, memoir, and oral reminiscence consistently recount the teacher's disciplined passing on of proper English and carrying out home visits — sometimes to signal the special promise of a child, sometimes out of desperation to help families. In language instruction, imitation of standard-ized elocution was the style of instruction. "I would hang on his lips, striving to memorize every English word I could catch and watching intently, not only his enunciation, but also his gestures, manners, and mannerisms," wrote a man of his evening school teacher.[17] The fictional teacher Sara Smolinsky, heroine of *The Bread Givers*, explicitly linked the attainment of professional status with perfect English:

> *Her brightest eleven year old ended "almost every sentence with 'ain't it.'" After she asked him to write "isn't it" one hundred times, he declared, "I got it all right now, Teacher! Ain't it?" Sara Smolinsky replied, "Oh, Aby! . . . And you want to be a lawyer! Don't you know the judges will laugh you out of court if you plead your case with 'ain't it?'"*[18]

In his 1952 memoir *A Walker in the City*, writer Alfred Kazin has a less benign memory of learning language by imitation as an immigrant Jewish child. It meant "reproducing [the teacher's] painfully exact enunciation. . . . This English was peculiarly the ladder of advancement. Every young lawyer was known by it." It meant also that "we were somehow to be a little ashamed of what we were."[19]

The teaching of writing presented a further challenge in breaking the silence of the foreign born. Mary Antin's beloved teacher Miss Dillingham, her "first American friend," as she characterizes her in the selection that follows, helped the young girl gather new words as if she were "gathering a posy blossom by blossom" (see p. 283). Miss Dillingham succeeded in having Mary's composition, "Snow," published in an educational journal. Her introductory letter attributed Mary's progress to the lessons of her classroom. "This is the uncorrected paper of a Russian child twelve years old, who had studied English only four months. She had never, until September, been to school even in her own country, and has heard English spoken *only* at school" (see p. 284). A sim-ilarly powerful image is conjured up by Mary Agnes Dwyer, who was ninety-three years old when I interviewed her for the piece in this chap-ter: "I would return to school at night," she told me of her 21-year-old self, "and there I would hold the hands of adults, guiding the pencil as I taught them letters" (see p. 288). It was as if the physical contact could pass on language skills needed for the new world literally *through* the teacher. Speaking of the immigrants she taught beginning in 1906 in an industrial city near New York City, she recalls her own sense of efficacy as a teacher and the reciprocity she came to see in the relationships: "They are the people I still love and remember, because *they believed in us*. We had a great deal to give and they needed it, but we needed them as well. They were going to be the future of our city, and they *were*, and they *are*, even now" (see p. 287).

We know little about classroom work carried out by African American teachers in the segregated Northern schools. Many African American children did not attend school regularly, and mainly those with well-educated families succeeded in winning places in competitive public schools like Boston Latin School and New York's Wadleigh High School for Girls. In general, African American parents seemed to prefer integrated schools, and desegregation was a core principle of the National Association for the Advancement of Colored People from its founding in 1906. Luckily for readers today, the *Black Women Oral History Project* recorded one woman's work at a unique institution, the Bordentown Manual Training and Industrial School for Colored Youth in New Jersey, the only state-supported segregated boarding school for secondary students in the North, which was established in 1886. Frances Olivia Grant (1895–1982) arrived there in 1917 and so experienced the influx of students as a result of the Great Migration. A Phi Beta Kappa, *magna cum laude* graduate in classics from Radcliffe, the daughter of a prominent Harvard-educated dentist, Grant remembers throwing herself "heart and soul" into work at Bordentown, where she was to stay for thirty-eight years. In her oral history reprinted in this chapter, Grant describes her surprise at the inadequate preparation of some teachers — besides not knowing their own heritage, they had never heard of Pushkin, of Dumas, she recalled indignantly. Using her New York connections and her own not inconsiderable intellectual powers, Grant infused the curriculum with African American history and culture, and, for the most outstanding students, instituted a program of guest lecturers, including Nella Larsen, Paul Robeson, and Elmer Carter, the director of *Opportunity*. Her goal: to instill in the pupils belief in themselves and pride in their heritage.

There was, of course, another facet to the teacher's power — her power to humiliate and cow her students. Here the muckraking journalists of the period were quick to open fire. Adele Shaw visited twenty-five

New York public schools in 1903, and found that in a number "there exists a rigidity that is like *rigor mortis.*" Here teachers snapped and sneered at children. "In one class the very way in which the teacher intoned 'You — are — not — still' gave me a sensation of quick fright that brought back the awful moment of my childhood when I saw a boy arrested. . . . 'Somebody — foot!' the same teacher shouted suddenly, and my circulation stopped. My own foot, I felt sure, had moved" (see p. 261). From schools like these, Shaw felt, would be graduated "brutal truck drivers" and "amateur criminals." To their credit, however, the journalists recognized that the patriarchal and even despotic culture promulgated by some administrators could undermine sound and humanistic practices of teachers. Shaw asserted that, "under unwise management, a trained teacher may be reduced to the level of one who has had no training.""The wrong kind of teaching," as Shaw saw it, took place where "the subordinate must be forever on the jump to accomplish the set end of her day's labor . . . to carry out [the principal's] conscientiously relentless will"[20] (see p. 261).

## Pleasing the Authorities: The Teacher's Proper Place

If, in a characteristic vignette of the teacher *outside* her classroom, the ghetto poor clear the sidewalk before her and men raise their caps as she passes, a characteristic vignette *inside* the classroom portrays the young female teacher trembling under the scrutiny of a supervisor or inspector. And well she might. Ward bosses were known to remove teachers on trumped-up infractions when a vacancy was needed for a party regular's daughter. Superintendents or their delegated authorities visited every classroom, often unannounced, and held public examinations of the pupils. Graded secretly, these examinations determined the teacher's status — her pay, her promotion, or her demotion. Indeed, so memorable were these episodes for teachers that numerous first-hand accounts of classrooms figure around a trope: males exercise power arbitrarily and maliciously over female teachers under their supervision.

In Myra Kelly's *Little Citizens*, the teachers so feared the surprise arrival of Timothy O'Shea, the associate superintendent for the area, that they devised a system of interclassroom communication to warn one another when he was in the building. Older teachers holding permanent licenses protected their younger sisters from "gum shoe Tim," then ministered to those women left either faint or hysterical from his criticisms. Tim is imagined as a man in love with power, animated by catching the teacher off guard and crushing her spirits. An observer of the New York City schools, writing in the same year as Kelly, portrayed supervisors as men who go about "from schoolroom to schoolroom, notebook and pencil in hand, sitting for a while in each room like malignant sphinxes, eyeing the frightened teacher, who in his terror does everything wrong, and then marking him [sic] in a doomsday book."[21] And in a more complex version of the same story in the turn-of-the-century mystery *The Crayon Clue*, the feisty female union organizer-in-waiting, "Billy" Pennington, eavesdrops on the district superintendent threatening Miss Forrest, her principal, with termination because her teachers refuse to buy texts from which he gets kickbacks. "If you continue to interfere with matters outside your province, I shall feel it my painful duty not to recommend you for reappointment," the superintendent says unctuously.[22]

Even in an enlightened public school, the Hancock School for Girls in Boston's North End, the "genial" principal forced a model teacher to become aware of how much she was "subservient to a higher authority." Marian Dogherty's first brush with Mr. Dutton was harmless. He merely opened the door to display her class to some visiting ladies, and heard her, while teaching the music lesson she hated, yell "shut up" at "the wretches" who were openly enjoying "the racket they were making." Later in the year, however, he came to hear the girls read. Her girls held their books properly "in their right hands, with the toes pointing at an angle of forty-five degrees, the head held straight and high, the eyes looking directly ahead," but they forgot to announce page and chapter. Mr. Dutton criticized; the teacher's heart sank, and she determined "that this sort of thing should never, never happen again" (see pp. 277–279).

Throughout her description of "The First Class," reprinted in this chapter, Dogherty uses language and imagery that show her acceptance of the school hierarchy with its clearly delineated chain of command. Children obeyed the teacher. In stepping up to her high platform, she confirmed that she was above them. When the children forgot to announce page and chapter, she had failed to perform her "duty" to the satisfaction of her "superior officer."

The heavy hand of school hierarchy was particularly heightened in regard to African American women teachers. Boston, New York, and Chicago differed somewhat in the degree to which they enforced desegregation laws that were on the books by the turn of the nineteenth century, but in all three cities, while African American elementary pupils could legally attend majority white schools, African American teachers were rarely hired to work with white pupils.[23] Indeed, until Mrs. Suzie Frazier sued the city of New York in 1895 to obtain a teaching job, for twenty-two years after segregation ended, New York hired no new African American teachers. In 1908, an Immigration Commission survey showed only three African American kindergarten and elementary school teachers in Boston and 1,456 African American pupils, forty-three African American teachers in New York City and 6,542 African American students, and in Chicago sixteen African American teachers, and 3,806 African American pupils.[24] Only in segregated school systems in the South were there any number of African American teachers. The reasons were simple: To be educated as teachers for desegregated schools, African American students had to attend high school and often normal schools to which they had little access. If they were considered at all, the standards of admission were often higher than for white students, and the atmosphere unpleasant. In addition, white teachers did not want to compete with African Americans for jobs. And most important, while most white parents did not object to some mixing of the races among young children, they often protested the presence of African American teachers in their children's classrooms, especially in high schools.

The results were that African American teachers who taught in majority white northern schools had to be paragons of virtue with extraordinary academic qualifications — especially those who taught in high schools. They were both the pride of their communities and public spectacles of sorts in their schools — the recipients, inevitably, of scrutiny. Gertrude Johnson Ayer (1884–19?) and Melva Price (1902–1996) were among the first African Americans to graduate from Hunter College and to attend Columbia University as graduate students. Both were also "firsts" in New York City schools. Ayer, who began teaching in 1905, was the first African American guidance counselor in an elementary school, became an assistant principal and then a principal in 1935. Indeed, she was the city's only African American principal in a Harlem School for twenty-five years. So unusual was her appointment as principal that Roy

Wilkins, the NAACP leader, wrote his congratulations in the NAACP magazine *The Crisis*. Extraordinary in every way, Melva Price knew twelve languages, including Sanskrit, Polish, and Russian; wrote chapters of her diary during her graduate school years at Columbia in ancient Greek, and was the first African American teacher of Latin at Wadleigh High School, the city's exclusive girls' school. Indeed, so unusual was Price that young African American girls recount sneaking peeks at her as they passed her door, and her appointment was celebrated in the African American community press in Boston and elsewhere.[25]

Also poignant was the situation of the teacher who was herself a recent immigrant.[26] Not just routinely obedient in her work, she actively sought from the school the social approval others looked for elsewhere. The school had taught her to be American, and now it had become a substitute for the family that frequently represented to her the shame and ignorance of her past. With affecting intensity, a Cleveland teacher spoke at a National Education Association convention: "I am an immigrant, a stranger in a strange land. . . . Please notice me, take hold of me, lead me. . . . Try to protect me from my own inexperiences. Take me in as a member of your great and glorious family. I want to belong."[27] Behind her plea was perhaps harsh generational and cultural conflict similar to that portrayed in Anzia Yezierska's frequently anthologized story, "Children of Loneliness." One week home from college, Rachel Ravinsky, the new "teacherin," precipitated a bitter shouting match with her parents by asking her mother to eat with a fork. "Pfui on all your American colleges! Pfui on the morals of America! No respect for old age. No fear for God," shouted her father. "Aren't you dragging me by the hair to the darkness of past ages," Rachel screamed back before running from the house into the "crushing daze of loneliness."[28]

It should not be surprising that teachers, for the most part, were more dependent on authority than rebellious against it. At the turn of the twentieth century, female teachers had no professional identity or organization to advocate on their behalf. Few were appointed to serve as principals or administrators. Many teachers were barely educated for their jobs; some supported themselves, parents, and siblings; increasing numbers were recent immigrants; and a good number, legally prevented from marrying while employed, were beholden to the schools for life-long employment. Indeed, one particularly pernicious way schools controlled older women teachers was to emphasize the "young-daughter-as-teacher" formulation. As *The Crayon Clue*'s predatory superintendent claims, he applauds the presence of the "joyous, attractive young women who enter [teaching] year by year," but cannot abide any woman past the "zenith" of age twenty-eight. She is "the old maid . . . in which sex feeling seems to have been left out of the composition."[29] Victorian ideology also encouraged the young woman to think of teaching as an extension of her life as a daughter, and as preparation for her true work — motherhood.

What teachers were experiencing in urban areas in the last decades of the nineteenth century was the rapid growth of bureaucracy that accompanied urbanization. With jobs at stake and relatively few protections against corruption, city governments, of which schools were just another department, made visible the raw exercise of male political power. In Boston, New York, Chicago, Philadelphia, and smaller cities, the schools were the fiefdom of local ward politicians who gave out jobs as rewards to loyal voters and to "buy" new ones. Teachers from many cities reported that positions were awarded by a system of "pulls." As a male teacher, acquainted with the state superintendent (a political appointee) and some principals, "confessed" in an *Atlantic Monthly* article of 1896, "[These well-connected men] 'pulled' me into a vacancy worth $1,650 a year."[30] Party members' daughters, it was also asserted, no matter what their qualifications, were given jobs, while well-trained but poorly connected teachers remained unemployed, unless they were willing to produce a bribe. In her "confession," also published in the *Atlantic*, Miss Amelia Allison (pseud.) described the pressure she came under because, in her perception, her father belonged to the wrong party — the party, as she notes, that actually *had* a platform or an "issue":

> *The party without an issue thought that they saw a chance to win. As our district was likely to have a close contest, it was suggested that my father be whipped into line. The only lash that he could be made to feel, they thought, was a threat to remove me. They sent their candidate for school trustee to our home, and he knocked timidly at the back door* . . . (see p. 306)

Although Miss Allison's family refused to be bribed, she did manage to keep her job through a succession of party changes. Her strategy was typical of the dedicated teacher who eschewed politics — shut the classroom door; teach so well that parents demand you for their children; hide your independence from your superiors.[31] As one can imagine, such a system of employment was not conducive to educational excellence. Rote memorization and strict discipline prevailed; classes were large, and teachers generally lacked formal preparation.

Beginning in the last decade of the nineteenth century, worldly, well-educated elites realized that big cities could not ignore their schools if they were to maintain civil order or, as the more liberal leaders thought, reduce poverty and inequality, and assist the poor in escaping from the worst abuses of labor under capitalism. Thus began two decades of campaigning to "take the schools out of politics."[32] Dubbed "the great school war" (a phrase coined by Nicholas Murray Butler, president of Columbia University [1902–1945] and founder of Teachers College), the New York elites led the struggle for "social efficiency," which pitted Protestant upper-class city leaders — lawyers, executives from the boardrooms of growing corporations — and social reformers like Julia Richman against Irish and German neighborhood politicians. At stake was the ownership of the city; and the reformers won the day.

With their children safely enrolled in private seminaries and academies, the reformers made the public schools their project. Graduates of prestigious colleges and members of social and philanthropic organizations, ninety-two of the new school board members in New York were lawyers, eighteen bankers, and the rest included writers, professors, philanthropists, university administrators, and doctors.[33] These men knew what kind of educational system they wanted — ordered, disciplined, with decision-making following the model of the business corporation. Thus the reformers elevated the superintendency to a position of great prestige, and spoke of the new system of education as "scientific." The president of the University of Chicago, William Rainey Harper, introduced the New York Superintendent of Schools William Maxwell to a convocation, saying, "I am convinced that next in difficulty and in importance to the work of the President of the United States stands that of the superintendent of schools of our great cities."[34] So the work of deciding a course of study, selecting books, hiring and supervising teachers, and creating a "learned profession" took on dimensions of national significance. John Dewey was among the few to point out the "obvious discrepancy" between the teacher's obligation to give lessons about democracy, *and* her obligation to *take* orders and remain silent at her workplace.

The new school reformers formed a national community with similar political strategies. New York began centralization in 1896, followed by St. Louis (1897), Baltimore (1898), Philadelphia (1905), Boston (1906), Chicago (1917), and San Francisco (1920).[35] The story of the takeover by "administrative progressives," as they are called by historian David Tyack, has been told variously: As business elites' interest in social control of grassroots and community-based education politics; as a story of democratic progress toward "modern" and professional school management; and, most convincingly, as a clash of interest groups, each with ideals and self-serving motives of their own.[36] From the perspective of teachers, whatever the analysis, neither a system run by partisan ward committees nor one run by professional managers directed by a central office provided an institutionalized voice in decision-making for teachers. For example, the Harper Commission in Chicago, an elite, all-male group, sought the opinions of education experts throughout the country in making its recommendations for the restructuring of the Chicago schools, but had no interest in teachers' expertise. The Commission relied on a strong superintendent advised by college presidents to select principals, and even to choose textbooks. The Harper Commission also asserted that more males were needed in schools, and that males should be paid higher wages than women. From the perspectives of both class and gender, then, female teachers were put in an awkward position. Many teachers would not have called themselves working class; rather they emulated the habits and manners of the very elite who were engaged in their explicit disenfranchisement.[37]

Perhaps unwittingly, the progressives helped teachers reconceptualize themselves as laborers in the system. Many teachers were quick to see that the messy, localized reign of politicians gave them both more freedom and job security than they would have under the judicious hand of the reformers. Under the ward system, teachers at least had seniority (the reformers wanted to promote teachers on the basis of a test, not seniority), their principals had power conferred by the local board, and the political structures were closely allied with the character and cultures of their neighborhoods. Billy Pennington, the union organizer of *The Crayon Clue,* expressed the changes in schools at the turn of the century:

*When I first began to teach, ten years ago, the teachers were regarded as a part of the school system. As the ones who, out of the whole system, came into daily, hourly contact with the children, they were consulted and their opinions listened to with respect. . . . The whole trend is now to treat us like factory hands. . . . It's a sort of death-in-life atmosphere; deadening and smothering.*[38]

Ultimately, teachers like Billy did overcome their own ambivalence about class identity, and thus they organized labor unions to confront the authority that ruled them. But that is getting ahead of the story.

In choosing teaching over secretarial work — the only other genteel profession open to women who were obliged to work — the teacher had signaled her desire for acceptance in a social class above her own. In granting the teacher so little agency and voice as a worker inside her school, the administrative progressives sent signals that she was not equal socially to their more educated wives and daughters. The teacher thus occupied a social space with double meaning; she was at once a success in her own eyes and those of the family to whose support she contributed, and at the same time not the match of upper-class graduates of schools like Vassar, Smith, and Wellesley. (Women's college graduates often chose volunteer philanthropic work, in settlement houses or in school improvement groups. They dominated the new fields of sociology and social work, and often viewed the teacher simply as an anonymous public servant.) The very small number of African American teachers experienced even more extreme social dislocation: Considered to have achieved an extraordinary victory in earning both a college education and a teaching position, the African American teacher was celebrated in her own community and excluded almost totally from the white social world to which she might have belonged by virtue of achievements had her skin not been dark.

One teacher expressed her bitterness at being excluded from her city's "very energetic women's clubs. They certainly have not considered what they might give to the teacher, nor what the teacher could give to them, for they hold their meetings at an hour when teachers are at work."[39] From a survey of teachers asking what they felt their own "position" to be came the following two opinions: One teacher told the story of attending a party given by a society woman for teachers the night following one for her own "set." On a tray, the young women noticed a small cake with a bite taken out of it, obviously left over from the previous night. At this revelation there were indignant looks, but the teachers' inviolable safeguard, the sense of humor, came to the rescue, and the holder of the telltale wafer lifted it up and proposed, sotto voce, "Here's health to us: the rag-tag and bobtail of the learned professions: beloved by children, tolerated by youth; forgotten by maturity; considered municipally, financially and socially as good enough for what is left." But the sense of humor apparently was not always an adequate defense. Wrote another woman, "The office girl or the typewriter is more of a social success because her evenings are free and her spirit is less fatigued; not because she has a mind or disposition equal to that of a teacher."[40]

### Enter the "lady labor sluggers": Teachers Organize

As Margaret Haley declared in 1904 to the General Session of the National Education Association (NEA):

> The teacher [is] an automaton, a mere factory hand, whose duty it is to carry out mechanically and unquestioningly the ideas and orders of those clothed with the authority of position. . . . The individuality of the teacher and her power of initiative are thus destroyed, and the result is courses of study, regulations, and equipment which the teachers have had no voice in selecting, which often have no relation to the children's needs, and which prove a hindrance instead of a help in teaching.[41] (see p. 312)

Haley's address, "Why Teachers Should Organize," reprinted in this chapter, was not a mere rhetorical gesture intended to stimulate debate on the working conditions of teachers. She stood before the NEA as business agent of the Chicago Teacher's Federation (CTF), founded in 1897 to advocate for better pay, job security, and a voice in decision-making for Chicago's elementary school teachers, and as president of the new National Federation of Teachers. To the credit of this "lady labor slugger" and her sister unionists were impressive victories. With CTF President Catherine Goggin, "Maggie" Haley had forced the state supreme court to wrest unpaid taxes from five public utility companies — money, they argued, that should have gone for teachers' raises. Subsequently, they took the Board of Education to court and won, after it earmarked the back taxes for school maintenance, not salaries. Haley also won a tenure law, a pension plan, and a system of teachers' councils that had some powers over curriculum and discipline.

Haley's visibility and ability to play for high stakes and win with the city's corporate and political elite attracted the attention of those considered the "real" workers — members of the Chicago Federation of Labor (CFL). "The time has come for the working men of Chicago to take a stand for their children's sake, and demand justice for the teachers and the children so that both may not be crushed by the power of corporate greed," declared John Fitzpatrick, the union president in a letter to the CFL in November 1902.[42] Astute politically and tireless in seeking alliances to promote the cause, Haley overcame the reluctance of genteel lady teachers to join with workingmen. After all, she argued, these men were a large voting block with an interest in public schools. And, furthermore, since women had not yet won the right to vote, Haley's voteless female constituents could campaign *through* and with male workers for candidates who supported a range of progressive issues: child labor laws, woman suffrage, direct primaries, and equal wages for men and women.

For the first two decades of the twentieth century, Maggie Haley, Catherine Goggin, and women in other big cities led unique female labor organizations of considerable power.[43] But until recently, their work has figured as a footnote among those who study labor history or the history of women in the professions. To labor historians, teachers were professionals, less interesting than "real" workers: To those interested in the professions, there was less to be learned from teaching than from jobs that restricted female entry.[44] But for recent scholars interested in women teachers themselves, the flash of female-led militancy raises important questions. What motivated the Maggie Haleys to organize, wield power, and fight in ways considered "unbecoming to the sex?" What was the relation between feminism, suffrage, and teacher organizing? What were the differences among women leaders of teacher organizations? And, beyond the scope of this book, but perhaps most important, why have women teachers not wielded such power in the new teacher union movement that began in the 1960s with collective bargaining?

Teacher organizing took place in a political environment that set the stage for the dilemmas that pursue the profession today: Are teachers workers carrying out mandates set by others, or are they professionals whose work is best characterized by the requirement that independent judgment be exercised? Gender added an even more complicating consideration. Women teachers attempted to reconcile two disparate movements — neither of which fit them well. To be effective as a union, they were best served joining a male militant, sometimes violent, high-profile labor movement. To accentuate their independence and professionalism, they were best identifying with the increasingly visible "new woman," that modern female who wanted to live independently, perhaps not marry, to vote, to have a career, and to speak her mind.[45] Like workers, teachers wanted better pay and working conditions; like the troublesome new woman, teachers wanted a voice in making the decisions that affected their work. But in truth, women teachers could justly be positioned as a unique exploited "class" or caste — not akin to laborers who used their hands and muscles in factories, sweat shops, and the trades; not parallel to the new woman in education, aspirations, social standing, or sophistication. Dan Lortie catches that identity best when he characterizes the profession as "special, but shadowed."[46] And that ambiguity remains unresolved in tensions about the compatibility of teacher unionism and professionalism even today.

In regard to labor unrest, throughout the later decades of the nineteenth century and then increasingly in the early twentieth, progressivism and socialism came to define the oppositional voices in urban politics. The Russian Revolution brought experienced labor organizers to the East Coast cities, and class warfare erupted in factories, sweatshops, mines, and mills. Union membership doubled between 1897 and 1901 to one million; it was two million by 1904. African American and white women, especially Jewish women "nurtured in the cradle of Russian socialism," made major contributions to worker movements.[47] Some labor union issues — child labor laws, worker safety, and exploitation of piece workers at home — were certainly women's issues, and had repercussions in classrooms. And teachers certainly had siblings, neighbors, and friends caught up in strikes and labor disputes. Nonetheless, of the female teacher organizations, only the Chicago Federation of Teachers formed a close affiliation with labor — signaling that large numbers of women teachers and their leaders resisted full identification as workers while simultaneously appreciating the power of organizing.

In regard to inspiration from and alliance with the "woman move-ment," as it was called, woman teacher organizations again straddled a divide. Although they sought help and often got it from club women, unmarried teachers were not the social equals of the female social reformers, many graduates of elite colleges. The club women faced fewer material constraints and had relationships with and some influence over corporate school reformers, especially through marriage. For example, club members in both New York and Chicago supported centralization bills that teachers opposed. Furthermore, teachers were of necessity more deeply engaged in the roughhouse politics of the state and local government than the club women of their day. Once centralization had taken power away from principals and vested it in the mayor's office and the state legislature, teacher organizers were forced to play on a large public stage. A particularly interesting example of women's organizing around job issues for which women's clubs and feminist journalists did provide support was the "one issue" campaign of the New York City Interborough Association of Women Teachers (IAWT). The campaign also showed some of the fissures between the broader women's agenda and teachers' interests.[48]

Under the leadership of Grace Strachan, a fearless district superin-tendent turned labor leader, the campaign began in response to one result of centralization. In 1900 New York State gained from the bor-oughs the legal power to set teachers' salaries for the five New York bor-oughs. To the surprise of teachers who had initially supported the move, the state set minimum salaries for women at $600, and at $900 for males. Further similar discrepancies appeared between veteran teachers, principals, and high school teachers. The rationale for salary discrimina-tion was that women were mentally and physically inferior to men; that teaching was a temporary career for a woman, but a life's work for a man; that men supported families while women supported only themselves; and, that if women's salaries were raised, more might choose not to marry.[49] The Interborough Association of Women Teachers, formed in 1906 from the Women Teachers' Organization, like the Chicago Federation of Teachers took "equal pay for equal work" as its slogan and appealed to the proletariat of the profession — female elementary school teachers, who were the lowest paid women in the system. Strachan's argument was that women had the same right to economic independence as men. Family responsibility had no place in fixing salary:

> *I hold that salary is for service, and should be measured by the service ren-*
> *dered, irrespective of the size, weight, color, complexion, race, previous con-*
> *dition of servitude, height, length of nose, location of ear, character of cos-*
> *tume, religion, size of shoe, height of heel worn, hair or lack of hair on the*
> *face or head, number of children, nephews, nieces, aunts, grandfathers, par-*
> *ents. . . . I'm sure if a man comes to sweep off the snow from your front stoop,*
> *you do not ask him if he is married and how many children he has, in order*
> *to fix the price for his work.*[50]

In addition, she pointed out, the unmarried woman teacher often supported elderly relatives who would not assist her in her old age while the
married man had children as "an endowment policy" for his.[51]

The Irish leadership of the IAWT, schooled in the rough-and-tumble
of ward politics, argued their case in the mass media and sought allies
among local politicians and in women's clubs. From 1907 on, backed by
a membership that reached 14,000 in 1910,[52] Strachan took her case to
city hall and the state legislature. Delegations of teacher lobbyists traveled to Albany, absenting themselves without pay from their schools, and
causing the city Board of Education to bellow its disapproval of women
taking political positions, especially when they contradicted the Board's.
The Board even tried to gag Strachan and accused her of neglecting her
supervisory duties. Using her usual grand rhetoric, she had written as the
*official* report of her absences: "Work in a cause destined to uplift the
moral standards of the school system, and hence the community, the
State, the nation, and the world — the establishment of justice for the
women workers in our public schools."[53]

In 1911, with newly elected Democrats as governor and mayor, the
New York legislature passed a law granting these voteless women their
equal pay. The bill said that salaries would be determined by merit, length
and degree of experience, and grade level taught.[54]

Comparing the equal-pay campaign in New York with Haley's campaign in Chicago illustrates the complex relation of teacher organizations, not only to club women but also to women's issues within teacher
organizations. Margaret Haley framed the issue of equal pay not as a
women's issue as Strachan had done, but as an issue of a living wage and

benefits. These she called the rights of any working person. In her view, teachers shared the plight of other exploited workers, and only in organizing unions would the power of the bosses be tempered. Within this framework, Haley supported woman suffrage and organized labor with far more passion and woman power than did Strachan. Tensions about these views plagued the CTF throughout its history, and it is fair to say that even when Haley won tangible material benefits for her membership, Chicago teachers, like teachers in other cities, were politically conservative, worried about maintaining the respect of the upper classes, and not inclined to support militancy except on their own bread-and-butter issues. Ironically, although she was overtly more woman focused, Strachan's brand of one-issue politics was much closer to the views of the teachers who supported suffrage largely as a path to better pay. Only small numbers of teachers embedded women's rights in the larger leftist labor struggle.[55]

That gender discrimination spurred women teachers to action there is little doubt; indeed, the equal-pay campaign was certainly marked as a campaign for fairness to women. Nor is there doubt that the way the enlightened reformers flaunted their patriarchal power must have been more galling to teachers than dealing with poorly educated ward politicians, who did not presume to tell teachers how to teach. But while Grace Strachan's rhetorical flourishes may have served to cheer her constituents on — she declared that "The Interborough Association of Women . . . send greetings to all its sisters, and promises that the degradation and belittling will disappear 'as mists of the morning'" — by 1920, teacher activism had faded from the political landscape in New York City. In Chicago, in 1917, with her membership dropping dramatically, Margaret Haley withdrew the CTF from the labor movement to save her organization. In the end teachers' goals were limited: teachers fought to protect themselves from intimidation and exploitation by supervisors, autocratic superintendents, and patrician boards, and to gain better pay and more security. Once the twin catalysts of the labor movement and the woman movement diminished in influence and World War I and the Great Depression loomed, teachers too retreated from activism and outright militancy.

# The True Character of the
# New York Public Schools

*Adele Marie Shaw*

From Adele Marie Shaw, "The True Character of the
New York Public Schools," *The World's Work,* Vol. 7, No. 2
(December 1903), pp. 4204–4221.

*In the years 1903 and 1904, New York writer and teacher Adele Marie Shaw
(1865?–1941) wrote a series of six "first hand studies of American public schools."
While Shaw aligned herself with the progressive reformers of her time, comment-
ing on overcrowded school buildings, schools' lack of sanitation, and the despotism
of administrators, her articles also provide one teacher's view on the modern school
system. A teacher herself, Shaw placed great importance on the role of teachers in
"Americanizing" their immigrant students. Today's immigrant children, she
claimed, are tomorrow's citizens. In a series of arguments, Shaw looks back on
women's traditional roles as mothers and the ideal of republican motherhood, and
imbues teachers with the ability to transform a "cityful of Russian, Turks, Austro-
Hungarians, Sicilians, Greeks, and Arabs, into good Americans," thus insuring the
salvation of New York City. Shaw's articles are radical, not because of her beliefs
about the importance of teachers to society, but for her insistence that this importance should justify a series of reforms, including administrative reform and equal
pay for women teachers.*

    *Shaw's and others' claims for teachers' rights become more problematic when
seen within the context of the nativist sentiments at the turn of the century. One
of Shaw's final recommendations was to restrict immigration into America, thus
relieving public schools from the burden of educating immigrant children. In her
writings, immigrant children emerge as unclean, uneducated, and potential crimi-*

nals — only the teacher and her "Americanizing" influence will reform them. In contrast, Mary Antin, a Russian Jewish immigrant whose writing appears later in this chapter, credited her parents and her community, along with her teacher, for instilling a love of learning in her. While Shaw's nativist feelings are not unusual for a woman of her background, they do hint at the cultural, social, and political views that sometimes alienated white, middle-class teachers from their immigrant students.

A highly educated woman herself, Shaw graduated from Smith College and served as head of the English department at Newtown (Queens, N.Y.) High School. She enjoyed a substantial career writing for Scribners Century, McClure's, and other national magazines. The series Shaw wrote on the public schools, of which the following is excerpted, garnered considerable attention and was published in The World's Work.

Twenty-three Million Dollars This Year Well Spent But Wholly Insufficient — Good Work of the Present Board — But Unspeakably Unsanitary Conditions in Some of the Schools — How Physical Examinations Are Conducted by Doctors and Nurses — Bad Methods and Bad Manners — The Improvements under Way — The Problem Presented by Immigration

The future of this country is more than ever in the hands of the public schools. We hear the statement often and are not startled. Now and then we rally (in our newspapers) to shout "Hands off!" to the sectarian and to the politician, and "Three cheers!" or "Down with fads!" to the reformer, but, unless some boy or girl in our own household raises the cry of injustice, we bother ourselves very little about the schoolroom influences that are making or spoiling American children.

What citizen or parent, for instance, who has no official connection with the public schools, has within a year been inside a schoolroom? or knows whether the work done in the public school nearest him is good or bad?

### The Problem in New York City

I chose New York City as the starting point in a study of the public schools of the United States because New York's problem is so difficult that once solved it would shed a calcium light upon the problems of other places. No other municipality had ever to meet a problem so difficult, so peculiar, and at the same time so all-embracing. With eighty-five per cent of its population foreign or of foreign parentage; its salvation dependent upon the conversion of a daily arriving cityful of Russians, Turks, AustroHungarians, Sicilians, Greeks, Arabs, into good Americans; its average citizen ignorant or indifferent concerning educational ideals; its present effort weighted with the ignorance and corruption of the past, the city has a problem of popular education that is staggering. . . .

### Can Any Amount of Work or Money Really Solve the Problem?

There were enrolled in the public schools last year 588,614 pupils. This year there is an increase in the day schools of 40,408 (enrolled pupils). September 30th there were 89,316 children in part-time classes. When we consider that 73,226 of these should have been provided for during the Tammany administration, and that the new buildings when completed will furnish 21,447 more sittings than are now needed, we can guess in some fashion at the stupendous energy, skill, and determination of the present Board of Education. In the history of the world I doubt if money was ever more wisely expended than the $23,000,000 used in 1901–2 by the present managers of the public schools of this city. How many parents have any knowledge of the enormous gain of the past two years? How many, comparing poor conditions with the best, are ready to say, "Make it all good, *no matter what it costs.*"

And it will cost. For the first time in our history all children of school age are registered and cared for, all truants are followed up, all recreant parents coerced. This alone adds an army to the school registers. Under this administration more children live and fewer die. This, as well as immigration, crowds the schools. And all the time, back of this growth by avulsion and by restoration, are the natural accretion and expansion of a great and attractive city whose normal increase is almost forgotten behind the descending avalanche of aliens.

What in the face of growth like this are 20,000 or 200,000 sittings? Unless Tammany returns forever to power (and that is not possible), East Side babies will go on improving; fewer tiny coffins will be needed, and more schoolroom chairs. Unless legislation dams the encroaching flood, more babies will be brought here and more babies will be born here than ever before. And unless New York ceases to draw like the magnet it is, its population will be swelled by contributions from the North and the East and the South and the West of our own country.

No one denies that New York's growth is abnormally large, its adoption of aliens abnormally confiding. If it hopes to Americanize a school population chiefly of foreign parentage it must use abnormal means. Last year one school had free baths; 1,000 baths were taken in that school in one week. Every school in the thickly settled districts should have free baths. If you sniff at "frills" and say, "Give them the three R's; let them get clean at home," you forget that they will not get clean at home, and that if they stay unclean in school every child and every home is endangered.

To educate the children of our adoption we must at the same time educate their families, and in a measure the public school must be to them family as well as school. To do this and not to neglect, as we are now forced to neglect, the children who are here, needs not twenty-three million dollars in a year, but five times twenty-three millions. If we withhold it we surrender the city to crime and to disease.

### Scenes from Primary School Rooms

In order to make a fair picture of the work, good and bad, that is done in New York public schools, since the beginning of the school year I have visited twenty-five of the schools where little New Yorkers are trained. These schools were very carefully selected, both for location and for such other considerations as should make them representative of the elementary system, so that the change from building to building has often been as great as the change from tropic to pole. Some children spend their entire school life under a *regime* that would make criminals of harmless mollusks, and some from kindergarten to graduation know only the influences that strengthen and establish.

In one of these primary schoolrooms an eager little girl is reciting,

*Down in the meadow where the stream runs blue*
*Lived an old mother fish and her little fishes two.*

You suspect something amiss with the natural history, but you know the atmosphere is gentleness and good-will. Across the corridor the woman whom the children call "a murder" is devoting herself to "discipline."

The lower-grade teachers bear the heaviest burden of the public school system. Their classes are too large, and the demands made upon

*"Playground in Poverty Gap."* Teacher-journalist Adele Marie Shaw protested conditions of the kind pictured here. Some ghetto school play spaces described by Shaw were even worse, located in dank, airless basements. Photograph by Jacob A. Riis, early 1890s.

them are exacting.

### The Material the Schools Must Work On

In a Brooklyn school not far from the Bridge I visited a room where sixty-five very small children were packed into a space properly intended for twenty. A bright-faced young woman was steadying a sleeping baby upon his third-of-a-seat while she heard the remaining sixty-four recite. By the end of the hour she had the sleepy one at the blackboard delightedly making a figure.

"He and his brother here are little Cubans," she explained. "They speak no English, but the brother can already imitate anything the rest can do."

I saw the small class a few days later and the two were already melted into the rank and file and were losing the distinctly foreign look. Soon they will begin to be ashamed of their beautiful Spanish name, and will revise its spelling in deference to their friends' linguistic limitations.

Esther Oberrhein in the entering class changes to Esther O'Brien in the next grade. Down in Marion Street a dark-eyed son of Naples who came last spring as Guiseppi Vagnotti appeared in September as Mike Jones.

The adaptability of childhood modifies more than the names. Mr. Hewitt, in looking for "types" to photograph, remarked the extraordinary homogeneousness of uppergrade children. Swedish, Norwegian, Italian — all were *American*. With every "type" the primary teacher must deal. With the cruel-fingered boy who "fell from a window a year ago and isn't quite right," to the big girl just landed guiltless of any tongue save her native Yiddish, the same magic must be made to work; the fusing and amalgamating force of interest kept at white heat. It is exhausting labor.

Did you ever try to teach sixty-five or even fifty-five little children how to thread a worsted needle? Did you ever take care of a mere dozen for a morning? If you did, you will admire and not carp at the woman who keeps her temper, treats them like human beings, and teaches them to speak English and tell them a story, even if she does say, as I heard one, "Don't that come in lovely," "somewheres," and "O my goodness."

The good primary teacher has the power of making you forget your environment. It was in the cavernous dimness of a very dreary room that I became so absorbed I overstayed my hour. It was here that Garcia, Mendelssohn, and Joshua sat in the same row and made well-proportioned pictures with yellow crayon, and a nasturtium for model. Whether it was drawing or arithmetic, there was apparently not a minute of the day when pleased attention and earnest effort languished. The teacher was a thin, delicate girl who gave her entire mind, and soul, and heart, and strength to her task. Philanthropists who never taught, and even superintendents who have, urge such teachers to spend the remnant of their force *in visiting the homes of their pupils,* and praise is accorded those who add to an already suicidal labor the taking of their flocks upon excursions. The excursions are admirable, a wonderful stimulus to the children who share them, but why not appoint wise, wholesome, responsible men and women and give them a salary as "conductors." Let the teacher go as a guest. Otherwise we shall always have the unconscientious too much in evidence while the sensitive and magnetic are killed off.

On the fifth floor of "No. 20" (Rivington, Forsythe, and Eldridge Streets in Manhattan) are the reading-room, library, sewing-room, cooking-room, girls' gymnasium, boys' gymnasium, modeling-room, draughting-room, [QA: drafting room?] and carpentry room. The principal of No. 6 (Miss Clara Calkins) can make her children happy, busy, and self-controlled in a building bare of even common necessities! What would she not accomplish for body and spirit in a building light, sanitary, and well equipped? It was at No. 6 that the photographer, taking a picture of the old form of assembly room, made by sliding walls (with no corridors), exclaimed at the remarkable stillness of the six classes during a long exposure. "If this is public school training," he said, "then I wish the children that come to my studio could have it. It's *extraordinary*."

### Some Examples of Wonderful Work and Model School Buildings

At 141 and 110 in Brooklyn I found the ideal principal and the modern building together. In both, sunshine — warmth and light — pervaded the place and the work. If there is any place where a citizen may find hope for the solution of an apparently insoluble problem it is in the new schools of the lower East Side of Manhattan. Let him see the cheerful athletes on the roof playground of No. 1 (Henry and Oliver Streets); let him watch the boys and girls fresh from the shower baths of 147 (Gouverneur and Henry Streets); let him see the "little mothers" and the ambitious newsboys in the evening study rooms of the recreation centres; and let him visit that humane product of a real civilization, the ungraded class for the mentally handicapped at school No. 1. Such schools are making self-supporting men of probable paupers, good men and women of probable criminals, and good American citizens of thousands and thousands of children whose parents speak no English, and learn loyalty to government only by seeing what it does for their offspring.

The mere physical gain in these improved schools is a constantly rising scale of inventive excellence. I have pored literally hours over the plans for the new 106, realizing in them dreams that have been often scoffed at as "impossible." Here, easily accessible from the street, is to be a vast auditorium, that with its toilet rooms and special approaches can be shut off from the upper building. Weary mothers that would never have climbed four flights of stairs will slip in here to free evening lectures and rest worn eyes on stereopticon views of lake and country, sometimes the valleys and mountains of their native land. A laboratory is not in itself beautiful. But a laboratory filled with youthful workers, learning the dignity of toil and the way to think, is more than beautiful. To the patriot it is hope and assurance.

If I were to attempt the guidance of a visitor to New York schools I should not let him escape till he had seen 159, visited 77 (whose former principal, Miss Richman, is now district superintendent), had a glimpse of 170 (east of Central Park at 111th Street), and seen at least the outside of 63 and 175 in the Bronx. These are mentioned almost at random, picked out from a long list of schools that would inspire the interest of any real American from Cape Nome to the Florida Keys.

## The Medical Inspector and the Nurse

In these modem schools education begins as far as possible, with the production of sound physical conditions in the child. The common sense of this method is plain to the cultivated man, but ignorant parents are chronic objectors to time thrown away on the care of the body. "You must stop teach my Lizzie fisical torture she needs yet readin' end figors mit sums more as that, if I want her to do jumpin'I kin make her jump," was an exasperated mother's protest.

It is this dead weight of ignorance that fell at first upon the shoulders of the medical inspectors and the nurses. . . .

As a rule, the doctor's toil is briefly over. The nurse's lasts all day. . . . The nurse's tact, humanity, and firmness are phenomenal. Everywhere she soothes eyes that look like martyrdom when the lids are drawn down, treats skin diseases of which ringworm and a scabby eruption are the most common, and examines heads.

The patients I saw were so little and so plucky I found my circulation quickening in admiration. Not a child whined or begged off, and not one cried out at the smart. The thing that goes straight to one's heart is the satisfied and utter confidence with which they settle back into the nurse's hands. They like to be cared for.

"Did your big sister use the kerosene?" asked the nurse, parting a mop of hair to peer carefully at the forest within.

"Yes, ma'am," replied the afflicted one.

"Tell her to put on more, so it will soak all through, and come to me tomorrow," was the day's direction.

The vermin present is of many kinds. In old days, it seems, those that hopped found undisturbed delight in varied exploration; those that crawled, abode and multiplied. But the day of the hopper and of the crawler alike is over — or would be over if the city could afford to give the same care to all neglected children that it gives to some. . . .

## The Dark Side of the Picture

New York children do not have equal chances, physically, in the New York schools. Yet the custom of seating two children (and in crowded classrooms I frequently saw *three*) at the same desk cannot be done away with till money can be spared for new furniture and space allowed for single desks. A New York physician has said that ninety-nine out of a hundred girls are deformed by the schoolroom postures before they reach the high school; curvature of the spine is one of the commonest effects of schoolroom chairs. Yet the new course of study, which insists upon a sensible change of position, with calisthenics and deep breathing at frequent intervals, is condemned by old-fashioned teachers as "wasting time." At present the attention given in the lower schools to keeping children straight and well developed varies with the caprices of the individual instructor.

The conditions of public education should provide for the right growth of body, mind, and character; and proper physical training demands good air, cleanliness, and freedom from degrading surroundings. Good air in the months of September and October is not hard to obtain, yet in nearly every classroom that I entered the atmosphere was foul. Sometimes even the assembly hall and the corridors were distinctly offensive. A room in which forty-six little girls live and work five hours in the day contained only one outside window. The miserably flickering gas over their heads consumed the oxygen needed by starved lungs, and yet on the three warm days during which I visited this class I did not once see the window opened more than a few inches. The scourge of New York is consumption; the preventive of consumption is fresh air; and these children say "Draught" as they might cry "Tiger!"

## A Murderous Hole of Darkness

The darkness would be less oppressive in such cases if the gas that bums on cloudy days in certain rooms of half the schools I saw, and on all days in some, was good gas, but its feeble uncertainty adds a melancholy to the gloom. In one dim assembly hall I groped my way to a platform on either side of which was drawn a cloth curtain. Behind the curtains two classes went on in simultaneous confusion, and I talked with the principal in a kind of cloth-bound cave, with grammar on one side, arithmetic on the other, and a "bad boy" awaiting discipline down in front.

The gas jets that eked out the scanty daylight in the curtained recesses had in one instance been replaced by Welsbach burners, and as one of the teachers said, "They're always breaking, and then they're worse than nothing."

The windows of this building opened on two sides into tenement back yards, whose washings were strung within a few feet of the children's desks, and whose sheds and water-closets just below were close to the schoolhouse wall.

Because of the stench that had floated in the windows, complaint had been made of the yard closets, and I was told that they had been closed and the air purified. I was not conscious of any unpleasant odor, but the closets were not entirely out of use.

In this building both principal and teachers appeared to take great pains with ventilation, but the conditions of their labors were more than difficult. The playground space was a small dark basement divided so as to give the girls the larger share. Sunken between the tenements and the school building was a narrow court not so large as a good city back yard, where 500 boys "went out to play." On rainy days they are often crowded so close in the hopeless darkness of the basement that there is barely standing-room. The teacher in charge of the playground must stay in this cell, though to see what is going on is impossible, and although on winter days the place is miserably cold for her and for the boys. . . .

### The Wrong Kind of Teaching

Nor is there any greater equality in the conditions in which the New York public-school child develops mind and character.

The well-to-do, who furnish the principal support of the public schools, send their children elsewhere. Three-fourths of New York's elementary teachers could not get positions in private schools.

"Who told you to speak out?" "*You've* paid attention!" scolded or sneered at a boy who is struggling to express an independent thought, will not make him a ready user of the gifts with which he is endowed.

The tone of continual exasperation in which more than one class is addressed would blight the forthputting powers of a Macaulay. Truancy from some of these classes should be imputed to a child for righteousness. In one room, where a geography recitation was in lumbering progress, I volunteered the beaming comment: "These seem like nice boys." "I haven't found them so," answered the teacher sourly, and a sudden animation and general straightening lapsed into stodginess. . . .

In one school in which I spent the better part of two days I did not once hear any child express a thought in his own words. Attention was perfect. No pupil could escape from any grade without knowing the questions and answers of that grade. Every child could add, subtract, multiply, and divide with accuracy; every child could and did pronounce his reading words with unusual distinctness. The chant in which recitations were delivered was as uniform as everything else. "Wren: w is silent. The only sound of r; the second sound of e; the only sound of n," was as near the heavy accentuation as I can get. It was the best and the worst school I ever saw. The best, because no pains, no time, nothing had been spared to bring it up to the principal's ideal; and the effort had been crowned with entire success. The worst, because it ignored absolutely any individuality in the pupils and rewarded them for nothing more than a mechanical obedience to another's thinking. . . .

### No School Better Than This School

In this school there exists a rigidity that is like a *rigor mortis*; it forbids such a natural outgiving of the natural teacher as the syllabus suggests. Here the subordinate must be forever on the jump to accomplish the set end of her day's labor, and while the principal is calm, pleasant in manner, and God-fearing in her life, most of the teachers who carry out her conscientiously relentless will are harassed, visibly worn, harsh, and unkind.

The children are apparently callous and happy in their indifference toward their environments. I saw a small boy whose elbow was suddenly jerked and shaken sneak a little mischievous grin toward the back of the room.

In one class the very way in which the teacher intoned "You — are — not — still" gave me a sensation of quick fright that brought back the awful moment of my childhood when I saw a boy arrested and haled away by a policeman. "Somebody — foot!" the same teacher shouted suddenly, and my circulation stopped. My own foot, I felt sure, had moved.

No child in this school ever "raises his hand" above the level of the shoulder excepting during the arithmetic recitation, when pencils that are not in actual use are held in the clenched fingers of the right hand, the right elbow resting on the desk, the left hand laid flat on the other side.

"My answer is — " began an infant arithmetician.

"Don't say that in my class" . . .

"Don't stand in my class with pencil, pen, or book in hand," snapped the teacher.

"Indeed! But you'll please sit down," was the sneer that greeted a wrong answer.

Neither the principal nor her first assistant, who was both sweet and gentle, "snapped," but the manner of one of the younger teachers who seemed a "kind of right-hand man" gave me an overwhelming desire to rescue the class committed to her, and to do it, if necessary, by physical violence.

In this school, probably the only one of its kind in the world, there is at least no indirection, no flabbiness. The apparent cruelty that kept me "on edge" is not half so fatal as the actual cruelty of methods known elsewhere.

"You dirty little Russian Jew, what are you doing?" seems even more ruinous to a child's spirit and temper.

The school most unrelieved in badness had no principal in evidence. Opposite the name of the "head" in charge I wrote in my notebook: "Coarse, fat woman, sensual look, youngish, diamond earrings, talks dialect." This woman's methods are summary, but according to her lights. If a child gets in her way she throws him out, lifting him by any portion of his person that "comes handy." From such a school graduate the brutal truckdrivers, the amateur criminals who, having little better in their minds, devise much mischief.

That the imitative powers of childhood are startling; that the teacher's thoughts, feelings, aspirations even, transfer themselves on invisible wings to the members of her class, proves itself every instant of the day. Yet in a majority of the schools I was continually embarrassed by the discourtesy with which the children were addressed—or ignored. There is sentimentalism that forgets the teacher's difficulties and there is "plain good sense." It is not sentimentality to recognize rudeness as rudeness even when its object is a child. What possible end but a common misery is to be attained by pointing out the "bad boy" to a stranger? What sort of example is the taste that discusses quick-eared children even in lowered tones when they are present "Get on to those eyes!" brought me a glance quite uncomfortable but already self-conscious. "He is a degenerate!" procured a sullen look of blank defiance that changed to sullen watchfulness as the talk went on.

## About School Boards and Examination

The stupid discourtesy of a good deal of schoolroom behavior is a direct reflex of the treatment of the teacher or the would-be teacher by the Board, and its employees. . . . How deeply the teachers resent the very treatment they too frequently "pass on to the children" only they and their intimates know.

"I could have borne it better," said a much-tried soul, "but from the Superintendent down every man made me feel he was the sole owner and proprietor of the city schools and that I had intruded on his private business."

Not long ago a New York teacher had occasion to be examined, and after several written requests that elicited no information she was sent by her principal to the office of Mr. Z —. Mr. Z — was the wrong man, but he directed her to Mr. Y — . It was "not Mr. Y —'s day," so she returned at another time and waited long upon a desolate bench until the interview was secured. Mr. Y — was also the wrong man, but he kindly conducted her to Mr. X —, to whom she was evidently non grata.

"I can't see you today," he snarled with the air of an angry plutocrat dismissing a persistent beggar.

The teacher went. As she retired, Mr. Y —, who seemed to have a vein of true humanity, instructed her that she must fill out a certain printed blank and present it to Mr. X — before she left the building for the day.

She filled the paper and with trepidation reentered the presence of the summary X —. For an hour she sat waiting before him while others who came later were received and dismissed, till, time failing, she ventured to approach the desk.

"I told you I couldn't see you," raged the indignant authority.

She halted, and, explaining deprecatingly, dropped the document upon the nearest support and fled as incontinently as self-respect would permit.

It took six journeys from her remote borough by steam and trolley before this unfortunate teacher was able to get that examination.

All servants of the Board are not like this, all buildings are not old, all teachers are not faulty. Mr. Snyder is the architect and head of the building department, and, busy as he is, his courtesy never fails, nor is he the only one of the authorities who can be approached without revolt. Moreover, in old buildings no less than in new are to be found a great corps of gently bred, enlightened teachers spending and being spent in the service of the city. All this ungracious setting forth of the dark side of things is the necessary and unpleasing task of one who tries to show that the opportunities of New York children are not all alike and not all good.

## The Pay of Teachers

The most rational of all the good salary bills . . . made advance in the pay of teachers dependent on merit as well as on length of service. At present, length of service alone governs the advance in salary.

There are certain injustices in the distribution of salaries. It is an injustice that a woman who is principal of a school of 2,500 children should receive $750 less a year than a man head of a high school department, and $150 less than a woman high school assistant. If the men now wailing in the newspapers about their inability to secure elementary school positions would equalize the salaries so these should no longer be like animals male and female, they would have their positions. Economy now keeps them out. Everywhere women teachers have to keep order for the men who are getting so many hundreds more for their virile authority! No influence effeminizes the schools so fast as the average man teacher. Men like Mr. Doty, who will rule in the beautiful 106, are not common in the public schools. Men's or women's, the New York salaries are generous and promptly paid. They should command the best service in the world. That they do not is chiefly because our energy is increasingly absorbed in providing for immigration.

## General Conclusions

Four conclusions stand out in my mind as the result of these weeks of visiting New York public schools and of study of the huge problem.

1. New York City has the most difficult educational problem in the country. It stands in a class by itself and has difficulties that no other city presents.
2. Under the present school administration it is doing wonderful work toward solving that problem.

3. But conditions still exist that put the complete solution of the problem beyond the reach of any normal effort and expense.
4. The only remedies for such conditions are the restriction of immigration and a vast increase in expenditure — larger than has yet been dreamed of.

# The Inquisition of the Teacher, or, "Gum Shoe Tim" on the War-Path

*Myra Kelly*

From Myra Kelly, *Little Citizens: The Humours of School Life* (New York: McClure, Phillips & Co., 1904).

*Excerpted from Myra Kelly's 1904 book* Little Citizens, *this piece illuminates the typical structure of power in the urban public school of the era. The associate superintendent, accompanied by the intimidated principal, inspects each classroom. A man beyond the teachers in years, the superintendent enjoys the power he can wield over young, attractive — and nervous — women. The teacher has no opportunity to speak on her own behalf. Kelly's writing in general reflects the common prejudices about foreign ethnic groups, and illustrates as well a tone of condescension and "cuteness" often found in writings by and about teachers. Kelly's Miss Bailey makes light of the children's tattered dress, and she herself is portrayed more as a housekeeper than as an educator.*

*Myra Kelly (1876–1910) was born in Dublin and immigrated to New York as a child with her father, a physician. A teacher in a Lower East Side school, she was also the author of several books of sketches and stories. S. S. McClure, the editor who published her first work in his magazine, said of her in his introduction to* Little Citizens, *"She loved her little people, and in depicting them made an imperishable classic."*

On the first day of school, after the Christmas holidays, Teacher found herself surrounded by a howling mob of little savages in which she had much difficulty in recognizing her cherished First-Reader Class. Isidore Belchatosky's face was so wreathed in smiles and foreign matter as to be beyond identification; Nathan Spiderwitz had placed all his trust in a solitary suspender and two unstable buttons; Eva Kidansky had entirely freed herself from restraining hooks and eyes; Isidore Applebaum had discarded shoe-laces; and Abie Ashnewsky had bartered his only necktie for a yard of "shoe-string" licorice.

Miss Bailey was greatly disheartened by this reversion to the original type. She delivered daily lectures on nail-brushes, hair-ribbons, shoe polish, pins, buttons, elastic, and other means to grace. Her talks on soap and water became almost personal in tone, and her insistence on a close union between such garments as were meant to be united, led to a lively traffic in twisted and disreputable safety-pins. And yet the First-Reader Class, in all other branches of learning so receptive and responsive, made but halting and uncertain progress towards that state of virtue which is next to godliness.

Early in January came the report that "Gum Shoe Tim" was on the war-path and might be expected at any time. Miss Bailey heard the tidings in calm ignorance until Miss Blake, who ruled over the adjoining kingdom, interpreted the warning. A license to teach in the public schools of New York is good for only one year. Its renewal depends upon the reports of the Principal in charge of the school and of the Associate Superintendent in whose district the school chances to be. After three such renewals the license becomes permanent, but Miss Bailey was, as a teacher, barely four months old. The Associate Superintendent for her vicinity was the Honourable Timothy O'Shea, known and dreaded as "Gum Shoe Tim," owing to his engaging way of creeping softly up back stairs and appearing, all unheralded and unwelcome, upon the threshold of his intended victim.

This, Miss Blake explained, was in defiance of all the rules of etiquette governing such visits of inspection. The proper procedure had been that of Mr. O'Shea's predecessor, who had always given timely notice of his coming and a hint as to the subjects in which he intended to examine the children. Some days later he would amble from room to room, accompanied by the amiable Principal, and followed by the gratitude of smiling and unruffled teachers.

This kind old gentleman was now retired and had been succeeded by Mr. O'Shea, who, in addition to his unexpectedness, was adorned by an abominable temper, an overbearing manner, and a sense of cruel humour. He had almost finished his examinations at the nearest school where, during a brisk campaign of eight days, he had caused five dismissals, nine cases of nervous exhaustion, and an epidemic of hysteria.

Day by day nerves grew more tense, tempers more unsure, sleep and appetite more fugitive. Experienced teachers went stolidly on with the ordinary routine while beginners devoted time and energy to the more spectacular portions of the curriculum. But no one knew the Honourable Timothy's pet subjects and so no one could specialize to any great extent.

Miss Bailey was one of the beginners, and Room 18 was made to shine as the sun. Morris Mogilewsky, Monitor of the Gold-Fish Bowl, wrought busily until his charges glowed redly against the water plants in their shining bowl. Creepers crept, plants grew, and ferns waved under the care of Nathan Spiderwitz, Monitor of the Window Boxes. There was such a martial swing and strut in Patrick Brennan's leadership of the line that it informed even the timid heart of Isidore Wishnewsky with a war-like glow and his feet with a spasmodic but well-meant tramp. Sadie Gonorowsky and Eva, her cousin, sat closely side by side, no longer "mad on theirselves," but "mit kind feelings." The work of the preceding term was laid in neat and docketed piles upon the low book case. The children were enjoined to keep clean and entire. And Teacher, a nervous and unsmiling Teacher, waited dully.

A week passed thus, and then the good-hearted and experienced Miss Blake hurried ponderously across the hall to put Teacher on her guard.

"I've just had a note from one of the grammar teachers," she panted. "'Gum Shoe Tim' is up in Miss Greene's room. He'll take this floor next. Now, see here, child, don't look so frightened. The Principal is with Tim. Of course you're nervous, but try not to show it. And you'll be all right, his lay is discipline and reading. Well, good luck to you!"

Miss Bailey took heart of grace. The children read surprisingly well, were absolutely good, and the enemy under convoy of the friendly Principal would be much less terrifying than the enemy at large and alone. It was, therefore, with a manner almost serene that she fumed to greet the kindly concerned Principal and the dreaded "Gum Shoe Tim." The latter she found less ominous of aspect than she had been led to fear, and the Principal's charming little speech of introduction made her flush with quick pleasure. And the anxious eyes of Sadie Gonorowsky, noting the flush, grew calm as Sadie whispered to Eva, her close cousin:

"Say, Teacher has a glad. She's red on the face. It could be her papa."

"No. It's comp'ny," answered Eva sagely. "It ain't her papa. It's comp'ny the whiles Teacher takes him by the hand."

The children were not in the least disconcerted by the presence of the large man. They always enjoyed visitors and they liked the heavy gold chain which festooned the wide white waistcoat of this guest; and, as they watched him, the Associate Superintendent began to superintend.

He looked at the children all in their clean and smiling rows: he looked at the flowers and the gold fish; at the pictures and the plaster casts: he looked at the work of the last term and he looked at Teacher. As he looked he swayed gently on his rubber heels and decided that he was going to enjoy the coming quarter of an hour. Teacher pleased him from the first. She was neither old nor ill-favoured, and she was most evidently nervous. The combination appealed both to his love of power and his peculiar sense of humour. Settling deliberately in the chair of state, he began:

"Can the children sing, Miss Bailey?"

They could sing very prettily and they did.

"Very nice, indeed," said the voice of visiting authority. "Very nice. Their music is exceptionally good. And are they drilled? Children, will you march for me?"

Again they could and did. Patrick marshaled his line in time and triumph up and down the aisles to the evident interest and approval of the "comp'ny," and then Teacher led the class through some very energetic Swedish movements. While arms and bodies were bending and straightening at Teacher's command and example, the door opened and a breathless boy rushed in. He bore an unfolded note and, as Teacher had no hand to spare, the boy placed the paper on the desk under the softening eyes of the Honourable Timothy, who glanced down idly and then pounced upon the note and read its every word.

"For you, Miss Bailey," he said in the voice before which even the school janitor had been know to quail. "Your friend was thoughtful, though a little late." And poor palpitating Miss Bailey read.

"Watch out! 'Gum Shoe Tim' is in the building. The Principal caught him on the back stairs and they're going round together. He's as cross as a bear. Greene in dead faint in dressing-room. Says he's going to fire her. Watch out for him, and send the news on. His lay is reading and discipline."

Miss Bailey grew cold with sick and unreasoning fear. As she gazed wide-eyed at the living confirmation of the statement that "Gum Shoe Tim" was "as cross as a bear," the gentle-hearted Principal took the paper from her nerveless grasp.

"It's all right," he assured her. "Mr. O'Shea understands that you had no part in this. It's all right. You are not responsible."

But Teacher had no ears for his soothing. She could only watch with fascinated eyes as the Honourable Timothy reclaimed the note and wrote across its damning face: "Miss Greene may come to. She is not fired. — T.O'S."

"Here, boy," he called; "take this to your teacher." The puzzled messenger turned to obey, and the Associate Superintendent saw that though his dignity had suffered his power had increased. To the list of those whom he might, if so disposed, devour, he had now added the name of the Principal, who was quick to understand that an unpleasant investigation lay before him. If Miss Bailey could not be held responsible for this system of inter-classroom communication, it was clear that the Principal could.

Every trace of interest had left Mr. O'Shea's voice as he asked: "Can they read?"

"Oh, yes, they read," responded Teacher, but her spirit was crushed and the children reflected her depression. Still, they were marvelously good and that blundering note had said, "Discipline is his lay." Well, here he had it.

# Schoolteacher's Nightmare

## *Mary Abigail Dodge*

From Mary Abigail Dodge, *Our Common Schools*
(Boston: Estes & Lauriat, 1880).

*Published in her 1880 work* Our Common Schools, *Mary Abigail Dodge's (1833–1896) poem portrays a woman teacher at work on a weekend night with her record book. A humorous look into a tired teacher's mind, the poem also hints* at how the growth of school bureaucracies changed the job of teaching. Dodge's teacher drifts off to sleep with her head full of statistics and school reports, alluding to the increasing pressure and responsibilities forced upon teachers by bureaucratization of big-city schools. While the poem uses humor to address questions about the effectiveness of the school system, Dodge was much more open about criticizing American schools in her other works. As a teacher, feminist, and journalist, Dodge attacked the school system in her book, Our Common Schools, for degrading women teachers by forcing them to undergo petty and minute supervision and other humiliations.

A prolific essayist and humorist, Dodge wrote under the pseudonym "Gail Hamilton." She published at least eight books between 1863 and 1872. She also edited a magazine for children, and wrote for such publications as Atlantic Monthly. Woman's Wrongs (Boston: Ticknor and Fields, 1868) is a spirited defense of the woman's rights movement, reprinted by the Arno Press (1972) with the pamphlet it attacked, "Women's Rights," by Rev. John Todd (Boston: Lee & Shepard, 1867).

'Twas Saturday night, and a teacher sat
Alone, her task pursuing:
She averaged this and she averaged that
Of all her class were doing.
She reckoned percentage, so many boys,
And so many girls all counted,
And marked all the tardy and absentees,
And to what all the absence amounted.

Names and residence wrote in full,
Over many columns and pages;
Yankee, Teutonic, African, Celt,
And averaged all their ages,
The date of admission of every one,
And cases of flagellation,
And prepared a list of the graduates
For the coming examination.

Her weary head sank low on her book,
And her weary heart still lower,
For some of her pupils had little brain

And she could not furnish more.
She slept, she dreamed; it seemed she died,
And her spirit went to Hades,
And they met her there with a question fair,
"State what the per cent of your grade is."

Ages had slowly rolled away,
Leaving but partial traces.
And the teacher's spirit walked one day
In the old familiar places.
A mound of fossilized school reports
Attracted her observation,
As high as the State House Dome, and as wide
As Boston since annexation.[1]

She came to the spot where they buried her bones,
And the ground was well built over,
But laborers digging threw out a skull
Once planted beneath the clover.
A disciple of Galen wandering by,
Paused to look at the diggers,
And plucking the skull up, looked through the eye,
And saw it was lined with figures.

"Just as I thought," said the young M.D.,
"How easy it is to kill 'em — "
Statistics ossified every fold
Of cerebrum and cerebellum.
"It's a great curiosity, sure," said Pat,[2]
"By the bones can you tell the creature?"
"Oh, nothing strange," said the doctor, "that
Was a nineteenth century teacher."

# The First Class: A Reminiscence

*Marian Dogherty*

From Marian Dogherty, *'Scusa Me Teacher*
(Francestown, N.H.: Marshall Jones, 1943).

*"I can no more forget that first class than a man forgets his first love or a warrior his first battle." So proclaimed Marian Dogherty in her 1889 account of teaching in Boston's model public school for immigrants, the Hancock School for Girls. Dogherty's powerful analogy suggests that, for many women, teaching was both a challenging professional experience and a deeply emotional one. Her narrative of her first year teaching illustrates the "perfect" fit between mothering and teaching — a love of children. Perhaps more than any other author in this book, Dogherty's description of her students reveals her own beliefs about children's many gifts. Like countless of her contemporaries, Dogherty does make note of her immigrant students' lack of hygiene and takes steps to educate the children on bathing, but overall her descriptions convey a love and caring toward her pupils, not a condescending attitude. Her acute observations of their characters reveal her appreciation of their cultural diversity and individual strengths. Dogherty taught for many years in Boston and authored a second work on teaching literature. Little else about her is known.*

The odd thing about the first class is that while other classes may fade more or less from the memory, that first group given to the young green girl in a September of long ago, emerges strong and clear, with the distinction of a well cut cameo. I remember that first day of school, though it is more than forty years ago, better than I remember yesterday; I recall its events, its emotions, more vividly than this morning's. It was a pleasant time to be alive. The whole world though it may have been a smoldering volcano, was apparently at peace. There was positively not a thing to worry about except to acquit oneself with credit in a happily chosen profession. Of course the pay was small or so it seems today. But at that time it seemed to me ridiculously large: thirty-eight dollars a month was the handsome beginning, and one looked forward to an increase of four dollars each month after the first year. I wondered how I could spend it all! My happiness was complete and I felt such a feverish urge to start that I left home at half past seven though school began at nine and though it was a short half hour's ride. It was good to be in the open car, to breathe in the fresh September morning air, to ride through shaded quiet streets not yet awake, to see the gardens of petunias and asters, to feel the chill from the river as we went over the old bridge from Cambridge to Boston and finally to become a part of the turbulent city.

When I reached the master's office and told him it was hard to wait for the school term to begin, he shook with ill-suppressed laughter. That puzzled me. What was funny? Did he not feel that way, too?

Then he ushered me to the room that was to be mine. It had fifty-six desks besides extra movable ones, in case the class should be larger. School rooms were hospitable in those days. There was always room for one more. Fifty-six and sixty were average classes. There was a high platform where the teacher sat. This was her throne and helped to fix her above the rest of the world in the minds of the children. If they desired converse with her, they had to step *up*; when they returned to their own quarters, they must step *down*. Now, the platform is no more. As an institution, it is gone, and with it went a little of that reverence for the teacher, so wholesome for the child, so pleasant for her, — that reverence which like mercy is twice blessed, blessing him that gives as well as him that takes.

At quarter of nine on that first day, the children came eagerly in, stiffly starched, and shining from recent scrubbing. They were radiantly happy. It was the fourth grade and they had left forever the ignominy of a primary school. Report had it that they were to have "geographies" and "rithmatic" books. No longer would they be slightingly referred to as "in the third reader." Such books were forever past. They would now hold in their hands a story-book, and read real stories and "pomes." Rumor whispered that they would carry these books home and prepare lessons by the evening lamp, but rumor was a fickle lady, and not to be believed too trustingly. Still all things were possible and it might be that books would no longer be regarded as too sacred for transportation to the home fireside, now that they were entering the august grammar department. Thus, encumbered by a large, flat volume of marvelous redness, easily recognized as a "jography," they could stick their tongues out merrily at those miserable little ignoramuses that still wal-lowed in the multiplication table. So, there was reason for their elation. Moreover, there was to be a new teacher. The one who had occupied that room was now too old to teach and had got married (she had reached the decrepitude of thirty-three). Would the new one be young or old, nice or cross?

I can no more forget that first class than a man forgets his first love or a warrior his first battle. Others might be better, but they would be without that mystic something that the first always has. They were chiefly Jews and Italians, with an Irish girl here and there like the plums in a pudding. Little embryo American citizens with interesting traditions of European life and a background of European oppression behind them. Some were dreamy and indolent; others promisingly alert; some with plain evidence of intellect in their small faces; others heavy with stupidity. Yet, all were peculiarly respectful. Depraved indeed is the child who exhibits his naughty propensities on the first day! The good are too happy and the bad do not *dare* lest they be banished to the class just left. Even the janitor seemed to them a celestial being, for when he shuffled in and banged the furniture about, an awe rested on their innocent faces, because he was a part of that great system that held them in its benign but awful hand.

There were many fascinating people in that first class: little Maria Ragucci, for instance. If only Sir Joshua might have seen Maria before painting his "Angels' Heads"! Then there was Sarah Bloominsky, Russian, and even at that tender age, darkly tinged with anarchy; big, brow-beating Sarah who matched her mulishness with mine, and generally came out ahead. And Immaculata! It took me some time to understand just why she had been so called. It certainly did not relate to the externals of face or of raiment, for Immaculata's acquaintance with soap and water was openly superficial. Rather had her mother with prophetic wisdom thus named her for the purity of spirit which successfully shone through the various layers of dirt. Immaculata had two accomplishments. When she was not chewing her tongue, she was begging permission to wash her hands. She was our Lady Macbeth; moreover she seemed no more successful than the tragic queen in removing the stains. This mania of hers developed after I had delivered a series of talks on the beauty of water and the efficacy of soap. I had told them in confidence that in certain high classes of society, daily immersion is not unknown; at this point, looks partly horrified, wholly incredulous were exchanged. "If you expect anything like that, you will be bitterly disappointed" the looks emphatically stated. Such things, I admitted, were wholly unreasonable, but would it not be a capital way to begin each new week, at least, with a scouring, an "altogether" as the vulgar termed it?

These talks had their effect, for Immaculata presented herself one morning, and with the shining eyes of the conqueror, exclaimed excitedly, "Oh, teacher, teacher, like that I had *two* baths, one here!" as she whacked her chest, "and one here!" indicating with a red and clean hand her entire face.

"That's fine, Immaculata, perhaps the next time you will have three!"

Rome was not built in a day and Immaculata had made a beginning. When she no longer felt that paralyzing distrust of water that held so many of her fellows in its grip, I deemed the time ripe to speak on behalf of the comb. Immaculata had soft brown hair that fell into curls as easily as the water falls into spray. These curls clung fetchingly to her smooth neck and untroubled brow; that is to say they so clung on Monday; the rest of the week they went, like the wicked in Isaiah "every one to his own way" until on Friday, complete lawlessness reigned. As the transforming effects of a daily combing were portrayed, Immaculata's eyes sparkled with pleasure, and soon she kept in her desk a little pocket comb which she took out at all sorts of unseemly times, flourishing it ostentatiously. In executive session I explained that there was a time and season for all things, but still, Immaculata would forget. Then, for five consecutive mornings, I read solemnly from the third chapter of Ecclesiastes: "To everything there is a season and a time to every purpose under the heaven: a time to be born; a time to die; a time to plant and a time to pluck up that which is planted."

The rhythms sank into Immaculata's ear, and on the third day their import penetrated her cerebrum, for while reading, I caught her eye, wherein was an understanding twinkle which said more plainly than her tongue could have done, "I get you, teacher, it's all right from now on;" and it was, for though Immaculata's curls continued to be irreproachable, the comb was never seen again. . . .

Even now, I cannot think of Mary Morton without a smile; Mary, sallow and thin and plain, but radiant with intellect and spirit. Mary belonged peculiarly to the sisterhood of saints, a limited order in the public schools. She had her human side, however, and on rare occasions displayed it.

It was the physiology lesson, and in those days we were required to acquaint those tender innocents with certain of their interior organs, the more picturesque ones, so to speak, like the heart and stomach and the intestines. It was hard to work up any real interest in such things, — to convey to an indifferent little girl, for instance, the appalling length of her small intestine. To announce, statistically, that this portion of her digestive tract measured fifteen to eighteen feet would have been the work of a dullard and would have been received with unsuppressed yawns. To present figures is not the fine art of teaching. But to picture the thing with vividness, to make them *see* this wonderful creation so adroitly folded in their little insides, that was teaching! To this end, I explained that were we to behold this particular portion of the alimentary canal of only *one* of them placed lengthwise in a straight line, it would reach from end to end of the school room. At this, there issued from a remote corner a prodigious whistle: a whistle that expressed many things, amazement, consternation, horror, unbelief. A roar of laughter went up from the class, which was possessed of a healthy sense of humor. Mary's crimson cheeks betrayed her. So she was human after all, and quite capable of challenging the teacher when she became too theatrical.

At the same time that Mary's whistle broke the silence, little Margharita exclaimed reverently, "Oh, my God!" Do not mistake this for profanity. It was merely the human spirit's salutation to its Creator as the awfulness of his work dawned upon her understanding.

I had meant to be graphic, and had succeeded in being grotesque.

Somehow, I never could mention the small intestine again, and if those girls who came after the illustrious first class went through life never suspecting that they were the happy possessors of such an organ, I hope it did them no real harm.

That year we had with us Katie Colori. Are you still enlivening this planet, Katie, with your look of the slums and your heart of gold? How you shuffled across the floor, in those sadly worn shoes of yours, revealing the soiled and naked feet! Your hair was matted with innumerable snarls, but the sunlight of your smile so dazzled the eye as to blind it to these imperfections. Do you remember the day of my disgrace, Katie? Do you recall after all these years, just where you sat, in the first seat of the last row, beside the eastern window where the sun came in each morning and played about your unkempt hair and pretty eyes? I dare say that you do not remember that terrible morning. I dare say that you never even suspected that your teacher *was* disgraced.

It was Monday morning and on Monday morning came the music period. If there was a time in the week when my spirit rebelled it was in that half hour given over to sweet melody. Throughout the week for the most part, I could maintain an equable temperature, but in the music time, the thermometer rose as with a fever. Music was the skeleton in our closet. The children knew it, and the teacher knew it, and on Monday he rattled his bones frightfully.

In order that other classes might not be entertained by the bellowing of the musicians or the awful yet restrained tones of the teacher during these periods, I always took the precaution to close the door, or rather, Margharita, whose knowledge bordered on the uncanny, did so.

Now, on this particular morning, we were practicing "How can I leave thee, how can I from thee part?" The notes came with a desperate slowness; the altos rumbled in dreary monotones while the sopranos screeched in discord. The teacher was beside herself, the more so that the wretches so openly enjoyed the racket they were making. So, as usual, she lost her temper. She brought down her baton, and said with ominous control, that if the next attempt proved no better, the music books would be closed and *remain so for one entire week.* Now such a threat would not in itself have depressed them, for though they did love to roar discordantly, they knew very well that I was temperamentally unfitted to teach music and sure to give evidence of that unfitness. What depressed them was the manner of delivering it for with children the manner is everything.

With a chastened demeanor, and a more earnest effort at accuracy, they resumed their singing, and the result was a little less painful, a shade nearer the printed score. I accepted it because I knew I had to, and we closed our books feeling that all was well.

As I left the side of the room and came in view of the door, I noticed that it was slightly ajar. Now, every teacher has *tête-à-tête* talks with her class, little private reckonings of the sort that every family enjoys, and she is no more willing to admit the public than the family is. So, naturally, as we had a family row, I felt disturbed to see the door open. Betraying, however, none of the anxiety I felt, I asked, "Has the door been open throughout the lesson?" and they shouted, "No, ma'am!" Then Katie spoke up, "Teacher, like that, the boss come in wid some ladies, yes ma'am."

So that was it! The genial master had entered innocently to show off a nice little class and had suddenly changed his mind. "About when did Mr. Dutton and these ladies come?" I asked, for I was determined to know the worst. I got it, too, for Katie yelled with inaccuracy but force, "Teacher, like that, they come in wen you said shut-up." Katie never suspected the pain, and the mortification her free translation of my English wrought. "Thou stickest a dagger in me," I exclaimed, but she thought I was only talking to myself. . . .

It was with that first class that I became aware that a teacher was subservient to a higher authority. I became increasingly aware of this subservience to an ever growing number of authorities with each succeeding year, until there is danger today of becoming aware of little else. A young teacher, however, eager to accomplish, forgets happily all the machinery of organization until it is forced upon her attention. It was unmistakably borne in upon me a few months after I had begun to teach. The genial principal came in one day to see how things were going with the new teacher. He took his seat on the platform beside me, thus temporarily sharing the throne, and announced that he would hear the little girls read.

The children were delighted to have any visitor, but especially a man, for the feminine influence preponderates in the public school. So, everything started pleasantly enough until one child, the first to read, failed to state the page on which the new chapter began. Our principal was a stickler for the proprieties, and the proper way to read in the public school in the year 1899 was to say, "Page 35, Chapter 4," and holding the book in the right hand, with the toes pointing at an angle of forty-five degrees, the head held straight and high, the eyes looking directly ahead, the pupil would lift up his voice and struggle in loud, unnatural tones. Now, I had attended to the position of the toes, the right arm, and the nose, but had failed to enforce the mentioning of page and chapter, for two reasons.

In the first place figures seemed to me a cold douche on the interest of a story and in the second place, I never could master Roman numerals myself and the chapters were always printed in those detestable x's and v's and l's. This grave omission at the very outset irritated the good man and he said in his most professional tone, "Perhaps, tomorrow, your teacher will tell you about Roman numerals." That was the first blow. I had failed to perform my duty and my superior officer had hinted as much with the additional suggestion that on the morrow I mend my ways. My heart sank. Would the children suspect? I watched them carefully. No, they were unconscious of everything excepting that they were having what in those days was termed a "perfectly bully" time.

Whenever the master would ask them a question, they would answer hastily, "Yes, ma'am."

"Say 'yes, *sir*' when you are talking to a gentleman," he said very sternly, and they replied cheerfully, "Yes, ma'am." This annoyed him doubly. Not only there was their lack of good taste, but what seemed like disobedience as well.

The word "spice" then occurring in the reading matter, the examiner propounded the question, "What is spice, who can tell me that?" Hands were raised everywhere. Cheerfully would they give of their store, be it knowledge, or be it darkest ignorance. "Carrots" exclaimed one. "No, ma'am, it ain't, it's bananas," said another. "No ma'am, teacher, spiders," ventured a third. When vegetables and fruits had failed, they tried bugs. Never had they seemed more pleased with themselves or with the world in general. An unnatural calm became apparent in the master's manner. "Put down your hands, children," he said quietly, "and tomorrow your teacher will tell you about spices." "Yes ma'am" they shouted joyously, as though he had made them a gift.

This was a signal for closing the visit. It had been painful to him and painful to me, but they had enjoyed it thoroughly. Mr. Dutton was a large man and he rose from the chair with all his natural dignity. Then, deciding to let bygones be bygones, he said kindly, "Good afternoon, little girls," and they spake as one voice, "Good afternoon, Mr. Dogherty."

The door closed with a bang!

As for me, only centuries of the civilization process kept me safe. I had followed my primitive instincts — but it is no matter! Meanwhile, the wretches looked up pleasantly at me, as if wondering what entertainment came next on this diverting program. Determined that this sort of thing should never, never happen again, I made them say, "Good-night, Mr. Dutton" and "Good-morning, Mr. Dutton" over and over and over, until the walls reverberated with the name. Then I impersonated him, imitating his mode of approach, talking to them as he was wont, making it all as realistic as possible letting them practice saying, "yes, sir," and "no, sir," and "thank you, sir." I finally dismissed them, long after the closing hour in the twilight of day and a midnight of interest. According to custom I said, "Good night, Girls." In chastened but absent manner, they answered sleepily, "Good night, Mrs. Dutton."

# An Immigrant Student and Her Teacher

❧

## Mary Antin

From Mary Antin, *The Promised Land*
(Boston: Houghton Mifflin Co., 1912).

*For many of the immigrant children arriving on American shores in the early
1900s, the public school system was their first exposure to "American" middle-class
values. Written from a student's perspective, Many Antin's (1881–1949) chapter
from her book* The Promised Land *chronicles an immigrant child's learning journey. A Russian Jew, Antin depicts the classic belief that American schools would
transform immigrant children into patriotic Americans. Antin herself seems to
appropriate this dream, striving to conform to her teacher's ideal by pronouncing
English perfectly and reading from the works of great American authors. Perhaps
most telling in this work is not Antin's feelings about her teachers, but her feelings
about the English language itself. She describes her mastery of the language with
deep pleasure and pride. To Antin and many others, learning English allowed them
access to America's opportunities, to the exercise of agency, and for those who
became writers — to a public voice.*

*In 1901, Antin married a Lutheran scientist in Boston and moved to New York,
where she associated with a group of Jews influenced by Ralph Waldo Emerson's
transcendentalism.* The Promised Land, *published in Boston in 1912, was greeted enthusiastically, particularly by reviewers who considered it an antidote to
growing fears that the new wave of immigrants, many living in poverty, would turn
against America. Until she suffered a nervous collapse at age thirty-seven, Antin
moved in literary circles, lecturing for woman suffrage and against the restriction
of immigration. On the eve of World War II, Antin reclaimed her solidarity with
persecuted Jews in "House of One Father" (*Common Ground, Spring 1941*), an
essay pleading for social justice.*

### Initiation

It is not worth while to refer to voluminous school statistics to see just how many "green" pupils entered school last September, not knowing the days of the week in English, who next February will be declaiming patriotic verses in honor of George Washington and Abraham Lincoln, with a foreign accent, indeed, but with plenty of enthusiasm. It is enough to know that this hundred-fold miracle is common to the schools in every part of the United States where immigrants are received. And if I was one of Chelsea's hundred in 1894, it was only to be expected, since I was one of the older of the "green" children, and had had a start in my irregular schooling in Russia, and was carried along by a tremendous desire to learn, and had my family to cheer me on.

I was not a bit too large for my little chair and desk in the baby class, but my mind, of course, was too mature by six or seven years for the work. So as soon as I could understand what the teacher said in class, I was advanced to the second grade. This was within a week after Miss Nixon took me in hand. But I do not mean to give my dear teacher all the credit for my rapid progress, nor even half the credit. I shall divide it with her on behalf of my race and my family. I was Jew enough to have an aptitude for language in general, and to bend my mind earnestly to my task; I was Antin enough to read each lesson with my heart, which gave me an inkling of what was coming next, and so carried me along by leaps and bounds. As for the teacher, she could best explain what theory she followed in teaching us foreigners to read. I can only describe the method, which was so simple that I wish holiness could be taught in the same way.

There were about half a dozen of us beginners in English, in age from six to fifteen. Miss Nixon made a special class of us, and aided us so skilfully and earnestly in our endeavors to "see-a-cat," and "hear-a-dog-bark," and "look-at-the-hen," that we fumed over page after page of the ravishing history, eager to find out how the common world looked, smelled, and tasted in the strange speech. The teacher knew just when to let us help each other out with a word in our own tongue, — it happened that we were all Jews, — and so, working all together, we actually covered more ground in a lesson than the native classes, composed entirely of the little tots.

But we stuck — stuck fast — at the definite article; and sometimes the lesson resolved itself into a species of lingual gymnastics, in which we all looked as if we meant to bite our tongues off. Miss Nixon was pretty, and she must have looked well with her white teeth showing in the act; but at the same time I was too solemnly occupied to admire her looks. I did take great pleasure in her smile of approval, whenever I pronounced well; and her patience and perseverance in struggling with us over that thick little word are becoming to her even now, after fifteen years. It is not her fault if any of us to-day give a buzzing sound to the dreadful English th.

I shall never have a better opportunity to make public declaration of my love for the English language. I am glad that American history runs, chapter for chapter, the way it does; for thus America came to be the country I love so dearly. I am glad, most of all, that the Americans began by being Englishmen, for thus did I come to inherit this beautiful language in which I think. It seems to me that in any other language happiness is not so sweet, logic is not so clear. . . .

She whom I found in the next grade became so dear a friend that I can hardly name her with the rest, though I mention none of them lightly. Her approval was always dear to me, first because she was "Teacher," and afterwards, as long as she lived, because she was my Miss Dillingham. Great was my grief, therefore, when, shortly after my admission to her class, I incurred discipline, the first, and next to the last, time in my school career.

The class was repeating in chorus the Lord's Prayer, heads bowed on desks. I was doing my best to keep up by the sound; my mind could not go beyond the word "hallowed," for which I had not found the meaning. In the middle of the prayer a Jewish boy across the aisle trod on my foot to get my attention. "You must not say that," he admonished in a solemn whisper; "it's Christian." I whispered back that it wasn't, and went on to the "Amen." I did not know but what he was right, but the name of Christ was not in the prayer, and I was bound to do everything that the class did. If I had any Jewish scruples, they were lagging away behind my interest in school affairs. How American this was: two pupils side by side in the schoolroom, each holding to his own opinion, but both submitting to the common law; for the boy at least bowed his head as the teacher ordered.

But all Miss Dillingham knew of it was that two of her pupils whispered during morning prayer, and she must discipline them. So I was degraded from the honor row to the lowest row, and it was many a day before I forgave that young missionary; it was not enough for my vengeance that he suffered punishment with me. Teacher, of course, heard us both defend ourselves, but there was a time and a place for religious arguments; and she meant to help us remember that point.

I remember to this day what a struggle we had over the word

"water," Miss Dillingham and I. It seemed as if I could not give the sound of w; I said "vater" every time. Patiently my teacher worked with me, inventing mouth exercises for me, to get my stubborn lips to produce that w; and when at last I could say "village" and "water" in rapid alternation, without misplacing the two initials, that memorable word was sweet on my lips. For we had conquered, and Teacher was pleased.

Getting a language in this way, word by word, has a charm that may be set against the disadvantages. It is like gathering a posy blossom by blossom. Bring the bouquet into your chamber, and these nasturtiums stand for the whole flaming carnival of them tumbling over the fence out there; these yellow pansies recall the velvet crescent of color glowing under the bay window; this spray of honeysuckle smells like the wind-tossed masses of it on the porch, ripe and bee-laden; the whole garden in a glass tumbler. So it is with one who gathers words, loving them. Particular words remain associated with important occasions in the learner's mind. I could thus write a history of my English vocabulary that should be at the same time an account of my comings and goings, my mistakes and my triumphs, during the years of my initiation.

If I was eager and diligent, my teachers did not sleep. As fast as my knowledge of English allowed, they advanced me from grade to grade, without reference to the usual schedule of promotions. My father was right, when he often said, in discussing my prospects, that ability would be promptly recognized in the public schools. Rapid as was my progress, on account of the advantages with which I started, some of the other "green" pupils were not far behind me; within a grade or two, by the end of the year. My brother, whose childhood had been one hideous nightmare, what with the stupid rebbe,[3] the cruel whip, and the general repression of life in the Pale, surprised my father by the progress he made under intelligent, sympathetic guidance. Indeed, he soon had a reputation in the school that the American boys envied; and all through the school course he more than held his own with pupils of his age. So much for the right and wrong way of doing things.

There is a record of my early progress in English much better than my recollections, however accurate and definite these may be. I have several reasons for introducing it here. First, it shows what the Russian Jew can do with an adopted language; next, it proves that vigilance of our public-school teachers of which I spoke; and last, I am proud of it! That is an unnecessary confession, but I could not be satisfied to insert the record here, with my vanity unavowed.

This is the document, copied from an educational journal, a tattered copy of which lies in my lap as I write — treasured for fifteen years, you see, by my vanity.

*Editor Primary Education:* —

*This is the uncorrected paper of a Russian child twelve years old, who had studied English only four months. She had never, until September, been to school even in her own country and has heard English spoken only at school. I shall be glad if the paper of my pupil and the above explanation may appear in your paper.*

*M.S. Dillingham*
*Chelsea, Mass.*

### SNOW

*Snow is frozen moisture which comes from the clouds.*
*Now the snow is coming down in feather-flakes, which makes nice snow-balls. But there is still one kind of snow more. This kind of snow is called snow-crystals, for it comes down in little curly balls. These snow-crystals aren't quiet as good for snow-balls as feather-flakes, for they (the snow-crystals) are dry; so they can't keep together as feather-flakes do.*
*The snow is dear to some children for they like sleighing.*
*As I said at the top — the snow comes from the clouds.*
*Now the trees are bare, and no flowers are to see in the fields and gardens, (we all know why) and the whole world seems like asleep without the happy birds songs which left us till spring. But the snow which drove away all these pretty and happy things, try, (as I think) not to make us at all unhappy; they covered up the branches of the trees, the fields, the gardens and houses, and the whole world looks like dressed in a beautiful white — instead of green — dress, with the sky looking down on it with a pale face.*
*And so the people can find some joy in it, too, without the happy summer.*

*Mary Antin*

And now that it stands there, with her name over it, I am ashamed of my flippant talk about vanity. More to me than all the praise I could hope to win by the conquest of fifty languages is the association of this dear friend with my earliest efforts at writing; and it pleases me to remember that to her I owe my very first appearance in print. Vanity is the least part of it, when I remember how she called me to her desk, one day after school was out, and showed me my composition — my own words, that I had written out of my own head — printed out, clear black and white, with my name at the end! Nothing so wonderful had ever happened to me before. My whole consciousness was suddenly transformed. I suppose that was the moment when I became a writer. I always loved to write, — I wrote letters whenever I had an excuse, — yet it had never occurred to me to sit down and write my thoughts for no person in particular, merely to put the word on paper. But now, as I read my own words, in a delicious confusion, the idea was born. I stared at my name: Mary Antin. Was that really I? The printed characters composing it seemed strange to me all of a sudden. If that was my name, and those were the words out of my own head, what relation did it all have to me, who was alone there with Miss Dillingham, and the printed page between us? Why, it meant that I could write again, and see my writing printed for people to read! I could write many, many things: I could write a book! The idea was so huge, so bewildering, that my mind scarcely could accommodate it.

I do not know what my teacher said to me; probably very little. It was her way to say only a little, and look at me, and trust me to understand. Once she had occasion to lecture me about living a shut-up life; she wanted me to go outdoors. I had been repeatedly scolded and reproved on that score by other people, but I had only laughed, saying that I was too happy to change my ways. But when Miss Dillingham spoke to me, I saw that it was a serious matter; and yet she only said a few words, and looked at me with that smile of hers that was only half a smile, and the rest a meaning. . . .

What . . . was my joy, when Miss Dillingham, just before locking up her desk one evening, presented me with a volume of Longfellow's poems! It was a thin volume of selections, but to me it was a bottomless treasure. I had never owned a book before. The sense of possession alone was a source of bliss, and this book I already knew and loved. And so Miss Dillingham, who was my first American friend, and who first put my name in print, was also the one to start my library. Deep is my regret when I consider that she was gone before I had given much account of all her gifts of love and service to me.

About the middle of the year I was promoted to the grammar school. Then it was that I walked on air. For I said to myself that I was a student now, in earnest, not merely a school-girl learning to spell and cipher. I was going to learn out-of-the-way things, things that had nothing to do with ordinary life — things to know. When I walked home afternoons, with the great big geography book under my arm, it seemed to me that the earth was conscious of my step. Sometimes I carried home half the books in my desk, not because I should need them, but because I loved to hold them; and also because I loved to be seen carrying books. It was a badge of scholarship, and I was proud of it. I remembered the days in Vitebsk when I used to watch my cousin Hirshel start for school in the morning, every thread of his student's uniform, every worn copybook in his satchel, glorified in my envious eyes. And now I was myself as he: aye, greater than he; for I knew English, and I could write poetry. . . .

# My Mother's Principal and Mine

⟨ ⟩

## Nancy Hoffman

### From a personal interview with
### Mary Agnes Dwyer, October 3, 1977.

*Mary Agnes Dwyer (1885–1979) was ninety-three years old when I interviewed her in Passaic, New Jersey, a city near New York City. She had been a principal at No. 10 school for some years when my mother served under her as a substitute teacher in the 1930s. I was a pupil at her school, beginning in 1947 as a kindergartener through fourth grade, when my family moved to another town. A woman of great dignity, her white hair swept into a pompadour, she told me her story sitting erect and alert in an armchair in her perfectly kept apartment. Like many other women of her era, teaching and administering had been her social life and her work, and she held proudly the title Miss Dwyer, which announced she had never married.*

*Dwyer's account illustrates not only the experience of teaching immigrant chil-*

*dren, but also the important role women educators played within immigrant communities. She remembers with pleasure the time spent in community members' homes, helping them with their English, answering questions, and addressing the needs of their children. She witnessed the major textile strikes of the 1920s that roiled Passaic and Paterson, in which some of her students' families took part. Dwyer's narrative also illuminates the web of interpersonal relationships that supported teachers. Her visits to the homes of her students helped her to better understand their cultural backgrounds and gain the support of their parents; and her friendships with others in the teacher community ultimately led to her own promotion to principal. Among her enthusiastic supporters and admirers were my mother, my mother's dear friend Miss Edith Kondell — Miss Dwyer's long-time school secretary who arranged this interview for me — and my aunt Alice Miller, a Passaic teacher for twenty-five years.*

The problem of schooling children today isn't anything as it was to teach the immigrant in 1906. I began at twenty-one, in 1906. And it was only a matter of the children being trained and particularly taught the English language. The parents were vitally involved. They came to the school as students. We used to have them from 7:30 to 9:30 in the same classrooms. Unpaid, we went back to teach them after a day's work. They are the people I still love and remember, because they believed in us. We had a great deal to give and they needed it, but we needed them because they were going to be the future of our city — and they *were,* and they *are,* even now.

When I look back at the Doctors Ehrenfeld, Reshnevs, Starks, Meyer Rothwax as a little boy, and his parents, the Cinnamons, Pashmans, I find people who are still close to me in friendship and remembrance. I was very young and I had a lot to learn. I was eager to accept what these people were bringing to all of us — their culture, their intellectual integrity, their desire to have their children have the best. They trusted us and loved us, and we did the same. Now, that was Number Two school. . . .

We did not need the PTA. There were always families that had emergencies, as during the woolen strike, and in happier days, too. The woolen industry strike went on for thirteen weeks. The teachers carried kerosene lamps into their homes. They bought the oil. People who had never touched those types of lamps before learned how to use them, because the parents hadn't the money just then, and everybody was in dire distress. Of course, we had to keep the children in school, and we did all we could. That was when Mrs. Barry of the Barry manufacturers, she and her associates, lovely women, came down into our school, put aprons on, and made warm soup, a regular soup kitchen.

I went up into the homes and saw how those people lived, and I loved the experience. I'd never seen anything like it before.

The immigrants who were not able to speak English were willing to come and study. We labored, holding their hands to teach them to write. They never were tired, always eager and ambitious for success. They never thought in terms of money, but they thought in terms of what there was to do in this great big place they had just come to, and they promised us that they would speak as much English as possible to the children in their homes. So it was a learning experience for the children and an exercise by the parents.

I think that period in Passaic was the highest peak we ever reached in the schools. We had 100 percent cooperation from every organization — Red Cross, Salvation Army, and all of the fraternal organizations as well. They were never too busy to stop and listen to us. And they got things done we didn't seem to count in those days. One little incident makes me very happy when I remember it. Many of those children came to school with their shoes practically off their feet. There was a cobbler on the corner — we called him a shoemaker, but he was really a cobbler. He would mend the children's shoes, polish the shoes; the children would be in their stocking feet in the school. In the late afternoon, one of us, a teacher or maybe one of the secretaries, would go around to pay for the shoes. They were in excellent condition, and he never charged any of us five cents. Then there were occasions when accidents would happen and we would have to find the parents before the child could be taken care of. We had several marvelous doctors who would come in at our personal call, and who could get anything done. No red tape. Today teachers aren't really able to allow their own initiative to come out to solve something. You have to go to this agency and that agency and see three or four people, or five people, before you can get anything done.

I was the middle child in a family of six brothers, three sisters, and an adopted sister. I always wanted to teach dolls — even all the empty chairs were pupils. We had access to many wonderful books. My father was an avid reader and he wanted to read with us and instruct us. He was particular about what we read. The boys were away in boarding schools as they came along, and I reached the point that I was interested in going, too. My mother never wanted me to go to boarding school.

*Miss Mary Agnes Dwyer, recalled by the author as "my mother's principal and mine," served in New Jersey schools from 1906 to 1951.*

We were shielded in our home. I insisted, because I knew what I wanted to do, and I couldn't do it unless I went away from home and boarded at a teacher's college. There was then a normal school in Trenton and in connection with it, there was a model school. You would go to the model school and take all your examinations. There were opportunities there, but things grew to be a little slow for me; I wanted to do it all in hurry, because I knew that I was the middle one in the family, and there were other ones to come along — I had a strong sense of responsibility, which is good. I had it all my life. I took six periods a day excepting Saturday, when we had a limited course. I did it so that I could get out, and get home again, and get to work.

I went to Trenton in 1901. I would have been sixteen. I had had a tutor. We were living in Garfield at the time, for one year. A Mrs. Rossi taught me trigonometry, Latin, which we needed, geometry, which was easy for me, and German. Those were the subjects we had to take in order to receive the entrance examinations. In the model school, I then completed the tests. Every test that you were exposed to, you had to receive at least 85 percent. Then you were permitted to take the pedagogy for that subject which was necessary for the license in that subject. So it was three and a half years — in Trenton, the model school, and the teachers college. I was able to get my license and my degree.

During all those years we had the opportunity of talking with people like Booker T. Washington, about Tuskegee and the situation with the blacks at that time. He had great faith in them, and I have lived to see some of his dream come true. I really have. I sat one afternoon with him and I listened and I learned. But I was so young, I was not yet 21. I taught my first class in 1906, in September, in Number Two school. I was twenty one and I didn't know anything about the foreign people at all, but it was the greatest experience of my lifetime to have been privileged to work on the east side of Passaic. The mills came — the Botany, Forseman, and the others — and the people came. It was as a magnet, pulling them because of the industry, and to me as I look back on it, it was the richest time we ever had in the city. . . .

*Malvina Rosenberg Hoffman, the author's mother, as a young normal school student, posing with her brother and friends. She later taught under Miss Mary Dwyer.*

Parents sent us disciplined children. We had forty, and they were different sizes. If it hadn't been for the home and the respect that the teacher had from the parents, we wouldn't have been able to do it, any more than teachers are doing it now.

The biggest problem that the teachers had, especially the young ones, was their idealism. I like it that way, but they have to temper their judgment. If they're very young, it's hard. . . .

Each term there was some new thing. We had to go to college to keep learning. I remember when the work-study-play system came in — the Gary System. At Number 10, and in other schools where there were seventh and eighth grades, the children were in school half a day, and working at one of the mills the other half, a real mill.

The teachers worked as hard as the students. The teachers didn't have much money — I got $450 a year. That meant that we taught all day, every day; we visited homes after hours; and we assisted various organizations, where we could, in order to keep "in" with organizations that could help the schools.

The only restrictions on teachers were that they be on time and be decent. They were trusted, they weren't bound in. Many of the teachers lived in this building, and in other apartments; some lived in private homes. The girls went into New York a lot to the opera. They had season's tickets. Then the teachers' association became a very strong organization, and through the association, the musical agencies in New York arranged for us to have the finest speakers and lecturers. As an officer of the association, I once introduced Zimbalist, and held his Stradivarius.

I was fifteen years a teacher, and all this time I was studying at Columbia and Fordham and NYU to get my administrative credits. I hadn't thought I'd move from Number Two school, but then there was a vacancy at Number 10. I went to Number 10 in the twenties, and I worked very hard because it was all so new. They had introduced the work-study-play system at Number 10 at that time, and it was a heavy thing, because we had all the continuation school people. We had half a day in the factory, half a day in school, and I was getting interested in that sort of thing.

Then a vacancy opened up for assistant principal, and Alma Smith pushed like fury, and kept at me. She said, "You're just wasting your time. Why don't you advance? The salary's better." I wasn't sure I was going to be happy away from the children. You never are, really. When you're with the children, you're living it all. The minute you go on, you're not. And then you're an authority, and some of the things that were close between you and your associates are no longer there. It's very hard.

There were people in that building who really wanted the promotion. They were "in." They knew everything. I was a Johnny-come-lately, and I had to learn. But Edith Kondell's lovely uncle, Mr. Brezlawski, was on the board, and Mr. Sylvester. They both approached me, and asked me to write and ask for the job as assistant principal. I said to them, "Well, if the board wants me . . ." Eventually I had to do it, because Alma Smith wanted me in there. She was very good at pushing what she wanted. She was loyal, and she was a magnificent person. We all have our own faults. . . .

Mr. Millar, the principal, hadn't been feeling well. He was in the school, though, on a Friday afternoon . . . and he dropped dead Saturday morning. The pressure began. The girls wanted me to be principal. There were a couple of men trying to get in, but the girls wanted me. So Mr. Brezlawski came to call on me. Edith was with me, then. He really insisted that I have Edith type a letter, which she did do, right there. He presented it, and that was the beginning. . . . It was a good life.

I learned much more about teachers. I remember one young girl. She brought a boy in. The boy was in a dreadful temper. She had caught him by the hair. She threw him into my office and said, "I don't like the way he looks at me." I looked at her, waited, moved a few things on my desk, and said: "Won't you sit down a minute." She did, and I said to the boy, "You go out and wait in the other office, and I'll send for you in a minute."

She sat down, and I said, "What could he do but look at you? He couldn't touch you, he couldn't answer you back, he couldn't throw anything."

She said, "I know, but he was angry."

I said, "You were too, dear."

She eventually gave up teaching, because she was quick-tempered, and she didn't have a something that has to be within you if you're going to try to form character and teach essentials.

It's a God-given something, and you never get away from that, never.

# Teaching in an African American Boarding School

⟿

## Frances O. Grant

From Ruth Edmonds Hill, ed., *The Black Women Oral History Project, Vol. 4: The Arthur and Elizabeth Schlesinger Library* (Westport, Conn.: Meckler, 1991), pp. 364–387.

*Frances O. Grant (1895–1982), an African American teacher and educator, was interviewed in 1977 by her former colleague from the Fieldston School, Maurine*

*Rothschild, as part of the* Black Women Oral History Project *of the Schlesinger Library at Harvard University. Born in Boston in 1895, Grant was the older of the two daughters of Fannie Bailey and George F. Grant. Her father, a prominent dentist, was the inventor of the artificial palate and the first African American president of the Harvard Odontological Society. Their home was a gathering place for African American young people who were to become notable figures in the educational and professional worlds. After completing the six-year course at Girls' Latin School in 1913, Grant enrolled at Radcliffe College, where she was the first African American woman elected to the Iota Chapter of Phi Beta Kappa. In 1917 she graduated* magna cum laude *in classics.*

*The following fall, Grant began teaching at an all–African American public boarding school in New Jersey, the Bordentown Manual Training and Industrial School for Colored Youth, established in 1886. Convinced that students needed both a liberal arts education and skills marketable in an economy that shut off many options for African American people, she argued for and won a curriculum that included four years of high school and a trade certificate. She was successful in getting the state to approve a five-credit course in Negro history. The school remained the only state-supported segregated boarding school for secondary students in the North until it closed in 1955, a "victim" of* Brown v. Board of Education. *An intellectual and scholar, Grant introduced her students to key African American cultural figures and to the European classical tradition. While at Bordentown, Grant was active in the National Organization of Teachers of Colored Children and the National Association of College Women. In 1949 she received her master's degree in education from New York University. For ten years after Bordentown closed, Grant taught Latin at the Fieldston School in New York City.*

"I was born on June 30, 1895, and had two of the best parents that anyone could ever have had. My father was born in 1846 in Oswego, New York. He came of a family that had part of an underground railroad station, taking slaves over the border into Canada, and many a time he told me of waking up at night and seeing these slaves taken out of the haycarts, and all smuggled over the border. A situation and a memory that was very, very poignant. My mother came from Virginia, and was the daughter of Maria Bailey, who belonged to the family of Leighs from Fairfax County. My grandfather was white. . . .

I went to the primary school, and then to the grammar school. The primary school was highlighted for me by the procession in 1902 of the

IWW, the Industrial Workers of the World, that later came under Gomper's organization, the American Federation of Labor. And they were protesting the imprisonment of three revolutionaries: Bill Haywood, Moyer, and Pettibone. The offshoot of this was that my first-grade teacher, Gertrude O'Brien, marched with the cigarmakers' union, and my father, who was something of a Tory, was outraged by this lack of what he considered professional attitude. I rather thought my whole education would stop there. Then I went to the Bowdoin Grammar School. At the time teaching in he Bowdoin Grammar School, and one of the early Negro teachers in the city of Boston, was the sister of my father's first wife. Of this I should have been proud; but I found less to be proud of when I found out that everything I did in school got home before I did.

One of the teachers that had the greatest influence in my life was my sixth-grade teacher, Eudora Pitcher, a real gentlewoman. She decided that I ought to go to Girls' Latin School. At that time, admission to the Girls' Latin School was by competitive examination, and she got permission from my mother for me to take the examination. I passed, and in the fall of 1906, I went to the Girls' Latin School. It was a six-year stint; one had six years of Latin, for which one got only four years' credit for college admission; three years of Greek, and two years of French, and contact with some of the most competent and interesting teachers, probably, in my experience. I feel that Girls' Latin School period influenced me greatly, because it inspired me with the desire to teach, and to be like some of the people who were working with me. One of them was Mary Randall Stark, who taught me Latin and Greek, and became my friend over the years. . . .

When I graduated from the Girls' Latin School, I was fortunate enough to win what then was the considerable prize of $25. I think we have to throw that into perspective, when we realize that the tuition at Harvard at that time was $100, and the tuition at Radcliffe, $150. So that the $25 prize meant a great deal more then than it did today, and I graduated at the head of my class. While I was in the high school, there was a friend and fellow student named Natalie Walker. She was the editor of the paper and the envy of most of us. She went to Radcliffe, and I was so very fortunate when I found myself there as a freshmen, in the fall of 1913, to see Natalie Walker assigned to me as my senior advisor. She went through college, graduated *magna cum laude*; that was the first year that Radcliffe got Phi Beta Kappa, and she made Phi Beta Kappa. So that I always felt that if I could do what my senior did, I'd be very much delighted. Fortunately, I was able to do that. Therefore at my fiftieth when she came back, she sent me a little corsage with an inscription, "From a senior to a freshman who both achieved." . . .

When I got into Radcliffe in the fall of 1913, there were rumors of war. And they persisted. The next year, however, came the *Guns of August* situation, and friends of mine who were in Europe had had a hard time getting back. At school we all were very, very tense; Americans, who do nothing by halves, had decided that everything German must go. No German in the schools, no German music — Schubert, Wagner, out. Karl Muck, of the Boston Symphony, was deeply chastised because he would not play "The Star Spangled Banner" before symphony concerts, remarking that the music was an old drinking song and had no place in classical music. . . .

When one goes through crises and survives, the crises always seem less; as I think back over the many situations that have come in my life, I recall the first very serious one, the hysteria that followed the bombing of the *Lusitania*. There were mass meetings everywhere, one big one at Tremont Temple; the decision to go to war immediately; the attempts by Woodrow Wilson, who had been reelected on the platform, "He kept us out of war," to try to stem the hysteria of an angry public. But on April 6, 1917, we entered World War I. I'll never forget the service that morning at prayers at Radcliffe, when Albert Parker Fitch, dean of the Theological School, spoke to us and gave us some idea of what war was going to be.

This was the year that I and many of my friends were getting out of college. At that time Negro families of substance sent their boys and girls to the northern colleges. Among the students at the time I was at Radcliffe was Ellis Rivers, a Phi Beta Kappa from Yale, who was studying at the Harvard Law School. He later became Judge Rivers. And William Augustus Hinton, at the Harvard Medical School, who was to invent the serum that replaced the Wasserman test. And so it went. But with the onrush of war was a question of what was going to happen with these young men of training and ability, whose entrance into the regular army service seemed a little bit out of the question. W.E.B. DuBois, who was then one of the officers of the NAACP, the National Association for the Advancement of Colored People, had campaigned strenuously for an integrated officers' corps. When that seemed impossible, he finally decided that he would settle for a segregated officers' training corps, and one was set up at Des Moines, Iowa. There went Ellis Rivers, Louis Wright, and a great many others whose names were going to be prominent in the history of Negro progress of that period.

Perhaps it's a truism to say that a secure childhood makes a happy adult. My childhood was a particularly happy one. My parents were fond of each other, and fond of us. They never talked down to us, but talked with us, and for the most part, we felt we could go to them with problems that we had. I remember one little incident which indicates how wise they were in dealing with us. My father had a little cupboard in which he kept wine and cookies, and my sister and I one day found it unlocked. So we went in, and childlike, not realizing that the consistent depletion of the cookies would somehow be discovered, found ourselves detected. Our parents who could have scolded us, or punished us, or spanked us, talked with us. I remember my father saying, "What I have is yours. All you have to do is ask me for it. You don't ever have to take anything that way." We felt so chagrined, that the experience probably did much to cement what was already a very close relationship. . . .

[W]e were surrounded by people who had put great emphasis on education — my cousin had graduated from Radcliffe in 1900, and taught in the Cambridge public schools; we had friends who were in the civil service, post office, worked in the library, as well as people in professions. There was a little bit of snootiness, I guess we shall say, because we took a rather dim view of persons who had opportunities for education but had not taken advantage of them. We had a summer place in Arlington, Massachusetts, and at that time my father's daughter by his first wife was quite a belle. When students came to Harvard for summer school, our house was rather a gathering place. There during my summers were the people who were to figure in the educational world: W. R. Valentine; Leslie Pinckney Hill, principal of Cheyney; W. T. B. Williams, assistant to Booker T. Washington in Tuskegee, and many, many others. . . .

My father died in 1910. . . . [His] death produced not only complete chaos as far as our lives were concerned, but brought to me the first realization that being Negro made a difference in what I could have and what I could get. We had to leave the old brownstone at 108 Charles Street, and seek other lodgings. As a child, I remember going around and seeing a place here and there for rent and coming back and saying to my mother, "Well, we can take this and we can take that," and her reluctance to tell me that that probably was not possible. As I said, my grandfather was white and my mother was very fair. She went out to hunt an apartment and secured one, a few steps from the Girls' Latin

School. No one asked her whether she was white or colored. We signed the lease, and when we, who were light brown, appeared, then the trouble began. The accusation was that she had secured the place under false pretenses, which of course was not true, because no one had asked her whether she was white or colored. But in order to break the lease, the man who owned the apartment sold it, and we were consequently evicted. Because of the prominence of my father, the situation made quite a *cause célèbre,* and I was given permission by the board of education to finish my education at the Girls' Latin School by registering at the Roxbury home of my half-sister, who had married and was living there. This was my first real poignant introduction to prejudice.

At college, you met a very cosmopolitan group, and I knew that among my close friends — people of all ethnic groups and all social and material classes — was Isabel Coolidge, who was frankly fond of me, and could afford to be as I constituted no particular threat to her; Julia Reynolds, the daughter of a South Carolina judge; Anna Shaughnessey, of a first-class Irish family; Doris Hellman, extremely clever, a young Jewish girl; and several traditional Boston WASPs. I played the piano, I was the class pianist; I was able to make posters because I did a little bit of sketching; I got into a good many of the Radcliffe clubs. Most of them were matters of grade. You went into the English Club, you got a certain number of grades; you went into the Latin club, you got a certain kind of grades. I had chosen to specialize in classics. I was particularly fortunate in being at Radcliffe when the great in that field were there. My instructor in Livy was Edward Kennard Rand, Pope Professor of Latin, and my advisor for the four years that I was there; Charles Burton Gulick, in Greek; Clifford Hershell Moore, in Latin composition. So it went. The desire to emulate my mentor, and my own personal pride in achievement, made me study very, very hard. When it came to the end of my junior year, and I didn't make what I had hoped to make, Phi Beta Kappa, I said, "Well, we'll see what we can do the last year."

In the fall of 1916, I came to my mailbox in Fay House, and there was a little note from Dean Brody congratulating me on having been elected to Phi Beta Kappa. I had known nothing of it and rushed over to the bulletin board in Fay House; there was my name with two others as having been elected on the basis of junior year grades and November hour exams. As I came down the steps of Fay House, I met President LeBaron Russell Briggs, who of course had formerly been dean at Harvard. He stopped me and said, "Miss Grant, your father would have been proud of you." I thought that was so sweet; everybody adored him; he was just a perfect dear of a man. When commencement came, I decided to go up for honors in classics, and getting honors in classics demanded two things; one had to take second-year honors in classics, which I did; then, to take five three-hour examinations; one in Greek literature, Latin literature, Greek composition, Latin composition, and general classic background. By the time I had finished those fifteen hours, my mind was a complete blank. I couldn't even tell you whether the sun was shining or not. It all came out as I had hoped. I got a *magna cum laude* in classics, was elected to Phi Beta Kappa, and saw the close of four delightful years at Radcliffe in June 1917. . . .

In 1917, after I got out of college, I was able to get a job through the influence of Eva Hall. Eva Hall graduated from Radcliffe in 1903 and was teaching in Cheyney, Pennsylvania, under the principalship of Leslie Pinckney Hill, who was a close friend of W.R. Valentine.

It was a rather interesting situation. On a hill in Bordontown, New Jersey, known as "Old Ironsides," had been a school established by the A.M.E. church. The estate originally belonged to Charles Parnell. Charles Stewart, the commodore of the battleship *Constitution*, which was moored down on the Delaware River just below the bluffs, married his daughter. . . . When I came up to the Bluffs to the school in the fall of 1917, I found myself for the first time in life in a completely segregated outfit. Mr. Valentine, who was the principal, had been brought there by Calvin Kendall. Calvin Kendall, at one time, was the superintendent of schools in Indianapolis, and Mr. Valentine was a teacher in a public school there. Mr. Valentine had felt that the ordinary public school education was inadequate for the group of young Negro boys and girls whom he taught, and that they needed something else to make it possible for them to go into the world, and make a living. So he had suggested that some of them be taught shoemaking, lathe work, and that sort. His experiment was so revolutionary, in a way, that John Dewey had written him up in *Schools of Tomorrow*. When Calvin Kendall was called to Trenton in 1913 and asked to take over this A.M.E. school which the state agreed to subsidize, he remembered W. R. Valentine, and called him from Indianapolis, so that when I ascended the little hill in 1917, W.R. Valentine was in charge. His wife, Grace, was a New Englander, from New Haven, Connecticut, and she and I formed an evil alliance against the prejudices that we encountered.

It was interesting, because the classes ran from the sixth to the tenth grade, which I considered immediately an impossible situation. After much stewing and much argument we were able to persuade Mr. Valentine to lop off the bottom and build to the top. I felt that you either had a seven-eight-nine situation, or a nine-ten-eleven-and-twelve. It took us ten years to do it. We did it, with considerable blood-letting, I must say. Then it was a question, also, of getting certification for the school. At the time that Mr. Valentine took over, there were teachers there who were earnest, but not too skilled. And the students were overage for the most part, earnest again, but I felt were not being held up to the highest standards. I guess perhaps one of my faults is that I feel if you're going to do anything, you have to do it right. Then I wasn't prepared to make allowances for anybody, black, white, grisly or gray. I didn't feel that because I was in a wholly Negro setup, that there should be a set of Negro standards. I felt that there should be standards, and that the students, if they were to go out in the world which was not wholly Negro, must be taught to meet the standards of that world. So that we eventually got state certification for the high school course. One of the interesting aspects of it was that we were able to include a five credit course in Negro history. . . .

The textbook at that time was Carter Woodson's *The Negro in Our History*. I might say that I knew Carter Woodson personally, knew him over the years. He was a delightful, crotchety old man who'd been all over the world, full of all kinds of prejudices and male chauvinistic attitudes, but feeling definitely the story of the Negro had not been adequately told. I think his book is still today a classic. Also, Mr. Valentine was able, in later years, to draw people to Bordentown. We got rid of a lot of what I call old wood. He brought Lester Granger down there as extension worker; and William Hastie, who later became Judge Hastie; Ben Johnson, the runner; and several others. He was able to bring these young people — Charles Ray, who was the first Negro captain of a football team at Bates — these young people were an inspiration, because they were people who had succeeded in the same kind of atmosphere that these young boys and girls were operating in.

When the great migration of the twenties came, we were flooded. . . . [A]fter the war, the Negroes left the South with the breakdown of old King Cotton, and came North in vast numbers. There were the great riots in Detroit, and Washington, various places. We got a large group of overaged students. At one time I was teaching boys and girls who were almost as old as I; the advantage of this situation was that most of them realized they had a great deal to make up.

We went into the organization of the trade situation, and that was very, very crucial. New Jersey had five trade schools, which were controlled by the union. The schools were rated by the Department of Education on their placement. Therefore, it was very important for the schools not to train students they couldn't place, or to train them for jobs in which they were not placeable. This, of course, and the prejudiced attitude of New Jersey automatically excluded a great many students from getting any kind of trade education. Therefore the school was fortunate in setting up trades: auto mechanics, printing, carpentry, domestic science, sewing and art. A great deal has been said, and is still being said today, about the inadequate training of the trade school in many industrial situations. Some of the operators prefer on-the-job training, they feel that it is superior. In many cases I imagine that it would be. The trade schools, while they were subsidized, found it very hard to reproduce any of the situations of industry, and they never had money enough, of course, to keep up with the mechanical changes in industry.

At the same time, half a loaf is better than none, and we were fairly successful in training. We made it a requirement that a student, to graduate from the school, must complete four years of high school and have a trade certificate. Certainly, over the year, that paid off. Our students have been most successful. . . . [I]n 1975, twenty years after the school closed, they gave a testimonial dinner for me, and over 500 students were there. They were all successful, and all holding onto the spirit of Bordentown, and appreciative of what Bordentown had done for them.

I think, also, it's interesting, when you have a boarding school with boys and girls, that some kind of entertainment and extracurricular activities have to be set up. The boys had a military setup, which was very good for the discipline. They were interested in their officers and so forth and so on, and they drilled and had the uniforms, and so forth. But we tried, and I'm not being modest about this at all . . . I was very energetic in setting up as many types of extracurricular activities as we could have that would involve as many students as we possibly could. So many of these Negro boys and girls had been in setups where they weren't a part of anything. When it came to the school play, or the school paper, or this, that, or the other, they automatically knew there was no chance for them.

So that the first thing we did was set up a school paper, called *The Ironsides Echo.* I sponsored it, and it was published without intermission up to 1948, the only omission being the year the printer was in France in World War I. Mr. Valentine, as all principals, I suppose, with a job on the line, was always cautious. But I felt that if we were publishing the school paper, I'd like to put it up against other people who were publishing school papers. So with rather disheartened approval, we entered the Columbia Scholastic Association, and won seconds and thirds over the years. Then later we went to the National Scholastic Association, out of the University of Minnesota, and won two firsts. Of course, therefore, my point of view was justified. . . .

We had chapel exercises once every day from 11:30 to 12:00. That period, when I first came there, was a matter of dull giving out of notices and so forth and so on, and I had the feeling that there ought to be something else. So we did a lot of organization, and we gave every trade an opportunity to explain the trade; and when certain situations were coming up, maybe one would be a rally for a football team, when we had the Christmas post office, one would be an advertisement for the post office, and in that way, again, we involved the students. In every type of situation in which they appeared, there was this little element of pride with their followers, and their feeling that they were definitely a part of something.

Most of them had come from situations where the school play was a lot of old ladies of the women's sewing circle talking at each other. Well, we went into dramatics, and we gave plays. We gave good ones. We didn't try to do things we couldn't do. I remember the first one I gave was Mary Antin's *Arrowmaker*. I picked it for two reasons. First, the Indians made the costuming and the relationship interesting. Then we gave several of the Negro plays, *Rider of Dreams,* and a good many of the others. . . .

So that we felt very definitely that we were involving the students, and with their sense of involvement came a type of loyalty and a strong feeling of working together, and I remember during the war, some of them wrote . . . about coming into Paris on trucks and all, and seeing somebody and jumping out of a truck and hailing somebody that you had seen at Bordentown. *The Ironsides Echo,* in addition to entering these competitions, set up a large exchange; white and Negro schools exchanged with us. When the war broke out, we sent *The Ironsides Echo,* over a hundred, to everybody all over the world. And interesting enough, when some of the soldiers came on back, not necessarily wounded, but on leave, they would come by the school and leave us five or ten dollars to pay for the postage, and tell about getting *The Ironsides Echo* when they were in foxholes in New Guinea, and having a little sense of belonging, and having the feeling that somebody cared and was interested. . . .

I had been very, very distressed when I came there, at what I felt was the inadequacy of a good many of the teachers. Perhaps that was a false impression of superiority, but I just felt that they were teaching with very little background. There was a minister at the time, a Reverend Roundtree, who had been a minister to Liberia, and he and two of the others organized the association called the National Organization of Teachers of Colored Children. We worded it in that way, so that white teachers who taught Negroes, if they wanted to belong, could. But our concentration was on the Trenton, south Jersey area. . . . [I]n the industrial areas in the North that wasn't possible, but below Trenton they were segregated. We had, really, a sort of crash program; we tried to not only get the teacher, but to get the teachers in touch with material. At that time, in Philadelphia, there was an agency that did a lot of printing of pictures of famous Negroes, very much like the Perry pictures. We bought those and circulated them.

Now in this teachers' organization, we had meetings every month, and then there was a big meeting at the end of the year. At those monthly meetings we reviewed the Negro books, kept them up to touch with all the things, because most of these Negro teachers were products from two areas; one from southern schools, and others, from the teachers' schools in Trenton and thereabouts, where they heard nothing that offered any kind of pride in their race or their people. I remember that from the Trenton area, two or three of them sent over some teachers for us . . . Well, they never heard of Pushkin, they never heard of Dumas, they didn't know that Matzeliger had invented the shoe-lasting machine — they were completely ignorant, and unfortunately perfectly happy. So that we were able to introduce the element of doubt, which is always a first step to achievement, and some of them went completely overboard, and did all kinds of things to interest the students. Belief in yourself — in this I go back to my early parents — and some pride in your own heritage, was so necessary in these days, when the students had been brought up to feel that Negroes didn't do anything, didn't have anything, couldn't go anywhere. This was very, very important, and I can remember several little instances, where children would say, "Oh, I didn't know that, I didn't know this," you know. I remember years later when I was in Russia, in Odessa, and I saw this statue of Pushkin, and the children playing around it just the way they played around the Lincoln statue in Newark . . . you realized, you see, that coming up and living with a reality rather than a legend is so important.

In addition to this organization, which I feel did a great deal, also, we tried to bring to the children people who had achieved. Mrs. Valentine had a lot of connections, I had a lot of connections, I had friends from New York who had connections, So we were able, by a series of what we used to call "monthly teas," and we put them on a scholastic basis — the students who made the best records were eligible. Among the guests were Paul Robeson; Bud Fisher; E. Simms Campbell; Elmer Carter, who was the director of Opportunity; Nella Larsen, who wrote *Passing*. They would come down on Sunday afternoons; sometimes they'd come down Saturday and Mrs. Valentine would put them up. We'd serve tea, and the whole situation served two purposes; it gave the children an opportunity for a gracious experience, the learning how to manage a tea, how to act at a tea, how to dress for a tea, how to conduct themselves with people that they were meeting. It served many, many purposes outside of their direct contact with people. They adored Simms Campbell and Paul Robeson, who were both very, very warm, and related to them very, very closely. . . .

The desegregation amendment from the Supreme Court put everybody in New Jersey on alert, in spite of Earl Warren's damning phrase, "in due time," which gave everybody a loophole. Jersey felt that it was time to do something, and one by one, the segregated school systems broke. It was interesting that, of the seven institutions in the state of New Jersey, only two were under the Department of Education: Manual Training School, and the School for the Deaf. So that while the city and towns began to integrate, the state was the last. It's always been my feeling that Bordentown could have integrated, but there was a tremendous pull of politics, and a tremendous feeling of prejudice against the integration of a coeducational boarding school. The state really made no honest attempt to do it. They invited a couple of white students into the boys' dormitory, and it lasted about a couple of days. The thing to do, of course was to have integrated from the top. The School for the Deaf was integrated, and I've always rather ironically felt that the state felt that if you were deficient in some respects, you could accept the integration; if you were of sound mind and sound body, it was out of the question! But they finally decided that they would close the school. Well, those of us who were involved, and had put the best part of our lives in it, were willing to have the school close. But we were not willing to accept the Department of Education's statement that they closed it because they couldn't integrate it. We felt that was unfair to everybody; it put us on the spot. The students rallied, they had great sessions in Trenton and great this and that and the other, but of course the die was cast. In 1955 the school was closed.

# Public Schools "Owned" by Politicians

*"Amelia Allison"(pseud.)*

From Amelia Allison, "Confessions of Public School Teachers," *Atlantic Monthly* (July 1896), pp. 97–110.

*In an age of urban reform, no government institution, even the public schools, was free from scrutiny. In a series of muckraking articles designed to "get schools out of politics," the* Atlantic Monthly *revealed the underbelly of school administrative practices for all to see. Teachers wrote in and told of the widespread system of using "pulls" or personal influence to get jobs, being passed over for jobs based on political affiliations, and the lack of salary standards. The articles also revealed the degree to which "publishers of textbooks" have influence "in the selection and retention of school officers," a revelation about the relation between business interests and the school appointment process. While "Confessions" has a sensationalist ring to it, it nevertheless illuminated some of the conditions that gave birth to teacher unions in the early 1900s. To protect themselves from the caprice of politicians, teachers worked within the system to support a tenure system.*

*In a brief introduction to the series, the* Atlantic *describes the writers as "successful teachers whose work has been continuous for period of from ten to thirty years" and whose names are withheld for "obvious reasons." We can assume, then, that "Amelia Allison" of the selection below is an assumed name. We do not know more about the identity of the author.*

During the period of my preliminary service as teacher in the public schools, my name was reported for a permanent place, and was "on the slate" when it left the teachers' committee. My father was at that time a voter with the party in power; but the teacher who was number five on the list had a kinsman on the board, who saw that unless she was appointed during his term she might never be. One of the trustees, therefore, brought in a charge of "cruelty to a boy" against me, and, without an investigation, my name was taken off, and number five was elected. To fail of appointment when it was my right was astonishing; but to have any one believe that I pulled a boy's ears till he could not put his head on a pillow hurt me deeply. I began an investigation on my own account, and I discovered that number five's sister was the guilty teacher. The boy's father appeared before the board and explained. The teacher was not even censured; but I had lost the permanent position.

For a year I went from one school to another, teaching for six weeks in the high school. When not busy in a schoolroom, I was visiting, studying, or reading. I attended the teachers' meetings and was surprised to find so many who had no opinion to express on important subjects. When the year had passed, I was put on the permanent list. I was assigned to a first-year school of fifty-four scholars. Most of them were beginners, and some "leftovers." I felt ready for my work. But my greatest trial was when Superintendent Goodenough selected my room as his place to doze, or really to sleep, while my little people were doing their work. He was never known to praise a teacher's work while she was in service. The only consolation was that he praised teachers who died, or regretted that it was always the "bright teachers who married." I might never marry, and therefore I could with confidence look forward to his praise only at my funeral.

A change in the political control of the city took place, and the party long in power was defeated. The other party decided to do without a supervisor for a year. Superintendent Goodenough, therefore, was dropped. It was a monotonous year. But I had now a chance to throw away the old and to use the new. I made all kinds of word and number games; I bought new readers for my supplementary work; I learned new songs, and I looked up kindergarten games.

The next August the board elected a superintendent, and there was no politics in this election. But there was much anxiety as to what kind of man he would turn out to be. Superintendent Quincy, a live New Englander, came, and he brought a breeze. At first he said little. He asked me what I had read. The next time he brought Mr. Michael Brannigan, chairman of the teachers' committee. He said, "Miss Allison is doing the kind of work I want. Has she your permission to carry it on?" Mr. Michael Brannigan was kind enough to abstain from any action that affected me. Superintendent Quincy rid us of many harmful practices. He held grade meetings; he required the schoolrooms to be empty fifteen minutes after the close of school; and no corporal punishment could be inflicted and not reported.

My scholars liked to come to school, and now they numbered eighty-seven. They sat on the edge of the platform, and even on the floor against the wall. I suggested that some come in the morning, and the others in the afternoon. This was done, and one little girl said, "Miss Allison is the best teacher, for we have to go only a half day, and we learn as much as they learn all day at the other schools." I found the work easier, and just as many were promoted to the next class as before.

This year I obtained my state certificate, and I felt that I could now be called a teacher. But a great misfortune threatened me just as I began to feel secure. My father had left the "party without an issue," and had become a member of the "party with a principle." Election time came, and the "party without an issue" thought that they saw a chance to win. As our district was likely to have a close contest, it was suggested that my father be "whipped into line." The only lash that he could be made to feel, they thought, was a threat to remove me. They sent their candidate for school trustee to our home, and he knocked timidly at the back door and made known his errand. In a very few minutes he walked rapidly away. His party was defeated, — luckily for me, no doubt, for a local politician was asked how a teacher whose work was good could be dismissed without "charges." He replied, "We always have charges when we need them." This is the only time that I ever heard of danger to a teacher in our city because of her father's political faith. The rule has been, once a teacher, always a fixture, even when glaring deficiencies could not be hidden, and complaints were "too numerous to mention."

But Superintendent Quincy was too progressive, and his church was on the wrong street. Perhaps he might have been kept if one of the teachers had not wanted the salary. This teacher always reminded us of the line of a hymn,

I can tarry, I can tarry but a term.

He never sat down; but he stood by the door with his coat and hat in his hands, as if something were urging him on.

About this time there was a vacancy in the grammar school, and the superintendent asked me if I would take the place. I liked my work, and declined the empty honor. It meant longer hours for no greater salary; for we are paid according to length of service, and there is no strife for promotion. Of course principals of the higher schools get more pay, but not principals of buildings, unless there are grammar schools in them.

In the middle of the year the superintendent left to study a profession, and a man who had "taught his way through" one of our best normal schools became his successor. At last this superintendent fell a victim to church influences, and he gave place to a young teacher whose church was right, but whose political party was wrong. "He had no principles to hinder," as one of our legislators said, so he turned his back on the party which claimed his first vote, and the position was his. He was younger than most of the teachers, but see how wise he was! He would come into the classroom and say, "Go to page 73 this month." He delivered extempore speeches at the teachers' meetings, and we wondered what it had all been about. In the three years that he was in service he never listened to one recitation in my room. He generally came to gather statistics or to dole out pages of textbooks. I did what I could to keep pace with the other schools, but I felt that there was nothing done thoroughly. At last came his turn to be decapitated, and his successor, who now holds the office, is the best of the long succession of superintendents. They say that he may not be here next year. It is time for a change.

For two years I have had a real grievance. Miss Wellpaid has a school of the same grade as mine, but mine requires more personal work. Yet Miss Wellpaid receives $260 a year more than I am paid, and my salary is the same as that of her assistants, who have no responsibility. Everyone admits the justice of my claim, and the board promises to equalize the salary. Children who, by school district lines, ought to attend Miss Wellpaid's school ask six months ahead if I will save them seats if there be room for outsiders. I will not take one of these pupils, even when they bring a demand from two trustees. Once, however, I was obliged to take two of them. They had an order from the president of the board, and a doctor's certificate which said, "It is bad for the health of these girls to attend Miss Wellpaid's school." I must be a "natural healer" of the woes of school life.

Is there nothing to make up that missing $260? Yes, many things. The ambition of every child in the building is "to go to school to Miss Amelia Allison." Ask a kindergarten child who will be his next teacher, and he will generally say, "Miss Allison." One of the ways of inciting good behavior and perfect lessons is to promise a visit to my school. Then I have once more my little people grown tall, sitting in my classes, glad to anticipate my desires about their work and play. Half of my present school have been in my first-year grades. When they argue that it is not late enough in the week to be Friday, one girl says, "We have only two days in our room, and they are Monday and Friday; nothing between." 1 have also notes of appreciation from parents, and I think with Whittier: —

> And when the world shall link your names
> With gracious lives and manners fine,
> The teacher shall assert her claims,
> And proudly whisper, "These were mine!"

# Why Teachers Should Organize

*Margaret Haley*

From Margaret Haley, "Why Teachers Should Organize,"
*National Education Association Addresses and Proceedings*
(St. Louis, 1904).

*When "Maggie" Haley (1867–1939) stood before the National Education Association to make the case that teachers should organize, she had already established herself as a power in Chicago politics and within the teaching profession. The turn of the century had seen significant growth in labor unions in Chicago, with consequent strikes, disputes, and unrest, as industry attempted to counter labor's power. Haley allied herself with the progressive wing of the union movement and, in a precedent-breaking move, engineered a formal alliance between organized labor and the Chicago Teachers' Federation. She saw in the union movement not only a chance to improve teachers' wages and working conditions, but also an opportunity to exercise the democratic ideals she discusses in the speech that follows.*

*For Haley, democracy meant the empowerment of working people, among whom
she counted "public school and industrial workers," or "manual and mental workers." In their alliance, she saw the defeat of commercialism — the end of the sub-
ordination of the worker to the machine. The workplace democracy she advocated,
the attention to child labor, woman suffrage, municipal ownership of utilities, and
security for workers in tenure and pension plans posed a powerful alternative to
the single-issue campaigns that had previously brought teachers together.*

*Haley was born and educated near Joliet, Illinois. She taught in Chicago until
1901, when she became full-time business agent for the Chicago Teachers'
Federation. Besides her activity on behalf of that union, Haley was active in the
Women's Trade Union League, the Public Ownership League, and the Labor Party.
A force for women's rights and the rights of grade school teachers within the
National Education Association, Haley was the first woman to speak from the floor
at an NEA convention. Haley worked with other women educators and advocates
of teachers' rights — notably Catherine Goggin, for a time president of the
Chicago Teachers' Federation, and Ella Flagg Young, superintendent of schools in
Chicago and first woman president of the NEA (1910).*

The responsibility for changing existing conditions so as to make it
possible for the public school to do its work rests with the people, the
whole people. Any attempt on the part of the public to evade or shift
this responsibility must result in weakening the public sense of civic
responsibility and the capacity for civic duty, besides further isolating
the public school from the people, to the detriment of both.

The sense of responsibility for the duties of citizenship in a democracy is necessarily weak in a people so lately freed from monarchical
rule as are the American people, and who still retain in their educational, economic, and political systems so much of their monarchical inheritance, with growing tendencies for retaining and developing the essential weaknesses of that inheritance instead of overcoming them.

Practical experience in meeting the responsibilities of citizenship
directly, not in evading or shifting them, is the prime need of the
American people. However clever or cleverly disguised the schemes for
relieving the public of these responsibilities by vicarious performance
of them, or however appropriate those schemes in a monarchy, they
have no place in a government of the people, by the people, and for the
people, and such schemes must result in defeating their object; for to
the extent that they obtain they destroy in a people the capacity for

*Margaret Haley, "lady labor slugger," fought for the advancement of teachers. She became business agent of the Chicago Teachers' Federation in 1901 and was one of the first presidents of the National Federation of Teachers.*

self-government.

If the American people cannot be made to realize and meet their responsibility to the public school, no self-appointed custodians of the public intelligence and conscience can do it for them. Horace Mann, speaking of the dependence of the prosperity of the schools on the public intelligence, said:

> The people will sustain no better schools and have no better education than they personally see the need of; and therefore the people are to be informed and elevated as a preliminary step toward elevating the schools.

Sometimes, in our impatience at the slowness with which the public moves in these matters, we are tempted to disregard this wise counsel.

The methods as well as the objects of teachers' organizations must be in harmony with the fundamental object of the public school in a democracy, to preserve and develop the democratic ideal. It is not enough that this ideal be realized in the administration of the schools and the methods of teaching; in all its relations to the public, the public school must conform to this ideal.

Nowhere in the United States today does the public school, as a branch of the public service, receive from the public either the moral or financial support needed to enable it properly to perform its important function in the social organism. The conditions which are militating most strongly against efficient teaching, and which existing organizations of the kind under discussion here are directing their energies toward changing briefly stated are the following

1. Greatly increased cost of living, together with constant demands for higher standards of scholarship and professional attainments and culture, to be met with practically stationary and wholly inadequate teachers' salaries.
2. Insecurity of tenure of office and lack of provision for old age.
3. Overwork in overcrowded schoolrooms, exhausting both mind and body.
4. And, lastly, lack of recognition of the teacher as an educator in the school system, due to the increased tendency toward "factory-izing education," making the teacher an automaton, a mere factory hand, whose duty it is to carry out mechanically and unquestioningly the ideas and orders of those clothed with the authority

of position, and who may or may not know the needs of the children or how to minister to them.

The individuality of the teacher and her power of initiative are thus destroyed, and the result is courses of study, regulations, and L equipment which the teachers have had no voice in selecting, which often have no relation to the children's needs, and which prove a hindrance instead of a help in teaching.

Dr. John Dewey, of the University of Chicago, in the *Elementary School Teacher* for December, 1903, says:

As to the teacher: If there is a single public-school system in the United States where there is official and constitutional provision made for submitting questions of methods of discipline and teaching, and the questions of the curriculum, text-books, etc., to the discussion of those actually engaged in the work of teaching, that fact has escaped my notice. Indeed, the opposite situation is so common that it seems, as a rule, to be absolutely taken for granted as the normal and final condition of affairs. The number of persons to whom any other course has occurred as desirable, or even possible — to say nothing of necessary — is apparently very limited. But until the public-school system is organized in such a way that every teacher has some regular and representative way in which he or she can register judgment upon matters of educational importance, with the assurance that this judgment will somehow affect the school system, the assertion that the present system is not, from the internal standpoint, democratic seems to be justified. Either we come here upon some fixed and inherent limitation of the democratic principle, or else we find in this fact an obvious discrepancy between the conduct of the school and the conduct of social life — a discrepancy so great as to demand immediate and persistent effort at reform.

A few days ago Professor George F. James, dean of pedagogy of the State University of Minnesota, said to an audience of St. Paul teachers:

One hundred thousand teachers will this year quit an occupation which does not yield them a living wage. Scores and hundreds of schools are this day closed in the most prosperous sections of this country because the bare pittance offered will not attract teachers of any kind.

Professor James further maintained that school-teachers are not only underpaid, but that they are paid much less proportionately than they received eight years ago.

It is necessary that the public understand the effect which teaching under conditions is having upon the education of the children.

A word, before closing, on the relations of the public-school teachers and the public schools to the labor unions. As the professional organization furnishes the motive and ideal which shall determine the character and methods of the organized effort of teachers to secure better conditions for teaching, so is it the province of the educational agencies in a democracy to furnish the motive and ideal which shall determine the character and methods of the organization of its members for self-protection.

There is no possible conflict between the good of society and the good of its members, of which the industrial workers are the vast majority. The organization of these workers for mutual aid has shortened the hours of labor, raised and equalized the wages of men and women, and taken the children from the factories and workshops. These humanitarian achievements of the labor unions — and many others which space forbids enumerating — in raising the standard of living of the poorest and weakest members of society, are a service to society which for its own welfare it must recognize. More than this, by intelligent comprehension of the limitations of the labor unions and the causes of these limitations, by just, judicious, and helpful criticism and co-operation, society must aid them to feel the inspiration of higher ideals, and to find the better means to realize these ideals.

If there is one institution on which the responsibility to perform this service rests most heavily, it is the public school. If there is one body of public servants of whom the public has a right to expect the mental and moral equipment to face the labor question, and other issues vitally affecting the welfare of society and urgently pressing for a rational and scientific solution, it is the public school teachers, whose special contribution to society is their own power to think, the moral courage to follow their convictions, and the training of citizens to think and to express thought in free and intelligent action.

The narrow conception of education which makes the mechanics of reading, and arithmetic, and other subjects, the end and aim of the schools, instead of a means to an end — which mistakes the accidental

*Ella Flagg Young, close associate of Haley and a leader in progressive education, began her career as a grade school teacher. She became a professor of pedagogy at the University of Chicago and, in 1909, superintendent of the Chicago Public Schools. Photograph by* Chicago Daily News.

and incidental for the essential — produces the unthinking, mechanical mind in teacher and pupil, and prevents the public school as an institution, and the public school teachers as a body, from becoming conscious of their relation to society and its problems, and from meeting their responsibilities. On the other hand, that teaching which is most scientific and rational gives the highest degree of power to think and to select the most intelligent means of expressing thought in every field of activity. The ideals and methods of the labor unions are in a measure a test of the efficiency of the schools and other educational agencies.

How shall the public school and the industrial workers, in their struggle to secure the rights of humanity thru a more just and equitable distribution of the products of their labor, meet their mutual responsibility to each other and to society?

Whether the work of coordinating these two great educational agencies, manual and mental labor, with each other and with the social organism, shall be accomplished thru the affiliation of the organizations of brain and manual workers is a mere matter of detail and method to be decided by the exigencies in each case. The essential thing is that the public-school teachers recognize the fact that their struggle to maintain the efficiency of the schools thru better conditions for themselves is a part of the same great struggle which the manual workers — often misunderstood and unaided — have been making for humanity thru their efforts to secure living conditions for themselves and their children; and that back of the unfavorable conditions of both is a common cause.

Two ideals are struggling for supremacy in American life today: one the industrial ideal, dominating thru the supremacy of commercialism, which subordinates the worker to the product and the machine; the other, the ideal of democracy, the ideal of the educators, which places humanity above all machines, and demands that all activity shall be the expression of life. If this ideal of the educators cannot be carried over into the industrial field, then the ideal of industrialism will be carried over into the school. Those two ideals can no more continue to exist in American life than our nation could have continued half slave and half free. If the school cannot bring joy to the work of the world, the joy must go out of its own life, and work in the school as in the factory will become drudgery.

Viewed in this light, the duty and responsibility of the educators in the solution of the industrial question is one which must thrill and fascinate while it awes, for the very depth of the significance of life is shut up in this question. But the first requisite is to put aside all prejudice, all preconceived notions, all misinformation and half-information, and to take to this question what the educators have long recognized must be taken to scientific investigation in other fields. There may have been justification for failure to do this in the past, but we cannot face the responsibility of continued failure and maintain our title as thinkers and educators. When men organize and go out to kill, they go surrounded by pomp, display, and pageantry, under the inspiration of music and with the admiration of the throng. Not so the army of industrial toilers who have been fighting humanity's battles, unhonored and unsung.

It will be well indeed if the teachers have the courage of their convictions and face all that the labor unions have faced with the same courage and perseverance.

Today, teachers of America, we stand at the parting of the ways: Democracy is not on trial, but America is.

# Equal Pay for Equal Work

❧

## Grace C. Strachan

From Grace C. Strachan, *Equal Pay for Equal Work*
(New York: B. F. Buck, 1910).

*Inspired by the successes of the Chicago Teachers' Federation, Kate Hogan, a New York City seventh-grade teacher, organized the Interborough Association of Women Teachers (IAWT) in 1906. The goal of this union, which at the height of its membership in 1910 boasted 14,000 teachers, was "equal pay for equal work." Grace Strachan, the enterprising superintendent who headed the union's executive committee from 1906 on, led the battle for equal pay on the state level. Her essay here was brought about by a proposal by male teachers to raise female teachers' salaries from an annual pay of $600 to $750, a salary still below their own. Strachan's response to this proposal, swift and to the point, was published on June 10, 1909, in a* New York Times *article entitled "Tell Men Teachers They Sha'n't Meddle. Women in the Schools Flatly Inform Them That Their Aid Is Not Wanted."*

*In choosing to launch a "single-issue" campaign focused on a compelling area of inequality, Strachan and the Interborough Association of Women Teachers demonstrated a different approach to reform than the Chicago Teachers' Federation's, which favored a broad political platform. What they shared, however, was a commitment to pursuing collective action as a means of strengthening women's power.*

### Preface

Salary — A periodical allowance made as compensation to a person for his official or professional services or for his regular work. — *Funk and Wagnalls.*

Notice the words, "a person." Here is no differentiation between male persons and female persons.

Yet the City of New York pays a "male" person for certain "professional services" $900, while paying a "female" person only $600 for the same "professional services." Stranger still, it pays for certain experience of a "male" person $105, while paying a "female" person only $40 for the identical experience. These are but samples of the "glaring inequalities" in the teachers' salary schedules.

Why is the male in the teaching profession differentiated from the male in every other calling, when his salary is concerned?

Why does the city differentiate the woman it hires to teach its children from the woman it hires to take stenographic notes, use a typewriter, follow up truants, inspect a tenement, or issue a license?

Why are not the appointees from the eligible lists established by the Department of Education, entitled to the same privileges and rights as appointees from Civil Service lists from other City and State Departments?

Some ask, "Shall the single woman, in teaching, be given the married woman's wage?" I do not know what they mean, But I say, "Why not the single woman in teaching just as much as the single woman in washing, in farming, in dressmaking, in nursing, in telephoning?"

Again, some ask, is there such a thing as "equal work" by two people?

Technically, no. No two people do exactly the same work in the same way. This is true of all professional and official work. Compare Mayor Gaynor's work with Mayor McClellan's. Will any one say their work as Mayor is "Equal Work"? And yet the pay is the same. Do all policemen do "Equal Work"? Yet they receive equal pay. So with firemen, school physicians, tenement house inspectors. The taxpayers, no doubt, believe that, judged by his work, Mayor Gaynor is worth a far higher salary than many of his predecessors. But a great corporation like the City of New York cannot attempt to pay each of its employees according to the work of that particular street cleaner or fireman or stenographer, and so must be content with classifying its positions, and fixing a salary for each. So should it do for its teachers. That is all we ask.

### The Family-to-Support Argument

It is rather a sad commentary on our profession that its men members are the only men who object to women members of the same profession getting the same pay for the same work. Who ever heard of a man lawyer fighting a woman lawyer in this way? A man doctor arguing that another doctor should give her services for less pay simply because she happened to be a woman? And leaving the professions, what attitude do we find the men who form our "Labor Unions" taking on this question? They form a solid phalanx on the side of "Equal Pay." The most powerful of all unions in many respects — "Big Six" — has a By-Law making it a misdemeanor to pay a woman less than a man working at the same form. All Labor Unions fight "two prices on a job."

Is it not sad to see men, American men, shoving aside, trampling down, and snatching the life preservers from their sisters? I say life preservers seriously and mean it literally. For to the woman obliged to support herself, is not her wage earning ability truly a life preserver. How can any man except one whom she is legally privileged to assist, take from a woman any part of the wages she has earned and remain worthy even in his own eyes? The excuses he makes to himself and to others in the attempt to justify his act, tend to belittle him more and more.

And yet some men whose blood sisters have by teaching provided the money to enable them, their brothers, to become teachers, oppose those very sisters in their efforts to obtain "Equal Pay for Equal Work." Can one ask for stronger proof of the insidious danger to our manhood which lurks in unjust standards of salary for service rendered? The true man, the good man, ought to put the woman who earns a respectable living, on a pedestal, as a beacon of encouragement to other women to show them one who wanted clothes to wear, and food to eat, and a place to live, and who obtained them by honorable labor.

I am firmly convinced that while teaching is a natural vocation for most women, it is rarely the true vocation of a man. And that those who enter the profession without the love for it which overshadows even the pocket returns, invariably deteriorate. Their lives are spent largely among those whom they consider their subordinates — in position or in salary, if not in intellect — the children and the women teachers. They grow to have an inordinate opinion of themselves. No matter how ridiculous or absurd or unfair may be the attitudes they take and the things they say, there is no one to say, "Nonsense!" as would one of his peers in the outer world. The novelist David Graham Phillips in the following description of one of his characters expresses my opinion better than I can myself: "Peter was not to blame for his weakness. He had not had the chance to become otherwise. He had been deprived of that hand-to-hand strife with life which alone makes a man strong. Usually, however, the dangerous truth as to his weakness was well hidden by the fictitious seeming of strength which obstinacy, selfishness and the adulation of a swarm of sycophants and dependents combine to give a man of means and position."

Recently in one of our schools, a male assistant to the principal resigned. The vacancy thus caused was filled by a woman. This woman is doing the same work as the man did, but with greater satisfaction to the principal. *But* she is being paid $800 a year less than the man was.

In another school I know there was a woman assistant to principal. As a grade teacher she had married and resigned, expecting — as most girls do when they marry — that she wouldn't have to work outside the home any more. But her husband became a victim of tuberculosis, and they went to Colorado in search of health for him. Time passed, their funds were exhausted, the invalid was unable to work, and so they came back, and the wife — after certifying, as our by-laws require, that her husband was unable to support her and had been so for two years — was reappointed. Later she secured promotion to assistant to principal. During the day she labored in a large, progressive school, composed almost wholly of children born in Russia, or of Russian parentage. At night she taught a class of foreign men. Now, although she actually had a family to support, she was receiving $800 a year less than a man in her position would receive. A married man? Oh, no, not necessarily. He might be a millionaire bachelor, or the pet of a wealthy wife—it is only necessary for him to be a "male" assistant to principal. Possibly on account of her family responsibilities, probably because she was ambitious, she strove for a principalship. During the school year, she traveled to Columbia University and took post graduate courses after school and on Saturdays; during the summer, when she should have been resting, she was studying with Professor This and Professor That. Last September she took the examination for a principal's license: in October, she died — typhoid, the doctors said. The husband she had cheerfully and lovingly supported for years survived her but a few weeks.

Why have I dwelt on this? To show the absurdity of the "family wage" argument of the male teacher. . . . Under a system of equal pay, where services should be paid for irrespective of sex, some women who now marry would remain single. But there are some men to-day who remain single because of relative economic independence, which they desire to maintain. These men are, however, relatively few. Women are as instinctive and as normal as men are, and independence, which they feared to lose, would prevent very few from marrying when they could make marriages which were attractive to them. Independence of women would improve marriage, since fewer women would marry because of necessity. By the same means divorce would be decreased, and human happiness would have a boom.

Our Association early in 1908 gathered some statistics. They showed 377 women — eleven of them married and six widows — supporting 707 others besides themselves. These teachers are all women, but the people depending wholly upon them or partly upon them are their mothers or their fathers or both or a brother or a sister or a niece or a nephew. These are actual figures collated from written answers to our questionnaire.

You see, then, that here is an average of two people for every woman to support besides herself. Now, what salary is offered to these young women of twenty-one years of age, after they have spent all these years in preparing for the position of teacher? What salary is she being paid by the City of New York, the greatest city in the world, with the greatest public school system in the world? $11.53 a week. A woman in charge of one of the stations in the city gets more than that. Does the latter have to spend as much money on clothes? No. She can wear the same clothes from one end of the year to the other if she wants to, and not be criticized. But I know when I go into a classroom, among the things that I notice is the teacher's dress — whether it is neat, whether it is appropriate. She must be a model for her class. Besides, the teacher must live in a respectable neighborhood and make a good appearance at home and abroad, and she must continue her studies in order to give satisfactory service.

# NOTES

## Introduction

1  From an unpublished "Utterance," or prose poem, spoken at the University of Massachusetts, Boston, 1977.

2  Frances R. Donovan, *The Schoolma'am* (1938; reprinted New York: Arno, 1969).

3  The early 1980s saw the historians Geraldine Clifford, Jacqueline Jones, and Polly Kaufman publish respectively, "Eve: Redeemed by Education and Teaching School," *History of Education Quarterly,* 21 (Winter, 1981), 479–492; *Soldiers of Light and Love, Northern Teachers and Georgia Blacks 1865–1873* (Athens: University of Georgia Press, 1992); *Women Teachers on the Frontier* (New Haven, CT: Yale University Press, 1985); as well as Linda Perkins' *Fanny Jackson-Coppin and the Institute for Colored Youth, 1837–1902* (New York: Garland, 1987). The more recent works referred to include: Donald Warren, ed., *American Teachers, Histories of a Profession at Work* (New York: Macmillan, 1989); Kate Rousmaniere, *City Teachers: Teaching and School Reform in Historical Perspective* (New York: Teachers College Press, 1997); and Patricia A. Carter, *"Everybody's Paid but the Teacher": The Teaching Profession and the Women's Movement* (New York: Teachers College Press, 2002). Among works on contemporary women teachers are Kathleen Weiler, *Women Teaching for Change: Gender, Class, and Power* (New York: Bergin & Garvey, 1988); Sari Biklen, *School Work: Gender and the Cultural Construction of Teaching* (New York: Teachers College Press, 1995); Madeline Grumet, *Bitter Milk: Women and Teaching* (Amherst: University of Massachusetts Press, 1988); Michele Foster, *Black Teachers on Teaching* (New York: New Press, 1997); and Jane Miller, *School for Women* (London: Virago, 1996).

4  Geraldine J. Clifford, "Man/Woman/Teacher: Gender, Family and Career in American Educational History," in *American Teachers: Histories of a Profession at Work,* ed. Donald Warren (New York: Macmillan, 1989), 293.

5  "Life of Horace Mann," Vol. 3, *Annual Reports of the Secretary of the Board of Education of Massachusetts for the Years 1839–1844* (Boston: Lee and Shepard, 1891), 427.

6  Friedrich Froebel (1782–1852) was a German educationalist and originator of the "kindergarten system." He believed in the efficacy of play and creative engagement in the development of young children.

7  In *The One Best System: A History of American Urban Education* (Cambridge, MA: Harvard University Press, 1974), David B. Tyack established this link.

8  Carl Kaestle, *Pillars of the Republic: Common Schools and American Society, 1780–1860* (New York: Hill and Wang, 1983), 124.

9  Kaestle, *Pillars of the Republic,* 124

10  Arthur O. Norton, ed., *The First State Normal School in America: The Journals of Cyrus Peirce and Mary Swift* (Cambridge, MA: Harvard University Press; reprinted from London: Humphrey Milford, Oxford University Press, 1926), 180–181.

11  Richard Bernard and Maris A. Vinovskis, "The Female Schoolteacher in Antebellum Massachusetts," *Journal of Social History,* 10 (1977), 332–345; Geraldine J. Clifford, "Teaching as a Seedbed of Feminism," unpublished paper prepared for the Fifth Berkshire Conference on Women's History, Vassar College, 1981, 3, 12.

12  Clifford, "Teaching as a Seedbed of Feminism," 1.

13  Michael Fultz, "African American Teachers in the South, 1890–1940: Powerlessness and the Ironies of Expectations and Protest," *History of Education Quarterly,* 35, No. 4 (Winter 1995), 408.

14  W. E. B. DuBois and Augustus Granville, *The Common School and the Negro American* (Atlanta: Atlanta University Press, 1911), 104, quoted in Linda Perkins, "The History of Blacks in Teaching," in Warren, *American Teachers,* 352.

15  Fultz, "African American Teachers in the South," 418.

16  This typology comes from R. W. Connell, *Gender and Power: Society, the Person and Sexual Politics* (Stanford, CA: Stanford University, 1987), 127.

17  Grumet, *Bitter Milk,* 24.

18  Weiler, *Women Teaching for Change,* 52.

19  David Angus and Jeffrey E. Mirel, *The Failed Promise of the American High School, 1890–1995* (New York: Teachers College Press, 1999), 9.

20  Herbert Kliebard, *The Struggle for the American Curriculum, 1893–1958* (New York: Routledge, 1995), 1.

21  Kliebard, *The Struggle for the American Curriculum,* 75.

22  Clifford, "Teaching as a Seedbed of Feminism," 19.

23  Anna Julia Cooper, from *A Voice from the South by a Black Woman of the South* (Xenia, OH: Aldine Printing House, 1892; reprinted New York: Oxford University Press, 1988), 78–79.

24  Darlene Clark Hine, "Rape and the Inner Lives of Black Women in the Middle West: Preliminary Thoughts on the Culture of Dissemblance," *Signs,* 14 (Summer 1989), 912–920.

25  Mary Helen Washington to Anna Julia Cooper, in Cooper, *A Voice from the South,* xxxvi.

26  Report of a Committee of the National Education Association on Teachers' Salaries and Cost of Living, Ann Arbor, National Education Association, 1913, 240–241, as quoted in Tyack, *The One Best System,* 259.

27  Phillip Sterling, ed., *The Real Teachers* (New York: Random House, 1972), 305, 307.

28  Author's interview with Grismaldy LaBoy and Julissa Medina, Brown University, Department of Education, Spring 2001.

## Chapter One — Seminary for Social Power

1  Minerva Leland Papers, A-78, Schlesinger Library on the History of Women in America, Radcliffe Institute for Advanced Studies, Harvard University, Cambridge,

Massachusetts.

2 Richard Bernard and Maris A. Vinovskis, "The Female Schoolteacher in Antebellum Massachusetts," *Journal of Social History,* 10 (1977), 332–345; John L. Rury, "Who Became Teachers? The Social Characteristics of Teachers in American History," in *American Teachers, Histories of a Profession at Work,* ed. Donald Warren (New York: Macmillan, 1989), 23; Valinda Littlefield, "Introduction," in *Facts on File Encyclopedia of Black Women in America: Education,* ed. Darlene Clark Hine (New York: Facts on File, 1997), 16.

3 Louisa May Alcott, *Work: A Story of Experience* (1873; reprinted New York: Penguin, 1994), 207.

4 Minerva Leland Papers.

5 The term *common school,* used in the nineteenth century for schools held "in common" or "owned" by all citizens, designated what are today called public schools.

6 In a study of Boston and Florida teachers in the 1970s, Dan C. Lortie thus characterizes the "social ambiguity" that has "stalked" teaching. He believes the "real regard" shown teachers has never matched the "professed regard." Lortie attributes this ambiguity in part to "the relative position of the young and the female in the nineteenth century." *Schoolteacher: A Sociological Study* (Chicago: University of Chicago Press, 1975; reprinted with a new preface, 2002), 10–12.

7 David B. Tyack, *The One Best System: A History of American Urban Education* (Cambridge, MA: Harvard University Press, 1974); Bernard and Vinovskis, "The Female Schoolteacher," 10; Geraldine J. Clifford, "Teaching as a Seedbed of Feminism," unpublished paper prepared for the Fifth Berkshire Conference on Women's History, Vassar College, 1981; and Carl Kaestle, *Pillars of the Republic: Common Schools and American Society, 1780–1860* (New York: Hill and Wang, 1983).

8 Rev. A. D. Mayo, "The Kitchen and the School-room," *National Teacher,* 2, No. 5 (May 1872), 155.

9 Amy Dru Stanley, "Home Life and the Morality of the Market," in *The Market Revolution in America: Social, Political, and Religious Expressions, 1800–1880,* ed. Melvyn Stokes and Stephen Conway (Charlottesville: University Press of Virginia, 1996), 83.

10 Mayo, "The Kitchen and the School-room," 155.

11 Quoted in Willie Lee Rose, *Rehearsal for Reconstruction* (New York: Oxford University Press, 1964), 229.

12 Quoted in Robert L. Reid, "The Professionalization of Public School Teachers: The Chicago Experience, 1895–1920" (Ph.D. diss., Northwestern University, 1968), 12, note 30.

13 "The School Mistress," *Harper's New Monthly Magazine,* 57 (September 1878), 608.

14 Joan Jensen, *Loosening the Bonds: Mid-Atlantic Farm Women, 1750–1850* (New Haven, CT: Yale University Press, 1986), 172.

15 Littlefield, "Introduction," 2. According to Linda M. Perkins, the Quaker manager approved Fanny Jackson-Coppin as principal of the school because she was best qualified, despite the Quaker view that women should not become "too educated." "Heed Life's Demands: The Educational Philosophy of Fanny Jackson-Coppin,"

Journal of Negro Education, 51, No. 3 (1982), 183.

16 This chapter focuses on New England. Much of the country lagged behind the Northeast in both the spread of common schools and the employment of high percentages of women, especially the South.

17 See Linda Kerber, "Separate Spheres, Female Worlds, Woman's Place: The Rhetoric of Women's History (1988)," in *Toward an Intellectual History of Women: Essays by Linda K. Kerber* (Chapel Hill: University of North Carolina, 1997), 169; and Stanley, "Home Life and the Morality of the Market," 80.

18 Stanley, "Home Life and the Morality of the Market," 84.

19 Edith Abbott, *Women in Industry* (New York: Appleton, 1910), 55, quoted in Mary P. Ryan, *Womanhood in America* (New York: Franklin Watts, 1975), 105.

20 Warren, *American Teachers,* xiv.

21 Henry F. Bedford, ed., *Their Lives & Numbers: The Condition of Working People in Massachusetts, 1870–1900* (Ithaca, NY: Cornell University Press, 1995), 4, 125.

22 Percy Wells Bidwell, "Population Growth in Southern New England, 1810–1860," *Quarterly Publications of the American Statistical Association New Series,* No. 120 (December 1917), 813.

23 "Letter III. What Is an American?" in *Letters from an American Farmer,* J. Hector St. John Crevecoeur, reprinted from the original edition, with a prefatory note by W. P. Trent and an introduction by Ludwig Lewisohn. Available online at http://xroads.virginia.edu/~HYPER/CREV/contents.html

24 Richard J. Altenbaugh and Kathleen Underwood, "The Evolution of Normal Schools," in *Places Where Teachers Are Taught,* ed. John I. Goodlad, Roger Soder, and Kenneth A. Sirotnik (San Francisco: Jossey-Bass, 1990), 138.

25 For exploration of statistics and formulation of the hypothesis that rural and urban labor markets for teachers made different demands and that rapid feminization accompanied the growth of urban graded schools, designed "for" women teachers, see Myra H. Strober and David Tyack, "Why Do Women Teach and Men Manage? A Report of Research on Schools," *Signs,* 5, No. 3 (Spring 1980), 494–503.

26 Jensen, *Loosening the Bonds,* 169.

27 A quantitative study by Joel Perlmann and Robert A. Margo refines the theory that school boards hired women because they were cheaper. They argue that the departure of males may have been an unintended consequence of boards' decisions to upgrade schools. In extending the school term and setting more stringent qualifications, boards did not realize men would leave. The alternative explanation is that boards decided to hire female teachers equally or more talented than males for the same wages and a more demanding work load. *Women's Work? American Schoolteachers: 1650–1920* (Chicago: University of Chicago Press, 2001), 100–103.

28 Alcott, *Work,* 157, 335.

29 Catherine Beecher to Mary Dutton, 8 February 1830, Collection of American Literature, quoted in Kathryn Sklar, *Catherine Beecher* (New Haven, CT: Yale University Press, 1973), 97.

30 *Common School Journal,* 12, No. 236 (August 1850), quoted in Michael B. Katz, *The Irony of Early School Reform* (Cambridge, MA: Harvard University Press, 1968),

118; *Boston School Committee, 1857–58,* 10, 11, quoted in Katz, *The Irony of Early School Reform,* 120.

31 Horace Mann (1796–1859), leader among the pre–Civil War schoolmen, served for over a decade as secretary to the first Massachusetts Board of Education. His controversial annual reports spell out the philosophy and vision of the common school movement. Henry Barnard (1811–1900) was the first secretary of the Connecticut Board of Education. A theorist and scholar of American and European education, Barnard wrote and lectured on education throughout his life and founded the *American Journal of Education.* For Cyrus Peirce, see text.

32 Christine Ogren, "A Large Measure of Self-Control and Personal Power: Women Students at State Normal Schools During the Late-Nineteenth and Early Twentieth Century," *Women's Studies Quarterly,* 27 (Fall/Winter 2000), 211; Altenbaugh and Underwood, "The Evolution of Normal Schools," 144.

33 Altenbaugh and Underwood, "The Evolution of Normal Schools," 167.

34 The establishment of normal schools symbolized the elevation of teaching to a profession thought to require special training; however, normal schools prepared only a small number of teachers on into the twentieth century. Other teachers attended summer institutes held on college campuses; some took a year's training in high school; but most simply met the requirement to have completed a year of school beyond the grade they wished to teach.

35 Arthur O. Norton, ed., *The First State Normal School in America: The Journals of Cyrus Peirce and Mary Swift* (Cambridge, MA: Harvard University Press, 1926), 83.

36 Norton, *The First State Normal School in America,* 81, 87, 90–91.

37 Norton, *The First State Normal School in America,* 86.

38 Norton, *The First State Normal School in America,* 183–184.

39 Jergen Herbst, *And Sadly Teach: Teacher Education and Professionalization in American Culture* (Madison: University of Wisconsin Press, 1989), 35.

40 Herbst, *And Sadly Teach,* 36.

41 Herbst, *And Sadly Teach,* 107–08.

42 Herbst, *And Sadly Teach,* 186

43 Herbst, *And Sadly Teach,* 170.

44 Clifford, "Teaching as a Seedbed of Feminism," 17.

45 Lortie, *Schoolteacher,* 10–12.

46 "Domestication" is the phrase used by Paul Mattingly in *The Classless Profession* (New York: New York University Press, 1975). He characterizes the attitudes of two generations of normal school leadership as follows: 1830–1860, upper class, "authoritarian and benevolent" with an emphasis on "intellectual discipline, spirituality, and self-possession"; and 1860–1890, lower middle class, with an emphasis on skills and teaching methods, and the assumption of shared values. From 1890 on, he argues, the superintendency became the socializing force for teachers. (For an example of the superintendency's force, see chapter three of *Woman's "True" Profession.*)

47 For an argument that the normal school had declined by the late nineteenth century see Mattingly, *The Classless Profession,* chapter seven, "From Inspiration to

Domestication," 134–168. Working without the benefit of feminist analysis, Mattingly misses the point made by Ogren: that late-nineteenth-century normal schools opened doors to independence and self-sufficiency for young women of modest means.

48 Ogren, "A Large Measure of Self-Control and Personal Power," 221–222.

49 Arthur Clarke Boyden, *Albert Gardner Boyden and the Bridgewater State Normal School: A Memorial Volume* (Bridgewater, MA: Arthur H. Willis, 1919), 144–145, as quoted in Ogren, "A Large Measure of Self-Control and Personal Power," 217.

50 Clifford, "Teaching as a Seedbed of Feminism," 59–60.

## Endnotes for Chapter One Documents

1 "This threefold process, in some studies, as the Philosophy of the Mind, of which an entire view should be taken, requires the whole term; in others, as in geography and history, parts may be taken, and the pupils made thorough in each as they go along. In mathematics the three steps of the process are to be gone through with, as the teacher proceeds with every distinct proposition. But still, there will, in every well-instructed class, be this three-fold order prevailing, and during the term, requiring a beginning, a middle, and an end; the first of the term being mostly devoted to teaching, and the middle to reciting, and the last to acquiring a correct manner of communicating" [Editor's note in the 1861 publication].

2 "We would observe, at this point, that the chirography of Mrs. Willard's letter, a copy of which now lies before us, is exquisitely neat, and boldly distinct. One element in her success, has been, no doubt, her beautiful penmanship, inherited from her father and carefully cultivated, as important to her education objects" [Editor's note in the 1861 publication].

3 A nineteenth-century term signifying the choice not to marry; it had a positive connotation, unlike its counterpart, "old maid."

## Chapter Two — A Noble Work Done Earnestly

1 Letter from Henry Stanton to Elizabeth Cady Stanton, April 1861, E. C. Stanton Papers, Library of Congress.

2 Estimates vary for the number of teachers who went south to teach. Jacqueline Jones, in *Soldiers of Light and Love: Northern Teachers and Georgia Black, 1865–1873* (Chapel Hill: University of North Carolina Press, 1980), and Robert C. Morris, *Reading, 'Riting, and Reconstruction: The Education of Freedmen in the South, 1861–1870* (Chicago: University of Chicago Press, 1981), estimate that about three-fourths to three-fifths of teachers were women; a small percentage were African American, with African American males predominating.

3 Morris, *Reading, 'Riting, and Reconstruction,* i.

4 *Freedmen's Record,* 1, No. 5 (May 1865), 70–71.

5 Ware was among the first teachers to go south. Her letters are published in

Elizabeth Ware Pearson, ed., *Letters from Port Royal (1862–1868)* (New York: Arno Press and New York Times, 1969).

6   *Woman's Work for the Lowly* (American Missionary Society, 1874), as quoted in James McPherson's *The Abolitionist Legacy: From Abolition to the NAACP* (Princeton, NJ: Princeton University Press, 1975), 165, from Jacqueline Halstead, "'The Grand Opportunity': Wisconsin Yankees Teach the Freedmen, 1866–1876," unpublished seminar paper, University of Wisconsin, 1971, cited with permission.

7   See bibliography for autobiographical accounts. The Arthur and Elizabeth Schlesinger Library on the History of Women in America, part of the Radcliffe Institute for Advanced Study at Harvard University, houses the collections of the Beecher-Stowe family, including Catherine, and individuals such as Lydia Child. Of quite another order are the novels by A. W. Tourgée and W. E. B. DuBois: *Bricks without Straw* (1880) and *The Quest of the Silver Fleece* (1911); a web version of the Tourgée novel can be found at the University of North Carolina's website: http://docsouth.unc.edu/nc/tourgee/tourgee.html#p369. Both authors used fiction to explore racial issues in the South using teachers as lead characters.

8   Farah J. Griffin, ed., *Beloved Sisters and Loving Friends: Letters from Rebecca Primus of Royal Oak, Maryland, and Addie Brown of Hartford, Connecticut, 1854–1868* (New York: Knopf, 1999). Indeed, our inability to know the denouement of the teachers' lives is tantalizing; there are hints of suffrage activism to come, of work on civil rights issues in the North, and of transgressions of social mores based on the experience of living in an interracial society in the South.

9   Rupert Sargent Holland, ed., *Letters and Diary of Laura M. Towne* (1912; reprinted New York: Negro Universities Press, 1969), 8. In considering the observations about race below, it is important to remember that even among Northerners, abolitionists like the schoolmarms were far outnumbered by people persuaded that the intent of the Civil War should be to preserve the Union, not to end slavery. Decisions about slaveholding were to be left to the states. There was little general interest among whites in assessing African Americans' intellectual and moral capacities, or in taking on their education as a cause. Thus the Port Royal Experiment was highly unusual. On January 15, 1862, General W. T. S. Sherman requested that teachers be sent to Port Royal, South Carolina, to teach ex-slaves left on plantations under control of the Union Army. Joined by Quaker missionaries, philanthropists, and abolitionists, the teachers set themselves up to prove that the newly freed persons could become economically self-sufficient and well educated despite the harm done to them by slavery. The best-known work on the experiment is Willie Lee Rose, *Rehearsal for Reconstruction* (New York: Oxford, 1964).

10  Linda Warfel Slaughter, ed., *The Freedmen of the South* (Cincinnati, Ohio: Elm St. Printing, 1869), 126. Additional biographical information available at http://www.las.iastate.edu/kiosk/1622.shtml.

11  Mary Ames, *From a New England Woman's Diary in Dixie in 1865* (Springfield, MA: Plimpton Press, 1906), 88–89. The Unitarian teachers Laura Towne and Elizabeth Hyde Botume left explicit statements favoring African American female suffrage — still by law more than half a century away, and de facto even further.

12 Griffin, *Beloved Sisters and Loving Friends,* 119, 134. Morris, *Reading, 'Riting, and Reconstruction,* 89.

13 Elizabeth Hyde Botume, *First Days Amongst the Contrabands* (1893; reprinted New York: Arno Press, 1968), 247.

14 Ames, *From a New England Woman's Diary,* 88–89.

15 Henry Swint, *The Northern Teacher in the South, 1862–1868* (1941; reprinted New York: Octagon Press, 1967), 94.

16 Henry L. Swint, ed., *Dear Ones at Home* (Nashville, TN: Vanderbilt University Press, 1966), 21.

17 Letter from teacher Arthur Sumner to his cousin Nina, August 1864, Penn School Papers, Southern Historical Collection, University of North Carolina.

18 Botume, *First Days Amongst the Contrabands,* 29.

19 Botume, *First Days Amongst the Contrabands,* 62, 63.

20 Ednah D. Cheney, July 9, 1865, Cheney Papers, Boston Public Library, Boston.

21 In Stanley, *The American Freedman* (New York Branch, American Missionary Association, December 1867), 361.

22 Morris, *Reading, 'Riting, and Reconstruction,* 174.

23 Morris, *Reading, 'Riting, and Reconstruction,* 189–190. Morris quotes the *Chicago Tribune* as it was quoted in *Forty-Eighth Annual Report* (Boston: American Tract Society, 1862), 35, 149.

24 *Pennsylvania Freedmen's Bulletin,* December 1865. Cited in Rose, *Rehearsal for Reconstruction,* 150.

25 *Freedmen's Record,* 3, No. 4 (April 1867), 54.

26 Morris, *Reading, 'Riting, and Reconstruction,* 115. Morris cites the *Tenth Semi-Annual Report on Schools for Freedmen, July 1, 1870* (Washington, DC: Government Printing Office, 1870), 49–54, 75–80.

27 Details from an unpublished senior thesis by Judy Cohen (University of Massachusetts, Boston, 1977).

28 Letter from Amy Williams to D. E. Emerson, March 5, 1878, American Missionary Association archives. Quoted in McPherson, *The Abolitionist Legacy,* 171.

29 Maria Waterbury, *Seven Years Among the Freedmen* (Chicago: T. B. Arnold, 1891), frontispiece.

30 Perhaps on account of their substantially informal authority, the teachers seemed to tolerate their own disenfranchisement and that of African American women. Several, however, made comments to the effect that when women got the vote, the African American men would have to give up their notions of "being higher than women generally." Botume, *First Days Amongst the Contrabands,* 233.

31 John Chadwick, *A Life for Liberty* (New York: G. P. Putnam's, 1899), 215–216. Although Greeley represented "good government" and presented an alternative to Ulysses S. Grant's patronage policy, most abolitionists opposed him because they feared he would "forgive" the South and remove freed people from federal protection.

32 Holland, *Letters and Diary of Laura M. Towne,* 271.

33 Holland, *Letters and Diary of Laura M. Towne,* 222.

34  W. E. B. DuBois, *The Souls of Black Folk* (Greenwich, CT: Fawcett, 1961), 31, 83.
35  Michael Fultz, "African American Teachers in the South, 1890–1940: Powerlessness and the Ironies of Expectations and Protest," *History of Education Quarterly,* 35 (Winter 1995), 418.

## Endnotes for Chapter Two Documents

1   This was the day that the Confederate capitol fell, and the war ended.
2   Member of Boston Committee on Clothing and Supplies.
3   A Quaker expression meaning "working group."
4   Stuart Banfield, a teacher from Dover, New Hampshire.
5   "Probably Anna Lowell, of the New England Freedmen's Aid Society, Boston" [Editor's note in *Dear Ones at Home*].
6   The reference is to Lydia Marie Child's *The Freedmen's Book.* See selection, p. 181.
7   Members of the black family with whom Mary Ames and Emily Bliss shared the house.
8   President of the Salem Female Anti-Slavery Society.
9   Annual Fourth of July meeting of the Massachusetts Anti-Slavery Society.
10  Miss T. is Laura Towne. See selection, p. 209.
11  The white man John Brown (1800–1859) led a slave attack on the U.S. arsenal at Harper's Ferry, West Virginia. He was hanged for treason.
12  Toussaint L'Ouverture (1743–1803), black leader of a revolutionary liberation movement in Haiti.
13  Forten made several trips away from the islands, then returned.
14  Miss Murray is Ellen Murray.
15  Towne was actually thirty-seven.
16  A staple of the teachers' diet was oysters.
17  From the area of the Combahee River.
18  H is Laura Towne's brother Henry Towne.
19  W. is Laura Towne's brother William Towne.
20  Francis R. Cope, of Philadelphia, who acted as financial agent for the Penn School.
21  Operetta by Gilbert and Sullivan.

## Chapter Three — Teaching in the Big City

1   Catherine Brody, "A New York Childhood," *American Mercury,* Vol. 14, 53 (May 1928), 62.
2   Anzia Yezierska, *Bread Givers* (1925; reprinted New York: G. Braziller, 1975), 269.
3   Tillie Olsen, "Utterance" (unpublished prose poem).
4   There were some special "steamer" classes for overage and non-English-speaking children, but most children simply entered grade one, no matter what their age.
5   William Elsbree, *The American Teacher* (New York: American Book, 1939), ch. 17, quoted in David B. Tyack, *The One Best System: A History of American Urban Education*

(Cambridge, MA: Harvard University Press, 1974), 60.

6 This chapter benefits deeply from David Tyack's now classic work, *The One Best System*. Along with providing the analysis that has influenced most subsequent research on urbanization and bureaucratization, Tyack attended throughout to the relation between gender and the growth of bureaucratized schools.

7 A ten-volume project of the Arthur and Elizabeth Schlesinger Library on the History of Women in America, Radcliffe College, edited by Ruth Hill, *The Black Women Oral History Project* (Westport, CT: Meckler, 1991) includes recorded and transcribed autobiographical memoirs of seventy-two women talking about their lives and developing careers from the 1920s through the 1980s. Among them are numerous women who spent some time as teachers, but only one, Frances O. Grant, devoted a career to teaching in the Northeast. An excerpt from the oral history is included in the selections for this chapter. In her lively book, *City Teachers* (New York: Teachers College Press, 1997), Kate Rousmaniere includes the voices of many teachers who worked in New York in the 1900s–1920s.

8 This is how Alfred Kazin characterized the teacher of immigrants in *A Walker in the City* (New York: Harcourt Brace, 1951), 18.

9 Myra Kelly, *Little Citizens* (New York: McClure, Phillips, 1904), 161.

10 William Maxwell, "The Personal Power of the Teacher in Public School Work," in *National Education Association Addresses and Proceedings* (Cleveland: National Education Association, 1908), 118.

11 U.S. Bureau of the Census, *Historical Statistics of the United States, Colonial Times to 1970* (Washington, DC: Government Printing Office, 1975), 115.

12 New York Superintendent Maxwell boasted of little Russians and Italians, six months after landing, "declaiming with tremendous fervor Patrick Henry's apostrophe to liberty or telling in their compositions about the day when their forefathers landed on Plymouth Rock." Maxwell, "The Personal Power of the Teacher in Public School Work," 119.

13 Julia Richman, "The Immigrant Child," *National Education Association Addresses and Proceedings* (Asbury Park, NJ: National Education Association, 1905), 113.

14 Quoted in Tyack, *The One Best System*, 232.

15 This was an average wage of 86,730 city elementary school teachers in 1905. In all but four of forty-eight cities surveyed, unskilled municipal laborers and sewer workers earned more. Stenographers earned about the same amount. *Report of the Committee on Salaries, Tenure, and Pensions of Public School Teachers in the United States to the National Council of Education, July 1905* (Washington, DC: National Education Association, 1905), 54.

16 Richman, "The Immigrant Child," 121.

17 Abraham Cahan, *The Rise of David Levinsky* (1917; reprinted New York: Harper & Bros., 1960), 129.

18 Yezierska, *Bread Givers*, 272, 273.

19 Kazin, *A Walker in the City*, 18–21.

20 See Joseph Mayer Rice, *The Public School System of the United States* (New York: Century, 1893), 39.

21  Charles B. Gilbert, *The School and Its Life* (New York: Silver, Burdett, 1906), 85, quoted in Tyack, *The One Best System,* 97.

22  Minnie Reynolds, *The Crayon Clue* (New York: Mitchell Kennerley, 1915), 2.

23  Michael W. Homel, *Down from Equality: Black Chicagoans and the Public Schools, 1920–41* (Urbana-Champaign: University of Illinois Press, 1984), 4. Segregation was ended by law in Boston in 1855, in New York City in 1883, and in Chicago in 1865. Boston data is available at http://www.nps.gov/boaf/abielsmith5.htm.

24  Tyack, *The One Best System,* 117.

25  David Ment, "Patterns of Public School Segregation, 1900–1940: A Comparative Study of New York City, New Rochelle, and New Haven," in *Schools in Cities: Consensus and Conflict in American Educational History,* ed. Ronald Goodenow and Diane Ravitch (New York: Holmes and Meier, 1983), 83. See also Gertrude E. Ayer, *Gertrude Elise Ayer Papers, 1931–1966,* New York Public Library, call number Sc Micro R-4842.

26  The Immigration Commission found that in 1911, 43 percent of teachers were second-generation immigrants. Magazines such as *School* reveal in their lists of appointments and retirements many new Jewish teachers and retiring Irish ones around 1905. See Richard J. Altenbaugh, ed., *The Teacher's Voice: A Social History of Teaching in Twentieth-Century America* (Bristol, PA: Falmer Press, 1992), 136.

27  Helen Horvath, "Plea of an Immigrant — Abstract," in *National Education Association Addresses and Proceedings* (San Francisco: National Education Association, 1923), 680–682, quoted in Tyack, *The One Best System,* 233.

28  Anzia Yezierska, *Children of Loneliness* (New York: Funk & Wagnalls, 1923), 122.

29  Reynolds, *The Crayon Clue,* 120.

30  Anonymous, "Confessions of Public School Teachers," *Atlantic Monthly,* July 1896, 101.

31  "Confessions of Public School Teachers," 107.

32  Tyack, *The One Best System,* 188.

33  See Diane Ravitch, *The Great School Wars* (New York: Basic Books, 1974); also Tyack, *The One Best System.*

34  William Rainey Harper, as quoted in Robert L. McCaul, "Dewey's Chicago," *School Review,* 67 (Autumn 1959), 265. Quoted in Tyack, *The One Best System,* 135.

35  Tyack, *The One Best System,* 147–148.

36  Carl Kaestle, book review, "Class Schools," *Chicago History* (Summer 1984), 71–72.

37  Marjorie Murphy, *Blackboard Unions: The AFT and the NEA, 1900–1980* (Ithaca, NY: Cornell University Press, 1990), 28.

38  Reynolds, *The Crayon Clue,* 10.

39  "Confessions of Public School Teachers," 104.

40  William McAndrew, "Public School Teaching," *World's Work,* 5 (March 1903), 3188–3189.

41  Haley was the first woman (and the first grade school teacher) to speak from the floor of the NEA. Previously, women's papers were read aloud by men.

42  Quoted in Julia Wrigley, *Class Politics and Public Schools: Chicago, 1900–1950* (New Brunswick, NJ: Rutgers University Press, 1990), 28.

43 In this section, I use the term *organization* to signify an organized group of teachers, including non-labor-affiliated associations and labor unions. Haley's organization was affiliated with labor; Grace Strachan's association was not.

44 Kate Rousmaniere makes this point in the introduction to *City Teachers,* 5–7.

45 Patricia Carter, "Becoming the 'New Women': The Equal Rights Campaigns of New York City Schoolteachers, 1900–1920," in Altenbaugh, *The Teacher's Voice,* 40–45.

46 Dan C. Lortie, *Schoolteacher: A Sociological Study* (Chicago: University of Chicago Press, 1975; reprinted with a new preface, 2002), 10–12.

47 James R. Green, *The World of the Worker: Labor in Twentieth-Century America* (New York: Hill and Wang, 1980), 61, 73.

48 Women teachers were particularly divided on the issue of suffrage — some argued that men could represent their interests as voters while they represented themselves through their associations, in the legislature, and among women's organizations.

49 Carter, "Becoming the 'New Women,'" 44.

50 Grace Strachan, *Equal Pay for Equal Work* (New York: B. F. Buck, 1910), 41.

51 Strachan, *Equal Pay for Equal Work,* 11, 18.

52 Wayne Urban, *Why Teachers Organized* (Detroit: Wayne State University Press, 1982), 91.

53 Strachan, *Equal Pay for Equal Work,* 298.

54 Carter, "Becoming the 'New Women,'" 40–58.

55 Urban, *Why Teachers Organized,* 99.

## Endnotes for Chapter Three Documents

1 In the 1870s, Boston incorporated several large suburbs that were previously separate villages.

2 Pat and Paddy were derogatory or slang names for the Irish immigrant.

3 "Rebbe" is the Yiddish word for "rabbi."

# ABOUT THE AUTHOR

Nancy Hoffman is vice president for the Youth Transitions Cluster and director of the Early College Initiative at Jobs for the Future, a national nonprofit policy organization located in Boston. She has taught and been an administrator, most recently at Brown University. She has also worked at Temple University, Harvard Graduate School of Education, and the Fund for the Improvement of Postsecondary Education. Hoffman was a founder and faculty member at UMass Boston's College of Public and Community Service in the early 1970s. Hoffman went south to teach in the freedom schools established during the civil rights movement of the 1960s — one hundred years after the schoolmarms in chapter two of this book.

Hoffman holds a B.A. (1964) and Ph.D. (1971) in comparative literature from the University of California, Berkeley, with a specialization in the Renaissance. She is the author of *Spenser's Pastorals* (Johns Hopkins University Press, 1979) and *Woman's "True" Profession: Voices from the History of Teaching* (2nd ed., 2003). With Florence Howe, she edited *Women Working: Stories and Poems* (Feminist Press, 1979) . She has also coedited three volumes of *Women's Studies Quarterly:* "Women, Girls, and the Culture of Education," "Women, Race, and Culture," and, most recently, "Keeping Gender on the Chalkboard: Notes for a New Century of 7-12 and Teacher Education." Hoffman chairs the board of directors of the Feminist Press, the oldest women's press in the United States. She writes on education policy and women's studies and has been particularly engaged in improving access to and success in college for inner-city high school students.

# INDEX

Adams, John, 28
Adams, Mary S., 79, 82-84
"Allison, Amelia," 240, 304-08
American Missionary Association, 122-
    23, 125-26, 128, 134, 157, 192-209
Americanization of immigrants. *See*
    immigrants, assimilation of
Ames, Mary, 124, 130, 165-70
Ames, Mary Clemmer, 146-48
Antin, Mary, 234, 252, 280-86
    love for English, 282
    gratitude to teachers, 252, 281, 282
    "Snow," 234, 284
    writing, 280-86
assimilation of immigrants. *See* immi-
    grants, assimilation of

Barnard, Henry, 38, 49, 326
Beecher, Catherine, 3, 9-10, 18, 24, 26-
    27, 33-38, 66-79, 233
behavior codes for teachers, 10, 19
biographies of teachers, 3, 49-66, 85-
    93, 141-58, 170-80, 230-31
black women teachers, 3, 8, 12-15, 19,
    25, 39, 93-103, 141-46, 170-80,
    192-209, 292-304
Bliss, Emily, 124, 165
Board of National Popular Education,
    66, 79
boarding around, 58, 61-63, 82-83
Boston Educational Commission, 159
Boston School Committee, 229
Botume, Elizabeth Hyde, 129-31, 134,
    136, 185-91, 328-29
*Bread Givers,* 228, 234
Brody, Catherine, 228
Bureau of Refugees, Freedmen and
    Abandoned Lands, 122, 125, 134,
    139, 169, 218, 220

certification of teachers, 60-61, 266,
    289, 299
Chase, Lucy, 130, 133, 159-65

Chase, Sarah, 130, 159-65
    as organizer, 159-62
    opinion of interracial education, 130
Chesnutt, Charles W., 10, 15, 138, 217-
    26
Child, Lydia Maria, 13, 133, 181-84
"Children of Loneliness," 239
class size, 20-21, 63, 65, 83-84, 89,
    165, 254-55, 305
Clinton, DeWitt, 56-57
Codes of behavior for teachers. *See*
    behavior codes for teachers
"Confessions of Public School Teachers,"
    304
Cooley, Rossa B., 136
corporal punishment, 60, 89, 203, 306

Dame schools, 2, 29
*Dear Ones at Home,* 159
democracy and education, 120, 126,
    207, 232, 241-42, 308-15
Dewey, John, 16, 21, 241, 298, 312
diaries of teachers, 85-93, 165-73, 210-
    17
Dickey, Sara Ann, 136
Dodge, Mary Abigail, 269-71
Dogherty, Marian, 20, 232, 237, 272-
    79
domestic education, 71-72, 78, 300
*The Domestic Receipt Book,* 34
domestic work, 105-06
domestics, 7, 72
Downing, Lucia B., 11, 30, 58-66
DuBois, W. E. B., 12, 125, 138-39, 295
Dwyer, Mary Agnes, 234-35, 286-92
    education of, 288-89
    work among immigrants, 234-35,
        287-88
    decision to become principal, 291
*Educational Biographies, Memoirs of
    Teachers, Educators and Promoters and
    Benefactors of Education,* 49
employment opportunity for women, 7-

11, 72-75, 138

English as a second language, 229, 233-34, 288

equal pay for equal work, 247-48, 307, 311, 316-20

*Equal Pay for Equal Work,* 316-20

*Evils Suffered by American Women and American Children,* 34, 66

feminism, 11-12, 43-44

feminization of teaching, 2-4, 6, 10
   and status of profession, 4-5, 8, 10, 13-14

*First Days Amongst the Contrabands,* 185

*The First State Normal Schools in America: The Journals of Cyrus Peirce and Mary Swift,* 85

Forten, Charlotte L., 127, 131, 135, 170-80, 183, 330 n. 15

*The Freedmen of the South,* 146

The Freedmen's Aid Association, 181

*The Freedmen's Book,* 13, 181-84

Freedmen's Bureau. *See* Bureau of Refugees, Freedmen and Abandoned Lands

freedmen's school teachers,
   attitudes toward blacks, 121, 123-24, 126-30
   black protection of, 151
   black women, 145, 170-80, 192-209
   commitment to black equality, 121-24, 127, 137
   community influence, 124, 135-38
   credentials of, 120, 123
   diaries of, 145, 165-80
   W. E. B. DuBois' opinions of, 139
   illness, 166-67
   interracial relationships, 124, 128
   letters of, 159-65, 192-209
   life-long commitment, 135-58
   loneliness, 139, 174, 219
   political activism, 137
   relationships with each other, 128
   relationships with students, 127-30

freedmen's schools, 122
   absorbed into public system, 134
   classroom conditions, 131-32
   curriculum, 132-33

French, Austa, 130

Fuller, Anna, 11, 103-17

Gardner, Anna, 133-35

Gary System, 290

Goggin, Catherine, 244-45

Grant, Frances O., 292-304

"great school war," 241

Haley, Margaret, 21, 244-45, 248-49, 308-15

Hampton Institute, 134, 138, 165

Hancock, Cornelia, 136

Hancock School for Girls, 237, 272

Harper, Frances E.W., 133, 182-83

Hart, Emma. *See* Willard, Emma Hart

Hartford Female Seminary, 36

Hoffman, Nancy, 286-92, 321

Hoffman, Malvina, 290

Hogan, Kate, 316

Holley, Sallie, 119, 128, 136-38

home visits, 233

illness,
   among teachers, 166-67

immigrant students, 281-86, 288

immigrant teachers, 239

immigrants, 15, 229
   American fear of,
   assimilation of, 38, 231-33
   number and nationality, 34, 231-32
   social problems of, 232
   teachers' involvement with, 233
   *See also* Irish immigrants, Jewish immigrants

Industrialization, 6, 31

Interborough Association of Women Teachers, 247, 249, 316

Irish immigrants, 231-32, 274
   *See also* immigrants

Jackson-Coppin, Fanny, 3, 20, 39, 93-103, 135-36, 324-25 n. 15

James, George F., 312-13

Jewish immigrants, 231, 233-34
   *See also* immigrants

*The Journal of Charlotte Forten,* 170

journals of teachers. *See* diaries of teachers

Kazin, Alfred, 234

Keller, Helen, 85

Kelly, Myra, 231, 236, 265-68

Ku Klux Klan, 137, 152-54

labor organizing, 308-16

labor unions, 20, 46, 237, 243, 245-49

Lee, Ellen P., 18, 79-82

Leland, Minerva, 24-25, 34
*Letters and Diary of Laura M. Towne,* 209
Lexington Academy, 39-41
*Life and Education of Laura Bridgman,* 85
A Life for Liberty, 329
*Little Citizens,* 231, 236, 265
Lortie, Dan C., 246, 324
L'Overture, Touissant, 132, 176, 178-79, 330
Lowell, Mass., 73

Mann, Horace, 4, 7, 38, 44, 311
"The March of Progress," 217-26
married women, 8, 32
Maxwell, William, 231, 241
Miner, Thomas, 50-51, 53
Mingo, 182-84
Moultrie, Marion, 22
Munro, Abby, 136
Murray, Ellen, 128-29, 178, 209, 212

National Education Association, 15, 21, 232, 239, 244, 308-09
National Federation of Teachers, 244, 310
*From a New England Woman's Diary in Dixie in 1865,* 165-69
New York City public schools, 235, 251-65
    assimilation of immigrants, 253
    African American teachers, 238
    centralization of, 242
    class size, 259
    condition of facilities, 259-60
    health care for students, 253, 258
    number of students, 238, 253
    political control of, 237, 247, 249
    teaching licenses, 263
    wages, 72, 264
normal schools, 15, 25, 27, 40, 42-43, 66, 79, 85-96, 98, 100, 134-35, 238, 289-90
    and professionalism of teaching, 40, 238
    and state support of education, 39-40, 43, 91
    *See also* teacher education

occupational choice, 25, 28
    and class, 14
    and marriage, 7, 37
oral histories of teachers, 230, 235, 292-303

*Our Common Schools,* 269-71

Perkins Institution, 85
Philadelphia public schools, 170
Phillips, David Graham, 318
politics, 126, 132, 137
    and public schools, 217-18, 248
"The Port Royal Experiment," 126, 170-80
practice teaching, 13, 26, 101, 233
professionalization of school administration, 15, 229, 242
professionalization of teaching, 39-40, 246
*The Promised Land,* 280
public school administration, 135, 229
    attitudes toward teachers, 20-21, 236
    political influence on, 134, 233, 242
    regulation of teachers, 311, 229
Putnam, Caroline, 128, 136

Reconstruction, 137
Richman, Julia, 232-33, 241
Rutledge, Julia, 159-65

Salary. *See* wages
Schofield, Martha, 136
school administration. *See* public school administration
school nurse, 189, 259
"The Schoolmarm," 103-17
'Scusa Me Teacher, 20, 272
seamstresses, 10, 71-72, 78
*Seven Years among the Freedmen,* 149
Shaw, Adele Marie, 233, 251-65
shouts, 127, 169, 176
Slade, William, 79
Slaughter, Linda Warfel, 146-47
Smolinsky, Sara, 234
Stanley, Amy Dru, 32-33, 45
Stanley, Sara, 3, 20, 123, 128, 132, 135, 192-209
stereotypes of teachers, 107, 138
Strachan, Grace C., 3, 247, 249, 316-20
student-teacher relationships, 22, 121, 129, 235, 287
Swift, Mary, 37, 40-41, 43, 85-93

Taylor, Susie King, 122, 141-46
teacher education, 135, 185
    *See also* normal schools
teachers' colleges. *See* normal schools

teachers' lack of authority,
teaching,
    patriarchal structure in, 14, 21, 236,
    249
teaching licenses, 237, 266, 289, 319
temperance, 26, 147
Towne, Laura M., 136, 170, 178, 209-
    17
    letters and diaries, 126-27, 129,
    137, 209-17
    life-long commitment to teaching,
    126
    political activism, 128, 137-38
Troy Female Seminary, 43, 49, 57
Tyack, David, 26, 242

urbanization, 6, 31, 240

wages, 74
    equalization of, 313, 316-20
    sex discrimination in, 242
*A Walker in the City,* 234
Ware, Harriet, 124
Washington, Booker T., 289, 296
Waterbury, Maria S., 123, 136, 149-58
"Why Teachers Should Organize," 254,
    308-15
Willard, Emma Hart, 3, 9, 30, 49-57
    early education of, 50-52
    first school, 49, 53-57
    first teaching job, 49, 52-53
    plans for Troy Seminary, 43, 49, 57
women principals, 39, 206, 264, 286-
    92
women's role in Civil War, 5, 11, 119-
    20, 141-45

Yezierska, Anzia, 228, 239
Young, Ella Flagg, 314, 319

# PHOTO CREDITS

FRONTISPIECE: Female teacher giving certificates to two young boys from the North Bennet Street School, Boston, May 1919. Photograph courtesy of The Schlesinger Library, Radcliffe Institute, Harvard University.

INTRODUCTION, P. 1: "A Visit to the Library of Congress." Photograph by Frances Bejamin Johnston (1854–1962), one of the first American women to achieve prominence in this medium. Johnston photographed Washington, D.C., public schools and The Hampton Institute for a series on contemporary life of the American Negro for the 1900 Paris Exposition. The Hampton album was displayed in 1966 at the Museum of Modern Art, New York City. Library of Congress, LC-USZ62-4550.

CHAPTER 1, P. 23: Group of young women studying plants in Washington, D.C., normal school. Photograph by Frances Benjamin Johnston, ca. 1899. Library of Congress, LC-USZ62-100290.

P. 50: Emma Willard School, Troy, N.Y.
P. 69: The Schlesinger Library, Radcliffe Institute, Harvard University.
P. 107: Library of Congress, LC-USZ62-57258.

CHAPTER 2, P. 119: Sallie Holley and Caroline Putnam with their students in front of the Holley School in Lottsburgh, Virginia, ca. 1897. Photograph from the Samuel May Papers, courtesy of the Massachusetts Historical Society.

P. 155: Samuel May Papers, courtesy of the Massachusetts Historical Society.
P. 190: The Schlesinger Library, Radcliffe Institute, Harvard University.
P. 212: The Penn School Collection. Permission granted by Penn Center, Inc., St. Helena Island, S.C.

CHAPTER 3, P. 227: Saluting the flag in the Mott Street Industrial School, New York City. Photograph by Jacob A. Riis, ca. 1892. Library of Congress, LC-USZ62-13077.

P. 255: Library of Congress, LC-USZ62-34555.
P. 289: Brown University Library.
P. 290, Brown University Library.
P. 310: Chicago Historical Society, ICHI-26443.
P. 314: Chicago Historical Society, DN-0007581.

# REPRINTED WITH PERMISSION